Charlotte

THE ARCHAEOLOGY OF
ANCIENT SICILY

THE ARCHAEOLOGY OF
ANCIENT SICILY

R. Ross Holloway

Drawings by Anne Lovelace Holloway

London and New York

First published in 1991
by Routledge
11 New Fetter Lane, London EC4P 4EE

Simultaneously published in the USA and Canada
by Routledge
a division of Routledge, Chapman and Hall, Inc.
29 West 35th Street, New York, NY 10001

10/11pt Bembo, Linotron 300

Disk conversion by Touchpaper (Oxford) Ltd
Abingdon, Oxon.

Printed in England by Butler & Tanner Ltd,
Frome and London

British Library Cataloguing in Publication Data

Holloway, R. Ross
The archaeology of ancient Sicily.
1. Italy. Sicily. Antiquities. Excavation of remains
I. Title
937.8

Library of Congress Cataloging in Publication Data

Also available.

ISBN 0–415–01909–5

NED
TERRA SIT LEVIS TIBI

CONTENTS

LIST OF ILLUSTRATIONS

Drawings by Anne Lovelace Holloway, unless separately credited.
Photographs, except as otherwise credited and nos 159 and 162,
by the author.

PREFACE

This book is an introduction to the archaeology of pagan Sicily written at a time when the pace of discovery and the development of the interpretation of both old and new material has far outdistanced the information published in any language other than Italian.

It is a pleasure to acknowledge my debt to a group of archaeologists whom it has been my good fortune to come to know through our common endeavors and several of whom have aided me directly in making this book. Admiration accompanies my thanks to Prof. Luigi Bernabò Brea, formerly Superintendent at Syracuse and dean of Italian prehistorians. If I feel that I know Selinuntine sculpture better than that of any other center of Greek art, it is due to Prof. Vincenzo Tusa, retired Superintendent at Palermo, who has dedicated himself to Punic and Elymnian Sicily as much as to the Sicily of the Greeks. My excursions into Sicilian numismatics have been better for the encouragement of Dr Aldina Tusa Cutroni. To Prof. Giuseppe Voza, Superintendent at Syracuse, I am indebted for permission to photograph freely in the magnificent coin cabinet of the Syracuse museum, which is in the generous care of Sig:ra Giuseppina Tranchina and which she and I first knew under the curatorship of Sig:ra Maria Teresa Currò. My first excavation in Sicily was at Morgantina under the direction of the late Profs Erik Sjöqvist and Richard Stillwell, who together created the first American archaeological undertaking in Sicily. These early years coincided with the period of intense activity, nearby at Gela, of Prof. Dinu Adamesteanu and Prof. Piero Orlandini, two gallant archaeologists whose research was to take them, as it did me for a time, to southern Italy. Subsequently I worked at La Muculufa under the cordial guidance of my friend Prof.

Ernesto De Miro and of Dr Graziella Fiorentini, Superintendents at Agrigento. And more recently on Ustica I am engaged in excavation under Dr Carmela Angela Di Stefano at Palermo. At La Muculufa I enjoyed the wholehearted support of my fellow members of the Associazione Archeologica Licatese and the friendship of Dr Giuseppe Navarra, Notary of Licata. Additional courtesies were shown me by Dr Giuseppe Castellana, Director of the Agrigento Museum. Dr Brian E. McConnell, now field director at La Muculufa, has kindly read Chapter I and made numerous useful suggestions. Others I owe to my collaborator Dr Susan S. Lukesh, Associate Provost of Hofstra University. I am also grateful for the encouragement of my colleagues Prof. Rolf Winkes and Prof. Martha S. Joukowsky.

Citations and footnotes have been held to a minimum. Ancient authors are so thoroughly indexed that anyone wishing to follow up my few citations of their evidence will have no trouble doing so. The limitation of footnotes is intentional. In a book of this nature I have no desire to present the reader with what Prof. Rhys Carpenter described as 'That open sewer at the bottom of the page.' I have, however, compiled an extensive bibiliography of publications between 1980 and 1989 because these will not yet have found extensive citation. In the preparation of the bibliography I have had invaluable assistance from Miss Anne Leinster and Mr Robert Behrendt.

Brown University has helped me materially in two instances. I was enabled to spend an entire week in the magnificent new Archaeological Museum at Syracuse with the support of funds provided by the Center for Old World Archaeology and Art, and the collection and preparation of illustrations was aided by a grant from the Faculty Research Development Fund. The University's principal support, however, has been the resources of its libraries, which constitute one of North America's finest collections in classical archaeology.

The book owes its existence to the initiative of Mr Richard Stoneman, senior editor at Routledge, but it could not have been completed without the drawings made by my daughter, Anne Lovelace Holloway, who has also been, with her sister, my companion in the field, and without the watchful editing of my dear and learned wife, cataloguer of the Morgantina excavations in 1961 and 1962.

RRH

Providence, 1989

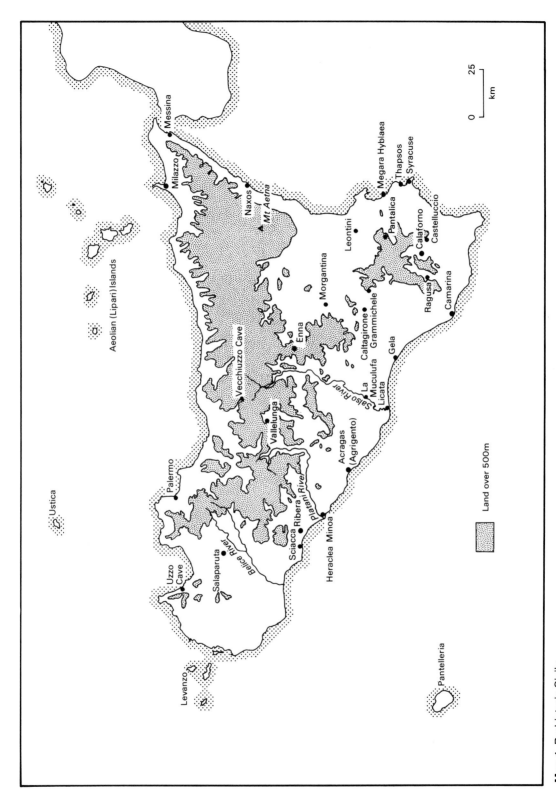

Map 1 Prehistoric Sicily

The Palaeolithic

Up to thirty years ago there was no evidence that man came to Sicily until the last great advance of the polar icecap and the Alpine glaciers in Europe was more than half over. This was approximately 30,000 years ago. The oldest known Sicilian flint tools from the rock shelter of Fontana Nuova (Marina di Ragusa) consisted of the sturdy blades, gravers, burins (pointed gravers) and scrapers that also characterize the opening phase of the Upper Palaeolithic in France (where the typological sequence used throughout Europe was developed).

During the excavation of the classical site of Heraclea Minoa at the mouth of the Platani River on the southern coast in the 1960s numerous flakes from prehistoric flintworking were found to have been employed as temper in the sun-dried brick of the city's fortifications. And just outside the walls flint tools were collected on the surface. Like the flakes which had found their way into the mud bricks, the tools belonged to a Lower Palaeolithic industry, and among them there was an amygdaloid hand ax, an object fashioned from a flint core, in shape like a pear with an extended neck, in size and weight approximating the head of a small sledge hammer. With this discovery (which has been extended by further finds of hand axes in various locations), the prehistory of Sicily leapt back half a million years.

At the same time Gerlando Bianchini, a bank manager from Agrigento, was patiently combing the countryside for traces of early man. His persistence and dedication were crowned by a series of discoveries which eclipsed even the Heraclea hand ax. At various sites Bianchini found the earliest form of tool lying on the surface of the ground. They are called 'chopping-tools' and consist of smoothed rocks from ancient beaches, large enough to fit the palm conveniently and intentionally chipped along one side (figure 1). The material is limestone or quartzite, as well as flint. The flaking is rudimentary, although it may either be in one direction or result from two operations carried out in opposing directions. 'Chopping-tools' antedate modern man, his Middle Palaeolithic cousin the Neanderthal, and their predecessor, Homo Erectus, who used amygdaloid hand axes. The 'chopping-tools' belong to an earlier era, extending back at least 2 million years, when beside the members of that slender lineage which led to modern man there were tool-using hominids known generically as Australopithecans.

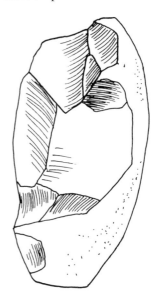

Figure 1 Chopping-tool

Although reports of the discovery of hominid physical remains in Sicily remain unconfirmed, Bianchini's work made it clear that, together with Africa, Asia and Europe, Sicily had witnessed the whole history of hominid and human industry. But there was a serious problem involved in this discovery: how had the hominids reached the island? Coming from Africa, where the remains of the earliest hominids have been found, any creature, it would seem, faced the barrier of the deep trench in the ocean floor between Sicily and Tunisia which ensured that Sicily remained separated from Africa even during periods of glacial advance when the sea level dropped sharply. The depth of the Straits of Messina, however, would not have prevented the formation of a land bridge at various times during the glacial age.[1]

Following the hominid tool-makers of the Lower Palaeolithic but coming before modern humans were the Neanderthals, a strain of man that was not destined to survive. The stone tools of the Neanderthals belong to what is called the Mousterian, a complex set of industries found over Europe, Africa and the Near East. The tool kits of Mousterian type are produced not from cores but from flakes, such as had already been employed in certain industries of the Lower Palaeolithic. The flaking technique, however, especially the retouching along the edges, is smaller and more closely spaced, creating an impression of precision and often of symmetry. It is doubtful whether there is a true Mousterian in Sicily; those few materials which might be associated with it may in fact belong to industries of the developing phases of the Lower Palaeolithic. No physical remains of Neanderthal type have yet been discovered on the island.

The appearance of modern man in Sicily (some time after 30,000 BC) is shown by the flint tools from Fontana Nuova (Marina di Ragusa) mentioned earlier. Otherwise, the initial phases of the Upper Palaeolithic are hardly documented in the island, and it is only in the latest stages of the Upper Palaeolithic, about 10,000 BC, that sites multiply. This is the time of the end of the last glaciation and the establishment of the landforms we know today. The Upper Palaeolithic inhabitants sought out shelter beneath rock outcroppings, and although they left their traces throughout the island, these are especially frequent on the north coast around Palermo. In this area the cliffs that dominate the coast were, in distant geological time, submerged in the sea. As a result they were eroded in vertical channels which often widen at the base to create hospitable shelter and from which large caves penetrate the mass of the formations.

The flint industry of these stations is termed Epigravettian, after the equivalent stage of the French sequence. It is based on small carefully shaped flakes worked into blades and bladelets, burins, other gravers and scrapers, all finished with minute retouch flaking on the edges. There are also small triangular or crescent-shaped microliths, perhaps arrow-tips. The miniaturization of the flint tools at the end of the Palaeolithic, generally for insertion in bone or wood handles or shafts, is a universal phenomenon. Hunting was man's livelihood, as it had been for eons past. The large animals of the Pleistocene (the Age of the Glaciers), the elephant, which existed in a dwarf variety during most of the period in Sicily, the hippopotamus, the hyena, all had departed. Their only surviving representative was Equus Hydruntinus, an ancestor of the donkey. But the Epigravettian hunters took wild boar, deer, fox, wild cattle and wild goat. As the period progressed the inhabitants of coastal sites show an increasing taste for shellfish.

For the first time, in the Epigravettian, archaeology brings us in contact with the intellectual world of early man in Sicily. The cave at Cala dei Genovesi on the island of Levanzo, close to the western extremity of Sicily, and joined to Sicily during the Late Palaeolithic, is the key to Sicilian Palaeolithic art. The Epigravettian deposit from the interior of the cave contained a detached slab of rock on which the figure of a bovine creature had been incised. This discovery serves to confirm the Palaeolithic date of other depictions on the walls of the same cave, together with rock engravings at other sites, especially those discovered in the caves of Monte Pellegrino overlooking Palermo. The same stratum in the Cave on Levanzo has also given a radiocarbon date just before 9,000 BC.

The style and the subject of the Levanzo bovine belong to the great tradition of Palaeolithic art in Western Europe. The firm outline of the creature and its attenuated horns are not too distant from the famous painted bovines of Lascaux; the other representations of bulls, cows, deer and horse on the walls of the Levanzo cave have even greater similarities to the animals of the mature phase of Franco-Cantabrian cave painting and engraving (figure 2). The drawing is assured and elegant. The bull is seen in all his massiveness and grandeur. The small wild horses lowering their heads to graze have all the nervous hesitation of their subjects in life, as does the movement of the stag in the same gallery. One wild goat is drawn in foreshortening, the body in profile but the head turned toward the viewer (figure 3).

The significance of these subjects and the reason for their depiction in the recesses of caves

is still far from clear. Few would doubt that they are governed by the same impulses that drew men to venture into the unlit depths of the earth. Was the object of man's adventures in the cave revelation of wisdom from secret sources or spectral ancestors? Was it the imparting of knowledge to cowering initiates? Was it preparation for the great endeavors of life, foremost among which must have been the hunt? Our answers to these questions can rely only on our ingenuity or ethnographic analogies to modern hunters and gatherers, whose intellectual attainments, complex and surprising as they may be, are probably a poor guide to the powers of the Palaeolithic mind. Nevertheless, despite these limitations, because of the work of André Leroi-Gourhan,[2] we can appreciate, in the French and Spanish caves, the logic of the placement of groups of images and thus their relation to a systematic pattern of thought. The Sicilian representations show that the inhabitants of the island participated in the same tradition.

Because they are late in the history of Palaeolithic art, the Sicilian engravings show a development toward scenes of human activity such as occur in the post-Palaeolithic art of Spain and Africa but are seen only fleetingly in earlier representations. The cave of the Cala dei Genovesi gives us a detailed sketch of a human figure in what must be ceremonial costume (figure 4). The figure wears a wide belt and above it a shirt or jacket which has decorative stitching or a fringe on its shoulders and sides. The figure clearly wears a hat, but although from the head alone one cannot be sure whether the figure is seen from the front or the rear, the fact that the toes of the left foot are shown makes it certain that this is a frontal view. The cap, peaked like a chef's hat, with stitching or a fringe shown as on the jacket, covers the whole face and apparently has no openings for the mouth, eyes or nose. Rather than a patriarchal beard, I would surmise that the engraving shows a long fringe attached to the headgear or possibly to the bottom of a beaded veil. Considering that the headdress effectively imprisons the wearer, the absence of arms from the shirt may indicate that it was a kind of straitjacket.

The individual thus restrained is flanked by two other figures. At the right there is an individual with bracelets on his arms, but no other detail of clothing, unless the peculiar form

Figure 2 Levanzo, rock engraving

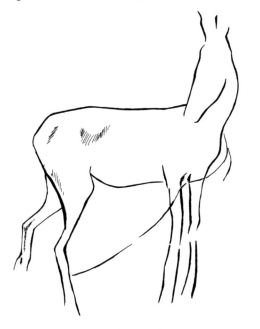

Figure 3 Levanzo, rock engraving

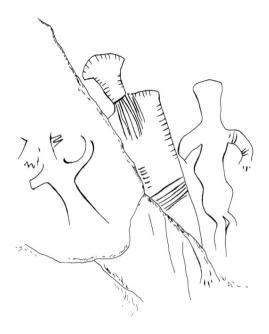

Figure 4 Levanzo, rock engraving

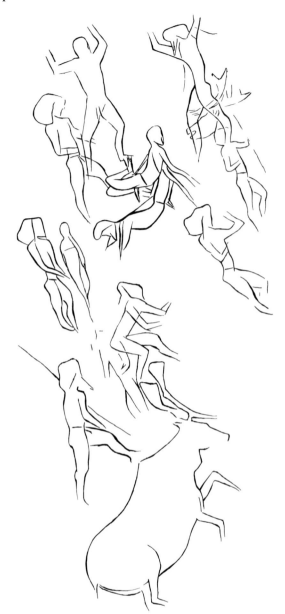

Figure 5 Monte Pellegrino, rock engraving

of his head is meant to suggest a hat like that of the central personage. At the left there is the partially executed sketch of another human, often said to be wearing a bird headdress because of his bill-like mouth. If we take the figures together, the two small ones seem to be dancing around the masked and hobbled individual in the center. Such a sense of deprivation and physical restraint in a setting of mystical mimicry would not be out of place in initiation ceremonies or in the mysteries of the shaman. A further possibility may be the rites of hunting magic with the central figure playing the role of the magically handicapped animal.

A similar scene, but with a larger group of actors, was found in 1952 in the small cave of Addaura on Monte Pellegrino, the sugarloaf eminence that rises from the sea and overlooks Palermo from the west. The rock face, on which the scenes were incised, receives illumination from the mouth of the cave. The ritual scene is part of a larger group of representations of bovines, deer, equines and humans (figure 5). It consists of eight large figures, presumably male, five of whom are dancing in an animated fashion (one stooping, two with arms raised) while another approaches and the last stands by accompanied by a small figure, very likely a

woman, whose size, cylindrical body and long lock of hair by her left side all contrast with the appearance of the men. The men seem to be naked save for a sack-like headdress. In one case this has a bill-like piece on its face not unlike the bill of the figure from the Levanzo cave. In the center of the circle there are two figures, both men. Both seem to be lying on the ground. They are restrained by cords which run down their backs from their necks to their legs. In the case of the upper figure the cord seems to reach the ankles. The result is that the figure's lower legs are bent backwards, preventing him from rising from the ground. The second figure, partially covered by the first, is evidently in a similar situation. Both have headdresses like the dancers, but it is impossible to say whether these are completely closed like the headdress of the Levanzo figure. The arms of the second figure are stumpy and may be held in some kind of jacket without openings for the hands.

The scene is thus very similar to the Levanzo engraving. It has been suggested that it shows an acrobatic performance, possibly connected with initiation ceremonies, or that the two figures on the ground are actually about to be strangled by the cords around their necks. But the representation of a hunting ritual in which two of the dancers play the part of captured and trussed-up animals is, I feel, more likely.

Animal representations in the grand tradition have been found in other caves on Monte Pellegrino and elsewhere in Sicily. Small smooth stones decorated with simple lines in rows were discovered on Levanzo, and they find parallels on the Italian mainland at the cave site of Praia a Mare on the southwestern coast of the peninsula. Otherwise, small scale carving or engraving (French *art mobilier*) is surprisingly rare in Palaeolithic Sicily. Recently, however, Giuseppe Navarra has published an extensive collection of figurines in compact sandstone, executed, according to his analysis, by pecking with stone punches[3]. He attributes these pieces to the early Upper Palaeolithic. The subjects represented are humans, male and female, as well as heads, isolated eyes and the elephant (figures 6 and 7). Although the need for sculpting the stone may have been much reduced by the natural state of the material itself, there is no question that these objects continued to excite interest down to the Early Bronze Age, when they appear in archaeological contexts (Adrano Museum, from the area around Mt Aetna).

The Palaeolithic survival in the opening millennia of the post-glacial age is termed the Mesolithic. In northern Europe, where it has been studied most thoroughly, the stone tool industries of the period reflect the fundamental change in man's sustenance brought on by the new climate. The tendency toward minia-

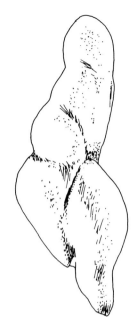

Figure 6 Licata, Navarra collection, sandstone figurine

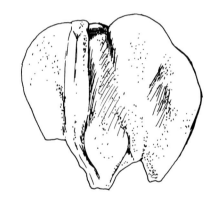

Figure 7 Licata, Navarra collection, sandstone figurine

turization is accentuated. In the economy hunting loses its absolute dominance and becomes associated on a more equal basis with gathering and exploitation of shellfish, where available. The Mesolithic in Sicily has been difficult to isolate and place in its environmental context, which would have been far different from that of northern Europe. However, recent excavations in the large cave of Uzzo, which overlooks the Gulf of Castellamare on the west coast of Sicily, have provided rich data for just this stage of Sicilian prehistory.

There was some Palaeolithic use of the cave, but the first major period shown by the excavations is the Mesolithic. Eight radiocarbon dates and two aspartic-acid racemization dates have been obtained for these levels. They range between $10,070 \pm 100$ BC and $6,280 \pm 80$ BC. The Mesolithic people of the Uzzo cave were still hunters, eating red deer, wild boar and birds. They gathered wild fruits. As the sea level rose, following the retreat of the glaciers in northern Europe, they turned increasingly to shellfish for food. The second stage of the Mesolithic, around 8,000, saw a dramatic increase in fishing. Among the quantities of fish bones from these levels there are vertebrae and fragments of ribs and jaws of at least three different types of Cetaceans.

This means that Mesolithic fishermen were pursuing dolphins and the like, an enterprise which required boats large enough for them to put out from the coast (figure 8). The beginning of deepwater fishing during the Mesolithic has also been observed in the excavations of the Franchthi Cave in Greece. Drawings of what are probably tuna fish, together with schematic human figures and bovines, in the cave at Cala dei Genovesi on Levanzo probably date from this time. Taken together, this evidence, both from Sicily and Greece, shows that the age of navigation began in the Mediterranean well before the movement toward village life and an agrarian economy.

Figure 8 Uzzo, scene of Mesolithic life, after drawing of M.T. Serafini

The Neolithic

We meet the Mesolithic people of Sicily in the Uzzo cave where six burials have been excavated and at the Cave of Molara in the Conca d'Oro behind Palermo where two other burials were found. The burials at Uzzo are all flexed inhumations, one or two occupants to the grave. There were no durable grave goods, flint tools, shell or jewelry. From their dental measurements, it seems that the Uzzo people were slightly built and more like Neolithic people; the dentition of the Molara burials, on the other hand, is larger and closer to Palaeolithic populations. On the basis of this admittedly limited evidence one has the impression of a Sicilian population which included descendants of older inhabitants of the island and relative newcomers, both participating in the Mesolithic development of the island.

The Mesolithic, in turn, was supplanted, at the opening of the sixth millennium BC, by an economy based on the cultivation of plants and the domestication of animals. With the Neolithic the material culture changes dramatically. Pottery comes quickly into use, as it did throughout the Mediterrranean and the Near East. Stone tools continue to be made, but the variety of tools is less, resulting in a preponderance of blades. The extreme miniaturization of the Mesolithic tools is given up.

The most notable changes of the Neolithic were demographic. As this new age developed the rock shelters were no longer adequate to house the increased population. The farmers moved onto their lands and created villages. Theirs were not the first houses. In Northern Europe large shelters had existed in the Palaeolithic, such as those erected on a framework of mammoth bones by hunters in Czechoslovakia and the Ukraine. But settled village life is a product of the Neolithic.

The impulses that led to the first Neolithic economies must be sought elsewhere. They are to be found in the Near East, beginning not long after 10,000 BC and developing over four millennia while Sicily remained an island of Mesolithic hunters and gatherers. It is not in Sicily that population pressure and the consequent post-glacial food crisis forced men into the roles of farmers and herdsmen. Sicily was brought into the expanding orbit of the new economic order only slowly, and only more slowly into the new social order of the agricultural village. Because the population does not seem to have outrun the food potential of hunting and gathering there can be no question of pressures in Sicily having produced a local Neolithic revolution.

The gradual development of the Mesolithic into the Neolithic is illustrated again by excavations in the Uzzo cave. By the beginning of the fifth millennium the residents of the cave were consuming small quanties of barley and of the three classic varieties of wheat (*triticum monococcum, dicoccum* and *aestivum*). The major factor in the diet was the meat of deer and wild boar. Increase in food sources came first from shellfish and then from fishing on the coast and in deep water for cetaceans (dolphins and the like) and sea perch. Sheep and goat appear in the Neolithic. Game then diminishes in importance. There was apparently a local experiment in domesticating the pig.

The excavators have interpreted this information as suggesting that a stable Mesolithic population at the Uzzo cave adopted a Neolithic economy piecemeal over a long period of time. It is true that as the Neolithic progressed those groups clinging to rock shelters for their homes were probably not the more progressive people of their day. Yet the Uzzo evidence does mean that there can have been no wholesale replacement of the Mesolithic peoples by invaders. In its acceptance of the Neolithic way of life Sicily's protected insular situation played a determining role. No less important, we may suppose, was the fact that Sicily remained underpopulated.

At the beginning of the sixth millennium pottery is first noted in the Uzzo cave. It belongs to that family of handmade vessels, their exteriors roughened by the impression of small sticks, seeds or shells, which appears as the earliest pottery in all parts of the Mediterranean. The fact that the earliest radiocarbon dates for this material are reported from southern France does not mean that pottery was invented there rather than in the Near East or in some other area. It means only that the invention was taken up with such speed that one cannot establish a point of origin. This pottery is purely functional. Its shapes are handleless, open containers. It is undecorated, although almost without exception commentators fall into the error of treating its corrugated surface as if the punch marks made intentional patterns. Anyone who has had to do with sheep has faced the problem of greasy hands. The roughened surfaces simply helped in getting a grip on the vase. The material from Uzzo belongs to a class of pottery called 'Pre-Stentinello', because it preceded the kind of pottery associated with the oldest villages of the island.

Stentinello ware has been synonymous with the Sicilian Neolithic since the excavations of Paolo Orsi on this site near Syracuse in 1890. Stentinello, together with the nearby villages at Megara Hyblaea and Matrensa in the same area and a second group on the slopes of Mt Aetna, has furnished most of our information about this culture. It is certain, however, that it was an island-wide phenomenon. Stentinello ware, like all Sicilian prehistoric ceramics down to the period of Greek colonization, is handmade, but it is far removed in purpose and appearance from the utilitarian pottery that preceded it and that continued to be made in the Stentinello villages. The new forms include containers with short or long necks set on bulbous bodies, goblets, and large bowls having a collar-like lip distinct from the lower body (figure 9). Occasionally this lower portion of the vessel is itself constructed of two sections meeting at an abrupt angle. The fabric of Stentinello ware is fine textured, and it is fired carefully to an even hardness. The color varies from gunmetal grey to a brown-black. The decoration is a refined folk art. The patterns were executed by incision, combing or stamping with small circular punches. The recesses were then filled in with paste of a color contrasting with the pottery surface. Like the designs of much early pottery, these decorations seem to be based on textile patterns and suggest the closely spaced weave of woollen fabric. The

patterns, therefore, are predominantly rectilinear. The potters worked with remarkable freedom in decorating their vases. The decoration may cover the entire surface of the vessel or be severely restricted. Among the patterns one can recognize herring bones, trailing fringes and crochet.

Into the designs of Stentinello wares, as presumably in the designs of the fabrics on which we suppose they were based, were worked amuletic images calculated to protect both the vessel and its contents. These are faces or simply eyes, single or in pairs (figure 10). They are evidence of the widespread and deeply rooted belief in the Evil

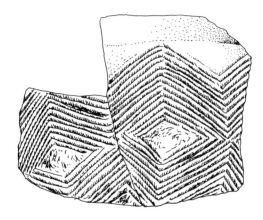

Figure 10 Trapani, Stentinello–style vase fragment from Uzzo

Eye, a superstition into which is channeled the fear of all the malevolent powers surrounding us and waiting to bring unsuspected woe. In many parts of the world, including Italy, belief in the Evil Eye is as strong today as it was seven thousand years ago. Its most obvious manifestation is in the glance of the envious neighbor or of the unconsciously unlucky 'jettatore' whose glance brings ill luck though no harm is intended. The best defense is an image of the very organ of danger, the eye.

The Stentinello villages were settled in the late sixth millennium. In the area around Syracuse they were delimited by ditches dug into the limestone formations. At Stentinello itself the ditch was reinforced by a mound or palisade on the inner side. It surrounded an area 253 by 237 meters (830 by 777 ft). Orsi's excavation concentrated on the ditch, where the richest deposit of cultural debris was located, but to

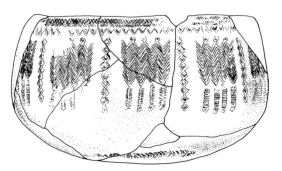

Figure 9 Syracuse Museum, vase of the Stentinello style from Naxos

judge from a single test trench made more recently, the village was composed of rectangular houses erected in perishable materials on a framework of posts. Until there is a thorough examination of the surface of this or one of the other similar villages, there will be no way to judge the density of buildings or to make an estimate of population. There is even less information at Matrensa and Megara than at Stentinello concerning the plan of the site. At Matrensa only sections of the ditch seem to have been completed.

Recently two other villages of this period have been investigated in the Agrigento region, at Serra del Palco (Milena) and Piano Vento (Palma di Montechiaro). At the former site hut foundations and remains of a subsequent enclosure wall, forming a compound without a ditch, have been excavated. At the second, where occupation began in pre-Stentinello times, there is an initial period of huts and a second period of more substantial dwellings. To this second stage belong the fortification walls preserved along one side of the settlement. Clearly there was no set pattern of the Stentinello villages. Stentinello burial customs are hardly known; one burial consists of an inhumation in a stone-lined grave.

Orsi collected faunal information at Stentinello which established the domestication of sheep and goats, cattle, pig and the dog, with the exception of poultry the entire barnyard of European history. Interestingly enough, there was no trace of wild game among the bones at the site. This information has not been significantly amplified by other publications, although one may soon expect detailed faunal and floral studies from recent excavations of Neolithic sites in Sicily.

The depths of the earth beckoned to the Stentinello people, just as they had to their Palaeolithic predecessors. Above Sciacca on Monte Kronio, which overlooks both the city and the sea beyond, there is a cavern known as the 'Hot-house of Saint Calogero' because of the thermal effect which heats air entering the cave and causes vaporization. The heat and humidity are such today that it is impossible to work in the cave for any length of time without protective clothing and fresh air piped into the explorer's suit from the surface. Despite these conditions, the cave was visited – certainly for religious reasons – beginning in the Neolithic.

The earliest pottery recovered on Monte Kronio is an incised ware closely related to Stentinello, but distinct from it, called the 'Kronio Style'. It is apparently a western Sicilian variety of Stentinello. The sequence is longer still in the Grotta del Fico on Monte Kronio where pre-Stentinello pottery appears and Palaeolithic and Mesolithic strata occur. The veneration of the forces felt to dwell in the cave did not end with the Stentinello Culture but continued into the fourth millennium. And it is this period, marked by pottery of the so-called Malpasso style, that has left the most macabre testimony to the demands of the cult. In another cavern deep in the hillside, one youthful participant in a ritual, carrying a large vessel, succumbed to the fumes. His skeleton was found in 1985 lying where he had collapsed over five thousand years before. In 'The Hot-house of Saint Calogero' there was found a tiny jadeite head (figure 11). The bird-like appearance of the head is also suggestive of a masked figure and recalls the Upper Palaeolithic beaks of some figures in the scenes from the Addaura Cave on Monte Pellegrino.

Figure 11 Agrigento Museum, jadeite head from Sciacca

Two figures of naked women summarily fashioned by pecking the surface of river pebbles are also attributed to the Neolithic. They come from deposits outside tombs of the first phase of the Early Bronze Age at Busoné near Agrigento (figure 12).

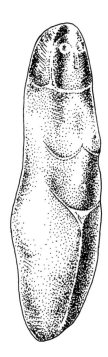

Figure 12 Agrigento Museum, figurine from Busoné

It is difficult to gauge the social organization of the Stentinello villages. Were they inhabited by single families, even extended families or clans? Or had that important threshold of society been reached at which members of distinct family groups associate, thus requiring the regulation of their disputes and relationships by a rudimentary public structure? If this step must be taken before society reaches the true village, then there is no reason to call the Stentinello settlements villages. There are too many indications of clan life persisting to a far later stage in the history of the ancient world. And size, even numbers of buildings within the settlement may be no guide to social complexity. There is never any guarantee that all the buildings of a prehistoric site were in use at the same time. It is often difficult to distinguish farm buildings from houses. Besides the dangers of fire in buildings presumably made of wattle and daub with thatched roofs, vermin would have made them uninhabitable after a certain time. And finally, the members of the clan may be numerous. In the traditions of an earlier age persisting in

Homer's *Iliad*, King Priam and his fifty sons lived within the walls of Troy, each with his own residence and family. In this bit of epic grandeur there is also reflected prehistoric reality.

Stentinello pottery is also typical of the Neolithic in Calabria, which therefore seems to have formed a cultural province with Sicily in what is also termed the Middle Neolithic. This period is contemporary with the flowering of Neolithic painted wares in Apulia and in Campania and precedes the appearance of the standard monochrome wares (Diana or Bellavista Style) which were produced in southern Italy and Sicily at the end of the Neolithic. Chronological precision is impossible but the Early Neolithic appears to be characteristic of the sixth millennium, the Middle Neolithic of the fifth millennium, and the Late Neolithic of the early and middle fourth millennium.

With the appearance of the Stentinello Culture Sicily came abreast of the Mediterranean and the Near East. Its people had learned to create their shelter rather than to accept what nature offered. They had learned to create their food supply rather than to rely on hunting and gathering. There were unquestionably losses as well as gains in this process. The Stentinello villagers found it necessary to defend themselves from their neighbors. And much of the intellectual richness of Palaeolithic imagination and art may have perished with the passing of the Mesolithic, although it has been argued with eloquence that the imagery of the arts of the Neolithic farmers across the Ukraine, the Balkans, Greece and Italy was a continuation of Palaeolithic symbolism and reflects no more than a mutation of Palaeolithic thought.[4] Certainly the jadeite bird-headed image from the 'Hot-house of Saint Calogero' lends itself to this interpretation.

It is impossible to say whether the appearance of the Stentinello Culture was the result of immigration of a new people from across the Straits of Messina. This has been the normal explanation of its origin, but the new ways may also have been learned by the old people of the island. In Sicily of the Stentinello Period, as in many sites on the Italian mainland, obsidian displaces flint as the preferred material for tools, whether blades, awls, or the small chips which seem to have been mounted as teeth in bone or wooden sickles. Obsidian is a dark-colored volcanic glass, with a regular fracture and a sharp cutting edge. Aside from distant Transylvania, the sources of the material are all on islands, Sardinia (Monte Arci) and Palmarola in the northern Tyrrhenian, Pantelleria between Sicily and modern Tunisia, and Lipari, in the center of the Aeolian Islands that are disposed like a three-pointed star off the north coast of Sicily. Stromboli, the easternmost of the group, is still an active volcano. Vulcano, south of Lipari, has thermal activity. The cone-shaped profile and geology of the other islands show them to be extinct volcanoes.

Obsidians have distinctive spectrographic profiles according to their sources and, therefore, we know that obsidian from Lipari was exported to southern and central Italy, to Sicily and to Malta. The immense quantity of blades found in the Neolithic sites of the Lipari Islands shows that finished tools were produced there for export, but it has also been argued from the diminution in size of blades of Lipari obsidian according to their distance from the source that cores were exported. Considering that Lipari was already settled in the Stentinello Period, it is less likely that collecting parties from Italy and Sicily would have had access to the deposits.

The settlements of Lipari are important for the record of pottery with designs painted on a light-colored ground (known as 'figulina' in Italian terminology) that was imported to the island. The earliest station, Castellaro, hidden in the interior of the island where an extinct volcanic caldera provides rich soil and a protected environment, has no traces of buildings but shows Stentinello pottery in association with a striking figulina ware, the surface of which is boldly decorated with red-orange designs. This is the 'Band and Flame Style', well known in the Neolithic of southern Italy and also represented by a famous example from the Stentinello village at Megara Hyblaea (one of seventeen sites in Sicily where examples of the style have been found). In the second phase of the period, occupation is first found on the acropolis beside the harbor of Lipari. Here the grey to black Stentinello pottery (both the decorated and coarse types) has been replaced by an elegant dark monochrome pottery, which should be contemporary with much of the Stentinello ware of Sicily. With it also appears a figulina ware in which the red-orange designs are edged in black (figure 13). Petrological examination of

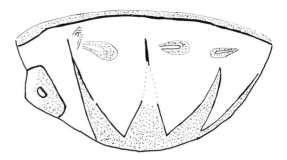

Figure 13 Syracuse Museum, Neolithic vase from Megara Hyblaea

the clay of this pottery suggests that, unlike the 'Band and Flame Style'. the 'Trichrome' pottery was locally made from clay brought from the north coast of Sicily. The inspiration for the 'Trichrome' figulina pottery also came from abroad, from the painted wares of Campania ('Grotta Felci Style') or the Adriatic area ('Ripoli Style'). The 'Trichrome Style' has a distribution in Sicily similar to the 'Band and Flame Style'. In the next phase of the stratigraphic sequence of the Lipari acropolis, 'Trichrome' pottery is replaced by 'Serra d'Alto' ware, named from the site near Matera in southern Italy, the region where this style is prevalent (figure 14). This is again a figulina pottery with designs on a light background. Its intricate designs are developed with great taste and restraint to produce an effect no less bold than that of the 'Band and Flame Style' against the surface of the vase. The shapes

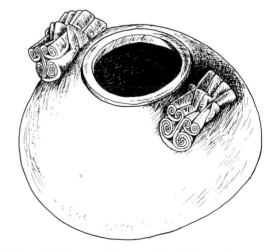

Figure 14 Syracuse Museum, Neolithic vase from Paternò

are typical of the period, two-part bowls and large cups, tall and squat containers and one-piece jars. The 'Serra d'Alto' handles are exceptional. Many are plastically modeled in shapes developed from spirals. All in all, this pottery, even more than its figulina predecessors, might be defined as ceramic fine art. Serra d'Alto pottery is again found in Sicily at some twenty sites throughout the island. One assumes that it occurs in association with Stentinello pottery, but the commonly cited occurrences are sporadic, and the most recent study of its distribution does not comment on specific contexts.[5]

The workings of prehistoric commerce are mysterious, largely because so few of the materials that were exchanged are preserved. But in the case of Lipari, obsidian was unquestionably a resource of singular importance on which the islanders could capitalize. Indeed, the first settlement of Lipari comes at the time when the obsidian trade was beginning. Most of what was brought to Lipari in exchange for obsidian has been lost, but what remains shows that the imports were both raw materials lacking on the island, clay for potting or grindstones or flint for stone tools for tasks where this material was preferred to obsidian, as well as exotic materials, and luxury goods, jadeite for amulets or pottery of the 'Band and Flame Style' and 'Serra d'Alto' types.

Widespread distribution of exotic materials was hardly a new thing in the Mediterranean and prehistoric Europe. The cowrie shells from an Upper Palaeolithic burial at Laugerie-Basse in the Dordogne came from the Mediterranean, and nearby in the Grotte des Enfants near Mentone there were found, in a context of the same period, other fragments of shell from a warm water source, possibly as far away as the Indian Ocean. Spondylus shells from the Aegean were distributed in quantity up the Danube and then into the Rhine valley during the Neolithic. From sources in northern Italy and Switzerland jadeite was exported during the same period to an area extending from Brittany to the Rhineland and including the British Isles. The objects in this material were largely small ax heads, some of which were never hafted or used but were prized as objects of prestige.

The trade in such precious, non-utilitarian materials poses a question for archaeological interpretation. Were they traded simply as goods like any others or was their exchange removed from what we normally think of as trade? If the latter alternative is true, we must envisage an entire class of precious objects and materials exchanged as gifts by individuals privileged to possess them. These ceremonial exchanges, so this reasoning runs, provided much of the impetus for the circulation of utilitarian goods. They were, so to speak, the fly-wheel that kept the drive wheel of commerce turning when inertia might have slowed it or brought it to a stop.[6]

It was only in the early twentieth century that recognition was given to the economic importance and to the elaborate mechanisms of ritual gift-giving among aboriginal groups of non-western peoples. The classic investigation of the sort was Bronislav Malinowski's study of the Trobriand Islands published in 1932.[7] In this area of Melanesia voyages are undertaken over great distances for the express purpose of effecting ritual exchanges of long necklaces of red shell and bracelets of white shell, which circulated in opposite directions around a vast circle of islands, thus balancing the exchanges. The 'kula', as it is called, was developed to such a degree that the circuit of these objects embraced a ring of islands 300 kilometers (186 miles) across and left the individuals along its route completely ignorant of more than a small portion of the circuit. It is the formal kula, moreover, that stimulates normal buying and selling of utilitarian goods along its course.

Clearly it is not necessary to envisage a system of the complexity of the kula as it existed at the beginning of the twentieth century to explain the circulation of goods in Neolithic Europe. But knowledge of the extent to which formalized exchange may be carried, and an appreciation of the power enshrined in exotic luxuries can aid in understanding how non-utilitarian goods were distributed so widely in the Neolithic and before.

Such knowledge has been salutary in many ways. It brings logic to what seemed illogical. The Potlach of the Indians of the Pacific coast of Canada and the United States is no longer viewed as a form of economic desperation in the face of a superabundant environment. And what Thorstein Veblen at the end of the nineteenth century ridiculed as the conspicuous consumption of the *nouveaux riches* now appears rooted in atavistic attraction to objects of prestige and magic.[8] Many items of adornment still in common use have a magical past. The first function of earrings was to protect against the Evil Eye, as it still is today in Mediterranean countries where girl babies' ears are pierced for gold studs. This mighty superstition can be traced back to the Palaeolithic when cowrie shells (because of their eye-like openings) appear to have served as amulets for the same purpose.

The problem presented by such tools of interpretation, usually, as in this case, drawn from ethnological parallels to a more recent era, is to know how closely they describe any specific exchanges in the past. How artificially tied to social obligations between families and between ritually designated partners was any economic activity? Gift giving and utilitarian trade are inseparable, even in the kula.

It is only prudent, therefore, to resist the temptation to overformalize the economy of the Sicilian Neolithic and imagine a ritual partnership behind the movement of every figulina vessel. The importance of religion in stimulating ancient trade goes beyond the attraction for magical substances. A shared cult place, admitting visitors beyond the limits of a family, becomes a meeting place and a market, as the fairs on saints' feast days throughout Europe testify to this day. That the exotic is especially welcome to the divinity is shown by the piece of Serra d'Alto pottery deposited in the 'Hot House' of Monte Kronio at Sciacca. But there can be no question that the custom of gift giving, the desire to manifest prestige through the rare and exotic, and the demands of magic aided immeasurably in the distribution of some goods. At the same time others, like obsidian, were traded for their utilitarian value. The result of these forces of integration is reflected in the similarity of Stentinello and related wares in Sicily and across the Straits of Messina in Calabria. And if the argument of the following section of this account is correct, there also came into play during the Neolithic economic forces more potent than the trade in obsidian: the wool and textile trade between Sicily and Malta.

The end of the Neolithic: Sicily and Malta

Some 70 miles (113 kilometers) south of Sicily is the island of Malta and its smaller neighbor Gozo. Malta is only 20 miles (32 kilometers) on its longer axis. But these limestone dots in the Mediterranean were the setting of an unusual Neolithic civilization. Nothing is known of its settlements. But its temples still stand, and they are among the oldest stone buildings in the world. Only some of the passage graves and cairns of Brittany are more ancient, and if these French tombs are excepted, Malta can claim the first large stone buildings in existence. Age, however, is not the only notable quality of the Maltese temples. In the course of the millennium and more over which they were constructed, beginning in the mid-fifth millennium and lasting to the end of the fourth, they achieved monumental size and established an unmistakable architectural style.

A steady output of energy from the islanders was channeled into temple construction. Twenty-three temples were known when David Trump compiled a list of them in 1972.[9] Since five temples occur in pairs, in addition to one group of three and another group of four, there are thirteen different sanctuaries.

The Maltese temple began as a small oval building entered on its long side. It became more complex as a series of such structures were joined together and small apses were added projecting from the oval ground plan. Save for the uprights of the doorways there was no use of large stone construction, certainly not of the mighty stone walling that qualifies the later buildings as Megalithic structures.

Maltese temple architecture emerges in all its grandeur, but with simplicity of plan, in the Temple of Ggantija on Gozo (figure 15). The plan of the primitive temple is faithfully preserved, but there are two sets of rooms combined in the same structure. The innermost chambers develop 'apses' on their long sides opposite the doorways. Shrines were installed in the 'apses', some of which are preserved because they were constructed of stone slabs.

The walling of the Ggantija Temple was built up in mighty courses of stone founded on massive boulders. The doorjambs of the southern entrances are 4 meters (13 ft) high. The first stone adjoining the doorway to the south is almost as long. Interior stucco and the fresh condition of the interior walls when excavated suggest that the temple was roofed. Models of the temples and a sketch on a wall block apparently made

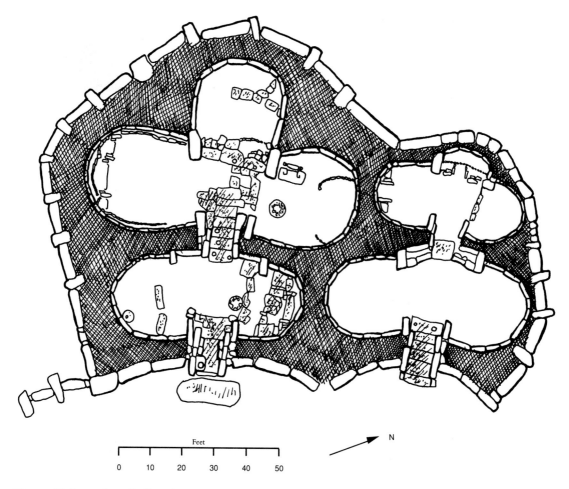

Feet

0   10   20   30   40   50

N

Figure 15 Gozo, Ggantija Temple

by a prehistoric visitor to pass the time while waiting in the forecourt of the Temple of Mnaidra confirm this (figures 16 and 17). Despite the massive fill surrounding the chambers, especially of the Ggantija Temple, one cannot restore a corbel vaulting here given the loose nature of the wall construction. A corbel vault is made by projecting each successive course of stone slightly toward the center of the vault and thus building up a vault without any true vaulting (a corbel arch is constructed in the same way). A lighter roofing of timber and thatch should be envisaged, and this is true as well for temples of a subsequent period in which the wall construction is firmer and the walling clearly begins to project over the enclosed space. Even here it is likely that the final covering was not of stone.

Important elements of the interior were decorated. Initially the surfaces were given an all-over pecking without designs but subsequently the spiral designs best known from the carved blocks at Tarxien came into fashion. Occasionally, in addition to floral ornament, sheep, pig or cattle were represented.

The development of Maltese architecture can be seen if one compares the Ggantija Temple with that of Hagar Qim (figure 18). The elements of the primitive plan are in evidence, but the apse-ended rooms have been combined so that the visitor no longer proceeds directly from the entrance to the central apse along the short axis of the building. Although the building that survives clearly had a long history of development and modification (one may note, for example,

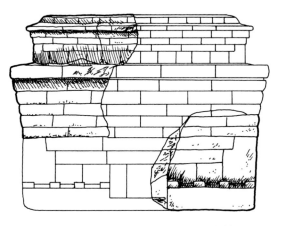

Figure 16 Valetta Museum, temple model from Tarxien

Figure 17 Mnaidra, graffito

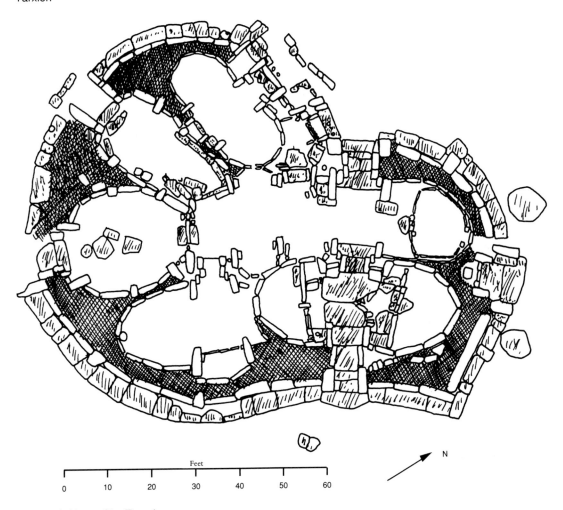

Feet

0   10   20   30   40   50   60

N

Figure 18 Hagar Qim Temple

the way one of the major rooms has lost an apse to its neighbor), the architectural whole is maintained by the exterior wall.

The masonry of Hagar Qim is carefully measured and squared. The facade of the temple we see today is exactly as the prehistoric masons left it (figure19). Only the two horizontal courses above the doorway have been replaced, but with the original blocks.

Figure 19 Hagar Qim Temple

Sir Themistocles Zammit's excavations at Tarxien, the most complex of the Maltese temples, produced significant information regarding the cult practices associated with these buildings. At Tarxien it seems that the interior shrines were true altars. In the recess in the base of one of them Sir Themistocles found a flint knife and, together with charred bones of sheep and cattle, some shells and pottery. Large stone basins were found in the temples and traces of burning on the floors suggest that the sacrifices may have been performed there. The divinity of Tarxien is surely represented by an over life-size statue of a woman preserved only in its lower part with oddly bulbous legs. The figure wore a fleece skirt. Smaller figures are preserved in their entirety. Representations of phalloi (male organs) and vegetation, as well as the sheep, cattle and pig already mentioned, show that the cult of the goddess had a definite fertility aspect. There are numerous figurines of women including some asleep on couches.

In an extremely important excavation made between 1961 and 1963 David Trump studied the temple at Skorba and uncovered a series of structures which preceded the existing temple on the spot. One of these structures was undoubtedly a shrine, in which there were found figurines and five goat skulls intentionally reduced to the horns and upper cranium. The other buildings were probably also shrines. Indeed, the earliest structure on the spot was an enclosure

wall, belonging to the fifth millennium and apparently delimiting an area almost the same as that of the later temple.

The Skorba excavations were also important in providing the first (and still only) series of radiocarbon dates bearing on the Maltese Neolithic. In this sequence impressed Neolithic pottery similar to Stentinello ware was being used in the later fifth millennium. The pottery of the Ggantija phase is early in the fourth millennium.

Also belonging to the period of the Megalithic temples is the so-called Hypogeum of Hal Saflieni. This is a series of underground halls, on three levels. The total floor area is 500 square meters. In part the walls and ceilings preserve spiral designs not unlike those found in the sculptural decoration of the temples. At two points, moreover, large niches and the surfaces around them are carved to resemble the shrines of the Megalithic temples (figure 20). Although the excavation

Figure 20 Hal Saflieni Hypogeum

of the Hypogeum was carried out at different times, and with different objectives, it is estimated that the chambers contained some 7000 burials. The pottery found suggests that the complex was built in the early age of the Megalithic temples and continued in use until its end. With the burials there was a wealth of small objects, principally figurines, including the sleeping lady type, pendants and beads.

The Hypogeum, therefore, reflects a world of belief and practice related to those of the temples. The Hypogeum is also a vast extension of the simple chamber tomb, which appears in Malta about the time of the early Megalithic structures. Initially there appear to have been a group of such tombs on the Hypogeum site, which was then enlarged with the Megalithic entrance to the chambers we find today.

The immediate impression made by the Maltese remains, whether the temples or the Hypogeum, is one of immense scale and therefore of notable resources, both material and human, devoted to their creation. That all this took place on two small islands in the fourth and fifth millennia BC simply adds to the mystery. Until the Skorba radiocarbon dates were obtained, these Maltese monuments were viewed as a provincial reflection of the beehive tombs and Megalithic walls of Mycenean Greece of the second millennium, while the Maltese taste for spirals was also seen as imitation of the art of the Aegean. These notions are now out of the question.

Some quiet reflection, and a modicum of ex-perimental archaeology, has shown conclusively that the Megalithic monuments of northern Europe, Stonehenge and the cairns of the British Isles and France did not need vast work forces for their construction. So there is nothing mysterious in a prehistoric population of 10,000 or so on Malta and Gozo carrying out the projects whose remains amaze us today. What needed to be explained was the organization and motivation of these projects.

Colin Renfrew has drawn an analogy between Malta and Easter Island, where rows of stone ancestor figures were erected by competing lineage groups. The traditional social organization of the area is not a state, but it is more than a family structure, being what has been called a 'chiefdom'. The chief is owed obligations by his people and in turn redistributes the gifts they make to him. Although his powers of coercion are limited, he is able to organize important undertakings. In this way an uncomplicated political structure might be capable of mon-umental building projects. Following this line of reasoning, Renfrew divides Malta and Gozo into six provinces, each related to a temple or temple cluster.[10]

The 'chiefdom' model treats Malta in isolation. It suggests how the temple-building process may have functioned, but it leaves unanswered the fundamental questions of why it began and how it could be carried to such lengths. Why did Malta develop in this way while the other small Mediterranean islands did not? What was par-ticular about Malta's situation? The answer may lie in its relationship with Sicily.

The relationship was close. The first pottery on Malta is a variant of Stentinello ware. Some forms of Stentinello decoration – impressions from true cardium shells, rocker decoration and lozenge stamps – have not been found. But the closely spaced patterns, the color and the texture of the pottery place them in the same family. And subsequently Maltese pottery, down to the end of the temple-building age, develops hand in hand with the Sicilian sequence. The Late Neolithic pottery of Malta is a polished red ware, found in bowls often having angular necks. The Late Neolithic pottery of Sicily is also a polished red ware, also frequently used for vessels with angular profiles. Early Bronze Age pottery in Sicily begins with simple incision on grey ware (the San Cono-Piano Notaro-Grotta Zubbia type), which is paralleled in the Zebbug pottery of Malta, itself following directly on the red ware in the mid-fourth millennium and representing a distinct break in the Maltese pottery tradition up to that time. One reason for the diffusion of Sicilian pottery of the San Cono-Piano Notaro-Grotta Zubbia type in Malta has become clear on the basis of results from the excavation of the Neolithic site of Serra del Palco at Milena in the area of Agrigento. At this site an enclosure of Neolithic date continued to be respected at the beginning of the Bronze Age. Votive deposits were made containing small jars of the San Cono-Piano Notaro-Grotta Zubbia pottery packed with ochre. The red variety of this natural pigment was valued as magical substance from early times. It was also used in Malta, especially with burials. Ochre is not native to the Maltese islands and must have been imported. Sicily is the nearest source, and a recent study, based on the discoveries at Serra di Palco, has suggested convincingly that in the Early Bronze Age Sicilian ochre was shipped to Malta in containers of San Cono-Piano Notaro Grotta Zubbia ware, which contributed to the new fashion of pottery in Malta.[11]

Obsidian reached Malta steadily, from Pantelleria and probably from Lipari. The flint used on Malta is probably Sicilian. The querns of volcanic stone are unquestionably so. The closest source for the alabaster of which some figurines were made would be the south coast of Sicily. Other imports, such as the fragment of Serra d'Alto ware from Skorba, may have passed through Sicily. On Sicily, the two hypogea of Calaforno in the southeastern part of the island are reminiscent of the hypogeum of Hal Saflieni.

The reconstruction of economic relations between the two islands in the Neolithic and the first stages of the Bronze Age has recently been elevated from the study of the durable materials preserved in archaeological deposits to the level of the consideration of the perishable materials which are not completely lost to us if we have the imagination to recapture their role in prehistory. We owe to Brian McConnell the exposition of the theory that the precocious development of prehistoric Malta was the result of Malta's textile trade with Sicily.[12]

The wool trade has a peculiar character which it has maintained over the long centuries during which documentary evidence is available, beginning under the Roman Empire. The centers of textile production import the raw material, often from great distances. Thus it has been observed:

> England became the chief centre of wool growing because the country was both suitable and sparsely populated, two factors which have always controlled where wool could be grown. They applied, first in England, later in Spain, and finally in Australia, and they constitute the reason why wool has rarely been produced where it is manufactured into cloth.[13]

Furthermore, the finished wool textiles are not infrequently returned to the source of the wool. To substantiate this apparently illogical phenomenon it is not necessary to consider the history of weaving in medieval Florence or England. One can find appropriate documents from Bronze Age Anatolia. Shortly after 2,000 BC a group of Assyrian merchants took up residence at Kanesh in Anatolia. Their archives have come to light during excavations and are invaluable for the light they shed on the interregional trade

of the period. This commerce was based on the exchange of raw materials (gold and silver) from Anatolia for Mesopotamian textiles and tin shipped from its source through Mesopotamia.[14] This kind of commerce can now be traced back into the third millennium thanks to the discovery of the archives of the Palace of Ebla in Syria.[15] We need not wonder that the shepherds of Sicily bought woolen textiles from the Maltese to whom they had sold the wool initially. There was no lack of sheep in Anatolia in the Bronze Age, yet imported textiles found a ready market there.

An important reason for this trade is the demands on the time available to the subsistence family that makes its own clothing. This pressure is obvious to any traveler who has watched peasant women spinning while walking along the road or in the midst of other tasks. But the textile industry that would capitalize on the peasant market for cloth must have organized its production well above the household level. So it is, according to McConnell's hypothesis, that the Maltese were brought to the level of social organization that is reflected in the Megalithic temples of the islands. The Maltese temples, no less than the Cathedral of Florence, are monuments to the wool trade.[16]

In Sicily the result of the Maltese wool trade would have been the establishment of a network of contacts and the maintenance of a homogeneous material culture, exactly as we see it maintained in the Stentinello period. The same cultural homogeneity marks the late Neolithic in Sicily. Lipari has provided the best group of Late Neolithic red ware, called Diana Ware after the area at the foot of the Lipari acropolis atop which the settlement stood during the fourth millennium. The angular profiles and tubular handles of this style are as characteristic as its color (figures 21 and 22). It was certainly common across Sicily, though none of the findspots, even Contrada Diana itself, tell us anything about a Diana village.

A major element of the succeeding phase of the Early Age of Metals in Sicily is known as San Cono-Piano Notaro-Grotta Zubbia after the three principal sites where pottery of this type has been discovered (figure 23). Excepting the huts of the period at Piano Vento (Palma di Montechiaro) near Agrigento, no villages are known. Our evidence comes from tombs, cham-

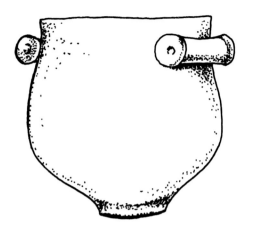

Figure 21 Syracuse Museum, vase of the Diana style from Matrensa

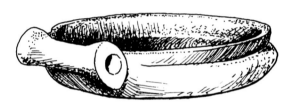

Figure 22 Syracuse Museum, vase of the Diana style from Matrensa

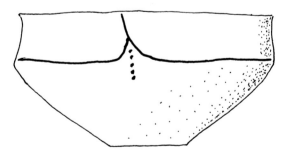

Figure 23 Licata, Navarra collection, vase of the San Cono-Piano Notaro-Grotta Zubbia style

ber tombs like those we have already met and known traditionally in Sicily as 'oven tombs' or 'tombe a forno', although the description 'entrance shaft and chamber' might be more precise (figure 24). The earliest chamber tombs known in Sicily have been excavated at Piano Vento. They were created by digging out a chamber in the compact subsoil. They stand at the head of the long history of the Sicilian chamber tomb, which came to be cut into limestone enlarged and embellished as the Bronze Age progressed.

Figure 24 'Oven tomb'

The pottery of the San Cono-Piano Notaro-Grotta Zubbia type has a decoration of sinuous and often solitary lines on a dark ground. The repertoire of shapes is dominated by bowls and jars. The first bronze blades known in Sicily also appear in these contexts. The pottery of the transitional phase between Late Neolithic and San Cono-Piano Notaro-Grotta Zubbia in a necropolis of chamber tombs at Piano Vento (Palma di Montechiaro) is also dark surfaced but the decoration is inlaid in large cut-out areas on the surface.

At the end of this poorly defined age in Sicilian prehistory the sense of cultural unity across the island is broken. Several pottery styles are known which reflect conflicting traditions. They are found in stratigraphic sequence in the important cave sites of Chiusazza near Syracuse and Vecchiuzzo in the mountains behind the northern Sicilian coast. This evidence suggests that they are successive, and if so, each endured a far briefer time than earlier styles. These new groups are the Chiusazza Style, pottery decorated with unsymmetrical designs in matt (dull) paint on a light background, the Serraferlicchio Style of decoration in black on a red ground, and finally the Malpasso Style, a monochrome red-surfaced pottery whose deep goblets and tongue-topped handles already suggest a knowledge of metal vases where such forms are natural to the material. The Malpasso style is characteristic of a necropolis of chamber tombs at Calascibetta near Enna in the center of Sicily. Although the chronology is very unsure, it is possible to hazard the suggestion that this diversity reflects the breakdown of the economic ties which had promoted uniformity in an earlier age. The abrupt end of the civilization that created the Maltese temples, based, at least in part, on the wool trade with Sicily, may have been at least part of the chain of events reflected in this change.

Similarly the demand for obsidian failed in the Early Bronze Age. The reason for the collapse of the trade may not really lie with the intro-duction of metal blades, which must have remained rare and expensive. Flint was the alternative for stone cutting tools. But in any case, following the period of rippled-surface finely burnished pottery called Piano Conte on Lipari, the islands, in the early Bronze Age, entered a period which has been interpreted as one of isolation and poverty.

The Early Bronze Age

In the four-fold scheme constructed by the great Paolo Orsi, the Castelluccian Culture represented the first phase of Sicilian prehistory following the Neolithic. Radiocarbon dates place one Castelluccian site, La Muculufa, around 2,200–2,100 BC. But considering the abundance of Castelluccian remains, it is obvious that this phase of Sicilian prehistory was a long one. The Castelluccian Age may well begin before 2,500 and continue into the early centuries of the second millennium.

Orsi's excavations at Castelluccio near Noto were made in 1892 and 1893. The site enjoys a magnificent position at the edge of the Hyblaean uplands to the southwest of Syracuse. The lime-stone plateau of this region has been carved by its streams into a maze of ridges separated by gorges. Travel is difficult. The soil is poor. It is still a region of herdsmen. From these heights Castelluccio looks south toward the sea from a position of security on an isolated spur of limestone. What must have been a small village occupied the top of the site. Erosion had erased

its remains, but Orsi recovered quantities of material from secondary deposits (referred to as a dump) on the side of the plateau.

The pottery of the Castelluccian Culture is brilliantly decorated in black on a red ground, which in reality is a slip applied over the light-colored surface of the clay (figure 25). Occasionally the black lines are bordered in white. The color pattern of Castelluccian wares thus has clear antecedents in Serraferlicchio pottery. The design patterns are wholly different. The Serraferlicchio potters inscribed their vases with diagonal stripes and introduced disconnected filling motives into the intervening spaces. This kind of decoration fitted naturally on vases whose globular shapes come from a fully ceramic tradition uninfluenced by metal prototypes. It is far different in Castelluccian. In its more complicated phases, the decoration is angularly precise and structurally interconnected. It devel-ops complex fields of diamond patterns, triangles, herringbones, wavy lines, and arching borders. The shapes of Castelluccian pottery are distinctive. There are the usual small cups, jugs and basins, but shapes become exaggerated and new eye-catching types are introduced. The most common among the latter is the open bowl on a pedestal, generally supported by handles connecting the two. The inventiveness of the Castelluccian potters appears in the elongation of the necks

Figure 25 Licata Museum, Castelluccian-style vase from La Muculufa

or bodies of jugs, combinations of asymmetrical handles and exaggerated rims and feet. Beside the painted wares there is a class of monochrome black pottery carrying incised decoration. Its shapes and decoration repeat those of the painted pottery.

Castelluccian pottery has regional subdivisions to a greater degree than even the most widespread of the preceding pottery styles, Stentinello and Diana for example. There are differences between tomb pottery, consisting generally of smaller vases with simple decoration, and the more elaborately decorated pottery from settlements. The Castelluccian ware from the area surrounding Mt Aetna is the simplest variety. The most familiar Castelluccian is from the area around Ragusa, where decorative motives appear in a developed but restrained fashion. Castelluccio itself has rather simple material from tombs, but the pottery from the village refuse deposits recovered by Orsi has abundant and undisciplined decoration. Agrigentine Castelluccian is different again, with a taste for elaboration of designs, a tendency which is carried farther in the Castelluccian of western Sicily. In fact, with some justice one might speak of the Castelluccian style as a loose union of regional groups.

This term is useful to describe cases where contemporary regional units are clearly in contact, but retain their own individuality. The pottery of the Castelluccian groups suggests close and frequent contact among them. On the other hand there is a period in Early Bronze Age Sicily (following the period typified by San Cono-Piano Notaro-Grotta Zubbia ceramics) when the evidence of pottery suggests local autonomy and isolation. At this time we seem to be witnessing the break-up of the network of communications which had been maintained, at least in part, by the Maltese wool trade and the Lipari obsidian industry. But in Castelluccian times there can be no question that regular contact was once more effectively established over much of the island. As we shall see below, one force operating in this direction was the political integration of the Castelluccian villages in regional confederations.

At Castelluccio Orsi also explored thirty-six chamber tombs which open directly onto the cliff face. The tombs revealed evidence of successive depositions, the earlier occupants unceremoniously swept toward the side of the tomb to make way for the newcomers. The pottery was somewhat meager and poor, but there were numerous stone amulets in the form of axes. There were almost no metal finds, only what is apparently the crosspiece of a small balance and some other fragments.

The glory of the Castelluccian necropolis is the architecture of the tombs. They are both single and double chambers. The chambers of the more elaborate tombs are recessed from the cliff face and are preceded by porticoes also cut out of the limestone formation. Two sculptured closing stones also remained to reward the excavator. The image sculpted on both is the same, a scene of copulation (figure 26). The male

Figure 26 Syracuse Museum, closing stone of tomb from Castelluccio

is reduced to a penis, the female has an armature-like body dominated by two gigantic spiral eyes. A better image for defending against the Evil Eye would be difficult to imagine. The eye, agent of evil but also protective charm, is joined by the second line of defense, any piercing horn or weapon that can penetrate the eye. Since the calamities of the Evil Eye frequently involve impotence, the swollen penis is an effective charm, and especially so because of the superficial similarity between the eye and the vulva. There is a long tradition of this superstition and charms against it in Sicily, which we have already seen operating in the decoration of Stentinello pottery.

Stone carving in an architectural setting raises the question of possible Maltese inspiration for Castelluccian tomb design. But the subject of the Castelluccian closing stones is not Maltese, nor is the portico architecture of the more elaborate tombs at Castelluccio. Furthermore, the Castelluccian Culture, to the best of our present information, arose at a time when the temple culture of Malta had already fallen into eclipse. This happened not long after the year 3,000. Subsequently the ruins of the temple of Tarxien were occupied by a cremation cemetery, which belonged to a new people who had no respect for the traditions of the past. Rather than Maltese influence, it seems that the porticoes of the Castelluccian tombs must reflect the architecture of buildings in Sicily which have yet to be discovered.

Maltese inspiration has also been claimed for the facade treatment of a group of Castelluccian tombs recently published from Donnafugata near the south coastal plain not far from Camarina. These tombs are built chambers rather than rock-cut, and the dirt face at either side of the doorways was faced with upright stones. The effect is not unlike that of the doorway of the temple at Hagar Qim, but the motivation is practical as well as decorative. The idea could easily have occurred independently to the Sicilian tomb builders as it did in Sardinia where a similar treatment is given to the facades of the so-called Giants' Tombs. Occasionally Castellucian tombs were approached by a short dromos (entry corridor).

Porticoed tombs such as are known at Castelluccio are also found at Cava d'Ispica and Cava Lazzaro in the same area but at the base of the Hyblaean plateau. A further instance is known from Monte Sole (Licata, figure 27). In this case the interior chamber is relatively small but it was entered from the portico through a rectangular vestibule.

Generally, however, the Castelluccian chamber tomb is a small cavity (barely 1.2 to 1.5 meters, 4 to 5 ft in diameter) cut into a limestone bank.

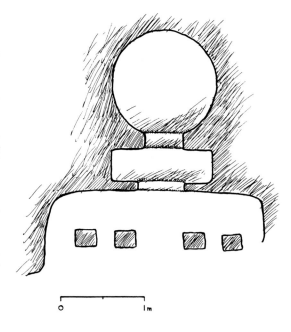

Figure 27 Licata, chamber tomb

The doorway may be slightly recessed, occasionally creating a porch before the tomb. Carving around the doorways, niches before the tombs, and multiple tomb chambers reached through a single door are known. Burial in natural fissures in the rock also occurs, following a tradition also known in the earlier phases of the Bronze Age. At La Muculufa, the area immediately outside such a burial cave was paved with simple rectangular terracotta tiles. The debris of funeral meals or sacrifices was found on this paving and has been noted elsewhere in association with Castelluccian tombs.

With the Castelluccians the chamber tomb came above ground. But the idea of the chamber tomb was already a thousand years old. We have met it in Malta not long after 4,000 and in fourth-millennium Sicily. In southern Italy the oldest chamber tomb, also of the underground type, belongs to a phase of the Neolithic contemporary with Diana pottery. The chamber tomb, however, appears in an area far more extensive than southern Italy and Sicily alone. It is known in the Near East, the Aegean, southern Russia; in the form of mortuary houses it occurs across the Eurasian plain. In the west it is met in the Iberian Peninsula and in France. In essence, the

Egyptian mastaba tomb is a chamber tomb. Some have traced the genesis of all chamber tombs to Egypt. Others feel that the Italian tombs are the oldest and therefore that the chamber tomb has its roots in the western Mediterranean.

Yet in this phenomenon perhaps we are witnessing social development rather than the propagation of an architectural form. Although there are exceptions, it appears that in much of the world in which the chamber tomb is found, its coming marks a distinct change in the relations of the dead and the living. Where previously the dead had found a place within the boundaries of the community, they are now given their own house and their own place. Thus one may detect a growing complexity in the life of the members of the community, no longer united in a single family or clan and no longer willing to tolerate the dead of other families in their midst. Once the idea of multiple burial in chamber tombs reached Sicily a tradition was established which was to endure, among the non-Greek peoples of the island, even after the coming of the Greeks in the eighth century. There is no compelling reason to attribute any of the modifications of the chamber tomb during its history in Sicily to any influence from other areas where it is also known, especially the Aegean.[17]

The appearance of the chamber tomb marches hand in hand with the spread of copper metallurgy. The two phenomena may be unrelated. But they suggest the ease with which social ideas and technological information travelled even in the fourth millennium. At an earlier date the same statement could be made about painted pottery and Neolithic agricultural practices. Once the way of the sea was open, knowledge and curiosity knew no boundaries.

A small Castelluccian settlement was excavated in the opening years of this century at Branco Grande on the sea near Camarina on the south coast of Sicily. Its circular huts measured approximately 6 meters (19 ft 8 in) in diameter. There were no interior posts to support the roof, and roof and walls were evidently made of light materials, probably wattle and daub for the walls and thatch for the roof. They rested on a low base of stone. The settlement was surrounded by a defense wall. A larger Castelluccian village has now been investigated at Melilli north of Syracuse (figure 28). Once again erosion had

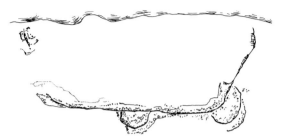

Figure 28 Melilli, city walls

destroyed all vestiges of the buildings, but the settlement, measuring some 90 meters (295 ft) across, was protected by a stout fortification wall. This structure was 3 meters (10 ft) wide and was strengthened by semicircular towers. Identical fortifications have come to light on the peninsula of Thapsos on the Bay of Augusta a few kilometers from Syracuse and Melilli. Thapsos was to be the site of a great Middle Bronze Age emporium. Once again there is no trace of the settlement, but it seems reasonable to attribute the wall to a Castelluccian community on the site.

These fortifications have great significance for the international relations of the Castelluccians. They are replicas of the fortifications with towers belonging to the later third millennium at Lerna in the Argolid in Greece, those on the island of Syros in the Aegean, and at Los Millares in Spain. Clearly, the knowledge of advances in military architecture travelled swiftly too.

Further Castelluccian domestic architecture has been revealed at Manfria just west of Gela. At this site excavation revealed two buildings which served as the centers of what were presumably two farmsteads, each with a house surrounded by sheds and silos. One of the main buildings is more than 10 meters (32 ft 9 in) long, the other half that size. Their floors were sunk below ground level, and the roof was supported by a series of posts set along the long axis of the building. The superstructure was again of perishable materials. Outside the two main buildings there were a number of very small silos and ovens. The cooking appears to have been done outside. The bone material shows that there was little hunting. Meat was obtained from sheep and goat, followed by pig with some cattle present. We may imagine agriculture was carried on with the same crops raised during the Neolithic. Chamber tombs on the ridge above the site served as the abode of the dead.

There is some question whether the buildings at Manfria are part of a true village or represent one, or possibly two, farmsteads. If the latter alternative is the case, we should not wonder at the presence of chamber tombs, characteristic of the multi-family community, at what may have been the holding of a single family. Fashions from larger centers of the Castelluccian world, of which one was surely modern Gela, would have influenced the residents of the farmsteads. From Gela comes one of the most interesting documents bearing on Castelluccian religion (figure 29). This is a group of seven phallos-like objects of terracotta found in a pottery plate. Such horns are omnipresent in Castelluccian surroundings. One might call them household gods, thinking of the equally primitive Roman *lares* and *penates*, but there is also something of the protective charm about them, much like the Greek herm with its prominent, often erect, penis. The symbolism of the phallic charm has already been encountered on the Castelluccian tomb portals.

Castelluccian mining is known from the area of Ragusa where the Castelluccians worked the flint mines of Monte Tabuto. They subsequently used the mining galleries for burials.

Up to this point there is little in our picture of the Castelluccians which would not seem appropriate to earlier ages. If one excepts the chamber tomb and their exiguous metal tools, the village life of the Castelluccians seems hardly

Figure 29 Gela Museum, dish with terracotta horns

different from the Neolithic. Evidence from one new excavation, however, suggests that Castelluccian Sicily may have known some form of political and religious confederation. The site in question is La Muculufa. Situated in the valley of the Salso River some 20 kilometers (12.4 miles) from its mouth, La Muculufa is part of a crest formed by limestone beds that are folded almost vertically in an east–west direction. As the Salso made its valley it wore a gorge through this barrier and stripped the peaks to their present bare state. The peak to the west of the river is known as Monte dei Drasi; the one to the east is La Muculufa. Together they are visible from Caltanissetta, 30 kilometers to the north.

During a brief period, perhaps no more than a century or two about 2,200-2,100 BC, as established by 21 radiocarbon dates, La Muculufa was the site of a Castelluccian village and sanctuary. The abandonment of the place may have been due to the failure of springs on the hill. The village was located at the foot of the exposed rock crest. To date six buildings have been excavated; most are similar to the huts from Branco Grande. One kitchen was preserved outside a hut. As excavation progresses, the entire village will be uncovered.

For the present the great importance of La Muculufa is its sanctuary. Situated at the eastern extremity of the long crest of the hill, it occupies a small platform lodged between the sheer wall of the peak and a second vertically inclined wall of rock which long ago split away from the main mass. On a clear day Mt Aetna appears on the horizon, and one can easily envisage the dawn at La Muculufa when the rising sun illuminates the sanctuary with a burst of light. Ancient religious observances often took place at dawn or soon thereafter, and it requires little fantasy to imagine the atmosphere of this miniature Delphi on such an occasion (figure 30).

The sanctuary had no covered buildings. Rather, artificial terraces were created to make level areas. One of the retaining walls is preserved intact. It rests against a large boulder at one end, and against the hillside at the other. It is almost 2 meters (6 ft 6 in) high. The wall is given a distinct batter, or inward inclination, as it rises. Unfortunately the area above this and its companion terrace wall to the north had been thoroughly disturbed in medieval times, but the Castelluccian strata were well preserved in front

Figure 30 La Muculufa, reconstruction of sanctuary by Anne L. Holloway

of the terrace walls. Here was found the mounded accumulation of innumerable fires and grouped around the last of them three vessels. Fragments of firewood (the bark had not been stripped from the logs) showed the intense heat over which lambs and kids had been cooked. It seems that these were butchered elsewhere, because few of the carcasses arrived at the sanctuary with their lower limbs. The pottery from the sanctuary is extraordinary. Technically it is superbly made and fired. Its decoration is often rich and individual, so much so that research still in progress suggests the possibility of identifying the work of individual craftsmen. And the contrast with the collection of pottery from the village site shows how much emphasis was placed on the use of fine ware in the sanctuary. There is twice as much decorated pottery in the sanctuary as in the village. And the sheer quantity of material from the sanctuary, as well as the group

of vessels left in place surrounding a ritual hearth, shows that these abundantly decorated vases were also intended to remain where they had been used as offerings to the gods.

Another observation made by Susan S. Lukesh, who is working with the pottery from the excavation, is that in the sanctuary there are groups of decorative patterns, one might say workshop pattern series, that do not occur in the village sample, at least up to now. Hypothetically it is plausible to suggest that there were outsiders coming to the sanctuary and making offerings, and there is further evidence to trace some of the 'foreign' decorative patterns to sites around the valley where surface collections have been made. Tentatively, therefore, one may identify La Muculufa as the seat of a cult common to the villages of the lower Salso Valley. And if the villagers met at stated intervals for religious purposes, it is a small step to envisaging a political side to their meetings. The entire history of ancient leagues and federations, whether in Greece or Italy, is full of such early political unions based on sanctuaries, the most relevant to the present context being the primitive Latin League which met at the sanctuary of Jupiter Latiarius on the Alban Mountain south of Rome. The sanctuary at La Muculufa is simply an earlier instance of the same phenomenon.

The Sicilian–Maltese wool trade of the fourth millennium had certainly been interrupted by the calamity that brought an end to the temple civilization on Malta. But connections with Malta were maintained by the Castelluccians. Just south of Syracuse, a trading station has been discovered at Ognina. Today the site is a small island at the entrance to a narrow harbor; earlier it was certainly a promontory projecting from the coast. There is both Maltese pottery of the Tarxien Cemetery type and Castelluccian ware at Ognina. The Castelluccian material, however, belongs to the dark surfaced monochrome variety, in some instances very difficult to distinguish from the Maltese sherds. This circumstance has led to some perhaps overhopeful identification of Maltese material at other sites.

From the west of Spain or southern France – came the so-called 'Bell Beakers' which have been found in Castelluccian contexts. We shall have more to say about these vases and their significance in discussing the Conca d'Oro Culture of the Palermo area.

The most eloquent testimony to the radius of Castelluccian contacts with the outside world comes from a group of singular bone plaques (figure 31). These objects are generally fashioned from the long bones of caprines, although one at least was made from an animal's incisor. They are worked so as to leave a row of button-like knobs down their length. The plaques are occasionally plain, but often they are delicately worked, the surface surrounding the knobs crisscrossed in a net pattern, the knobs themselves decorated with stars and wavy lines.

The plaques defy interpretation as functional objects. The curvature of the bone and the differences in size and shape make them impractical for any use that has been suggested for them, as decorations for dagger sheaths or the like. One school of thought would make them stylized female idols endowed with multiple breasts like the Artemis of Ephesus and other female divinities of Asia Minor. The Castelluccians, however, were not quite so abstract in their rendering of the human figure, as is shown by their terracotta figurines, some of them decorated, all of them at least as anatomically correct as gingerbread men. Paired holes at the ends of some of the plaques suggest that they were worn around the neck. So if not figurines, they may well have been amulets. They are found in tombs as well as in settlement contexts, which further suggests their importance as personal possessions. Such plaques, moreover,

Figure 31 Syracuse Museum, bone plaque from Castelluccio

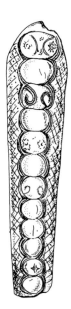

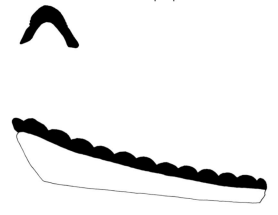

have been found far outside Sicily. There is a plaque from Malta, another from southern Italy, and in the east they have been found in Greece, at Lerna near Argos, and at Troy at the entrance to the Dardanelles, where three plaques were excavated by Schliemann. In all cases the contexts are of the late third millennium.

From Sicily there are seventeen plaques distributed widely over the Castelluccian territory. This evidence, compared with the sporadic pattern of distribution outside Sicily, shows that the plaques were made in Sicily and carried abroad by Sicilians. The routes along which they passed were the avenues by which ideas and techniques from the east came west. The design of fortifications, knowledge of metallurgy and the notion of the city of the dead all traveled in this way. Although one tends to attribute the diffusion of such concepts to easterners coming west, there is no reason to exclude the initiative of the Sicilians. To what degree formal ties of exchange and hospitality, a variety of the Kula system examined on pp. 12–13, were instrumental in the relationships must remain speculation. But it would be natural to assume that they played a part. And in the bone plaques one may possibly have items that belonged to such a fraternity and were actually exchanged among its members over an area from Malta to Troy.

Castelluccian ties with the east have been emphasized in studies of the decorative patterns of Castelluccian pottery by Giuliana Sluga Messina.[18] One of these is a cruciform figure developed from attached diamonds, or chains of the same figures (figure 32). These and other less unusual patterns, for example cross-hatched triangles, checkerboard patterns, chevrons and wavy lines, are compared by the author to the painted pottery of the Near East, especially Iran, and Anatolia, introducing the possibility of a migration of peoples from this area to the west and eventually to Sicily. But doubt falls on this theory simply because of the widely differing places and times from which these parallels are taken. In addition, there is a single crucial objection to it. The cruciform figure that forms the core of the argument is present in the west long before it appears on any eastern pottery. It occurs in the painting of the Grotta di Porto Badisco in Apulia, datable to the Mesolithic (figure 33). This configuration, like most geometric patterns of decorated pottery of the

Figure 32 Ragusa Museum, vase of the Castelluccio style from Castiglione

Figure 33 Grotto of Porto Badisco, painting

Neolithic and Early Bronze Age, may well come from textiles. Such figures, descendants of long forgotten amulets, are still made by children today. Their name in the English-speaking world, 'God's Eyes', indicates their origins all too clearly.

None the less, the question remains why the Early Bronze Age turned to elaborate decoration of its pottery after the monochrome styles prevalent in the Late Neolithic and at the opening of the Early Bronze Age. To be sure, the Castelluccian technique has its roots in the Serraferlicchio style, but this consideration does not explain the motivation for the flowering of geometric decoration we see, especially at La Muculufa and in the complex Castelluccian pottery of western Sicily. It is possible that the excavations of La Muculufa offer at least a partial explanation of this phenomenon. What is evident in the sanctuary of La Muculufa is the competition of different villages to make the finest and most beautifully decorated vessels to bring and deposit at the common gathering place. Just as tomb pottery tends to be banal, the pottery destined for the sanctuary was the finest that the offerer could obtain. This competition fueled displays of virtuosity by the Castelluccian painters, and ritual uses may indeed be the motivating force behind the rebirth of painted pottery itself. If so, the beginning of the new popularity of painted wares would coincide with the creation of the federal sanctuaries in the Early Bronze Age.

On the Aeolian Islands the third millennium witnessed the rise of what is termed the Capo Graziano Culture. There are several well-documented villages of this period in the islands. At first the villages are located close to the shore, for example Contrada Diana at the foot of the Lipari acropolis, Piano del Porto on Filicudi, the site above the port at Alicudi, and Point Peppa Maria on Panarea. Later the settlements move to the safety of the heights of the islands. The character of the villages remains unchanged, as shown by the type site of the Capo Graziano Culture, La Montagnola del Capo Graziano on Filicudi, or by similar sites in defensive positions, the Lipari acropolis and Serra dei Cianfi on Salina (figure 34). The huts are oval shaped. Their floors were generally sunk below the surface level. The superstructure was of perishable

material. On the acropolis of Lipari a significantly larger Capo Graziano building, 18 meters (59 ft) on its long axis, was separated from the rest of the settlement by an enclosure wall. This building, which clearly had some special function, and its neighbors were found below an impressive sequence of settlements superimposed one on the other. They cover a span of time that extends well into the first millennium.

Capo Graziano pottery is monochrome and grey in color with simple decoration of dots or incised wavy lines. The forms, from bowls to large containers, are generally simple ceramic types (figure 35).

Several features beside imported pottery show that from its beginning the Capo Graziano Culture was in touch with the Aegean. The huts were made with potsherd pavements characteristic of Greece in the later third millennium. As in the same area, but rarely encountered in the west, there were pits dug beside the huts. Small terracotta anchor-shaped hooks of uncertain use, but also known in the Aegean, are found. But the most significant of this group of characteristics is the vocabulary of signs which are incised on Capo Graziano pottery (figure 36). It may be debated whether these are distant relations of the so-called 'linear' scripts of the Aegean world; what is sure is that the islanders had come in contact with writing and now used written signs, even if in a limited way, themselves. Luigi Bernabò Brea, the excavator of the prehistoric sites of the Lipari Islands, has interpreted

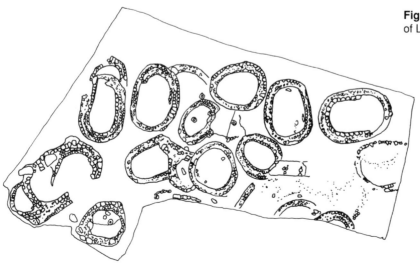

Figure 34 Filicudi, village of La Montagnola

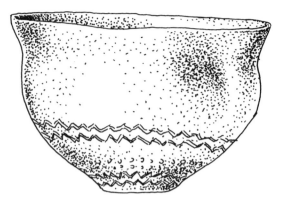

Figure 35 Lipari Museum, vase of the Capo Graziano style from Lipari

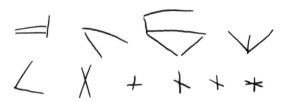

Figure 36 Signs incised on Capo Graziano and Milazzese-style pottery

this group of characteristics, as well as less specific parallels between Early Helladic pottery (late third millennium) in Greece and Capo Graziano ceramics, to mean that the Capo Graziano people arrived from the east.[19] At the very least one must agree that they provided a bridgehead for eastern contacts with Sicily. These were intensified at the end of the Capo Graziano period when Aegean pottery appears in the later villages of this group. These sherds from mainland Greece belonging to what is called Late Helladic I and II show that the Capo Graziano Culture persisted into the sixteenth century. Bernabò Brea has further suggested that together with intensified Aegean contact came piracy, which prompted the removal of the villages to defensible heights.

The coastal northeast of Sicily at this time also sees the arrival of inhumation burial inside large storage jars (pithoi). Instances are known at Messina and Naxos. This rite is typical of western Asia Minor and belongs to the same current of influence, and possibly migration, as the foreign characteristics found in the Aeolian Islands.

One element of Capo Graziano pottery, cups with ribbon handles swung well free of the body,

occurs in the pottery of contemporary sites on the north coast collectively representing what is known as the Rodi-Tindari-Vallelunga Culture. This group, in turn, is contemporary with the Castelluccian Culture, a synchronism shown by the tomb with elements of both cultures at Vallelunga on the border of the Castelluccian area in western Sicily and in another at Contrada Pergola (Salaparuta). Its influence is seen to the south in the tombs at Ribera. The pithos burials at Naxos, on the east coast, also contained Castelluccian material.

Capo Graziano vases are also found in western Sicily in the cemeteries of chamber tombs concentrated around Palermo which have been referred to as the Conca d'Oro Culture. (This is not a consistent 'culture' but rather a convenient term for the Early Bronze Age cemeteries of chamber tombs in the Palermo area.) The tombs are of the early underground type met in the San Cono-Piano Notaro-Grotta Zubbia area, although double chambers reached by the same entrance shaft are common. The pottery, too, continues the San Cono-Piano Notaro-Grotta Zubbia type of incised decoration, though the forms, most often small jars, are different. The most finely decorated pieces, of the so-called Moarda style, appear to be incised translations of Castelluccian designs (figure 37).

Figure 37 Palermo Museum, vase of the Moarda style from a tomb of the Conca d'Oro group

The tombs, however, were used over a long time. In them are found pieces of Serraferlicchio ware, the Castelluccian pottery with white edging to its black decoration often referred to as San Ippolito ware, and Capo Graziano ware as well. The burials of this area are important for the presence of bell beakers, showing contact with southern France or Spain (figure 38). This class

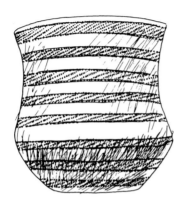

Figure 38 Palermo Museum, bell beaker from a tomb of the Conca d'Oro group

of pottery, which seems to be northern European in origin, is also found in the British Isles, the Low Countries, the Rhineland, as well as in central Europe and northern Italy. It regularly occurs in tomb groups with distinctive arrow heads, bronze blades and archers' stone wrist-guards. Tombs with this distinctive kit are apparently isolated from the general cultures in which they occur. The most recent interpretation of the Beaker Complex suggests that it is the equipment of a particular caste with membership over wide areas and across cultural boundaries.[20] This situation would perhaps have been similar to what has been tentatively envisaged for the Castelluccian bone plaques in our discussion above. It means that the beakers would have been important symbolic gifts even outside the geographical area where tombs with the full group of distinctive equipment appear. This explains the stray beakers found in Castelluccian territory even as far away as Manfria near Gela.

Bernabò Brea has defined the area of contact of the Capo Graziano Culture in terms which approximate our concept of the loose union of regional groups represented by the Castelluccian Culture. Besides the sites of the north coast of Sicily of the Rodi-Tindari-Vallelunga Culture and the important contemporary settlement now under excavation on the island of Pantelleria south of Sicily, this group of related units includes the Tarxien Cemetery Culture on Malta, whose pottery has some forms, for example small pedestal stands, and some incised decorative patterns in common with Capo Graziano. The Tarxien Cemetery Culture also shares the unusual burial rite of cremation with the Aeolian Islands in the period of the Capo Graziano Culture. The Tarxien Cemetery group were workers in bronze, amply demonstrated in the Tarxien cemetery, but not characteristic, as far as we know, of the Early Bronze Age people of Sicily.

The Middle and Late Bronze Age

As the Castelluccian Age was drawing to a close, events took place in the far distant Aegean which were to have great influence on the future of Sicily. The first signs of the transformation of what had remained an essentially Neolithic village society, as had the Early Bronze Age in Sicily, are visible around the Gulf of Argos and especially at Mycenae. The famous Shaft Graves, thirty in number and grouped in two cemeteries just below the acropolis of the site, are nothing more than greatly enlarged pit graves for multiple burials in which an impractical attempt has been made to create a burial chamber by installing a roofing some feet off the floor beneath the dirt fill of the shaft. The dazzling riches of the six tombs of Grave Circle A excavated by Schliemann and Tsountas have long been famous. The work of Mylonas and Papademitriou in Grave Circle B revealed the first and less opulently buried warrior barons of Mycenae. The character of these people is shown first by their skeletal remains, larger and better nourished than those of the commoners of the Argolid and second by the bones of the men bearing the scars of their bellicose existence. Their weapons were revolutionary, among the first swords in Greece, and terrifying they were, long rapiers which we see in the hands of a sinewy warrior shown in the act of dispatching his adversary on the magnificent gold ring from Tomb IV. Another weapon of the Mycenean princes was the horse and chariot. On the reliefs of the grave stelae (tomb markers) erected above the graves of Grave Circle A warlords appear in the act of running down their victims.

It was the Shaft Grave Dynasty that shows the first evidence of the expansive vitality that marks the centuries after 1,600 BC in Greece. Under their impetus central administrations of Near Eastern type came into being which channeled raw materials and human resources into industries producing for export as well as for home consumption. We know the economic aspects of Mycenean life best from the archives of clay tablets inscribed in the Linear B script found at Pylos and belonging to the end of the thirteenth century, as well as by the similar archives of Knossos in Crete which was under Mycenean control when these records were made, certainly within a century and perhaps less of the Pylos tablets. The best documented industry at Pylos is the manufacture of perfume, which was evidently shipped in the distinctive flasks with side spout but surmounted by a false neck with two handles attached to it which give the name 'stirrup jar' to the form. The trail of Mycenean pottery, and especially Mycenean stirrup jars, in the centuries from 1,500 to 1,100 BC is a long one reaching from the Levant and Egypt to Italy, Sicily, Sardinia and Spain. No less impressive was metal-working at Pylos, much of it intended for war. Cabinet work, textiles, both wool and linen, and faience, are no less prominent. And over all this activity there is the figure of the Mycenean monarch. Following the Shaft Grave Period he and his like were buried in the great underground 'beehive' or tholos tombs in which monumental building and skillful engineering were united to their task.

In many ways, and especially in the arts, the Myceneans followed the example of the Minoans in Crete, whose cities had first developed at the opening of the second millennium. But beyond the Aegean, Crete made contact only with Egypt and the Levant, not with the west, until about 1,200 BC.

Mycenean industry required raw materials on a scale unknown to the village societies of an earlier date in Greece. Timber, clay, agricultural produce and wool, even possibly silver and gold, could be had at home. Copper and tin, however, came from abroad. In an earlier day, the villages of Greece may have been content to exist on the borders of the Near East and to share its metal supplies, including copper from Cyprus and tin from those mysterious sources, possibly in Czechoslovakia or Anatolia, that had made possible tin bronze earlier than elsewhere at third millennium Troy. But the expanded Mycenean consumption of metal must have stimulated the search for new supplies. It can be no coincidence that Mycenean pottery appears in Sardinia in the fourteenth century, just at the time when Sardinian copper would have been of use to the intensified metal production of Italy and Sicily and of Mycenean Greece as well. Although physical analysis has not yet been able to give us a definitive answer as to the source of the Bronze Age ingots from Sardinia, it would be remarkable indeed if they were made from anything else than local ore. These same ingots, however, were cast in the peculiar 'ox hide' shape used in the eastern Mediterranean.

All this lay in the future when the Shaft Grave Dynasty was ruling Mycenae. But in one way the Shaft Graves illustrate contact with the west, just as do the first Mycenean sherds, belonging to this epoch, which have been found at Vivara in the Bay of Naples. The Shaft Graves are rich in amber. The source is Baltic, but the workmanship of the amber beads from the Shaft Graves suggests that the finished pieces may have come from England. The natural route they might have traveled to their destination in Greece was down the Rhone to the Mediterranean and then east past Sicily. By this same route Cornish tin could also have reached the Mediterranean. But there is no reason to suppose that the precious amber reaching Mycenae or the Mycenean pottery returning west required any more intense network of contacts than existed when the bearers of the bone plaques traveled from Sicily to the Aegean or when Aegean elements contributed to the formation of the Capo Graziano Culture.

The years following 1,400 BC mark a decided change in the relations of the Aegean and Sicily. Now begins the period of massive importation of Mycenean pottery into southern Italy, and there appear local imitations of the imported wares. The Mycenean material from Scoglio del Tonno (Taranto) was excavated in the early years of this century. Recently similar concentrations of Mycenean and imitation Mycenean pottery have come to light at Terme Tito near ancient Metapontum and further along the coast of Italy's instep at Broglio di Trebisacce. The Mycenean material in Sicily, however, is different both in quantity and in type. Leaving the Aeolian Islands aside for the moment, in Sicily proper we find vases almost exclusively from tombs. This distribution only partially reflects a bias in excavation. The material is concentrated in several necropolises around Syracuse. It is made up predominantly of small, closed vessels, of the type which would have held unguents or perfume (figure 39). This is unlike the repertoire of open vases, including a wide selection of large containers, characteristic of the Mycenean imports of southern Italy.[21] Swords of Aegean descent,

Figure 39 Syracuse Museum, Mycenean vase from Matrensa

if not of Aegean manufacture, accompany these vessels (figure 40). A pair of bronze basins from Caldare near Agrigento, found with bronze blades, (figure 41) and similar pieces from a tomb at Milena, inland from the same city, are imports as is the Mycenean jar found near Agrigento and for many years in a private collection there.

The single most impressive testimony to commerce between east and west is also Sicilian. On

the peninsula of Thapsos (just north of Syracuse) there existed, before the fourteenth century, a settlement of huts in the tradition of the buildings we have met earlier (figures 42 and 43). Typically the huts are round, but they may be oval or almost rectangular. They are generally larger than their Early Bronze Age predecessors. Their roofs were supported by interior posts. The hearth is now found in the interior of the building. The houses are randomly distributed over the settlement. In them there was found the Bronze Age Sicilian pottery known as Thapsos ware and imported Middle Bronze Age pottery from Malta. Thapsos pottery is grey monochrome ware with incised decoration. This is often limited to simple linear designs but birds, animals and fish are also sketched. The apotropaic (protective) eye is not unknown. There is also plastic ribbing on the exterior of the vessels. Aside from the usual group of cups and jugs, Thapsos pottery is distinguished for its development of the pedestal vase. These often reach

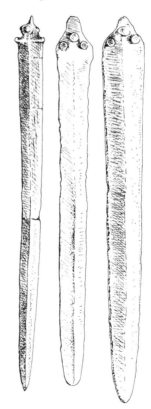

Figure 40 Syracuse Museum and Agrigento Museum, swords from Plemmyrion and Caldare

Figure 41 Agrigento Museum, basins from Caldare

Figure 42 Thapsos Peninsula, view from the west

Figure 43 Thapsos, reconstruction of hut after *La Sicilia Antica*

gigantic proportions (figure 44). There are enlarged versions of cups as well (figure 45). Such vessels are found in houses as well as tombs and seem to reflect a developed etiquette of dining and drinking. This was Orsi's impression of the group of skeletons and their vessels which he found in a tomb at Cozzo del Pantano near Syracuse. The chamber of this tomb mimicked

the round form of a Thapsos hut and reproduced its interior, even to the low bench around the inside of the exterior wall found in various huts of the period.

These tombs of the Thapsos Culture, both around Syracuse and elsewhere in Sicily, continue the tradition of the rock-cut chamber. At Thapsos itself they are approached by ramps cut in the rock, like the dromoi of Mycenean rock-cut chamber tombs (figure 46). The borders of the doorways are often drafted in receding facets, each given a slightly concave outline to produce a distinctive frame around the door. The interiors of the tombs may be large and may be multi-chambered. The chambers vary in shape. They may have niches in their walls. One particularly interesting tomb from Molinello di Augusta across the Bay of Augusta from Thapsos has a ramp whose walls are facetted to produce the effect of a series of separate panels lining the corridor to the tomb. The interior of the same tomb directly evokes a round Thapsos hut, even imitating the curve of a thatched roof and including a bench around the wall.

It is in rich tombs, at Thapsos and near Syracuse at Plemmyrion, Matrensa and Cozzo del Pantano,

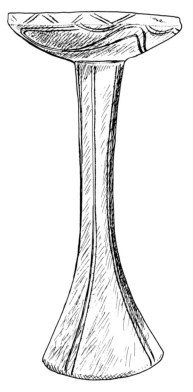

Figure 44 Syracuse Museum, vase of Thapsos style from Thapsos

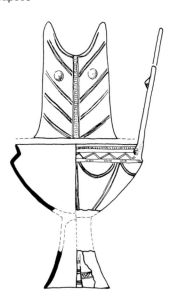

Figure 45 Syracuse Museum, vase of Thapsos style from Thapsos

Figure 46 Thapsos, ramp leading to chamber tomb

that the greater part of Mycenean imports in Sicily are concentrated. It may be debated to what degree the Thapsos tomb was influenced by Mycenean tholoi and chamber tombs. As noted already, the tradition of the rock-cut tomb is fully Sicilian, and elements such as the bench seem to recall fixtures of contemporary Sicilian houses and their Castelluccian predecessors. Even the entrance ramp is not necessarily Mycenean but has Castelluccian antecedents. However, there is a certain precise style and architectural self-consciousness about the tombs of the Thapsos Culture that is not necessarily the result of undisturbed local evolution.

At just this time architecture as it was understood in the Aegean and in the Near East had been brought to Sicily. Sometime after 1,400 BC the simple village of huts on the site of Thapsos was joined by a group of buildings that were unlike anything seen before in Sicily (figure 47). These are long rectangular structures measuring up to 20 meters (65 ft 7 in) on a side and grouped around paved courtyards. The streets outside are paved. But the rooms of the buildings open inward, not outward to the street. The concept of the buildings is the same as that of the Near Eastern port city warehouse as it is known from Enkomi on Cyprus. It is a generic form of storage building which survived over the centuries because of its functionality. It is the same design as incorporated in the Roman grain warehouse and its modern successors. Doubtless similar buildings existed

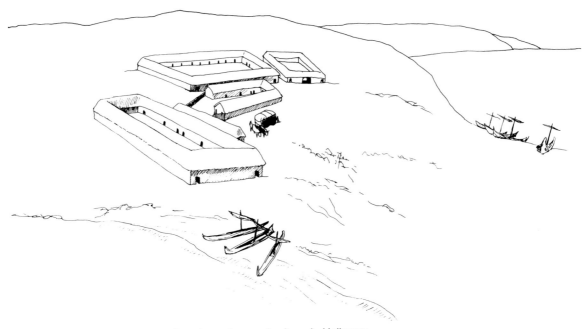

Figure 47 Thapsos, reconstruction of warehouses by Anne L. Holloway

throughout the Near East and in the port cities of the Aegean, where, however, they have yet to come to light. Still, Cyprus has a special tie with Thapsos. Three pieces of simple Cypriote pottery were found in a chamber tomb at Thapsos (figures 48 and 49). It seems probable, moreover, that the basins from Caldare (and Milena) are Cypriote products. Also eastern, though more probably Syrian than Cypriote, is the Late Bronze Age bronze statuette of a divinity from the sea

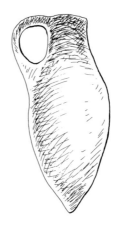

Figure 49 Syracuse Museum, vase of Cypriote style from Thapsos

off Selinunte (often called the 'Sciacca Bronze', figure 50). [22]

The warehouses at Thapsos are difficult to date precisely because no imported pottery is associated with them. [23] Because of the largely denuded surface of the peninsula nothing is preserved save the foundations of their walls and traces of the paving of the courtyards and of the streets.

The evidence of Cypriote or Levantine activity in Sicily makes it unavoidable to ask how the

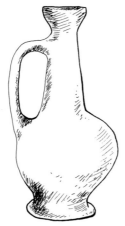

Figure 48 Syracuse Museum, vase of Cypriote style from Thapsos

Figure 50 Palermo Museum, bronze statue from the sea off Selinus

Mycenean products that came to Sicily were carried. It is all too easy to assume that a Mycenean vase was brought by a Mycenean ship and a Mycenean merchant. But who is to say that the ship was not Cypriote or Syrian and the merchant a Levantine rather than a Greek? The famous Late Bronze Age shipwreck of Cape Gelidonya off the Lycian coast of Turkey has been interpreted as a Cypriote vessel, carrying, of course, some Aegean goods, and the larger and richer wreck of a merchant vessel curently being excavated in the same area off Kaş seems also to have a similar eastern origin.[24] The existence of eastern urban architecture at Thapsos must preclude, it appears, any idea that only Sicilians were involved in the import trade. The architect of the Thapsos warehouses was a foreigner, and the entire complex can be little else than a foreign trading station on the coast of Sicily.

Until recently the Thapsos Culture seemed largely restricted to southeastern Sicily. Not only the important discoveries at Milena have altered this view, but also the identification of several cemeteries of chamber tombs to the west of Agrigento (Ribera immediately east of Sciacca

and Castelvetrano, Poggioreale, and Montevago in the Belice Valley), the discovery of Thapsos settlements in the Valley of the Belice in western Sicily, and most recently the excavation of a Thapsos settlement at Gaffe, Licata, which is as yet only in its initial stages.

In the Aeolian Islands the pottery of the Milazzese Culture shares many features with Thapsos pottery, especially pedestal bowls and ribbed decoration. Finely done incised patterns of chevrons often appear on several shapes of jugs and containers. The system of written signs on pottery, first found in the Capo Graziano Period, continues in a developed form. Bernabò Brea has interpreted these marks as signs of individual potters applied to the vessels before firing in order to distinguish the work of each. The buildings of the Milazzese Period which succceed those of the Capo Graziano Period on the Lipari acropolis are irregularly oval like their predecessors but have their drywall socles carried to a higher level. The sites of the villages are clearly chosen for defense, as typified by the site of Milazzese itself on the island of Panarea, perched on top of a precipitous headland joined to the island by a narrow isthmus (figure 51). The Milazzese villages not only contain a notable collection of Mycenean pottery of the fourteenth and thirteenth centuries but also received pottery imports from the Italian mainland (Apennine Culture). The burial customs of these people are known from a cemetery on the Milazzo peninsula across from Lipari on the north coast of Sicily. These are inhumations in large storage vessels, the rite introduced in Capo Graziano times. There is a further village of the Milazzese Culture on the island of Ustica, situated west of the Aeolian group between Sicily and Sardinia. The circuit of the Late Bronze Age city walls is still in place on Ustica, and in some stretches they stand to a height of 3 meters (9 ft 10 in). Within them are the remains of a town which the limited excavation carried out to date suggests had an urban density unknown on the sites of the Aeolian Islands.

The administrative centers of Mycenean Greece came under attack during the later thirteenth and twelfth centuries. Sometimes, as in the case of Pylos, they were destroyed and abandoned. At other places, Tiryns for example, a more modest town lived on and prospered, although the palace was no more. Greece was

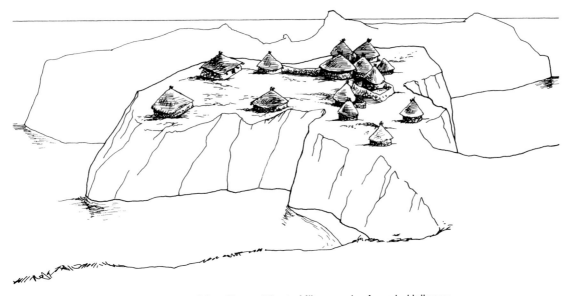

Figure 51 Panarea, reconstruction of the village of Punta Milazzese by Anne L. Holloway

becoming a village society again. At the same time displaced Myceneans found new homes in the eastern Mediterranean, Aegean Turkey, Cilicia and Cyprus.[25] Late Helladic III C Pottery, as the ware made just before and then following 1,200 BC is termed, is not known in Sicily, save for one jug from the Pantalica necropolis. It is found in quantity on Lipari. But Lipari, as we shall find, is now closely tied to the Italian mainland. And in this mainland orbit the period of Mycenean decline saw continued import of pottery, local imitation of these wares, and widespread assimilation of Aegean types in metallurgy. At the same time one exclusively eastern industry, the making of faience, began to be practiced in Italy (at Frattesina near the head of the Adriatic). Italian bronzes, and even an Italian ax mold, were carried back to Mycenean Greece. Crete begins to have contact with the west. Late Minoan pottery reaches Calabria, and in Crete an odd taste developed for a pseudo-Italian pottery evidently made on the spot. These phenomena suggest local substitutions for a diminished supply of Mycenean goods, now that the palace system of production was no more, and possibly the migration of artisans.

In Sicily the break with the Aegean was abrupt, but in some ways the effects of the contact through the emporion of Thapsos were lasting. To appreciate this fact, one must make the trek up the limestone hills north of Syracuse, adding miles to the journey to skirt the impassable gorges that divide the uplands into isolated and lonely ridges. Here, on a lonely promontory connected to the neighboring ridges only at a single point, there stands the site of Pantalica. In the gorges below the summit are some five thousand chamber tombs, three hundred of which were investigated by Orsi between 1895 and 1910. The burials began with the waning of Mycenean influence in the thirteenth or twelfth century and continued for several centuries thereafter. Located on the sheer cliffs, many in positions impossible to reach without ropes or ladders, the tombs can be capacious, a single large room or multichambered. They were the work of an industrious community. But the houses of the community have vanished or their few traces have yet to be identified on the hilltop which was resettled during the early Middle Ages.

By contrast the site preserves what was before the discovery of the Thapsos warehouses the only example of large-scale prehistoric architecture surviving on the island. Orsi called the remains the 'anaktoron', imagining them to have been the palace of an Aegean-style ruler. The building, at least in the surviving lowest courses, is made of great stone blocks, carefully fitted together (figure 52). As preserved it measures

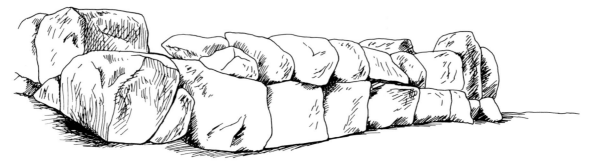

Figure 52 Pantalica, wall of the 'Anaktoron'

37.5 by 11.5 meters (123 ft by 37 ft 8 in) but this includes only two attached blocks of rooms, each forming a rectangle. Beyond them Orsi noted the remains of a large courtyard, which were destroyed after his first visit to the site.

The plan of the 'anaktoron' is unlike any Mycenean palace, save possibly the enigmatic building on the acropolis of Gla, which may have been more a storehouse than a residence. With its courtyard it is strangely reminiscent of the storehouses at Thapsos, which does not mean that its function was the same. A hoard of bronze implements was found in the anaktoron and it seems that a smithy was located in the building. But metal working as a palace industry is hardly contrary to Orsi's notion of a king at Pantalica. When the shadows of prehistory are dispelled by the first accounts of the Greeks in Sicily in the eighth century, we find this area under the control of the Sicel King Hyblon. It is not difficult to see him as the last of a line of kings of Pantalica. And, what is more, the other sites associated with the Pantalica Culture are all hill-towns surrounded by the necropolises on the slopes below. These few towns, Pantalica, Cassibile (near the coast south of Syracuse), Caltagirone, Monte Dessueri (inland from Gela), Monte Castellazzo di Palma di Montechiaro (between Agrigento and Licata), stand in contrast to the villages, farms and sanctuaries of the Early Bronze Age and the small settlements of Thapsos times. It is as if the population of the island had been concentrated in a few centers. This process of gathering a dispersed population into a new city was known to the classical world as synoicism. In tradition it was already practiced by Theseus when he created Athens in the Bronze Age. Synoicism required the leadership of a strong-

man, like Theseus or that ancestor of King Hyblon who founded Pantalica.

Throughout the long centuries of Sicilian prehistory we have visited up to this point, it has become clear that once the sea had been opened to navigation ideas and knowledge traveled speedily across great distances. Through Thapsos Aegean arms, reproduced in the weapons found in the tombs of the Thapsos Culture, arrived in Sicily. These were the tools of domination. No doubt with the arms came soldiers of fortune, the historical counterparts of Achilles, Agamemnon and Odysseus of saga. The result was a convulsion in Sicilian society. The population was uprooted and driven into the new towns founded by the Sicilian kings, a repetition in Sicily of the making of the Mycenean world initiated by the Shaft Grave barons. The organization of Late Bronze Age Sicily remained rudimentary compared to the palace system of production we know in Greece, no doubt because Sicily was so much farther from the advanced centers of the Near East which served as models for the Greeks. But the new order, perhaps because it was simpler, was more enduring in Sicily than in Greece.

The sequence of the Pantalica tombs and their grave goods (and of the related necropolises) was divided by Bernabò Brea into three periods.[26] In the earliest phase (also called Pantalica North after the tombs in this part of the necropolis) the pottery has a rich red surface (figure 53). There are shapes familiar from the Thapsos Period such as pedestal vessels, although they are smaller. In the Pantalica North tombs there are bronze violin-bow fibulae and simple arched fibulae (often with two knobs on their bows), both distinguishing marks of the period (figure

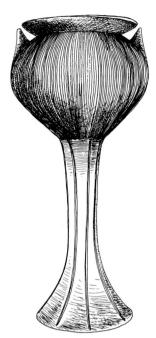

Figure 53 Syracuse Museum, vase of the Pantalica style from Pantalica

54), together with the curved-bladed daggers, swords with cast handle-tongues, and axes. The fibula is the modern safty pin. There is only a single piece of imported Mycenean pottery from these tombs (Late Helladic III C:1 shortly before 1,200 BC), but five bronze mirrors from the site have also been claimed as Cypriote imports.

The second major phase of the Pantalica necropolis (Pantalica South) appears to belong to the ninth and eighth centuries. The vase rep-

ertoire is much impoverished and shows carinated (angular) shapes like those known from Lipari and related to the pottery of the mainland Italian Late Bronze Age (Ausonian II). There is painted pottery decorated with patterns of crescents that can cover the entire surface of the vase (the so-called 'piumata' ware, figure 55). Among the fibulae the serpentine type predominates, together with a simple arched type with thickened bows having a rectangular rather than round cross-section. It appears that the Pantalica South necropolis was in use down to the eve of Greek colonization in the eighth century.

Between these two phases (and represented at Pantalica by a very small group of tombs) there is the Cassibile Period, named from the site of that name south of Syracuse and its necropolis of chamber tombs. It occupies the period from about 1,000 to 850 BC. Though in a less awesome location than that of Pantalica, Cassibile is again in a defensive position, 2 kilometers (1.25 miles) from the sea at the edge of the limestone plateau. There are other major necropolises of a similar kind. One is that of Dessueri in the valley of the stream of the same name behind Gela. Equally remote is the site of La Montagna at Caltagirone which commands the pass from the Geloan Plain into the upper Catania Plain.

Slightly beyond Caltagirone along this road to Catania is Grammichele, where in the locality Molino della Badia Orsi excavated one of the more important cemeteries contemporary with the Cassibile Period. This is a cemetery of simple inhumation graves covered by stone slabs, or burials in pithoi. The grave goods, both bronzes

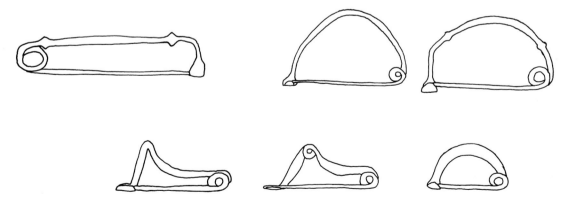

Figure 54 Types of Late Bronze Age and Iron Age fibulae, left to right, top to bottom, violin bow (with knobs), simple arch, simple arch (with knobs), elbow, elbow with double spiral, thickened arch

Figure 55 Syracuse Museum, vase of the 'piumata' style from Thapsos

and pottery, reflect connections with mainland-influenced Late Bronze Age culture found on Lipari. Not all of the Cassibile sites are protected and inland. The Greek settlers of Syracuse built their houses on the island of Ortygia over a stratum of this period (continuing into the Pantalica South phase), and a Cassibile tomb has recently been excavated in the same place. A similar Cassibile-Pantalica South deposit underlies the first Greek colony, Naxos. At Thapsos, moreover, there was activity at this time. Traces of the Cassibile Culture have been found over a wide area of Sicily, westward to the area of Agrigento and northwestward to Enna in the center of the island.

Cassibile pottery continues the Pantalica North and Thapsos tradition and adds to it the painted 'piumata' wares. Among the bronzes there now appears the 'elbow' fibula, while the simple arched fibula without knobs is now common. Other bronzes continue the Pantalica North types.

The social fabric of the Pantalica society has been discussed in an important paper by Laura Maniscalco.[27] She notes that in addition to an old tradition of the funeral banquet, so clearly present in the tombs of the Thapsos Culture and rooted in still older traditions, the Pantalica Culture also has tombs in which the grave goods define sex. The status of the warrior is also shown by the number of his weapons and possessions. In the cemetery of Molino della Badia where this tendency is strongest, the chamber tomb itself is abandoned for the simple pit grave or pithos burial. The earlier symbolism of the banquet belongs more to the world of the clan, the later emphasizes the individual. Following the examination of the same material by Anna Maria

Bietti Sestieri, one may observe that this change in social outlook accompanies the penetration of Sicily by cultural influences deriving from the Italian mainland, the influence of which is most pronounced in the Cassibile group and especially in the Molino della Badia necropolis.[28] It is to Late Bronze Age Culture of the mainland and its extension to the Aeolian Islands that we may now turn our attention.

Compared to Sicily, the mainland developed as if a Castelluccian era had extended to the end of the Bronze Age. The pottery of the mainland, belonging to the Apennine Culture, as it is called, is monochrome and dark surfaced. It is undecorated in the Early Bronze Age and then acquires rich impressed ornament both rectilinear and curvilinear in the mid-second millennium. In the Late Bronze Age, which endures through the ninth century, the pottery is again undecorated, but bronze working flourishes, showing contacts both with central Europe and with the Aegean. Hoards of bronzes are known from the mainland as early as the Early Bronze Age, but the multiplication of their number, as well as the increased output of bronze, which now includes personal ornaments such as fibulae and pins as well as arms, axes and other tools, says a great deal about the increased resources in metals and their use as a reserve of wealth at this time. Very little is known about the settlements of the Apennine Culture, but there were apparently villages not dissimilar to those in Sicily. Major sanctuaries seem to have been visited by persons from far distant places and the commerce associated with the sanctuaries formed links in the transmission of goods, especially bronzes, throughout the peninsula. In the Late Bronze Age, possibly as early as the thirteenth century, ties with central Europe, and especially with the Alpine region and the Danubian basin, intensify. The animal head handles in pottery and the repoussé decorations of bronzes appear in both areas. Cremation burials in distinctive biconical jars, which appear in Italy at the same time, may be offshoots from the same region. These burials mark what is called 'Proto-Villanovan', as distinguished from 'Sub-Apennine', the continuation of the established Bronze Age culture. These two phases overlap chronologically.

On the Aeolian Islands a catastrophe seems to have overtaken the Milazzese villages. They were destroyed and a new people, settling only on Lipari itself, brought with them a material culture which is essentially that of the Late Bronze Age mainland. The pottery of the new settlement on Lipari is characterized by carinated bowls with zoomorphic handles. Among the bronzes long pins are conspicuous. There are faience beads, probably from the new centers of manufacture at the head of the Adriatic. Amber makes its appearance as it does in Greece again at this time, proving once more that the Late Bronze Age was still a time of movement and exchange. In the later phases of the period, Ausonian II, the pottery develops from the style of the preceding phase (figure 56), although

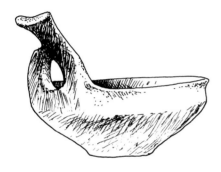

Figure 56 Lipari Museum, vase of the Ausonian II style from Lipari

'piumata' ware of the Cassibile type is also present. The Ausonian village on the Lipari acropolis has imported Late Helladic III B and C pottery, dating it in the thirteenth and twelfth centuries. Ausonian II continues to an indeterminate moment, possibly in the ninth century. The burial rite is cremation certainly related to Proto-Villanovan, although the distinct Proto-Villanovan urn is absent. These do occur, however, in what appears to be a true Proto-Villanovan outpost at Milazzo opposite Lipari on the north coast of Sicily. The largest building of the Ausonian II village on Lipari was built in the technique of Late Bronze Age mainland building, posts in the walls assisting in supporting the structure. This important structure, a carefully constructed long building with curved corners, was also distinguished by the bronze treasure, 75 kilograms, which was buried beneath its floor and reflects the same accumulation of capital in this form known from the mainland.

Bernabò Brea gave the name 'Ausonians' to the last prehistoric inhabitants of the Aeolian Islands from the legend repeated by Diodorus Siculus to the effect that Lipari was settled by the Ausoni, an Italic people from Campania, under the leadership of Liparus, the son of Auson. It seems that Hellanicus and Philistus, two of the earliest Greek historians, calculated the arrival of the Sicel people in Sicily three generations before the date of the mythical Trojan War. This would mean a calendar date in the thirteenth century. In this case, too, there seems every reason to accept the coincidence of the archaeologically established arrival of the new population of Lipari and the traditions (and admittedly speculative chronology) of the Greek historians.

There are two colonies of the Ausonian II Culture on Sicily. The first is at Leontini, the second is at Morgantina, both in eastern Sicily on the borders of the Catania Plain. The cemetery at Molino della Badia (Grammichele) is closely related. The name of Morgantina is derived from Morgetes, who, according to a tradition preserved in a fragment of Antiochus, the Syracusan historian of the fifth century, was the leader of a party which migrated to Sicily from the Italian mainland. The coincidence of tradition and archaeology is again so strong as to make it probable that some traditions regarding the end of the Bronze Age did survive in Sicily. But this is no proof that the ancients were always right, as we shall see in the case of the myth of Minos and Daedalos to be examined in the next chapter.

Contemporary records from the second millennium may be misinterpreted too. Egyptian inscriptions beginning in the reign of Mernephta (1,236–1,223 BC) record the defeat, on various occasions, of foreign peoples, in particular Libyans, and together with them, especially in the battles recorded by the reliefs and texts of Rameses III (1,198–1,166 BC) on the pylons of the Temple of Medinet Habu, a group of allies whose names have been interpreted as familar ethnics of people from the Aegean, Anatolia and the western Mediterranean. In this period of general troubles which also saw the end of states in the Aegean, the Hittite Empire in Anatolia and kingdoms in the Levant such as Ugarit, and clearly accompanied by population movements, the Egyptian documents might well, many scholars have reasoned, refer to one front of a much wider episode of 'barbarian' invasions of the Aegean and the Near East. Three names in particular can be taken as referring to the western Mediterranean: Shekelesh (= Siculi?), Tjeker (= Etrusci?), and Shardana (= Sardani?).

Not all students of the 'Sea Peoples', as they have become known, share the enthusiasm for these lexical equivalents or for the historical reconstruction in which they have been placed. The Egyptian records, the sceptics argue, may refer to no more than a rebellion of subject foreigners. Instead of being the Egyptian name for the Mediterranean, the term 'Great Green', used in these texts, may really denote the marshes of the Nile Delta and the 'islands' of the inscriptions may be no more than the areas of firm ground isolated amid its waterways.

Further problems arise from the names themselves. The Etruscans did not call themselves Tirsenoi (Greek) or Etrusci (Latin); they were 'Rasenna'. Sardinia (or its variant Sandaliotis) is not the original name of the island; it was Ichnusa. The Siculi were indeed one of three groups of natives distinguished by the Greeks when they arrived in Sicily in the eighth century.

Inscriptions of the Siculi of eastern Sicily survive and show that they spoke a language akin to Latin. They had probably not been in Sicily long, perhaps no longer than the Ausonians who came via the Aeolian Islands at the end of the second millennium. But it is far more reasonable to imagine their arrival in Sicily directly from the Italian peninsula, where there were also 'Siculi', than by a roundabout route through the Near East. At most any Siculi who played a part in Late Bronze Age events to the east were probably from the older group in central and southern Italy, an area physically closer to the Aegean. They would have been involved, however, in an historical scenario which otherwise relies on the identification of names, spelled after the Egyptian fashion only by consonants, with ethnic designations which in the west do not belong to the times and places with which they have been equated. Although there are reasons enough to believe in pirates in Sicilian waters and Sicilian travelers to the east centuries before the thirteenth and twelfth centuries, nothing compels one to include any Sicilians among the 'Sea Peoples'.

Background

To most of us ancient Sicily means Greek Sicily. The first Greek colonists came to Sicily in the eighth century BC, and the presence of the Greek cities is still apparent in the landscape. Until very recently modern Syracuse occupied the area of her ancient predecessor. At Agrigento (Greek Acragas) the ancient metropolis is hidden, but only barely so, in the sloping bowl that descends from the acropolis (and medieval town) toward the low ridge a kilometer distant where a line of three temples still marks the limit of the city. At Selinus an archaeological park keeps alive something of the deserted grandeur of the ruins. Sicily's Greek temples are more numerous than those of any part of the ancient Greek world. One of them, erected by the non-Greek (Elymnian) city of Segesta, and thus Greek only in architecture, has a setting which rivals even the mountain backdrop of Greek Delphi. But unlike the ruined temple at Delphi, the temple of Segesta is in the same condition now as it was on the day in the late fifth century when its builders interrupted their work. At Acragas and Selinus there are two of the grandest and most unusual Greek temples (the Olympieion at Acragas and Temple GT at Selinus). Selinus is home to some of the earliest Greek architectural sculpture. And in another art, coin design, Greek Sicily became preeminent for all time.

The non-Greek Sicilians, Sicels in eastern Sicily, Sicans in the central area, and Elymnians in the west, were never a serious threat to the Greeks. But the Greek cities were confronted by two dangers which made their existence precarious. The first of these was the imperialism of their own tyrants, especially the rulers of Syracuse, under whom subject cities were suppressed and populations reshuffled at will. The second was the threat of Carthaginian expansion. From at least the time when the first Greek settlers arrived in Sicily and possibly before, the Carthaginians (Phoenicians settled in North Africa) held a foothold in western Sicily on the island of Motya, situated hardly more than a kilometer offshore across a shallow lagoon. The Carthaginians went on to become masters in Spain and Sardinia. They mounted their first war of conquest in Sicily at the beginning of the fifth century but were turned back by the united forces of Syracuse and Acragas at the Battle of Himera (480 BC). Seventy years later they repeated their attack, and now with devastating success. Soon there was no Greek city save Syracuse that had not fallen victim either to the invaders or to the Syracusan counter-attack. Indeed the Greek population of the island was faced with near extinction on more than one occasion. It was supported by new groups of colonists drawn from the motherland, beginning under the tyrants of the early fifth century. Mercenaries, often from Oscan-speaking Italy, entered the service of the tyrants and remained to cause trouble when their service ended or the tyrant and his family lost power. From the mid-fifth century on several towns of the interior, and the city of Catane for a time, were in the hands of Campanian mercenaries. The struggle between the Greeks and Carthaginians continued intermittently during the fourth and third centuries until Rome entered the arena of Sicilian affairs in 264 BC and the struggle became one between Carthage and Rome. Rome triumphed. Sicily became partly a Roman province in 241 BC and completely so after 211 BC.

Had the writing of ancient history been

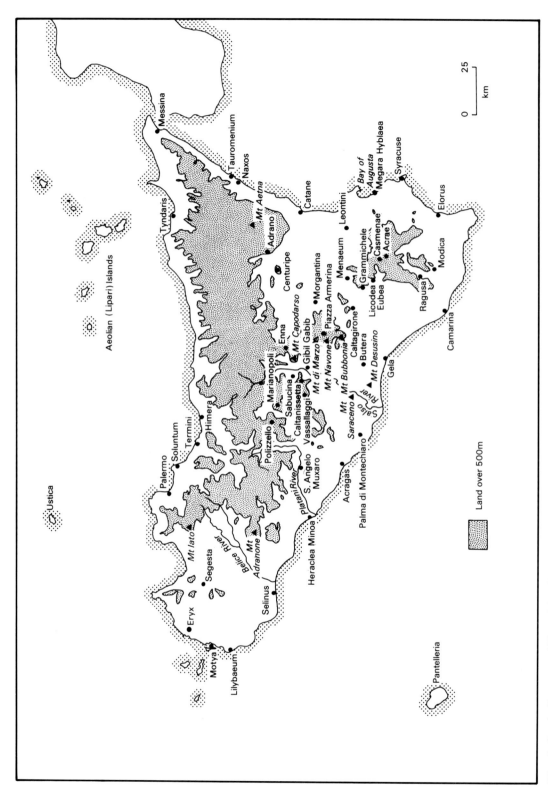

Map 2 Greek, Roman and Phoenician Sicily

Messina

Tauromenium

Naxos

Mt Aetna

Adrano

Catane

Tyndaris

Leontini

Bay of Augusta

Megara Hyblaea

Syracuse

Elorus

Centuripe

Morgantina

Menaeum

Grammichele

Casmenae

Licodea

Acrae

Eubea

Aeolian (Lipari) Islands

Mt Capodarso

Piazza Armerina

Enna

Gibil Gabib

Caltagirone

Modica

Mt di Marzo

Mt Navone

Butera

Ragusa

Marianopoli

Mt Bubbonia

Salso River

Sabucina

Mt Desusino

Gela

Caltanissetta

Vassallaggi

Mt Saraceno

Camarina

Polizzello

Himera

Soluntum

Palermo

Termini

Platani River

S. Angelo Muxaro

Palma di Montechiaro

Acragas

Ustica

Mt Iato

Belice River

Mt Adranone

Heraclea Minoa

Segesta

Eryx

Selinus

Motya

Lilybaeum

Pantelleria

Land over 500m

different and the survival of what was written better, Sicily might have gained a central place in the history of ancient Greece. It does so only in Thucydides' account of the ill-fated invasion of Sicily mounted by Athens in the years 415–413 BC. There exists no history of the wars of the Greeks and the Carthaginians such as Herodotus wrote for the wars of the homeland Greeks and the Persians, and there are no writings by a Sicilian to do for Syracuse what Thucydides did for the Athenian Empire. The works of the Greek historians of Sicily who were contemporaries of these events have perished and are known only through their echoes. Most of what is preserved comes from Diodorus, the compiler from Agyrium, who lived during the first century. Three of Plutarch's *Lives* are important for Sicilian history of the fourth and third centuries, those of Dion, Timoleon and Pyrrhus. There is a life of the late-fourth century Syracusan tyrant Agathocles by Cornelius Nepos. These sources, Thucydides' history of the Athenian invasion of 415 BC and scattered passages elsewhere, the most valuable in Herodotus, are all we have of the history of Greek Sicily before the Punic Wars.

It is surprising, then, that the beginning of Greek settlement seems to be among the best documented events in the Greek history of the island. This is largely because of the digression made by Thucydides at the opening of his account of the Athenian expedition. The historian recalls that Greek settlement began with the colony of Naxos, situated on the peninsula of Capo Schiso in the shadow of Mt Aetna. The venture departed from Chalcis on Euboea, the large island close to the coast of Attica and Boeotia. But, according to Thucydides, the Corinthian colony at Syracuse was founded within a year of Naxos. Leontini, on the southern edge of the Catania plain, was established, under the leader of the colony at Naxos, five years after Syracuse. Catane (modern Catania), another Chalcidian colony, was founded two years later. At the same time the Megarians, neighbors of the Corinthians north of the Isthmus of Corinth in Greece, sent out a party which, after two false starts, established Megara Hyblaea just north of Syracuse. In each case Thucydides gives the name of the leader of the colony, its oikist.

Thucydides' brief summary creates the image of a race for colonies leading to the domination of the east coast of Sicily by the Greeks within the space of seven years. The summary is not without its problems. Nowhere does Thucydides inform his reader how long ago these events took place. He says only that archaic Megara Hyblaea existed for 245 years before its suppression by the tyrant Gelon of Syracuse. True, Thucydides himself clearly had a notion of when these foundations were made. In the same passage he situates the arrival of the Sicels from Italy, 'Three hundred years before the Greeks came to Sicily'. But we must look elsewhere (to Herodotus and to the ancient marginalia to Pindar's occasional verse in honor of the Sicilian tyrants Hieron and Theron and their henchmen) to establish the dates of Gelon's rule at Syracuse (about 485 to 479 BC). Otherwise, there would be no way to calculate the handbook date of 728 for the foundation of Megara. But then an exact placement of the early Greek colonies in respect to later events was clearly not a matter of importance to Thucydides. Nor did he place the colonies with complete precision in relation to each other. Megara is only located 'about the same time' as Syracuse, and so the standard dates of 734 for the settlement at Naxos and 733 for the founding of Syracuse, calculated by assuming that Leontini was founded the same year as Megara, are in fact approximations.

Thucydides' summary continues by listing the settlements of the south coast. First there is Gela, a colony of Rhodians and Cretans founded forty-five years after Syracuse (688 BC by traditional calculation). Next comes Megara Hyblaea's colony Selinus established 100 years after the mother city (628 BC by the standard reckoning). Acragas, the colony of Gela, was founded after an interval of 108 years (580 BC figured from the Herodotean date for Megara). Finally, Camarina, Syracuse's secondary colony on the south coast, was inaugurated 135 years after Syracuse. Thucydides then mentions the Euboean settlement at Zancle (Messina) on the Strait across from Rhegium and Messina's daughter colony of Himera well to the west along the north coast, but there are no dates given for them. There follows the mention of two inland dependencies of Syracuse, Acrae and Casmenae, with dates in reference to the foundation of Syracuse, which makes it seem that Thucydides was using, and condensing, a Syracusan source, such as the work of his contemporary Antiochus. The possibility must be considered that this source was bent on proving that Syracuse should be ranked with the very first colonies and had come into being within months of the foundation of Naxos, which was universally recognized as the first Greek city in Sicily. (The first colony in the west was the Euboean settlement at Cumae north of Naples preceded by a Euboean presence, although not official colonization, on Ischia, the island nearby.) Moreover, not everyone in antiquity agreed with the version of early colonial history given by Thucydides, or at least with its dates. A hint of this comes from the date for the foundation of Selinus given by Diodorus Siculus. The Augustan writer falls far short of Thucydides as an historian, but his date for Selinus shows that an alternate chronology was known. Diodorus says that Selinus had existed for 242 years before its destruction by the Carthaginians in 409 BC. His source, therefore, thought that Selinus was founded in 658 rather than in 628, and if Selinus' mother city Megara was a full century earlier than the daughter colony, that city would have been founded in 758 BC. The French excavators of Megara Hyblaea have suggested a chronology which retains the traditional dates for Megara and Syracuse but lengthens the period over which the colonies of eastern Sicily were planted.

Euboean Colonies	Ischia	ca. 770 BC
	Naxos	ca. 750
	Cumae	ca. 750/730
	Zancle	
	(Messina)	
	Rhegium	ca. 730
	Catane	
	Leontini	
Corinthian Colony	Syracuse	735/730
Megarian Colony	Megara	ca. 730 (?)
	Hyblaea	

But even these dates may be more precise than is warranted by the manner in which Greek historians calculated dates. Numbers such as 45 years (the interval between the foundation of Syracuse and Gela), 135 years (the interval

between Syracuse and Camarina) and 245 years (the life span of archaic Megara Hyblaea) are all based on the translation of a count by generations into years, in these cases equating a generation with 45 years. Counts by generations could also be given equivalents of 30 years, 35 years or 33⅓ years (three generations to a century). Even the apparently eccentric date for Acragas, 108 years after the establishment of the mother city (580 BC), is actually based on a date of 100 years (three generations) before the Agrigentine tyrant Theron's triumph, in alliance with Gelon of Syracuse, over the Carthaginians in 480 BC. By thinking in generations we can appreciate better the margin of error in many dates in early Greek history. But the archaeological evidence, to be reviewed shortly, shows that, just as Thucydides thought, the Greek occupation of the eastern coast of Sicily in the mid-eighth century was carried out rapidly.

But why did the Greeks undertake colonizing ventures on such a scale in Sicily, and in southern Italy as well, in the eighth century and how were these ventures organized? In many ways the phenomenon is an astounding one. Settlers from communities which were apparently no more than groups of villages organized by kinship and under the leadership of aristocrats whose position depended on traditionally sanctioned authority succeeded in gaining control of southern Italy around its coast from Taranto to Naples and the coastal areas of Sicily save for the west of the island beyond Selinus on the south and Himera on the north. The same Greeks colonized Libya and in the century following the initial push toward the west they were to be active in colonizing the northern Aegean and ultimately the shores of the Black Sea. In the past the Greeks had moved overseas from their homeland to Asia Minor and to Cyprus, but these movements had more the character of migrations than of colonization. The colony was an offshoot of the parent community. The resources of manpower and equipment devoted to the venture were subtracted from what was available for those left behind.

Before examining the traditional explanations of colonizing we should take note of the relation of the earliest Greek poetry, the epics of Homer, to the colonizing movement. Although the date at which the *Iliad* and *Odyssey* were cast in their final form will never be established with certainty, they may be taken with some assurance to represent the poetic expression of the age that launched the Sicilian colonies. The wanderings of Odysseus are sailors' yarns of western waters mixed with folk tale and fiction, and it is no wonder that the attempts made to chart the course of Odysseus' voyages and to identify his landfalls have not been convincing. But his adventures are an impression of the west, of its dangers, its mysteries and, compared to Greece, its lush fertility. It is Scylla and Charybdis, the Cyclops, Circe and Calypso and the Lotus Eaters. The *Odyssey* also brings forward the portrait of a colony. This is Phaeacia, to which Odysseus comes as a castaway to be befriended and protected by the king's daughter Nausicaa. Her grandfather, Nausithous, had brought the Phaeacians thither, 'He walled the city, built houses, made temples for the gods and divided the farmland.' Although in legend he was leading the migration of an entire city, in Homer Nausithous is acting the part of the oikist of a Greek colony.

Appreciation of the significance of the oikist has been strangely absent from discussions of the motives for Greek colonization. The oikist was a venerated figure, endowed with a religious aura which was certified by the oracle at Delphi. (The oracle possibly offered less specific directions for the destination of the expedition than Delphi claimed at a later date.) In the foundation the oikist regulated the human and the divine. Like Nausithous he not only saw to the physical division of the land and the arrangement of the settlement but also assigned the gods their portion and position. On his death the oikist was heroized, and his tomb became the center of an official cult.

Generally one of two explanations is offered for the westward movement. The first is over-population and land hunger. The second is commercial ambition.

To sustain the hypothesis that commerce stimulated colonization one must prove that commerce was developed in precolonial times. For Sicily this is difficult. The most tangible evidence of precolonial contact is the Greek Middle Geometric (i.e. pre-750 BC) cup with pendant semicircles and the chevron cups (later but still Middle Geometric) from Villasmundo just north of Megara Hyblaea (figure 57).[1] These vessels were deposited as grave goods in large chamber tombs with precisely cut doorways that

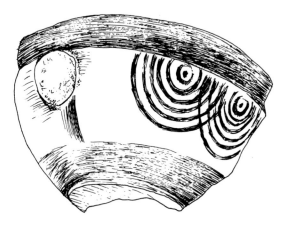

Figure 57 Syracuse Museum, fragment of Greek Middle Geometric pottery from Villasmundo

belong to the Pantalica tradition. The tombs held four to twenty burials accompanied by substantial numbers of grave goods. The cemetery was in use during the eighth and seventh centuries. In addition to the Middle Geometric pieces, the later tomb groups of the cemetery include other Greek cups of the types which are found in the earliest colonies (the Thapsos cup and its poor relation, the Aetos 666 cup, figure 58).

Figure 58 Syracuse Museum, 'Thapsos cup' from Megara Hyblaea

The priority of the early imports in the Villasmundo cemetery in respect to the colonial settlements nearby is clear. No examples of pendant semicircle cups or of chevron cups have been excavated at Naxos, Megara Hyblaea or at Syracuse.[2] What these imports represent is more difficult to determine. The same material has been found in Etruria and chevron cups are known from the native cemetery at Cumae from the period before the Greek colony. Greek

Cumae's predecessor on Ischia was the first Greek foothold in the west and on the basis of the excavations of the last decades Ischia's role has been interpreted as that of an offshore trading station importing Etruscan iron ore and working it into tools and weapons. These products were then sold to the mainlanders of Campania whose iron technology could not match that of the Greeks. The same Euboeans who were present on Ischia (which they shared with other peoples, not all Greeks, because some of them left graffiti in Aramaic) were also active on the Syrian coast and were surely among the most wide-ranging Greek traders of the ninth and eighth centuries. It appears that their island not only took the lead in overseas ventures at this time but also had maintained some contacts with the Near East even during the so-called 'Dark Ages' following the crises at the end of the Bronze Age. The Euboeans are thought to have been leaders in the development of metallurgy. And their experience in commerce overseas made their cities, Chalcis and Eretria, favored departure points for colonial ventures. The colony at Naxos and the two settlements of Leontini and Catane, which effectively gained control of the Catania plain, also departed from Euboea. Later Zancle (Messina) was founded as a pirates' nest by another Euboean group from Cumae. Euboean trade, therefore, was certainly a precursor of colonization, but was the commercial center on Ischia a sufficient stimulus for the colonizing movement? Similar emporia had existed in the west in the Bronze Age, in Sicily notably at Thapsos. The Bronze Age was also a time of outward movement for the Greeks of the Aegean onto the Asia Minor coast and into Cyprus. But the trading stations produced no Mycenean colonization in the west. At Ischia the pattern of Bronze Age commerce was simply repeated.

Something changed dramatically when the Euboeans moved to Cumae and then began to settle in Sicily. To say that land-hungry Greeks, victims of overpopulation or failed harvests, sought relief by emigration to the west, is to forget that the unaided farmer or herdsman had no way of reaching foreign shores. Without organization and without leadership he was helpless. The crucial factor in the establishment of the agrarian colonies was the willingness of the oikists and their kind to risk the dangers of the seas and unknown lands rather than to remain at home. There was something propelling aristocrats to abandon the known for the unknown and that something led to the colonizing wave that rolled westward from Greece.

One must not assume that the oikist of a colony was carrying out the policy of his homeland in a calculated venture of expansion. Whatever ties of dialect, traditions and sentiment continued to exist between the mother city and colony, the oikist and his party were effectively divorced from the mother city on their departure. Traditions clung to the names of the oikists which put them in a light far different from the reverential honor their memory enjoyed in the new settlements. Archias, the oikist of Syracuse, was guilty of manslaughter. Phalanthus, the leader of the Spartan colony at Taranto (Taras) was involved in an unsuccessful coup before leaving Sparta.

The personal fortunes of these two oikists alone do not explain the intensity of the colonizing movement in the eighth century. But recognition of the new political and social conditions faced by these leaders of the tribal society that seems to have been characteristic of Greece in the centuries after 1,000 may help us to understand why so many of their number were willing to lead colonial ventures. Greece in the eighth century was on the threshold of the city state. Slowly perhaps, but irreversibly, the rule of the assembly and of codified law was destined to replace the rule of inherited authority. We hear complaints against the old order from Hesiod, the didactic poet second only to Homer in the beginnings of Greek literature. Hesiod protests that the nobles ('kings' was their title) take bribes and dispense crooked justice. The aristocrats, for their part, must have smarted under attacks on their ancient privileges, which they were quickly losing. The depth of their uneasiness and their appetite for new horizons is also apparent in Homer. His audience wanted songs of the distant west, and he satisfied their desires with the *Odyssey*. For the same audience songs of affronted dignity also struck a responsive chord. And so selecting from the wide range of epic saga Homer composed the *Iliad*, the story of the Achaeans' affront to Achilles and his wounded pride. This crisis of the spirit, like the crisis of religious consciousness in seventeenth-century England which assured leadership from the ranks of the wealthy and educated for colonies of Nonconformists, Catholics and Quakers, provided the direction and the necessary investment in ships and supplies for the Greek ventures overseas.

The emigrating aristocrats could count on a band of their traditional dependents to accompany them. The nucleus of those following Archias to Syracuse came from one village of the Corinthiad, Tenea. And if their own community could not make up the quota of colonists, a joint venture, often with a second oikist, could be contemplated. This happened already when the first colony bound for Sicily went out to Naxos. Naxos was known as a Euboean colony, but the discovery in the recent excavations of an inscription to the goddess Enyo, who belongs to the Aegean island of Naxos, as well as the fact that the Sicilian city bore the island's name, shows that the settlers were a mixed group. In the seventh century the poet Archilochus was one of the adventurers from the island of Paros near Naxos who led the colony to Thasos in the northern Aegean. The colony assembled the 'misery of all Greece', as he termed it.

No doubt that misery did comprise the victims of population pressure and crop failure and these often invoked 'causes' of Greek colonization have again been championed in recent years. Advocates of the population growth hypothesis find support for their position in the demographic growth they find reflected in the cemeteries of Attica in the ninth and eighth centuries. The climate crisis school also uses evidence from Athens, the abandonment of wells in the eighth century in the market-place of the city. However, statistics from what is known of eighth-century burials in Attica are not particularly reliable and the closing of the market-place wells may be linked to very local conditions of the clay subsoil of Athens or possibly only to the development of the city. Neither the population or climatic problems envisaged by their proponents were severe enough to cause the Athenians of the day to become colonizers. They eventually turned to bloody revolution in the seventh century instead. This is not to deny that population increased in Greece before and during the colonizing period. There were surely years of bad harvests too. But those affected by these perennial pressures moved only when an outlet was provided by the departure of disaffected aristocrats for the west.

The first colonies

Looking across the site of any of a number of the Greek colonies in Sicily, one can almost hear the words of an oikist of another age who planted a colony on another continent. It was in 1683 that William Penn wrote to the Committee of the Free Society of Traders of London describing the city he had laid out the previous year in Pennsylvania. The Quaker proprietor of Pennsylvania had much in common with the Greek oikists of Sicily. He was an aristocrat and he was an exile of conscience. For Philadelphia he chose a location that any of his Greek predecessors would have approved. 'The Situation is on a Neck of land,' he wrote, 'and lieth between two Navigable Rivers, Delaware and Skulkill, whereby it hath two Fronts upon the Water.' The situation with two harbors is found, for instance, at Syracuse, Camarina and Selinus. Philadelphia's city plan was based on narrow streets (what the Greeks would have called 'stenopoi') and avenues (the Greek 'plateiai'). There was some difference, because Penn's plateiai (Market and Broad Streets today) were laid out to cross at right angles (an arrangement not found before the fifth century BC). But like the Greek planners, Penn reserved a space of ten acres in the center of the city for buildings of 'Publick Concerns'. For his own part William Penn would have approved the work of his predecessors in Greek Sicily and because of the excavations of the last four decades we know the physical characteristics of the first group of Greek colonies in some detail, and of these the best known is Megara Hyblaea.

The oikist of the Megarian enterprise, Lamis, did not live to see his colony succeed and contemplate its layout like William Penn. The Megarians landed first not on the landward side of the ample Bay of Augusta, where their city was eventually to be situated, but on the northern rim of the Augusta peninsula. Soon, however, the Megarians put aside the idea of an independent settlement and joined in the new Chalcidian colony of Leontini. The two factions in the colony quarreled, and the Megarians moved once again, this time to the old Bronze Age site of Thapsos, on the promontory projecting into the Bay of Augusta towards its southern end. Here Lamis died. When he came to excavate Thapsos Paolo Orsi found a reminder of the Megarian presence there. One of the Bronze Age chamber tombs was reused in the eighth century for a burial accompanied by a Late Geometric Corinthian cup of the type which has become known as the Thapsos Class. Was this the tomb of Lamis? We shall never know for sure, but it is more than likely that it was. At this point in the story of the colony King Hyblon enters the picture, helping the Megarians to establish their settlement in his territory on a low bluff which skirts the shore within the arm of the Bay of Augusta. By deciding to aid the floundering party of colonists this astute successor of the Kings of Pantalica was apparently looking to gain the adherence of a group of Greek clients to play off against the Greeks at Leontini and Syracuse, where Archias' Corinthian colony had been planted only after a battle with the natives. This clash inaugurated the Syracusan policy of heavyhandedness toward the Sicels which led to the creation of a separate class of serfs, the killyrioi (something like the Spartans' helots), in the territories under Syracusan control.

Although the site of Megara has been recognized since the Renaissance and Paolo Orsi devoted five campaigns of excavation to the cemeteries, the city of Megara has been made known almost exclusively by French excavators since the Second World War. Their work, under

the auspices of the archaeological authorities at Syracuse, came just in time to save Megara from the expansion of the petrochemical industries which have now occupied the entire landward side of the Bay of Augusta. There is no other site in Sicily where the triumph of archaeological observation over disorder is so apparent as at Megara Hyblaea. This is because the archaic city was razed to the ground and its population deported, the rich to citizenship at Syracuse, the poor to the slave market, by Gelon of Syracuse about 483 BC. The site was finally reoccupied and a new Megara arose in the fourth century. The archaic remains, therefore, have the character of the original letters on an erased and reused parchment.

Nevertheless, the results of twenty-five years' excavation and subsequent study have made it possible to visualize archaic Megara Hyblaea as clearly as William Penn's Philadelphia. The excavations are centered on the ancient market place (agora) and the street network surrounding it (figures 59 and 60). There can be no question but that the survey divisions followed by the street plan go back to the foundation of the colony. This is proved by the original houses of the colonists, seven of which can be studied on the spot and others of which can be plotted on the excavation plans. The houses are of the

Figure 59 Megara Hyblaea, general street plan

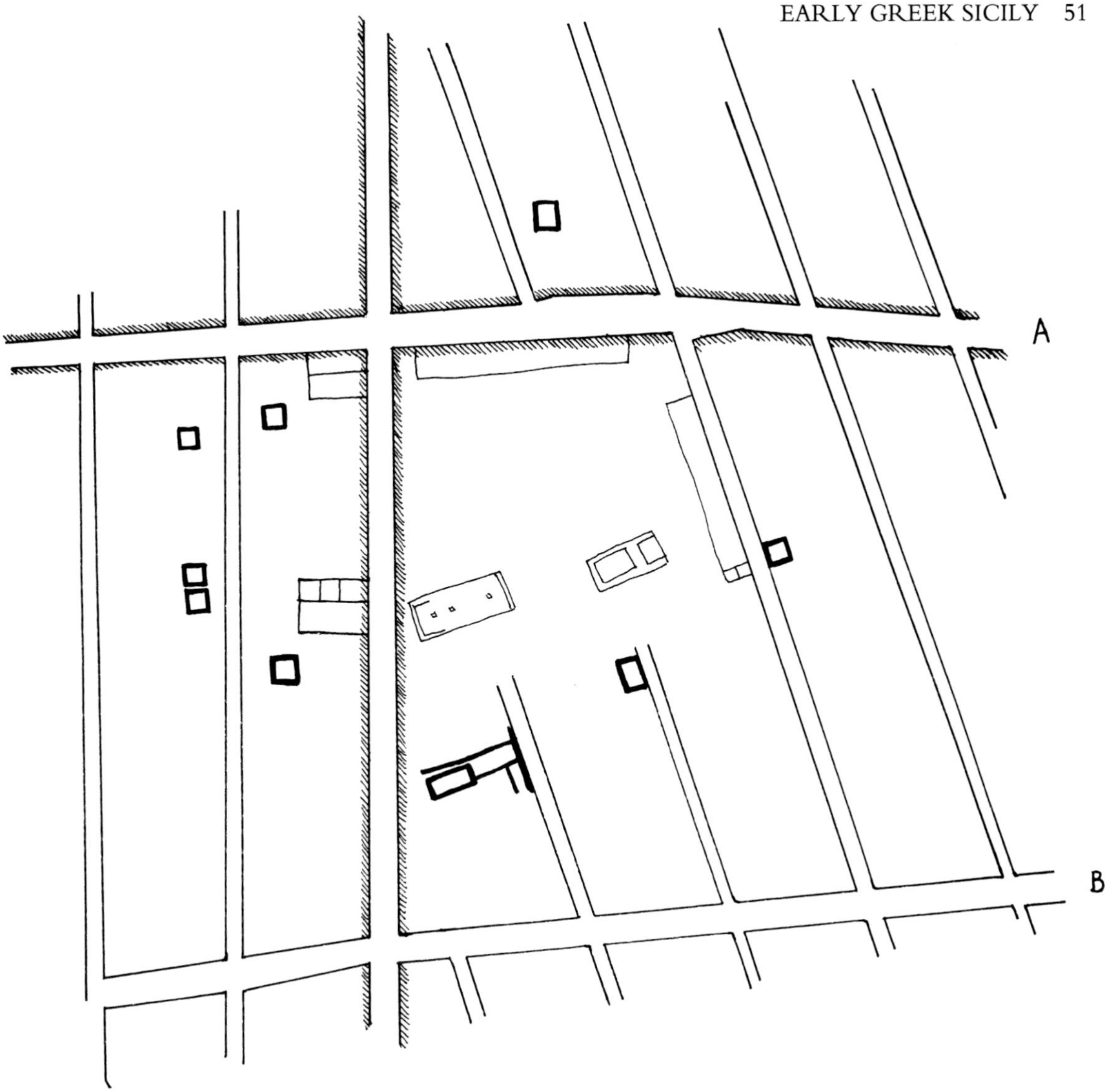

Figure 60 Archaic Megara Hyblaea, excavated area, houses of the eighth century in heavy outline, north at top

simplest kind, a single room 4.5 meters (14 ft 9 in) square or almost so (figure 61). All are oriented along the same alignments followed by the streets. The construction employed a technique of walling well known in the homeland. The wall base was made of polygonally shaped stones, their irregular facets providing stability for the rubble walling above. Such technique is known as Lesbian masonry, but the technique was widespread in Greece.

These houses must have served to shelter family and animals in a fashion not unknown to the poorer levels of European peasantry even in the twentieth century. It is commonly thought that the first Greek colonies were made up only of men, who eventually found wives where they settled (as was the case of the initial Theran venture at Cyrene in Libya). I find this interpretation difficult to accept for the Sicilian colonies. There is direct evidence to the contrary from the Fusco cemetery at Syracuse, where infants' graves are found already among the tombs of the first generation of settlers. Indeed, beside the earliest recorded tomb, accompanied by a Greek geometric amphora, there is a child's burial and with the child a little bronze horse.

Figure 61 Megara Hyblaea, house of the eighth century, after P. Auberson in *Mégara Hyblaea* ɪᴠ

Such objects were made for dedication; numerous examples come from the sanctuary of Zeus at Olympia. The Syracusan tomb, therefore, appears to have been that of an aristocratic child, who did not grow up to take his horses to the games at Olympia but was lovingly provided with the fine votive he might have carried with him. If children came from Greece, their mothers came too.

The alignment of the houses at Megara permits one to reconstruct the laying out of the city. The houses (excepting three to be considered shortly) backed on to the median line of the blocks. Thus, in the first stage of the division, strips of land 27–28 meters (88–92 ft) in width were set out in a north–south direction. The north–south streets were laid out only after the land division in the city had been made. All the streets in this direction are 3 meters (9 ft 10 in) wide (with one exception, C1 which borders the agora and is 5.8 meters or 19 ft wide). Eight of these north–south streets are within the excavation area. They are crossed by two east–west streets, 'B', 5.8 meters (19 ft) in width and 'A', which varies in width, 5.3 meters (17 ft 4 in) generally but widened to 6 meters (19 ft 8 in) where it borders the stoa built during the seventh century along the north side of the agora. Due to the asymmetry of the street plan, the length of the blocks varies between 110 and 116 meters (360 and 380 ft).

The agora was planned from the first day of the settlement. No building was erected there during the first century or so of the colony's existence, and this is not surprising since Greek politics and the commerce of the agora could be carried on without permanent structures. Greek religion, too, was often satisfied with an open-air setting until houses for the gods, such as were built in the seventh century, could be provided. The same simplicity is found in the sacred area of the upper city at Himera, where a single simple one-room shrine, Temple A, stood in the seventh century.

Although surveyed with great precision, the north–south streets have two conflicting axes. The cross streets, although parallel at the west end of the excavated area, change direction slightly at the agora and begin to converge as they cross the blocks east of the agora toward the harbor. The resulting street plan, for all the precision of the survey lines, is inexplicably asymmetrical. The two parts cannot be exactly contemporary, and two of the eighth-century houses, only one on fig. 60, show that originally the western orientation prevailed in this sector too. The eastern orientation, which produces the trapezoidal blocks to the east of the agora, is therefore a later development. It is not appreciably later because eighth-century houses were oriented on this axis too. It seems, therefore, that the original design, executed in the west at least up to the mid point of what became the agora, was a fully orthogonal scheme. Then the division system was extended eastward, but with a different orientation. This new alignment also determined the direction of the last element of the city plan, the two avenues 'A' and 'B', which begin perpendicular to the divisions west of the agora but continue eastward on converging lines. It would be hazardous to attribute the alteration of direction to some formal social division within the colony (Megara, the mother city, had five tribes). It has also been supposed that preexisting tracks or trails influenced the plan. But the conflicting axes are more likely due to factors which we still do not understand.

The scope and accuracy of the land divisions of Megara Hyblaea and of the other colonies of eastern Sicily must be recognized as one of the great achievements of the Greeks in the Late Geometric Age. Behind it is the authority of the oikist, or in this case of his successor. The houses of the colonists, rudimentary, almost identical and uniformly aligned, also speak of an authority which directed a common effort. As the street plan worked out not all the allotments in the city could be of equal size. The city plan, of course, was not a matter of inspiration at the moment of colonization. Behind it was the practice of land division in the countryside, which must have been well developed before the Greeks came west. In the colonies the regular division of the countryside has been documented at Metapontum in southern Italy. We may assume that the countryside inland from Megara was similarly surveyed and division made among the colonists.

During the seventh century the original houses in the area around the agora were enlarged and others built. The normal practice was to add other rooms to the original nucleus forming a row which was aligned across the width of the block (figure 62). Some of these enlargements came to occupy the entire width of the block, others were half that size, respecting the original median division lines. In addition to these frankly simple dwellings there appears one example of a more elaborate type of house with a courtyard and a portico in front of the suite of ground-floor rooms. It is possible that the portico also supported the balcony of an upper story. This is the so-called 'pastas' house, and the type is typical of Greek town architecture. Gradually the density of building around the agora increases, and a true townscape replaces the open character of the early years of the colony. It is quite possible that the agora of Megara was surrounded by the workshops and homes of tradesmen and artisans, just as we know the agora of Athens was. Around the agora there is little trace of anything that could be identified with the 'fat folk', the rich class who incited the conflict with Gelon and then took Syracusan citizenship while their unfortunate fellow citizens were sent to the slave market. Although the houses of the rich were undoubtedly simple, they are probably to be found in sections of the city as yet unexcavated.

Public buildings were erected in the agora and on its borders during the seventh century. There are foundations of two temples in the square. Neither had a surrounding colonnade, although one had a porch. Both have the proportions of length to width typical of temples at this time in central Greece and the Peloponnesos. The same proportions occur in a pair of structures placed side by side at the end of the block, forming the west side of the agora at its north end. These are interpreted as shrines to the founders of the colony, Lamis and his successor, who were naturally heroized and whose cult would have been practiced at the agora. Another structure of similar proportions just north of the agora may also be a shrine, and two circular structures in the second block to the west of the agora, which were covered over at the end of the eighth century, possibly had some religious significance. Also to the west of the agora was a building consisting of a court and three dining rooms opening off it behind a colonnade. (The dining rooms are identified as such by their off-center doorways, so situated to permit the arrangement of couches around the walls without overlapping the entrance.) This would have been a dining hall for public officials, like the tholos in the agora of Athens. Another and larger complex

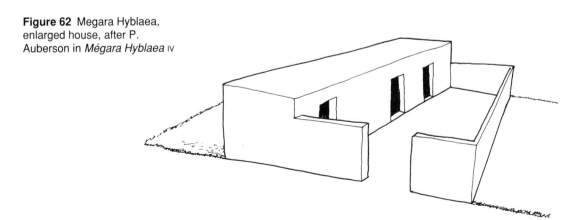

Figure 62 Megara Hyblaea, enlarged house, after P. Auberson in *Mégara Hyblaea* IV

just to the south of the agora may also have had some civic purpose. Two porticoes (stoas) enclosed the agora on the east and west.

The archaic fortifications of Megara, built shortly before the city fell into Syracusan hands in the 480s, will be considered in the section on military architecture. At the time of their construction, Megara Hyblaea was a city approximately 1 kilometer across.

The early pottery from Megara Hyblaea and its bearing on the absolute date of the settlement have been the subject of intense discussion. The material from the lowest strata of the city consists of the famous Thapsos cups, simpler straightsided cups (kotylai), pitchers (oinochoai) and wine mixing bowls (craters). This is material which is generally attributed to the third quarter of the eighth century. However, the pottery does not confirm any historical date. Quite apart from the coincidence that both of the usual calculations of calendar dates (728 or 748) fall within the range assigned to the pottery in question, the dates for this pottery were originally proposed on the basis of the calendar dates calculated after Thucydides' account of the first colonies. Fortunately the relative sequence now relies on excavations in Greece quite independent of Sicily. Moreover, there is other excavation evidence from Syria and Palestine, not without its own difficulties of interpretation but showing, none the less, that Greek Middle Geometric (the period represented by the finds at Villasmundo preceding the colonial settlements) belongs to the last half of the ninth and/or the first part of the eighth century. We are on safe ground, therefore, in attributing the Greek pottery at Megara to the mid-eighth century or slightly later, but the material does not add any precision in dating the arrival of the Greeks.

The value of the same material for establishing the relative age of the Sicilian colonies is quite a different matter. For years it seemed that one, the earliest, form of Thapsos cup found at Megara was not known at Syracuse, and thus the date for the foundation of Syracuse should be later than Megara's. This was in contrast to the generally accepted chronology based on Thucydides. This situation has now changed with the latest excavations at Syracuse where the missing variety of Thapsos cup has been found. On the basis of the pottery it is now impossible to argue the primacy of one site over the other.

Syracuse is the most appealing city in Sicily, and its island nucleus, Ortygia, home of Arethusa's fountain, is set between the open ocean and the great harbor like a graceful arch across the water. The narrow streets of the island between the Temple of Athene (now the Cathedral of Syracuse) and the Temple of Apollo on the landward side of Ortygia are ancient stenopoi, and other streets reaching the sea side of the island continue the same pattern (figure 63). It is now

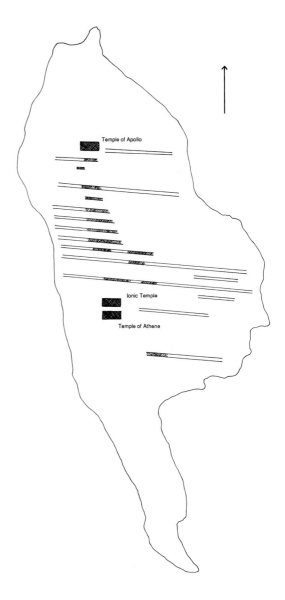

Figure 63 Syracuse, early street plan

clear that the street system goes back to the time of the oikist Archias because excavation beside the Temple of Athene (under the present City Hall) has found the same kind of single-room house known at Megara and also dating to the eighth century. What is more, the houses were oriented according to the general ancient street plan. The early pottery (as mentioned above) is indistinguishable from that of Megara Hyblaea.

Some remains of eighth-century Naxos are now known from the intensive excavations of recent years. One street intersection has been brought to light. Polygonal masonry is known here from a handsome terrace wall. The earliest pottery is like that of Megara and Syracuse but with the Corinthian material there is pottery characteristic of Euboea, two-handled transport jars (amphorai), craters and cups, occasionally with naturalistic decoration not found on Corinthian ware of the period (an exception is the tightly packed rows of miniature birds – reduced almost to a zigzag pattern – occurring in panels on small Corinthian cups, kotylai).

A fourth site on the east coast, south of Syracuse is not mentioned by Thucydides, but it was evidently settled during the first wave of colonization. This is Elorus where once again houses approximately 4 meters (13 ft) square and built with socle walls in polygonal masonry have been brought to light.

Sanctuaries

An episode in the history of Gela, recounted by Herodotus at the beginning of his sketch of the rise of the tyrants of Gela and Syracuse, illuminates the character of the aristocratic society of early Sicily. The forebears of Gelon, the future tyrant, were hereditary priests of Demeter at Gela. But the first in that public office, Telines, already had the 'sacred things' (hira) of the goddess in his possession before the civic priesthood was established. This story documents the transformation of proprietary cults into public institutions.

The cult of the mother Demeter and daughter Persephone, goddesses of the agricultural cycle, was an ancient one in Greece. We often think of it as particularly Sicilian because the story of Persephone's disappearance into the power of the god of the underground world, Hades, was localized at Enna, the Sicel city in the heart of the island. How this connection came to be made is difficult to say. An indigenous vegetation goddess may easily have become identified with Persephone. Enna enjoyed great prestige on this account. And the same worship became the most prominent cult shared by the Greek cities of the island. Simply by displaying 'the sacred things' of the goddesses, Telines was able to win back a group of Geloans who had fled in a body to the Geloan outpost of Mactorion (site uncertain). As the price of his intervention Telines demanded the public priesthood of the goddesses for himself and his descendants, thus preparing the way for his family's future power.

The Geloan secession brings to mind the secession of the plebs at Rome in the fifth century. This was a protest against the arbitrary advantages enjoyed, and abused, by the patricians, whose monopoly of religion gave them a monopoly of law and politics as well. We hear of a possibly similar case at Syracuse, when a group of citizens left for Himera in the seventh century. Such dissension, in Sicily as elsewhere, bred support for tyranny, epitomized by the name of Phalaris, who must have staged his coup at Acragas within a generation of the city's foundation. Phalaris was remembered for his oriental sadism and the bronze bull in which he roasted his victims, their screams transformed into a soft lowing by the artful construction of the nostrils of the animal. But tyranny was already a common experience in Sicily going back to the early years of settlement when Panaetius of Leontini conspired with the underclass to slaughter the aristocrats and install himself as dictator. Aside from a few such episodes we know next to nothing of the growing pains of the Greek cities of Sicily. Yet distinctions between the aristocrats and their followers must have been present from the beginning. Nothing assures us that the 'shares' of the colonists were equal, and with time the disparities simply grew worse. The apparent homogeneity of the early settlements masks real differences in privilege and power.

The clearest picture of religion in the early Sicilian colonies is afforded by the postwar excavations at Gela, the city on a long low hill beside the sea on the south coast of the island. The modest stream of the River Gela trickles into the Mediterranean beside the hill. A wide plain separates the city from the barrier of hills east and west and toward the interior. On the acropolis of Gela the seventh century saw the erection of a series of small rectangular buildings (figure 64: 1). One or more of these (depending on the interpretation of fragmentary walls) occupied the ground where the Temple of Athene (identified by the preponderance of Athene types among the terracotta figurines from the votive dump excavated nearby) was to be built in the next century. Another was situated immediately east of the temple. Their appearance is suggested by two models discovered in the Geloan sanctuaries. These structures were razed in the later sixth century when the major Athene temple was built. Still later another major temple of the Doric order, of which one column still remains in place today, was erected further east.

The shrines on the site of these major civic temples and a small shrine of Hera situated near the center of the early town were only part of the religious landscape of Gela in the seventh century. Along the flanks of the city and outside whatever defenses were erected in the early days of the colony there was another series of small shrines. Some of these had a long life, surviving the misfortunes of Gela even after the Carthaginian destruction of 405 BC and serving the renewed Gela of the fourth century. Others were frequented only in the archaic age. Seventh-

century material has been found in three of these shrines, although this does not preclude others being as old. The sanctuary of Predio Sola, situated on the seaward side of the site, judging from objects found within the shrine, only one corner of which was preserved, appears to have belonged to Demeter (figure 64: 2). The votive material was found partly below the wall of the shrine, showing that this was built well after the beginning of the cult, and partly in an upper stratum within the preserved angle of the walls. The appearance of these cult places is suggested by the models dedicated in the sanctuaries (figure 65). The terracotta casings of the eaves (revetments) show that the building was not without color and decoration. The votive objects were plentiful. Represented are both the abundant elegance of imported objects, their direct copies and a large element in which an awkwardness of popular votive art is apparent. The terracotta figurines of the lower stratum are standing images of the goddess, some with outstretched arms but most in that compact stance derived from board-like figures in wood, of which three precious examples were preserved by the sulphureous waters of the spring of the sanctuary of Contrada Tumazzu near Palma di Montechiaro to the east of Agrigento (figures 66 and 67). The technical term for these figures is 'xoanon'. There is a grandiose terracotta three-cornered lamp with

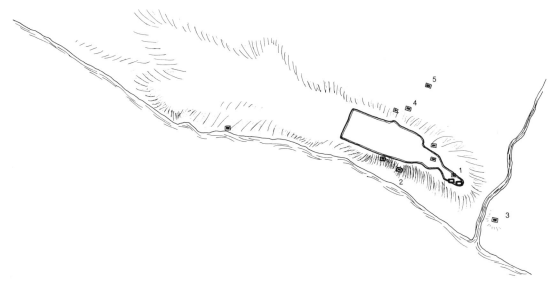

Figure 64 Gela, plan. (1) Acropolis, (2) Predio Sola, (3) Bitalemi, (4) Railroad Station, (5) Santa Maria dell'Alemanna

Figure 65 Gela Museum, terracotta model of shrine from Predio Sola

Figure 66 Gela Museum, terracotta figurine from Predio Sola

Figure 67 Syracuse Museum, wooden figures from Palma di Montechiaro, photograph courtesy of German Archaeological Institute, Rome, inst. neg. 37.650

rams' heads on the sides at the apices and human heads that served as spouts in between (figure 68). Discoveries from the famous Sanctuary of Demeter Malophorus at Selinus show that this piece copies imported Greek marble sanctuary lamps (figure 69). The largest element of the imported pottery is Corinthian, mostly handsomely decorated oil flasks. There are also bigger vessels, mixing bowls and cups (figures 70 and 71). A bold animal-tapestry style was the trademark of Corinthian oil and scent bottles of the late seventh and early sixth centuries. But there is also pottery from Ionia, Attica, Sparta and a faience scarab, apparently of genuine Egyptian manufacture (although faience scarabs were also made in Greece, notably on Rhodes). The material of the upper stratum is dominated by a group of forty-one masks of the goddess, locally

Figure 68 Gela Museum, terracotta lamp from Predio Sola

made but reproducing a prototype known throughout the Greek world. The major center of the diffusion of these objects is thought to have been Rhodes. They are found in tombs but are mostly associated with cult places of the underworld divinities, and in Sicily especially with the cult of Demeter and Persephone. The largest of the masks from Predio Sola is a full

Figure 69 Palermo Museum, marble lamp from Selinus

half-meter (1 ft 8 in) in height (figure 72). Others run as small as 10 centimeters (4 in) high. Each has an expression marked by the unemotional vitality of archaic Greek art, but this characterization is our reaction to objects which must have had an explicit function within the cult (figures 73 and 74). The nocturnal ceremonies of the worship of Demeter and Persephone explain the numerous lamps also found in the deposit (figure 75).

Francesco. Once again this is only a sample of a more extensive votive dump, to which offerings were consigned when shelf and wall space for them was exhausted in the sanctuary proper. The deposit numbers thousands of objects and includes exquisite examples of the finest luxury wares of the Greek east among its pottery. A small selection of this material is on exhibition in the Regional Archaeological Museum in Syracuse.

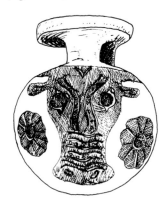

Figure 70 Gela Museum, Corinthian oil flask from Predio Sola

This material, a fraction of the original possessions of the sanctuary, illustrates how commonplace foreign goods were in the archaic colonies. A far larger and impressive body of material of this kind from an archaic sanctuary came to light at Catania in 1959 in Piazza San

Figure 71 Gela Museum, Corinthian oil flask from Predio Sola

The sanctuary at Bitalemi is just across the River Gela from the city (figure 64: 3). As

Figure 74 Gela Museum, terracotta bust of Demeter-Persephone from Predio Sola

Figure 72 Gela Museum, terracotta bust of Demeter-Persephone from Predio Sola

proved by a graffito on a sherd found there, it was a 'thesmophorion', the seat of a women's cult of Demeter and Persephone in which the cycle of life was imitated and assisted in ceremonies including the burial and subsequent recovery of fruits, vegetables and especially young pigs. Once again the structures of the sanctuary were of the simplest kind. Some were in mud brick, with no stone socle to protect the walls from humidity. As at Predio Sola the cult was in being before the buildings. The graffito explains that the vase it marked came from the 'tent of Dikaio'. Dikaio

was evidently one of the women participating in the mysteries. As at Athens she and her fellows occupied tents during the festival and at least part of ritual would have been performed in them. There were remains of ritual meals cooked on the spot, and an entire stratum of vessels dedicated to the goddesses by being buried in an inverted position. The terracotta figurines are more varied than those at Predio Sola. There are fewer masks, and with the other objects there was a deposit of formless bronze ingots. These are certainly money (Latin 'aes rude', 'crude bronze'), and with them there was found a cast piece bearing a large letter 'Xi', which is the abbreviation of 600 (such an object is known by the Latin term 'aes signatum' or 'marked bronze').

Another sanctuary, which began its life in the seventh century north of the hill of Gela near the modern railroad station, further illustrates the role of the sanctuary as a depository for money (figure 64: 4). This shrine is notable for the discovery there in 1956 of a hoard of 1,000 or more silver coins (870 were recovered), the latest dating to about 480 BC. Banking was a business of Greek sanctuaries, and we shall have

Figure 73 Gela Museum, terracotta bust of Demeter-Persephone from Predio Sola

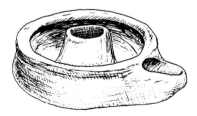

Figure 75 Gela Museum, terracotta lamp from Predio Sola

occasion to return to the Gela hoard when discussing Sicilian coinage.

Finally one should take note of the ancient sanctuary below the church of S. Maria dell'Alemanna, the patroness of Gela, located on a rise of ground again in the plain north of the city (figure 64: 5). Surviving terracotta revetments show that the sixth-century temple here was the largest at Gela. No other extramural sanctuary discovered thus far at Gela enjoyed such architectural splendor.

This review does not exhaust the sanctuaries of all periods known in the surroundings of the city, nor those situated at some distance, 'She of the Many Crowns' at Butera to the northwest (possibly Mactorion, the scene of Telines' encounter with the dissident Geloans) or the sanctuary at Feudo Nobile, located on the border of the Geloan territory toward Camarina.

The multiplicity of cult places around Gela in archaic times is not astonishing by ancient standards, but it reflects tellingly on the character of religion in the colonies. Religion came to the colonies as the possession of aristocrats. City cults developed slowly, as we have already seen at Megara Hyblaea, where a century passed before the erection of a temple in the agora. Meanwhile private cults, accessible, one may imagine, on the basis of tribal membership, which could be acquired in the colonies without true lineage ties, flourished outside the city walls. Demeter was the major goddess of this extramural world. The sanctuaries of Bitalemi and Predio Sola were hers, and probably that of S. Maria dell'Alemanna as well. (The deity of the sanctuary near the railroad station is unknown.) In the case of S. Maria dell'Alemanna the building of the great temple suggests a move toward city patronage and away from private control, such as was carried out in Athens in respect to the Eleusinian mysteries.

The cults of outlying places in the countryside must have owed their origin to the same aristocratic priests and their interests that are reflected in the sanctuaries closer to the center. Modern scholarship often speaks of the colonists' taking possession of the territory of the city through setting up of cults in the countryside, as if this were a civic undertaking. It is better understood as the manifestation of the Greek aristocrats' establishing the cults through which, in the beginning, they maintained a position of reverence and power among their countrymen.

At Syracuse the presence of civic cults outside the walls is shown by the sanctuary of Olympian Zeus located across the great harbor from Ortygia. The temple, which was a large and magnificent structure of stone, belongs to the end of the seventh century. On Ortygia there were notable cults of Apollo, Artemis and Athene. Like the Temple of Zeus, Apollo's temple was also built at the end of the seventh century. But precise information concerning the beginning of the cults on the island is lacking. The establishment of the shrines of gods on the mainland adjacent to Ortygia, again Apollo, but especially Demeter and Persephone, belongs to a second step in the development of the city.

Perhaps because Acragas was founded at a later stage of the colonizing movement, in 580 BC, this city displays the control of the city over religious life from the beginning (figure 76). As far as we know archaeologically, the cults of Acragas were organized in a ring around the city. On the acropolis was the temple of Athene. We

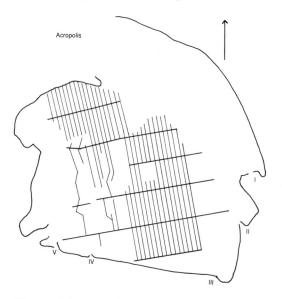

Acropolis

Figure 76 Acragas, plan, gates numbered I to V

know that the tyrant Phalaris began his rise to power as the contractor for this project. Nearby was the temple of Zeus Artabyrius from Rhodes. Then around the eight-kilometer circuit of the walls of the lower city shrines are positioned beside many of the gates. The temple of Demeter is above Gate I. (Most of the identifications of

Agrigentine temples, except for Olympian Zeus, are modern guesses.) Gate III is guarded by the temple of Hera. Gate IV has the temple of Heracles. At Gate V one is in the midst of the sanctuary of the Chthonian (Underworld) divinities. Acragas was never the home of aristocratic exclusive cults. Rather, from the beginning religion was an expression of the city.

The most impressive instance of a city's intervention in extramural sanctuaries is to be found at Selinus, the westernmost of the Greek colonies on the south coast of Sicily. The city occupied a bluff between two rivers, and the area extending inland from it. Anyone approaching Selinus from the sea in the years before it fell to the Carthaginians in 409 BC would have seen two groups of temples. The first rose within the city on the acropolis overlooking the sea. The second, including one peripteral temple as large as the Parthenon at Athens (Temple ER), its neighbor, one of the largest temples ever raised in the Greek world (Temple GT), and their companion (Temple FS) stood to the east across a small estuary. Unfortunately, there is no sure evidence of the divinities to whom these shrines belong.[3] But these magnificent buildings are an unerring sign that the city, not individual aristocrats, held control. This must have been true from the late seventh century when the first monumental building on the site of Temple ER was constructed.[4]

Extending along the foot of the sandy rise which borders the far side of the ancient harbor to the west of the acropolis there was a series of shrines rather different in character from those of the east hill. The best known of these is the justly famous Sanctuary of Demeter Malophorus (Demeter the Bearer of the Quince, a cult name brought to Sicily from Megara in Greece and transmitted through Megara Hyblaea to the daughter colony in the west of the island, figure 77).

The shrine of Demeter, enclosed within a wall forming a temenos ('divided off' land, the Greek term for a sanctuary reserve), also echoed the ancient shrine of the goddess at Eleusis, just over the border from Megara in Attica. Immediately outside the propylon (gateway), which dates to the fifth century BC, there was a well recalling the Kallichoros Well, which stood beside the gate of the sanctuary of Eleusis and beside which

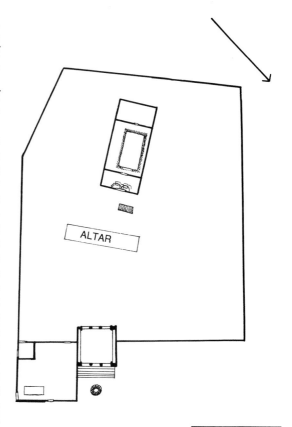

Figure 77 Selinus, Sanctuary of Demeter Malophorus, plan

Demeter collapsed in despair over the disappearance of her daughter. To the left of the entrance there was a separate shrine of Hekate, who also served as guardian of the Eleusinian shrine. In the center of the sanctuary there is a grand altar, also erected in the fifth century. Excavations earlier in this century showed that the altar covered a dense accumulation of charred remains of sacrificial animals, and a rich collection of vessels and terracotta figurines. In fact, the entire area within the temenos wall was given over to ritual deposits, frequently consisting of vessels deliberately buried in the sand in an inverted position as at the thesmophorion of Bitalemi. The remains have not yet all been exhausted, even after the excavations of recent years. The grand altar stood over a simply constructed archaic predecessor.

Behind the altar there is the temple itself (figure 78). Initially there was a simple rectangular structure of the kind we have already met at

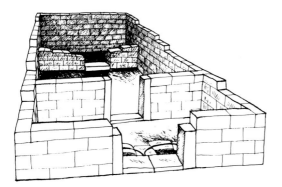

Figure 78 Selinus, Temple of Demeter Malophorus without fourth-century modifications

Gela. Subsequently the stone temple, of which much of the walling is still standing, was built. The plan is a large central chamber preceded by an outer room and followed by an inner chamber or adyton. The rear of the building was transformed under the Carthaginians after 409 BC, when the cult became associated with that of the Carthaginian goddess Tanit. The sand was mounded up behind the building (aided and possibly encouraged by natural drifting) covering the rear wall, which itself was rebuilt in a rough fashion showing that it was not meant to be seen. The same mound covered the rear roof and to strengthen this an arch was installed in the rear chamber. The temple now gave the appearance of being an entrance to the underworld. But how much earlier was the original construction? This is a difficult question to answer. Because of the simple plan of the building it has been assumed that it belonged to the early category of temples without peristyles. But the Malophorus temple was built from its foundations to its eaves in stone, and such building is difficult to find before the fifth century (figure 79). It dispensed with the terracotta revetments usual on archaic buildings. The molding of the roof line is also quite unusual. Unfortunately the excavation of the building took place before Ettore Gabrici, to whom the publication of the sanctuary is due, took charge of the excavations in 1915, and in the previous work the pottery against the foundations, which constitutes the objective evidence of the date of construction, had not been kept separate from other material. Even if it had been, one must remember that the sanctuary was one large deposit of votive material, which becoming mixed in the fill of the foundation trenches might, from superficial observation, suggest a misleadingly early date for the construction. Both the propylon and the grand altar belong to the fifth century, and I would date the first rebuilding of the temple to that date.

Next to the Malophorus Sanctuary there was a small shrine of Zeus Meilichios, who with his consort is represented on a series of crude stone uprights (stelae) crowned by two heads. Both the small temple and most of the other traces of activity here belong to the Carthaginian period.

To the south of the Malophorus sanctuary there is a second sacellum and temenos of similar character which is currently under investigation. To the north there are the remains called 'Temple M'. These may belong to a monumental altar or to a large fountain house which drew water from the nearby spring.

Thanks to the work of Gabrici, an important selection of material from the Malophorus Sanctuary was published in 1927. In essence it mirrors the votives we have encountered in the Demeter sanctuaries of Gela. The wealth of the sanctuary is shown by the exquisitely carved small marble figures of women in seated and reclining poses, possibly to be attributed to a dedication rather than to a small pediment, as is often maintained (they were meant to be seen in the round). The marble lamps of the sort which provided the prototypes for the terracotta lamp at Predio Sola were imported in the seventh century (figure 69). The grand altar was adorned with handsome scroll work at its ends. The group of small terracotta altars have handsome figured decoration, gorgons, lions and mythological scenes. The terracotta figurines belong to the same general categories we met at Gela, although there is a stronger presence of seated archaic goddesses than at Predio Sola and male figures appear among them, as at Bitalemi. In the material from the Malophorus Sanctuary we

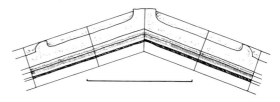

Figure 79 Selinus, Temple of Demeter Malophorus, stone cornice

also have the styles of the fifth century as well as the archaic. In addition to terracotta masks, there are terracotta busts of the goddess and among these are some of the grandest Sicilian terracottas of archaic times. The pottery follows the pattern of the Geloan sanctuaries with important representations of Corinthian, Attic, Greek island and Ionian vessels.

Appendix 1: the identification of Gela

Modern Gela has been known by the ancient name only since 1927. Formerly it was Terranova di Sicilia, the name given to the abandoned site when a new city was founded there by Frederick II in AD 1230. However, the ancient sources are by no means so precise as to make identification certain, and in some cases they are very difficult to reconcile with the topography of the site. These problems have been treated at length by G. Navarra, who argues the alternative solution, identifying ancient Gela with modern Licata located 25 kilometers to the west at the mouth of the River Salso.[5] Although little excavation has been done there Licata is far from a negligible archaeological site,[6] as demonstrated especially by the discovery of the Greek sanctuary located at Casalicchio on the inner border of the plain behind the city.[7] Licata is the findspot of an inscription, possibly of the third century BC, which uses the term 'People of the Geloans'.[8]

However, the Geloans were resettled by Phintias, tyrant of Acragas, in the early third century at a city which was named, in his honor, Phintias, but where the deportees may have continued to boast of their ancient identity. One piece of evidence would seem to weigh heavily in favor of identifying Gela with the commonly accepted site at Terranova. This is the foot of an Attic drinking cup (kylix) of the sixth century BC bearing a dedication to Antiphemus, one of the two oikists of Gela, and said to have been found with numerous other fragments of imported pottery.[9] The authenticity of this apparently decisive find was questioned by Biagio Pace, a scholar second only to Paolo Orsi in Sicilian archaeology before the Second World War.[10] Hardly more decisive is the graffito on the stone crown of a funeral stele in the form of a Doric entablature with roof above, to which

an Ionic column in relief is added as decoration in the pediments and found at Gela.[11] The graffito contains the word 'geloios' ('Geloan'), but it is hardly sure that Greeks proclaimed their citizenship in such informal messages only in their home cities. Furthermore, the most recent excavations at Gela have brought to light Greek pottery of the eighth century, thus antedating the supposed foundation of the colony. These sherds may be trade goods brought to the spot before the settlement or to an initial Rhodian station, Lindoi, which preceded the joint Rhodian–Cretan venture.[12] One must admit, therefore, that the question of the identification of Gela is one for which there exists only the weight of evidence rather than proof. The generally accepted identification is followed in this work.

Appendix 2: the Sanctuary of San Biagio and the Sanctuary of the Chthonian Divinities at Acragas

Two sanctuaries at Acragas have been associated with the beginnings of the city. One is the fountain complex at San Biagio near Gate I. A votive dump including some sixth-century material was discovered in the deep gallery penetrating the hillside behind the structure through which water reached the fountain house and its basins. The dump and the building, however, may have little to do with one another. Certainly the early date of construction originally claimed for the structure is dubious.[13] The so-called Sanctuary of the Chthonian Divinities is difficult to interpret. The three sacella containing altars and circular constructions were once taken to be typical manifestations of an archaic cult of Demeter and Persephone. One of the sacella, however, is the third in a succession of structures or planned structures, one of which at least may have been intended to be a peripteral temple. The area includes four such major temples, three reduced to little more than foundation trenches, the fourth transformed by an early nineteenth-century restoration into the picturesque 'Temple of the Dioscuri'. Despite the clearly archaic material excavated here by Piero Marconi in the 1930s, much information essential for the understanding of the area is lacking.[14]

Burials

Since evidence of the first tombs is scant everywhere except in the Fusco cemetery at Syracuse, the following remarks concern the archaic and classical periods as a whole.[15]

Together with the extraurban sanctuaries, the cemeteries of the Greek colonies could be found along the roads outside the walls. By far the greatest part of Paolo Orsi's undertakings in the archaeology of the Greek cities during his long tenure as Superintendent at Syracuse was the excavation of cemeteries. His monographs on Megara Hyblaea, Syracuse, Camarina and Gela are monuments to these efforts. The first colonists brought with them traditions of burial, both inhumation and cremation. Cremation was more expensive and consequently less frequently practiced, but the choice must have depended on family traditions, personal preference and fashion. At Syracuse the colonists continued to bury as they did at the mother city, Corinth, in trench graves sunk in the limestone rock. Feeling less crowded in their cemeteries, the colonists buried the body in the extended position, while it was usually contracted at home. At Gela cremation is far more prevalent than at Syracuse (50 per cent against under 10 per cent), but cremation was the almost universal practice for adult burials on Rhodes and predominated in Crete, the two homelands of the Geloan colonists. Camarina, though a sub-colony of Syracuse, was near Gela and acquired a taste for cremation from her neighbor. At Selinus, 85 per cent of the burials are inhumations. Children were commonly buried in storage vessels, generally amphorae (two handled vessels, principally containers for wine and oil). Since infant mortality has been estimated at about 50 per cent, children's graves are common. In soft ground tombs could be protected by tiles. Large nails found in tombs prove the use of wooden coffins, or, in the case of 'primary cremation' (burning of the body in the grave trench) the use of a wooden bier on which the corpse was placed. As time passed there was some elaboration of funeral practices. Stone and terracotta sarcophagi came into use, many of them decorated with architectural details, such as columns at the four corners of their interiors. Tomb chambers constructed of squared stone blocks began to be constructed at Megara Hyblaea. A number of these have been found empty. They seem to have been prepared for Megarian nobles who departed for Syracuse following Gelon's offer of citizenship. Another important cemetery of built chamber tombs is found at Mt Adranone (Sambuca di Sicilia), a secondary colony of Selinus. These span the sixth and fifth centuries. There are double as well as single chamber tombs and the grave offerings were exceptionally rich. They include bronze vessels as well as pottery.

Tomb goods were placed with the remains or deposited on the exterior of the tomb (although approximately one-quarter of the graves are without any gifts). Pottery is the best preserved class of offerings, and tombs could contain magnificent examples of imported Greek vessels with figured decoration. Smaller vases held the oils which were deposited with the dead. Children received the most elaborate sets of offerings, including toys. Women also enjoyed richer groups of gifts than men, and despite the general frugality in the Greek tombs, women occasionally had jewelry with them. Although a bronze vessel was sometimes used as an ash urn, no burials in Greek Sicily compare with the 'princely tombs' of the Etruscan and Italic peoples. (A single richly furnished burial of a warrior from near Leontini appears to have belonged to an Italic mercenary captain.) The grave goods also

do not mark social distinctions. Clearly expensive sarcophagi could hold burials without offerings, and it may be assumed that, as in more recent times, those of modest station might invest heavily in pretentious tomb furnishings. In any case, for the memory of the deceased among the living above-ground markers were more important than burial offerings. We hear of the monumental tombs of the Syracusan tyrants, and traces of late archaic tomb pavilions (aediculae) are known from Megara Hyblaea. Only two monumental tombs survive, both from the Hellenistic Age. The first is the so-called Tomb of Theron just outside Gate IV at Acragas. The structure consists of an upper and lower chamber. The upper chamber (the tomb proper) has false doors on each of its four sides. There are engaged Ionic columns at the corners. Above, there was a Doric frieze (alternating triglyphs and metopes, for the terms see the following section 'Temples'). The podium is plain and capped by a cornice. Another monumental Hellenistic tomb at Elorus consists of an underground chamber and above it a massive column in masonry now preserved to a height of 10.5 meters (34 ft 5 in). Originally the column must have been been several times as tall. Elements of the cornice and column drums of what may be another monumental tomb, or small temple, dating to the fourth century are known from Monte Saraceno. The cornice fragments are notable for the remains of painted decoration on their surface.

Statuary was another way to emphasize the importance of a tomb. A number of funeral statues are known from Sicily, two of the most interesting from Megara Hyblaea, the kouros (standing nude male figure) from the tomb of the doctor Sambrotides and the seated woman with suckling twins (Night with the twins Sleep and Death).

In the later sixth and fifth centuries pottery imported from Athens, where workshops of the highest artistic level were decorating their products with mythological subjects, becomes common in Sicilian Greek tombs. In some cities, Acragas for example, there developed the custom of fitting out tombs, men's tombs in particular, with sets of vases for the symposium or formal evening gathering for drinking, philosophy, politics, poetry and song. It is possible that some unusual scenes on vases used for the tomb reflect the particular interests of their owners while alive. This might explain the unusual vase with two figures labeled Sappho and Alcaeus (the two famous seventh-century Ionian Greek poets) from a fifth-century tomb at Acragas. Certainly the winged figures which decorate so many of the lekythoi (oil flasks) from cemeteries in southern Sicily (Camarina, Gela and Acragas) must have hinted at the liberation of the soul and a flight to a propitious hereafter. This notion was suggested by tales of the Isles of the Blessed and was taught by numerous secret cults.

In funeral imagery of the average tomb, however, we are in the realm of popular religion, of comforting associations rather than systematic theology. And consequently several divinities that appealed to the imagination could be enlisted as heralds of hope. Dionysus, god of wine but also the god of mystical transformation, was prominent among the divinities of salvation, beckoning with his band of ecstatic followers toward a blissful afterlife. A remarkable document of Dionysiac imagery from Sicily has recently been published (figure 80). It comes from Montagna di Marzo and is a lead sheet, 1.8 meters (5 ft 11 in) long and 0.4 meters (1 ft 4 in) in

Figure 80 Catania, private collection, lead sheet from Montagna di Marzo. Drawing courtesy of E. De Miro

height. On the surface there is engraved a scene of Dionysus riding in a cart and accompanied by his merry satyrs. The iconography is Athenian, derived from the Dionysiac rituals of the festival of the Anthesteria. A practically identical scene is preserved on an Attic black figure vase (one in which the figures appear in black glaze against the buff-colored clay background) and on a second black figure vessel which is either of Athenian or western Greek manufacture. The exact purpose of the lead sheet, which is a sporadic find now in a private collection in Catania, is unsure. If it came from the necropolis of Montagna di Marzo, where many discoveries have been made in the past, it would be natural to assume that it was the covering for a wooden sarcophagus. But in publishing this object, E. De Miro suggested that it was a cartoon in a painter's workshop.[16]

Dionysiac imagery explodes in the fourth century. The scenes on the red figure pottery (in which the background is now black and the figures are in the natural clay color) produced in Sicily and in southern Italy, mainly for funeral purposes, is dominated by Dionysus and thus with intimations of hope for comfort in the next life. The presence in tombs of the Archaic Period of terracotta figurines or masks of the types common in the sanctuaries of Demeter and Persephone points to a similar role for Persephone, the consort of Hades himself. She, like Dionysus, was associated with the mystery cults and the theology of the afterlife. This is the message of the gold plaques with instructions for the deceased on the journey to the underworld that have come to light in tombs in southern Italy. Figurines of a goddess with a bird suggest Aphrodite, goddess of the passions and attendant on marriage. Thus these figurines are also an expression of the theme of a union for the better in the afterlife. In the Hellenistic Age the theme of marriage, with Aphrodite and her son Eros (the Greek Cupid) attending, was to become a prominent part of funeral iconography.

Temples

We have seen that the simple shrine (in Greek, naiskos, in Latin, sacellum) erected for the aristocratically controlled cults of the early colonies was perpetuated in the stone temple of Malophorus (Demeter) at Selinus. An antechamber and an inner room (the adyton) are the only additional complexities in the plan. This type of temple had a long history. A building with a dressed masonry socle and what must have been a mud brick superstructure is known on the acropolis of Selinus. The seventh-century temple in the agora of Megara Hyblaea had a porch of columns, but its overall dimensions were still modest (figure 81).

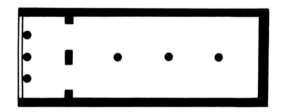

Figure 81 Megara Hyblaea, temple

An early stage of monumental temple building can be followed at Selinus. The mid-fifth century Temple E in the sanctuary on the eastern hill was erected over the remains of two earlier buildings, one of the late sixth century, the other, as established by the pottery from its foundation fill, belonging to the late seventh century. The earlier of the two was already a sizable temple ocupying the same space as the main chamber (cella) of the mid-fifth century temple (figure 82). The plan is restored hypothetically with two columns at the front between the wall ends (the so-called in antis arrangement) and a double interior colonnade to support the roof. A quantity of the dressed blocks for the

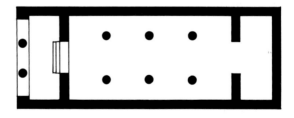

Figure 82 Selinus, Temple E(1)

walling, however, prove that this was already a stone temple. About 80 per cent of the terracotta roof tiles of the building survive, having served as fill for the subsequent constructions. In the fire which destroyed this early archaic temple clear traces of the clay and straw bedding on which the tiles rested were left on their surface. The tiles are gaily decorated in a checkerboard pattern of red, black and cream on their upper faces. Along the edge of the roof ran a chain

in Greece when Temple E1 was built. The palmette forms of the antefixes and ridgepole decoration are typically Corinthian as well, and so it seems likely that the Selinuntine temple followed Greek prototypes. The temple had monolithic stone columns. There are two sizes, one for the in antis columns of the porch, the other for the interior colonnade (figure 84). They and the surviving fragments of capitals are of the Doric order. The Doric order, most

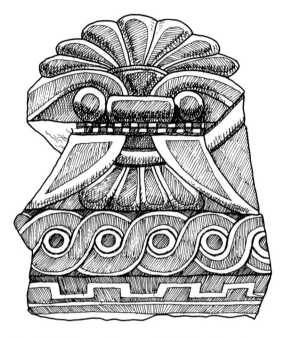

Figure 83 Palermo Museum, Antefix from Temple E(1) Selinus

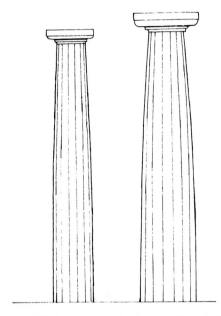

Figure 84 Selinus, restored columns of temple E(1)

of similarly colored, plastically modeled palmettes (in this position called antefixes, figure 83). They served to mask the joints between the tiles. The ridgepole of the roof was covered by a tubular tile, once more decorated with a line of free-standing palmettes along its crest. The tiles show, furthermore, that the roof of the temple did not end in a gable opening (the pediment), which we expect in Greek temples, but was inclined over all four sides of the building, a hip roof. The roof tiles combine a flat piece (the pan tile) with an angular cap to cover the joint with the adjoining tile. This is a typically Greek tile form, except that in Greece the pan tile and cover tile were usually separate. Roof tiles had been made for three quarters of a century at least at Corinth

familiar to us from buildings like the Parthenon, was the typical building style of mainland Greece (figure 85). The Ionic order, which we shall encounter in one major temple at Syracuse, was the design preferred in Asia Minor and in the Greek islands. In the early Temple E at Selinus the cushion-like member supporting the rectangular block of the capital (the echinus) has the wide form typical of the earliest Doric columns. A number of blocks one-half the thickness of the normal wall blocks are restored in the uppermost courses of the exterior wall, suggesting that at its top the outer wall courses were backed by wood. The same half-width blocks are worked back to two depths on their visible faces, so that projecting and retreating

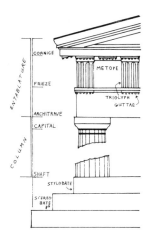

Figure 85 Diagram of the Doric order

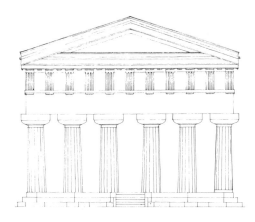

Figure 87 Syracuse, Temple of Apollo

surfaces alternated along the wall. The projecting surfaces were colored red, the retreating surfaces black. The result would have been related to that of the alternating grooved and plain elements of the normal Doric frieze (the channeled triglyphs and smooth-faced metopes).

The Temple of Apollo at Syracuse (of the Doric order) is one of the first Greek temples with an external colonnade (a peripteral temple, figure 86). The idea of the surrounding colonnade (peristyle) had been introduced around the middle

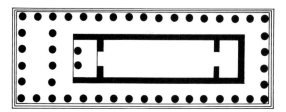

Figure 86 Syracuse, Temple of Apollo

of the seventh century in Ionian Greece (the earliest example being the Temple of Hera in the sanctuary of the goddess on the island of Samos just off the Turkish coast). We have no archaeological date for the Temple of Apollo at Syracuse, but its construction is generally placed around 600 BC, almost contemporary with the first peripteral temples in stone of the Doric order in Greece proper. The temple is a major achievement of stone engineering (figure 87). Its monolithic columns rise 7.9 meters (26 ft) in height. The stone architrave immediately above them was 'L' shaped, allowing the greater part of the architrave to be made of wood and

thus reducing the weight of the superstructure. There is no trace of stonework above this point in the peristyle, and by the standards of the primitive wooden Doric order the spacing of the columns was extremely close. It was so tight that a normal individual can easily touch columns at either side while standing between them. This spacing was clearly motivated by concern for the weight of the superstructure over the colonnade. The walls of the cella were entirely of stone. In plan the Apollo temple shows a simple sacellum with two columns in antis. Any interior columns supporting the roof are hypothetical. An adyton (inner room) followed toward the rear. The colonnade of the peristyle is doubled on the front of the building, a characteristic not found in Doric temples of the mainland but reminiscent of the doubled colonnades of temples in east Greece already existing at this time (Samos, for example). The temple was approached by a stairway in the center of its eastern facade, useful for access because of the height of the three-stepped podium on which the temple was placed (in the fashion of all normal Greek peripteral temples). The stairway was added after the completion of the temple. Farther to the east one would have found the altar of the temple. Such open-air altars served the ceremonies of the cults of the Olympian divinities, as distinct from the under-world gods like Demeter. The temple was thought of as the house, and the treasure chamber, of the god. Two handsome examples of archaic altars were found in the excavations around the fifth-century temple of Athene not far from the Temple of

Apollo. They were surely connected with the sixth-century temple. One is faced with a Doric triglyph and metope frieze. The other is decorated with palmettes and spirals.

The roof of the Temple of Apollo was protected by terracotta tiles. In place of the antefixes covering the joints between the tiles at the edge of the roof, such as are found in Temple E1 at Selinus, the Apollo Temple had an upright terracotta barrier called a sima. This was pierced at intervals by tubular spouts for the rainwater. Since the roof ended over the fronts of the building in a pedimental triangle, the spouts were not needed on the raking sima at the two ends of the building. The wooden beams supporting the edge of the roof (which projects slightly over the columns and superstructure of the colonnade) were also protected by terracotta covers, both on their exterior face and on the underside. (In completely stone buildings this member of the entablature was termed the geison, and the term may be extended to the wooden elements just described.) Both the terracotta revetments of the sima and the geison of the Apollo Temple were brightly decorated in red, black and cream.

This system of terracotta revetments, the sima and the geison cover below it, was typically Sicilian. Its appearance marks a clear break with the mainland Greek type of antefixes such as are present at Temple E1 at Selinus. An experiment leading to the new system is found in the terracottas of Temple A at Himera. This building, which was enclosed within the later Temple B, was a simple sacellum. From its roof there survives a lateral sima and geison cover made in one piece (figure 88). There is no cover for the underside of the geison. The Sicilian system evolved quickly from such initial versions

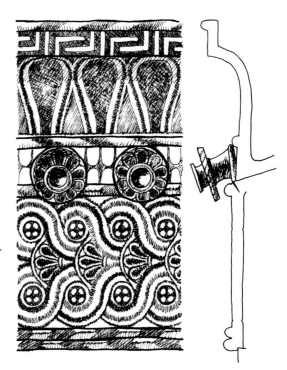

Figure 89 Syracuse Museum, lateral terracotta revetment from the Early Temple of Athene

into the elaborate roof terracottas we find in the major Sicilian sites and in southern Italy as well. Typical of its developed form are the revetments from the archaic Temple of Athene in Syracuse, belonging to the early sixth century (figure 89). The mainland Greek palmettes survive here as pendants attached below the fully Sicilian system of revetments. The broad band of the geison cover is decorated with an elaborate guilloche (interlaced) design. The raking sima has tongues, a checkerboard and rosettes, all between a pattern of St Andrew's crosses. The halfround moldings separating the main elements are given barberpole stripes, and the ends of the tulip spouts from the lateral sima are treated similarly. If one compares the Syracusan roof with the revetments made at Gela for the treasury of that city in the Panhellenic sanctuary at Olympia, the essential similarities of the Sicilian roof system are apparent. The general form is the same, although in the Geloan treasury, from the end of the sixth century, the raking sima cuts across the horizontal geison and sima rather than resting on top as in the older building at Syracuse. But the major

Figure 88 Himera Museum, terracotta revetment from Temple A

decorative motives are the same, and the general effect is similar. The repertoire of motives that adorn the Sicilian terracotta revetments was all present in portable art of the seventh century. We know pottery best, but we should not forget metal work, bone and ivory carving and textiles. As has been pointed out, the characteristically Sicilian deep cavetto molding of the sima developed from a shallower form (represented especially at Gela) which, in turn, can be matched, at a smaller scale, in Greek mainland architectural terracottas. So rather than an invention, the Sicilian terracotta revetments are a bold development from Greek prototypes.

In Sicily, the extension of stone building to the full elevation of the peripteral temple is first found in Temple C on the acropolis of Selinus (figure 90). The ground plan of this temple has much in common with the Temple of Apollo at Syracuse. There is the same simple interior structure, adyton, cella and entrance chamber (the pronaos) without the columns in antis of the Syracusan temple. The temple was approached by stairs its full width. The facade columns are doubled and the interior structure is longer and more slender than its counterpart at Syracuse, increasing the width of the surrounding colonnade, as was done in the Ionian temples (in which the peristyle was doubled all the way around the interior structure). At Selinus the interior chambers are raised above the peristyle, thus emphasizing that they were thought of as a distinct building within the colonnade. The temple measures 23.8 by 63.75 meters (78 by 209 ft). The builders began with monolithic columns (the first were erected at the southeast corner of the peristyle) but soon changed to columns made up of drums. Still, the number of flutes (vertical channels) on the columns is not consistent (sixteen or twenty) and unlike normal Doric columns, those of Temple C have

no trace of that slight bulging of the shaft called entasis which counteracted the concave appearance of a straight line against the sky. The elevation of the exterior order shows columns and capitals much like those of Temple E1 surmounted by a plain architrave and above that the distinctive Doric frieze of alternating triglyphs and metopes. The plaques with pendant knobs (guttae) are present, as on all canonic buildings of the Doric order in every part of the Greek world. (The plaques on the underside of the geison above the frieze, with three rows of knobs, are called mutules. Those below the frieze, having only one row of knobs, are called regulae.) However, there is a peculiarity at Selinus; the mutules over the metopes are only half the normal width. The roof terracottas are quite in the Sicilian style on the ends of the building, although the set that survives is not the original revetment of the building but a replacement made toward the end of the sixth century, which accounts for the new and more slender palmette chains included among the patterns. The shelf-like ends of the roof at the corners of the pediment are old-fashioned, recalling the hip roof of Temple E1. Along the flanks there is no Sicilian sima, but rather a line of intertwined palmette antefixes, again much like Temple E1. The lion's head spouts at the four corners of the building are in line with the coming fashions of the day.

Temple C occupies an interesting position in the rediscovery of archaic Greek art and architecture. It was investigated first in 1823 by two Englishmen, Harris and Angell (the former of whom lost his life to malaria contracted during their work at Selinus). At the time Greece had not yet emerged from her war of independence against the Ottoman Empire and the sculptured metopes of Temple C (to be considered shortly) were the first examples of early archaic Greek sculpture to become known in western Europe. In the later nineteenth and early twentieth century the date of the building was set in the second half of the sixth century on the basis of the roof terracottas, despite the patently early character of the metope sculpture and the equally early character of the architecture, both conveniently dismissed as simply representing the provinciality of a colonial city. Although there has been no excavation in the foundations of the temple to secure evidence of its date, recent investigations

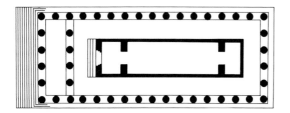

Figure 90 Selinus, Temple C

have provided grounds for placing the building before the mid-sixth century. This evidence comes from the east side of the sanctuary area, where in the mid-sixth century a stoa (colonnade) was built over a fill which extended the sanctuary in that direction. The pottery recovered from this fill is no later than what is called Middle Corinthian, the phase of Corinthian pottery which lasted from the opening years of the century until about 550 BC. If the extension of the sanctuary followed the erection of Temple C, as is natural to assume, then the temple must belong to the first half of the century. A date of 575 BC marks the middle of the span, although if the style of the scupture of the metopes is given the weight it deserves in the argument, the true date of the temple would be slightly earlier. Somewhat later than Temple C is Temple D, which is situated alongside Temple C to the north (figure 91). This temple has the wide passageways between columns and cella found in Temple C, and its interior plan is reminiscent of its neighbor. The second row of facade columns has been eliminated, but in the pronaos there are two columns in antis and in addition two half columns forming the ends of the antae themselves. The entablature was stone, as were the roof tiles, and thus this building completes the development of the Sicilian temple into a completely stone building. Like Temple C it had abbreviated half mutules over the metopes.

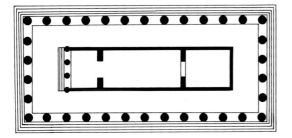

Figure 91 Selinus, Temple D

Temple F in the sanctuary on the eastern hill at Selinus belongs to the end of the sixth century (figure 92). Its ground plan repeats that of Temple C. The elevation, in stone, is that of a normal Doric order. This building was of the lengthened archaic type (fourteen columns on the flanks, six on the fronts). It had a doubled façade colonnade. Crowning the entablature was a

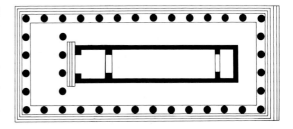

Figure 92 Selinus, Temple F

stone sima of 'Sicilian' type in which lions' heads were substituted for tubular spouts. At some time after its erection the peristyle was closed by partitions between the columns. There were apparently openings along the perimeter, but these had doors, thus creating a peristyle completely cut off from the exterior. The divinity of Temple F (as in the case of all the temples of Selinus) is unknown, and so one cannot gauge to what extent this unusual arrangement was meant to serve the cult. Although an extreme solution, the modified plan seems very much in line with Selinuntine thinking about the peripteral temple whereby the peristyle was considered a barrier surrounding the sacellum.

This concept and the increasing desire of Selinus, like other Greek cities, to display its wealth to the advantage of its gods led to Temple E and F's neighbor, Temple G (figure 93). Temple G is one of the largest Greek temples ever planned. It measured 50 by 110.4 meters (164 by 362 ft) and was to have eight columns on its facades and seventeen on its flanks. Its current state – the pile of gigantic blocks and column fragments to which it was reduced by an earthquake during the Middle Ages – has made detailed study of the temple well-nigh impossible. Current thinking is that the temple

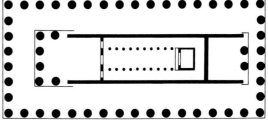

Figure 93 Selinus, Temple G

was not meant to be roofed entirely but that the peristyle was thought of as a colonnade around a court in which a sacellum stood as a separate building. The plan was maintained in its original form only at the eastern end. Most of the building was done, with modification of the plan, in the fifth century, and the temple was still unfinished, the columns unfluted, at the time of the Carthaginian sack of Selinus in 409 BC.

If Temple G was meant to rival the proportions of the gigantic temples of Ionian Greece (Ephesus, Didyma and Samos), a late-sixth century temple at Syracuse represents an attempt to transfer the Ionic order as it had developed in Asia Minor to Sicily (figures 94 and 95). This building was situated a few yards to the north of the Temple of Athene (both the archaic building whose roof terracottas we have examined and the replacement of that structure of just after 480 BC). The first suggestive fragments of the Ionic temple were discovered by Paolo Orsi, but the building was documented during the excavations of 1963–4. Only a preliminary publication of it has appeared. Its columns were Samian Ionic and like the columns of the great temple of Artemis at Ephesus

Figure 95 Syracuse, restored column of the Ionic Temple

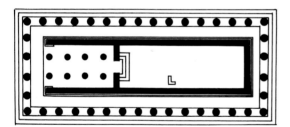

Figure 94 Syracuse, Ionic Temple

(which was assisted by donations from King Croesus of Lydia) the columns were meant to have bands of decoration around the bottom of their shafts. Enough of the capitals is left to show that they, too, were very close to the Asiatic Ionic of the day and were decorated with a rich pattern of palmettes on the side of their spirals. The ground plan did not allow room for a double colonnade like the great Ionian temples, but there may have been a deep pronaos with double rows of columns reminiscent of the Ionian models. Because of the great height of its columns (the height of an Ionic column was normally in the range of ten lower diameters) the Ionic temple

must have towered over its Doric neighbor, the early Athenaion. At some time, possibly when the tyrant Gelon came to power, work on the Ionic temple ceased. Gelon's temple, erected to commemorate the victory over Carthage in 480 BC, was the new Doric shrine to Athene. This choice was more than a matter of personal taste. The buildings we have been examining were the political instruments of ambitious men. And Gelon's abandonment of the Ionic temple, begun perhaps a generation before he seized power, has an air of political motivation.

Temple building had both a symbolic and economic objective. It glorified the gods and the city, which thereby succeeded in overawing the proprietary aristocratic cults that existed in the earlier foundations. In economic terms temple construction meant returning to circulation the money that otherwise would have accumulated in the coffers of the divinities concerned.[17] Public works meant public employment then as today.

Everyone profited, the individual laborer, the farmer whose oxen were employed during the slack periods of the agricultural year hauling stone from the quarries, and finally the magnate whose slaves earned day wages for their master. In fifth-century Athens, where we have more detailed information concerning the building program carried out under Pericles, there were more than hints of scandal. Phidias, the overseer of the project, was exiled as a result. This was an old story in Sicily. The director (epistates) for the building of the archaic Athenaion in Syracuse, one Agathocles, was haled before the oligarchic council of the city and convicted of misappropriation of materials. The size of the funds at the disposal of the epistates could also encourage more dangerous schemes. Phalaris of Acragas used the money destined for a Temple of Zeus to launch his tyranny.

The epistates of such a project viewed his work with pride. Indeed the earliest known Sicilian public inscription was cut on the top step of the foundations of the Temple of Apollo at Syracuse, just beside the stairway leading up to the temple's east facade (figure 96). The step is worn, and the upper parts of some letters in the middle of the inscription have to be restored, thus permitting variant readings. The most recent interpretation of the whole runs, 'Kleomenes the son of Knidieides made it for Apollo. And he included columns. They are fine works'.[18] The word just preceding 'columns' has given the most trouble. At one time it was read as a second proper name, thus suggesting that the inscription recorded the work of two master builders, one of whom took special credit for the columns. But the new reading, by Margherita Guarducci, giving only one name, suggests that Kleomenes was the 'epistates' of the temple. The verb 'to make' rather than 'to dedicate' implies a more active role in the project than we usually expect from donors or officials. Kleomenes clearly thought of himself as directly involved in the work. In this respect his final remark about the columns is significant. They were an addition

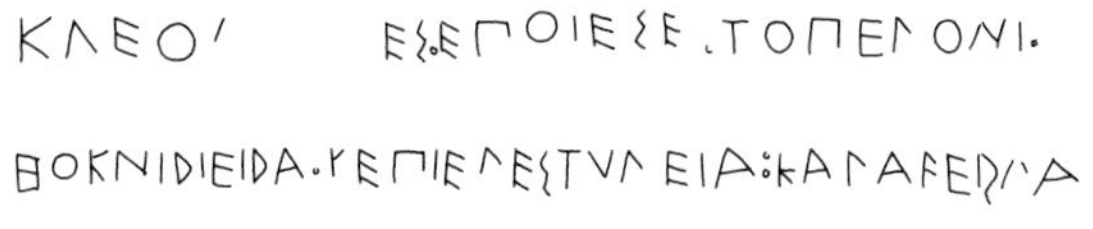

to what was expected, perhaps even to what had originally been planned. One is reminded of what the Alkmeonid family did for the temple of Apollo at Delphi when they supplied marble instead of limestone for the facade of the building. Their purpose was highly political: to win favor with the oracle and assist their plots to overthrow the Peisistratid government at Athens. We can only guess at Kleomenes' objectives. But largely on his own initiative, it seems, he erected the first peripteral temple at Syracuse and had no hesitation about recording the fact for posterity.

How did Kleomenes carry out his desire to give Syracuse its first temple with a monumental colonnade? In respect to anything that Sicily had seen up to that time he needed specialized quarrying, specialized transportation from the quarries (especially considering that he would be erecting monolithic columns 26 ft in height), specialized engineering on the site to raise the columns and roof the temple, specialized work to produce the roof terracottas, both the tiles and the decorated geison covers and sima, and the gorgon masks which seem to have decorated at least some of the metopes of the exterior. Like Phalaris at Acragas, if one can trust the tradition about the Agrigentine tyrant which eventually found its way into a fourth-century book on stratagems, he brought in foreign specialists. When the Spartans faced a similar situation in building the shrine of Apollo at Amyclae during the seventh century, they invited an Ionian architect, Bathykles of Magnesia, to oversee the project. We know that other famous Ionian architects (and engineers) travelled from one project to another. Kleomenes, who seems to have had Ionian roots (his father was known as 'The Cnidian'), may very well have looked in the same direction. The building was destined for a city that prided itself on its Dorian-Peloponnesian heritage, and so the order of the temple was Doric. But in the ground plan the doubling of the facade colonnade shows that the planners had Ionic prototypes in mind as well. The 'foreigners' who came to work on the Sicilian buildings found a good home and created the nucleus of the specialized building trades that must have existed in the major Greek cities of the island, where public building was well-nigh continuous during the archaic age.

The ambitions of a latter day Kleomenes may well have been behind the design of the Ionic

ΚΛΕΟΝ   ΕΣΕΓΟΙΕΣΕ.ΤΟΓΕΓΟΝΙ.

ΒΟΚΝΙΔΙΕΙΔΑ.ΥΕΠΙΕΛΕΣΤΥΛ ΕΙΑ:ΚΑΓΑΓΕΡΙΑ

Figure 96 Syracuse, inscription from the stylobate of the Temple of Apollo

temple at Syracuse. This building represents a conscious break with the Sicilian Doric temple. It was not the only such case, as is shown by Ionic capitals, the most impressive being from Gela. But it was certainly the most extreme and it fairly shouts for attention. Instead of continuing work on this Ionic pavilion, after the victory over Carthage in 480 BC Gelon erected a soberly canonical stone temple of the Doric style to replace the old Athenaion with its cheerful archaic roof terracottas. This building, much of which was preserved in place when it became the Christian cathedral of Syracuse, is the only Greek temple whose columns still shelter the mystery and the treasures of a religious cult. The simple grandeur of the Doric columns seen in the dim light of the interior as they tower over the faintly burning gold vigil lamps and the black ironwork of the grilles to the side chapels is a ghostly reminder of the splendors that were sheltered here when the temple was new. Through his new temple Gelon enunciated the architectural message of his regime.

Sculpture

The sculptural decoration of Greek temples includes some of the most prized works to have survived from classical antiquity. The sculptures of the Parthenon, the sculptures of the Temple of Zeus in the panhellenic sanctuary at Olympia, and the sculptures from the Temple of Athene-Aphaia on Aegina also testify to the way in which these scenes were devised to project a vision of the great divinities of the same shrines. It was a vision which materialized the gods for a people who traditionally conceived of their divinities in physical form. But unlike the cult statues of the same gods within the temples, the sculpture of the metopes, pediments, and continuous Ionic friezes materialized the gods in the midst of action, where their presence often takes on the character of an epiphany. Battles with monsters of the dim mythical past encountered by both gods and heroes in these scenes, or still more elemental struggles between titanic beasts reveal another, and basic, function of this kind of art. Its energy protects the sanctuary and the worshippers in it from the mysterious dangers that surround all living things. This fear, confirmed every day by accidents, crop failures,

sickness of men and animals, and death is embedded, for much of mankind, in the ancient belief in the Evil Eye. We have already met this superstition in the Sicilian neolithic, and it is still very much alive in the Mediterranean. The brightly colored architectural terracottas of the Sicilian temples and the complicated designs which decorated them belong to the same aesthetic as the painted cart of more recent times and the ribbons and bits of mirror protecting the mule in its traces. The bright colors (especially red in Sicily and Italy) startle the evil emanation, and, should they fail, the complexity of the ornament succeeds in ensnaring it. The decoration of Greek temples thus spans a wide horizon of sophistication from the most ill-defined superstition to the heights of theology and political allegory. And remains in Sicily bring us very near to the beginnings of Greek architectural sculpture.

One facing head of a gorgon in terracotta survives from the decoration of the Apollo Temple in Syracuse. The severed head of the gorgon Medusa, the very sight of which turned men to stone, is in its horrid self the embodiment of the Evil Eye and consequently, by the logic of superstition, an effective antidote. The gorgon's head from the Apollo Temple is now attributed to one of the exterior metopes of the building. There were surely other gorgoneia,

Figure 97 Gela Museum, terracotta gorgon's head from Gela

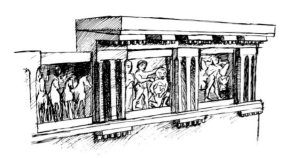

Figure 98 Palermo Museum, frieze and cornice of Temple C, Selinus

or other subjects, on other metopes, although, as we learn from better-preserved temples (notably at Selinus), the decoration may have been limited to the facades, or even the principal facade, of the temple. We illustrate a similar architectural gorgon from Gela (figure 97).

The east pediment of Temple C at Selinus was adorned by a monumental terracotta gorgoneion, restored as over 2.75 meters (9 ft) in height. But the fame of this building rests on the limestone metopes of the east facade. Three of these, reconstructed soon after the excavations of Harris and Angell, have long been familiar. Now, thanks to the patient work of Vincenzo Tusa, the sculptural fragments from Temple C have been analyzed and published, thus permitting us to form some idea of how the sculptured frieze was planned.[19]

On the restored metopes we have first Perseus in the act of severing the head of the gorgon, while Perseus' protector, the goddess Athene, stands by (figures 98 and 99). On another, Heracles strides along carrying two figures suspended like small game from a pole on his shoulder. The story is one of the burlesque adventures of the hero, who captured two simian individuals called the Cercopes when they tried to steal his weapons. From their trussed-up position they had an excellent view of Heracles' private parts, and their humor on the subject softened Heracles' wrath so that he released them. Finally, the sun god is represented standing frontally in his chariot drawn by two horses and flanked by two outriders. Although the earliest decorated metopes in Greece were terracotta with painted designs, the metopes of Temple C are high relief, almost freestanding sculpture transferred, as it were, to the narrow ledge of

the metope frame. The gaze of the figures is insistently frontal, which suits their apotropaic role, and their proportions have all the charming exaggeration of early archaic sculpture. Much of the apparent awkwardness of the proportions would have been compensated for by the steep angle of vision from the spectator at ground level up to the temple facade. The pleated edge of Perseus' chiton (shirt) and Athene's gown have been claimed as proof that these reliefs were executed well after the middle of the sixth century. However, these details were recut on the original surface of the stone in an effort to modernize the sculptures, apparently at the same time the new roof was put on Temple C in the later sixth century. Otherwise these sculptures with their simple heads and undifferentiated features, their block-like anatomy and lack of detail (save in the knee-joints) place them securely in the early archaic period, well before the middle of the sixth century. This date accords very well with the evidence noted earlier of the extension of the terrace before the temple at this time. The frontal composition of the sun god's chariot might appear advanced for this date. But just this composition is well attested in graphic sources before 550 BC. In making an estimation of these sculptures one must also remember that originally they were brightly painted and many details which were not modeled, such as the pupils of the eyes, were added in paint. Some traces of this decoration remain in the meander border of Athene's dress.

From the other fragments of the frieze we know that one metope contained a helmeted male head. There are also fragments of a second metope with a chariot group. In addition there are two other heads of women and the torso of a youth. All these fragments match the frontality of the figures of the three restored metopes. Another fragment which seems to belong to the Temple C metopes has a profile head of a woman. This fragment was part of a scene of struggle, because the hand of an assailant seizing the woman's neck is still preserved.

The subject of the frieze can be identified as an epiphany of the gods of the official city cults of Selinus thanks to an important inscription of the early fifth century which lists the members of the civic pantheon in a 'Te deum' of thanksgiving for victory in war. The inscription runs as follows:

Through these gods the Selinuntines are victorious.

We are victorious through Zeus and through Phobos (Ares),

Through Heracles and through Apollo and through

Poseidon and through the sons of Tyndareus (Castor and

Pollux) and through Athene and through Malophorus

(Demeter) and Pasikrateia (Persephone) and through

The other gods but especially Zeus.

Inscribing then the peace treaty in gold

Figure 99 Palermo Museum, metope from Temple C, Selinus, photograph courtesy of Alison Frantz Archive

Appending these names, dedicate it in the Temple of Apollo

Making Zeus' version an inscription.[a] And the gold

Shall weigh sixty talents.[b]

[a] Evidently the inscription on stone that has survived.

[b] The light Sicilian talent equivalent to about 20 gm of gold. The tablet of the inscription was to weigh 1 kg.

The gods of the metopes of Temple C correspond exactly to the pantheon named in the inscription. Heracles, Apollo (as the sun god) and Athene, seen assisting Perseus, are present on the restored metopes. The second chariot would have carried Poseidon, frequently shown mounted in a chariot in archaic Greek art. The two female heads would have served for Malophorus (Demeter) and Pasikrateia (Persephone). The youthful male torso might belong to one of the Tyndaridae (Castor and Pollux). The woman seized by another figure is best interpreted as Hera dominated by Zeus, as we find the couple portrayed on a metope of the fifth-century Temple E.

In this way the apparently random selection of subjects for the metopes of the building falls into place as an epiphany of the gods of the city. One may note that myth can serve to make a god's power manifest without the god being a major participant in the action. Thus Athene need only be the onlooker at Perseus' triumph over the Gorgon. Implied action, as on the part of the sun god (Apollo) in his chariot, is as effective as immediate struggle.

From a building which must have stood on the acropolis of Selinus and which was a predecessor of Temple C (possibly hidden under its podium like Temple E1 and 2 beneath Temple E) there comes a series of metopes which were found built into constructions of the Punic period of the city after 409 BC. The hypothetical building they decorated has been termed Temple Y. These metopes take us back one step from Temple C toward the painted terracotta metopes of the seventh century in Greece because although carved in limestone their style is based on drawing, emphasizing the figure in profile view, and they are in low relief. The subjects, however, bring together the same assembly of gods as the metopes

of Temple C. The surviving metopes have Apollo (shown with his sister Artemis and their mother Leto), Heracles overcoming the Cretan bull, Zeus (as a bull) in the act of carrying off Europa. The two most recently discovered metopes of the group show on one what is probably a scene of Malophorus, Pasikrateia and Hekate (?) and on the other Poseidon and his consort Amphitrite mounted in a chariot (figures 100 and 101). All these gods are members of the pantheon of Selinus. It seems, however, that the divine subjects were not sufficient to fill up the number of metopes to be decorated because there is an additional metope of the same size

Figure 100 Palermo Museum, metope from unknown temple, Selinus, photograph courtesy of Soprintendenza ai Beni Culturali ed Ambientali, Palermo

with a sphinx. The subject is a neutral apotropaic image.

The sculptures from the earliest temple thus far identified at Himera (Temple B) belong to the same period as the sculptures of Temple C at Selinus. They are in terracotta and apparently represented the struggles of Heracles. Un-

Figure 101 Palermo Museum, metope from unknown temple, Selinus, photograph courtesy of Soprintendenza ai Beni Culturali ed Ambientali, Palermo

fortunately they are very fragmentary and it is impossible to reconstruct the sequence of scenes. Other fragments of the same group are attributed to the pediment of the temple. The building itself was a sacellum without colonnade.

It is probably more than coincidence that early temples with sculptured metopes are found exactly on the frontiers of the Greek west, at Selinus and at Himera on the north coast, both cities on the border between Greek and Carthaginian Sicily. In Italy there is a similar case in the early temple in the sanctuary of Hera at the mouth of the Sele River just north of Paestum. This sanctuary is located on the border of the Greek regions and the barbarian (subsequently Etruscan) lands to the north of the river. The decorated metope frieze was not invented in the west. It was common property of Greek builders from the beginning of the Doric order. But its early flowering on the frontiers of the Greek world speaks eloquently of the way in which

these scenes were felt to make the gods of the colonists physically present in their new homes.

The scenes represented by these sculptures could easily have been based on the portable art which the colonists imported from the motherland. The prototypes were less often scenes on pottery than wooden inlays, metalwork and, we may suppose, textiles. We know this material best from the inlaid chest dedicated by the Corinthian tyrant Cypselus that was still to be seen in the Temple of Hera at Olympia in the second century AD when the guidebook writer Pausanias described it. Metope-like panels on metal-work with appropriate mythological scenes are also known from the Olympian sanctuary where they are found decorating the bronze overlays of the leather straps by which the Greek soldier held his shield. Such minor art was the major conduit through which the west stayed abreast of the visual arts of the homeland. The second channel was, of course, the arrival of craftsmen. The Selinus metopes, especially those of Temple C, testify to the transplanting of sculptors from the Aegean. Selinus, in fact, became the home of a school of sculpture working throughout the sixth and fifth centuries. To the later sixth century belongs a set of metopes for Temple F. The lower half of two metopes from the building survive. They were part of a representation of the battle of gods and giants, another myth where a pantheon of gods could be shown together.

The life of the sacellum without colonnade was far from over after the introduction of the peripteral temple. Major temples fronted by simple porches were still built, as at Camarina, and small shrines followed the old type. Together with the small sacellum there continued the tradition of antefixes along the roof edge, which had disappeared on major temples after the development of the 'Sicilian' sima. A terracotta model representing one of these shrines has been found at the native center of Sabucina near Caltanissetta, which was undergoing rapid Hellenization in the sixth century (figure 102). For all its crudity, the model embodies what its maker felt to be the essence of a Greek shrine of the day. The columns and the roof tiles of the building are carefully executed. Two antefixes, one a gorgon, one very similar to a gorgon although it is usually called a satyr (the part-equine creatures of the wild frequently seen

of the ridgepole tile (such as are known from Monte S. Mauro) and improperly placed at the pediment's corners. Finally two horsemen emerge from the ridgepole (there are traces of the base of a third such figure in the center of the roof-line). The Sabucina model thus encompasses both epiphany and apotropaic images on a small sacellum. Such figures, epiphanies of the Dioscuri (Castor and Pollux), were common on small Sicilian sacella. The best preserved such figure comes from Camarina, but there are fragments from Gela, Agrigento and Syracuse as well (figure 103). The horsemen on the roof, which reach their apogee in the marble horsemen from Locri Epizephyrii (on the instep of the boot of southern Italy) in the fifth century, are a characteristically western Greek form of architectural decoration.

There are antefixes from Greek sites in Sicily in the form of both gorgoneia and satyr heads, and the satyr-head antefixes are surely among the most original pieces of Sicilian Greek art. They are best known at Gela and Naxos. Antefixes were certainly made at Naxos, where the molds and kilns have been found outside the walls. Gela was probably a center of production as well. The Geloan group is especially famous (figure 104). Although belonging to the early fifth century, these satyrs are the direct descendants of artistic

Figure 102 Caltanissetta Museum, terracotta temple model from Sabucina

with Dionysus, the god of wine), appear in the pedimental opening, thus doubling the pedimental gorgoneia of Greek temples but warning us that antefixes in the form of heads were somehow felt to be akin to the gorgon mask. There are old-fashioned disc antefixes at the ends

Figure 103 Gela Museum, terracotta horse's head architectural group from Gela

Figure 104 Gela Museum, antefix in the form of satyr's head from Gela

Figure 105 Syracuse Museum, terracotta gorgon plaque

currents that created the sculptures of Temple C at Selinus. Furrows and swelling solids go to make up the satyr mask, which shares the intensity of energy that is stamped on every archaic image. All Greek satyrs are demonic, but the Geloan satyrs make the demon's energy explode into the forest of hair surrounding it. The Naxian antefixes have faces far less detailed than their Geloan counterparts, but the idea of the face emerging from its beard and hair is similar.

We find female antefixes that sometimes joined satyr heads in alternation along the roofs of sacella only in the native interior of the island.[20] We may presume that such female head/satyr head series existed in the coastal cities, as they did in the Greek motherland. Two elegant female antefixes come from Syracuse, where they seem to have decorated a funeral monument. Negro heads were used for antefixes too (unfortunately the Greeks apparently considered them ugly and apotropaic). There is a splendid mold for such a head from Megara Hyblaea.

The ability of the Sicilian workers in terracotta is especially well demonstrated in the surviving roof adornments discovered at Gela. In addition to the gigantic gorgoneion and fragment of a sphinx, there is the figure of a lion, a beast known as an implacable enemy of the Evil Eye and already present in the decoration of Temple C

(where the corner water spouts assume the form of lions' heads). The Geloan lion, with three similar companions, was apparently situated at the roof corners of a major temple of the city.

One of the best known pieces of early Sicilian Greek art is the small gorgon from the excavations around the Temple of Athene in Syracuse (56 cm or 1 ft 10 in square, figure 105). This gorgon is a close relative of the gorgon from Temple C at Selinus. Her running pose is the same, and like the gorgon of Temple C she holds the winged horse Pegasus under one arm. (Pegasus sprang from the neck of the gorgon at the instant that Perseus severed her head.) The Syracusan gorgon, however, has all the colors of terracotta working. The background is black. Her face gains the vitality of a red tongue and red and black pupils in her eyes, while the animated contours of the face are outlined in black against the cream background. Her wings, and those on her boots as well, have contrasting feathers of red and black. Her chiton is red, with an edging which utilizes the tongues, triangles and

Figure 106 Palermo Museum, head from Temple E

mouth and the traces of the eyes. What remains is an unmodulated oval not unlike that of the head of Athene from the Perseus metope of Temple C. The head is certainly that of a goddess because she wears a crown (polos). The hair was indicated in waves across the forehead and hung in a mass behind the head.

At twice the scale of the Selinus divinity the Laganello Head in Syracuse comes from a colossal cult statue (figure 107). It was found near the source of the Ciane, the small stream which flows into the Great Harbor of Syracuse from the west. The nymph of the river was venerated by the Greeks, and the Laganello head must be her image. Typical of its age, the head is a simple ovoid onto which, it seems, the features have been attached. The hair is done in large knobs and scallop curls across the forehead. This head too has a goddess' polos.

Together with the Selinus metopes, these heads testify to the accomplishments of the Sicilian sculptors at the opening of the sixth century. Although the Sicilians had no access to marble, their work in their native limestones has all the vigor and accomplishment of early archaic art in the homeland. Their materials, however, meant that a style imbued with an early archaic flavor was to continue in the island longer than one would expect in the centers of the motherland. This is evident, for instance, in the seated figure, slightly under life size, from Acrae, Syracuse's inland daughter city, and very possibly from the Aphrodite sanctuary there, and in the small upper body of a kore (standing young woman) from the same site. Both may be rather later in date than they appear at first glance, and the same may be said for the kore in high relief originally set in an architectural framework (an aediculum) from the second of Syracuse's inland outposts, Casmenae (Monte Casale).

Beside stone, the early Greek sculptor worked in wood. Nothing of this art is known in Greece proper save for some miniature and decorative pieces, but three kore figures at small scale have been preserved in the waters of a sulphur-laden spring near Palma di Montechiaro, which was a Greek cult place (figure 67). In general, the three correspond to the early archaic architectural sculpture from Selinus that we have just examined. But in one particular their style is distinctly that of the woodworker. The overfold of their long

Figure 107 Syracuse Museum, the Lagonello head

meanders familiar from roof terracottas. The source of the gorgon figure and her color scheme is Corinth. We find comparable representations in Greek roof terracottas. It is often assumed that the Syracuse gorgon is a roof ornament too. There is no compelling reason why this should be so, and the nail holes visible below the right leg and left thumb could be intended for attachment to an altar, chest or throne.

Two remarkable heads, which are rarely given their due in histories of Greek art, bring us face to face with the cult statues of the time of the Temple of Apollo at Syracuse and Temple C at Selinus. One head was found in the interior of Temple E at Selinus (figure 106). In all likelihood it was part of the original cult statue of Temple E1, preserved in the temple despite its various rebuildings. The head is life size. The surface is much abraded. The nose has vanished. One must look carefully to see the small straight

dress (peplos) above the waist is worked with a distinctly yoke-shaped line making a surface which turns out sharply at the edges. This edging and the gently curving surface of the garment seem natural for sculpture made with the adze and wood chisel.

This style also gives its essential qualities to the most original creation of Sicilian Greek art, the seated woman with suckling twins in limestone from Megara Hyblaea (figure 108). The statue was recomposed from 936 fragments after its chance discovery during the construction of one of the petrochemical plants south of the ancient city. It comes, therefore, from a necropolis of Megara Hyblaea and must be interpreted as a funeral marker. The usual reaction to this simple expression of maternal eternity is to claim it for an otherwise lost strain of native Sicilian art or to suggest that it is somehow dependent on the statues of seated dignitaries of Ionian Greece, with whom it has no more in common than it does with the seated figure from Acrae.

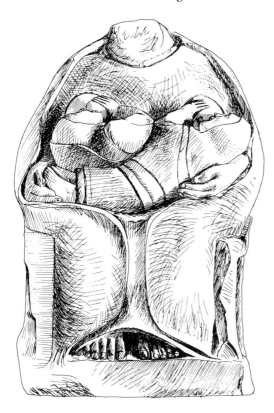

Figure 108 Syracuse Museum, statue of Night with the children Sleep and Death from Megara Hyblaea

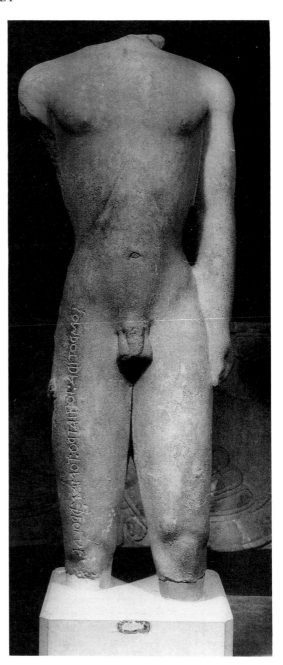

Figure 109 Syracuse Museum, Kouros of Sambrotides from Megara Hyblaea

The statue is limestone. It was certainly made in Sicily. Its iconography is clearly Greek, Night seated and suckling the twin children Sleep and Death, a group which appeared among the panels of the Chest of Cypselus at Olympia, where the names were written beside the figures so that there could be no doubt of their identity. One could not imagine a more appropriate image for a funeral sculpture. The composition is carried out with simplicity, but not without sophistication. Note, for example, the position of Night's hands, the right hand withdrawn behind the feet of one infant, the other extended beneath the back of the same. Night's cloak becomes a compositional device to surround the group and by closing over her legs, to support it.[21]

The style of the sculpture is that of the Palma korai transferred to stone. This way of working the surface created both the sharp edges of the cloak and the modeled surfaces of drapery behind them. Archaic Greek stone sculpture in the homeland, at least in so far as we know it, never achieved such independence from the stone-mason's techniques and style as in this statue.

From the cemeteries of Megara there also comes the earliest of the marble kouroi from Sicily. As the inscription on the thigh informs us, the monument is that of the doctor Sambrotides (figure 109). The proportions of the figure place it among the Greek kouroi made in the generation before 550 BC. The inscription, in the local alphabet, was certainly cut in Megara. But the material is Greek marble, and it is probable that the statue was imported. A marble sphinx from Megara falls into the same category, a tomb guardian either imported ready made or possibly the work of a mainland Greek artist using costly imported marble in Sicily. Whichever the case the work was up to the best standards of the day in the homeland and, like the kouros, it gives us some idea of the ostentation of the 'fat' classes of the city. We may reserve further discussion of the question of imports until we take up the group of late archaic marble kouroi from eastern Sicily.[22]

One might expect that an independent sculptural style could have developed in terracotta, the medium of which the Sicilians made such fertile use for their votive figures. This does not seem to have happened. Rather, large scale Sicilian terracotta sculpture followed models in stone. It is Acragas that provides us with a particularly interesting group of life-size heads that are translations of stone sculpture into terracotta. Freestanding terracotta sculpture was

clearly important, but save for the piece from Terravecchia di Grammichele on the border of the Sicel area, to be discussed later, little is preserved save in small fragments.

City planning

The cast of Greek city planning set by the earliest colonies remained the pattern for the archaic period and beyond. But the urban designs of the late seventh and sixth centuries were carried out on a grand scale. To the north of the acropolis of Selinus the street pattern as far as the fortifications of the post-409 city has long been known. Only recently, due to precise excavations along the projected axes of the street system, has it become evident that the streets originally extended the full width of the area between the two rivers (the Cotone on the east and the Modione (Selinus) on the west, figure 110). The grid also extended northward well beyond the limits of the small city of the fourth century. Eleven east–west streets (stenopoi) each 3.6 to 3.9 meters (11 ft 10 in to 12 ft 9 in) wide, and bordered at the northern and southern ends of the group of blocks thus delimited by two wider streets of 6 meters (19 ft 8 in), have now been documented. The north–south avenue crossing them (plateia) was 9 meters (29 ft 6 in) in width. The blocks would have been 29 meters (95 ft) wide. Further north on the Manuzza plateau the archaic city developed with a street plan on a different axis. The agora is thought to have been situated between the two. Not all details of the topography of Selinus have been established with certainty, but the similarity of its development to the two axes of the street plan of Megara Hyblaea is striking. The street plan of Selinus was in place in the sixth century, and its nucleus must go back to the foundation of the colony.

The date of the street plan of Acragas is uncertain (figure 76). When the great Temple of Olympian Zeus was built after 480 it was oriented according to the grid, but it is uncertain when the plan was put in place. The area covered is a vast one, but within it until very recently there has been no exploration of the classical and archaic levels outside of the sanctuaries near the walls. The blocks were about 35 meters (115 ft) wide (40 meters or 131 ft in the southern area) and varied in length from 269 to 310 meters (882 ft 4 in to 1,016 ft 10 in). The avenues were 10 and 12 meters (32 ft 10 in and 39 ft 4 in) wide; the cross streets were only 4.5 to 5.5 meters (14 ft 9 in to 18 ft) wide. The street plan remained in use until the sack of Acragas by the Vandals in the fifth century AD.

At Syracuse the early city soon expanded onto the mainland forming the district of Acradina. Here too recent excavations have revealed the orthogonal city plan, although there is no datable evidence of its use before the fifth century. The inland Syracusan sub-colonies, Acrae and Casmenae, both had regular plans. That of Casmenae is known from aerial photographic interpretation and recent excavation; its grid plan certainly goes back to the foundation of the city in 643 BC.

Himera, which marked the western Greeks' boundary on the north coast of Sicily, was an early foundation, settled in 648 BC according to traditional chronology. The site commands the mouth of the northern Himera river in the setting of the steep promontories of the coast and the hills behind them. The city occupied both one of the lower hills and a part of the narrow coast below. The upper city had a grid plan from an early time, but its urban layout is better known from the new plan of the fifth century. Himera, site of the Greek victory over Carthage in 480 BC and for a time subject to Acragas, had clearly suffered drastically for a new city grid to be imposed over the old town. The new plan is different from the city planning of the seventh and sixth centuries in that the streets are wider, but it does not show other development that occurred in subsequent grid plans of the fifth century. Now in place of the elongated blocks and streets and avenues of variable width one finds blocks with proportions length to width of 1:4 and avenues made twice the width of the streets. Naxos and Camarina show the new developments, and in fact their layouts are extraordinarily similar. The imposition of regular proportions in street widths and block sizes is related to developments in city planning known from Thurium in southern Italy (an Athenian colony) and from the Peiraeus, the port of Athens, plans both attributed to the urban designer Hippodamus of Miletus. But while these new

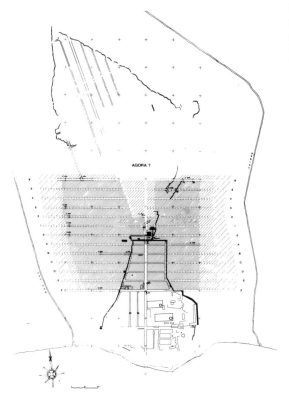

Figure 110 Selinus, plan after *Rendiconti dell' Accademia Nazionale dei Lincei* 1985, ser. 8, vol. 40

cities were designed in a series of squares formed by avenues crossing at right angles, the Sicilian cities kept the old formula of wide avenues running in a single direction.

Crafts

The best-known craft of Greek Sicily is terracotta masks and figurines, found both as votive offerings in shrines and occasionally in tombs. The archaic figurines begin with primitive (the so-called Daedalic) pieces, plank-like in body and surmounted by ill-proportioned heads which recall Greek work of the seventh century BC. Rigidly simplified seated figures of goddesses belong to the early sixth century. One, a figure adorned with multiple necklaces and a polos, was intended to evoke the statue of Athene Lindia on Rhodes, dear to the Rhodian colonists of Gela. Perfume jars from Ionian Greece in the form of standing girls holding a dove or flower became the prototypes for Sicilian imitations which developed both for the cult of Aphrodite and eventually, with a pig or torch in place of the dove or flower, for Demeter and Persephone. Athene types join the repertoire. The female types outnumber male figurines. In the second half of the century other Ionian prototypes led to the development of the votive mask, associated especially with the cult of Demeter and Persephone, for example at the Predio Sola sanctuary at Gela.

The bronze figurines of Sicily are not numerous, and it is often difficult to distinguish between imported pieces and those made on the island. There are some clearly early pieces of the seventh century, for example the Athene from Himera (figure 111). There are three (possibly imported) kouroi (standing nude youths) of Ionian stamp from Selinus. During the sixth century there is a group of handles for offering vessels (paterae) in the form of youths (many of them possibly from southern Italy). An impressive basin with ram's head handles from Megara Hyblaea is, however, probably of Sicilian manufacture.

Identification of pottery produced in the archaic Greek cities is difficult. Early Megara Hyblaea had a lively, but apparently short-lived, industry making polychrome potttery decorated with mythological scenes. Throughout the

Figure 111 Himera Museum, bronze figurine of Athene from Himera, photograph courtesy of N. Bonacasa

seventh and sixth centuries it is probable that much of the plain ware of Greek type was made in Sicily, but clear distinctions have not been made up to now. The Sicel cities of the interior were evidently better customers for imitations of Greek imports, as shown by a distinctive class of mixing bowls (craters) made for their consumption. In addition to the Greek and Ionian Greek vessels that were imported specifically for their contents (perfume, oil, and such), the Greeks of the coast made use of decorated mixing bowls and cups, which are also found in their tombs. At the end of the fifth century a modest offshoot of the Athenian pottery industry was established on the island. Its main centers of production were situated near Syracuse and Himera. One workshop of the fourth century producing red-figure vases (the designs appearing in the orange-red of the fired clay against a background of black glaze) was located at Manfria near Gela. Its work is related to other vases from

Leontini. A second group comes from the region of Mt Aetna. Finally, a distinctive development of the red-figure style with additional colors, blues, pinks and white, is found in the work of the Lipari Painter and his circle.

The Sicels

During the entire archaic age (down to 480 BC) and for at least a century thereafter, much of Sicily belonged to non-Greek populations. We have met them before, the Sicels in the east, the Sicans of the center of the island west of the River Himera, the Elymnians in the west, and finally, the Punic stations on the west and north coasts. The Punic settlements, Motya, Panormus and Solus, were the result of Carthaginian expansion at the same time as the first Greek foundations were made, or a very short time before. They will be examined at a later point. The Elymnians, who became the great foes of Selinus, have left almost no archaeological record in the archaic age. It is to the Sicans and the Sicels that we must turn to view the native world in contact with the Greek colonies during the first two centuries of their existence.

One can only assume that the story of the Sicans' coming from Spain was probably as fanciful as the identification of the Elymnians as survivors of Troy who fled west. But with the Sicels we are on firmer ground. They were relative newcomers to the island, having arrived from mainland Italy, as we saw in Chapter 1, at the end of the second millennium. Fragments of their language survive on inscriptions, especially from the area of Mt Aetna (Mendolito). It was related to Latin and the Oscan-Sabellian languages of the Italian peninsula.

Sicel cults persisted in a non-Hellenized form throughout historical times. At Adrano those who approached the god of the place were confronted by the god's mastiffs who admitted only the guiltless to the sanctuary. A similar emphasis on probity and conduct is shown by the cult of the Palici at a small lake near Menaeum. To swear by the two gods was to undertake an awful responsibility for the truth and to risk powerful reprisals for falsehood. Sicel religion is rooted in cults of the earth and its cavities rather than the sky. And in one case a Sicel goddess was embraced with enthusiasm by the

Greeks as none other than their own Persephone. Recent excavations near Lake Pergusa below Enna, where, in a meadow, Persephone was overtaken by Hades, have brought to light part of a sanctuary, in all probability that of a Sicilian vegetation goddess. Here in the fifth century a group of rooms was built over two grottoes. One of these was full of burnt material. Nearby there were a group of tombs also belonging to the sixth and fifth centuries. The material from the cult rooms is of the hybrid painted pottery produced in the Sicel communities (see pp. 88–9) together with simple types of Greek cups and lamps that were also made in various parts of the island. With them were pyramidal clay weights, usually interpreted as loom weights, but also found in sanctuaries (for example at the Thesmophorion of Bitalemi). There is, however, a notable lack, in so far as the excavations have been carried out to date, of the equipment of a Greek cult, especially terracotta busts and figurines.

The Sicel sense of identity and resentment toward the Greeks remained strong to a late date. In fact between 459 and 456 BC there was played out one of the most remarkable episodes in Sicilian history. Immediately after the fall of the tyrannies of Syracuse and Acragas, and undoubtedly counting on a weakening of the two powers as a result, a Sicel leader, Ducetius by name, raised the standard of autonomy and attempted to create a united Sicel league. Ducetius founded a Sicel capital at Menaeum, on the southern border of the Catania plain. He sought to extend his authority to the western edge of the plain where he succeeded in capturing Morgantina. He brought other towns, unspecified, under his control, including Inessa, the town on the slopes of Aetna to which the tyrant Hieron's settlers of Catane, largely Sicels, had fled when the Catanian exiles were restored by the new democracies (site uncertain). Some of the Sicels held aloof, however, and Ducetius' power was blunted by the united forces of Syracuse and Acragas when he attempted to invade the territory of the latter. At this point the story takes a bizarre turn, but one that illustrates how close the Sicels and Greeks had become, for all their pride and antagonisms. Defeated, Ducetius fled to Syracuse and in the guise of a suppliant implored the protection of his enemies. His wishes were granted and the would-be King of the Sicels departed in honorable exile for Corinth. Behind these events one can make out Syracusan corruption of the native leader and a far from noble Ducetius willing to sell out his fellow Sicels in exchange for a safe-conduct. Even more important to note is the ease with which Ducetius managed his affairs at Syracuse. He must have spoken Greek and been thoroughly at home in a Greek milieu, like members of the native elites of a more recent past who returned from the universities of England and France to lead revolutions against the colonial powers. Ducetius later came back to Sicily and led a Sicel colonizing venture on the north coast of the island, but that part of his life does not concern us here.

The archaeology of contact between the Greeks and the older inhabitants of Sicily is rendered difficult by that very symbiosis that we may term the Ducetius factor. A taste for Greek pottery in particular may disguise a Sicel site and make us take it for a Greek community. However, there are indicators of a more reliable nature. If we find public documents on an inland site in Greek, we may be confident that this was the language of the place. On the other hand, the continued use of the chamber tomb in the interior of the island, following the tradition that comes down from the Bronze Age, suggests fidelity to non-Greek customs.[23] Architecture, too, may be significant, but unfortunately very little Sicel domestic architecture is known.

A further problem involves the way in which archaeological research has developed. The overwhelming mass of evidence regarding the sites of the interior comes from the hinterland of Gela and Acragas, and to a lesser extent, Syracuse. These are precisely the areas of Greek expansion. If there were more information from settlement excavation in the region of Mt Aetna and in the mountainous districts between the Catania plain and the north coast, where the Sicel communities were not under such intense Greek pressure, the Sicels during the centuries of Greek colonization would be more concrete figures.

In eastern Sicily the Sicel communities on the eve of Greek colonization had significant ties to their past. The Pantalica tradition predominated but there were places, notably Leontini and Morgantina, where the material culture of the invaders who entered Sicily through the Lipari Islands (the Ausonians) clearly survived in its

new environment. The life of these villages had been neither uneventful or free from foreign contacts. We have seen how the tombs of the Pantalica Culture came to reflect more the family unit than the clan group. And foreign contacts with the eastern Mediterranean evidenced by large elbow fibulae and jugs with side spout strainers, both traceable to prototypes in the Syro-Palestinian area, are the precursors of the Greek contacts that begin in the eighth century. We have seen the earliest appearance of Greek goods in the chamber tombs of Villasmundo in the eighth century. At first Corinthian pottery appears alongside vases harking back to the Cassibile phase of the Iron Age. But it is rapidly joined by what are clearly imitations of Greek imports and then, as the seventh century develops, by a class of vases that adapts the decorations of Greek wares to traditional Sicilian shapes or modified versions of Greek vessels. Corinthian pottery, which dominates the Greek imports of the eighth and seventh centuries, was marked, down to the mid-seventh century, by a precise linear style of decoration using closely packed lines encircling the vase and a carefully circumscribed repertoire of motives found in the occasional bands of decoration. Generally these bands were of limited height. Only occasionally was a meander, inherited from the earlier geometric phases of Corinthian work, allowed to expand over a large surface of the vessel. Stylized water birds that appear almost as a line of question marks are the only vaguely representational designs of the eighth century. In the seventh century Corinthian wares are decorated, and often brilliantly so, but such pieces are uncommon and had no effect on inland Sicilian imitations. The Corinthian pottery of this age was made to high technical standards. The clay is clear and hard. The smaller vessels can be remarkably fine and thin-walled. The glaze is consistently opaque.

The first stage of adaptation and imitation of this export ware ('Thapsos' cups, for example, have never been excavated at Corinth itself) occurred in the Greek colonies. These products imitate the imports faithfully but lack the technical accomplishment of the originals. Such products must in many cases have been the sources on which the Sicel potter drew for his adaptation of the Greek style. What he did, as time went on, was to use the decorative system of the

Corinthian pottery but recombine its elements and apply them to shapes taken from his own traditions. This process appears in the seventh century at Villasmundo where technically inferior vases appear with Corinthian decoration. Such are the tall-necked 'amphora' with rudimentary handles on its shoulders, a typical Cassibile shape, and the open bowl with vertical lip that also derives from the Sicilian Iron Age. There are Greek shapes, too, the crater or mixing bowl among them. Other fabrics beside the Corinthian contributed to the design vocabulary of these native wares. They were the exports of Euboea, of other Greek islands and of the Peloponnesian centers outside Corinth. Their often more exuberant designs and non-Corinthian decorative motives such as the lazy S curve and the bullseye are also known in the pottery produced in the colonial cities. Megara Hyblaea, the nearest neighbor of Villasmundo, was the most likely source of inspiration for the nearby Sicels and certainly supplied them with its own products too.

The material from Villasmundo has not yet been published except in preliminary form. The site that has given its name to this period of Sicel adaptation to the Greek presence and to Greek goods is Monte Finocchito, south of Syracuse. The cemeteries here, predominantly rock-cut tombs, take us back a step further in time. In its early phase (ninth to eighth centuries) Monte Finocchito is still very much allied to the Cassibile and Pantalica South phases of the Iron Age sequence. The tomb groups are marked by metal fibulae with spiral bows. The repertoire of vases is the tall necked 'amphora' with rudimentary handles on the shoulder, the jug with side strainer, bowls, askoi (a vessel in shape like a modern urinal). The smeared decoration in dark on a light background which approximates a scale-like effect and is called 'piumata' ware was developed locally during the Cassibile period. The askoi can also carry rudimentary painted decoration, a tradition that goes back to the beginning of the Pantalica sequence. The second phase of Monte Finocchito has Greek imports and imitations like the earliest tombs at Villasmundo. The fibulae are of a new type, with a long pin, 'a staffa lunga', which was introduced just at the time Greek influence reached Sicily and Etruria. Which of these two Italic areas deserves the credit for this development is not altogether sure, but the Sicilian claim is a strong one. The same tendency toward local imitation of Greek painted design is found at Monte Finocchito, although the cemetery was not in use as long as that of Villasmundo and the processes of adaptation did not progress as far. Greek decoration was also translated into impressed design, for example in a splendid bowl of native shape bearing a wide Greek meander.

The further development of Siculan geometric pottery in the sixth century can be followed especially in the material from the chamber tombs of Licodia Eubea and related sites studied by Paolo Orsi. A typical vessel of this variety (from the Navarra collection, Licata) reproduces a Greek water jar (hydria, figure 112). The decoration perpetuates the lazy S curves of Greek utilitarian pottery and colonial wares. But the stylized water birds of the shoulder are derived from Protocorinthian pottery at least two centuries earlier than the piece in question. The wavy lines on the neck come from chevron cups of the eighth century. The old lives on beside the new. This is typical of peasant art, dependent on a metropolitan center, and perpetuating its styles in a timeless pastiche. Pottery of this type is characteristic only of the interior centers which perpetuated traditions distinct from those of the Greek cities. It is thus characteristic of the Sicels.

The necropolis at Licodia Eubea remained Sicel long after the Greek cities of the coast had

Figure 112 Licata, Navarra collection, Siculan water jar

succeeded in advancing their territories well inland. The site is only a few kilometers from Caltagirone, which was a Greek outpost, and from Grammichele, which appears to have been a mixed Greek-Sicel community (see pp. 91– 3). To the east, even closer in a direct line but in some of the roughest country of this part of Sicily, was the Syracusan outpost at Monte Casale (Casmenae). Yet Licodia Eubea was not absorbed into the Greek cultural orbit and despite imported pieces of some of the cheaper kinds of Greek pottery (small oil flasks and cups of the Attic type with some hastily drawn figure decoration) its tombs from a generation or less before Ducetius set up his Sicel capital just to the north at Menaeum are still fully distinct from those of their Greek neighbors.

Syracuse pursued an aggressive policy toward the inhabitants of the mountains of its hinterland. A site like Monte Finocchito seems to have prospered at first from the Greek presence. At least the density of tombs increases. But the tombs come to an end in the seventh century, no doubt as a result of the Syracusan policy of reducing the natives to the level of serfs (killyrioi). The end of the town at Monte Finocchito followed the settling of Acrae by the Syracusans in 663 BC (conventional Thucydidean date). Little survives from the seventh century at Acrae, but we have already noted the sculpture of the early sixth century there. To the same period as these early archaic statues belongs the temple of Aphrodite, which has only recently been properly studied and restored on paper (figure 113). This peripteral building, 40 by 18 meters (131 by 59 ft), is based on the temples of Apollo and Zeus at Syracuse. It has a deep porch and a second row of facade columns. The interior structure has a porch with two columns in the wall ends ('in antis'), followed by an antechamber

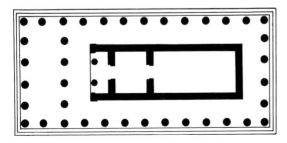

Figure 113 Acrae, Temple of Aphrodite

and then the naos proper. The order was Doric and was stone, including the overhang of the roof (the geison). But the order was highly decorative. The triglyphs of the frieze were ornamented with palmettes at the head of the flat fascias and with a running spiral on the band above. Beside the usual channels at the base of the curved element of the capitals (the echinus) there was also a bead-and-reel decoration, another Ionic addition, and a similar decoration appears behind the blocks bearing the Doric peg motive (the mutules) under the geison. There were the usual roof terracottas, of which only small fragments are preserved. The altar was decorated with a bold palmette at the center of its long side and sweeping volutes at the corners. This building must have been one of the most uncompromising signals of the Greek trans- formation of the mountainous territories behind Syracuse.

At Casmenae the street plan of the Greek settlement of 643 BC (conventional date) can be clearly discerned from air photography. The crown of this inhospitable hill ('Where the summer sun beats down without relief and where storms and ice reign in winter' - Orsi) is occupied by forty parallel streets running north-south. The city blocks between them are crossed only by narrow alleys between the houses, which seem to have occupied almost all of the subdivided space. Excavation among the houses has been limited, but it is clear that they are of the Greek 'pastas' type with living- and work- rooms organized around a courtyard. At the west end of the site Orsi identified a temple, which was peripteral, though possibly not in its earliest phase. The divinity was honored by a conspicuous deposit of arms (iron spear heads, daggers and arrow points) and miniature bronze models of helmets and breastplates. These offerings might be appropriate for the warrior goddess Athene, to whom the temple is attributed. Their quantity at Casmenae suggests that the colony functioned as a frontier bastion ('phrourion'). Certainly there was little agriculture on these exposed heights, only herding.

The final link in the Syracusan line of expansion was her colony at Camarina, founded in 598 BC (conventional date). Thereby the southeastern corner of the island was firmly secured for Syracuse. The border toward the interior was undoubtedly irregular and even fluid. The area of Modica and Ragusa was as stoutly Sicel as Licodia Eubea, and, of course, this Sicel corridor constituted a buffer between Gela and Syracuse. At Ragusa there are cemeteries with tomb groups similar to those of Licodia Eubea, but at this site the chamber tomb has given way to large burial shafts. The owners of these tombs were also capable of acquiring excellent Attic black figure vases, unusual for a Sicel community. Recent work has brought to light the source of these imports, a Greek settlement known from the cemetery at San Rito which existed cheek-by-jowl with the Sicels. The burials are

the usual Greek trench graves, some with sarcophagi or with coverings of tile, occasionally 'enchytrismos' (burial within a storage jar) and in one case a cremation. The tomb groups contain outstanding decorated pottery. There is a fragmentary archaic Greek inscription from the site, as well as an archaic stone lion funeral sculpture which stood in an aediculum of which one pilaster capital survives. Monte Casasia south of Licodia Eubea has both chamber tombs and a Sicel graffito on one of the vases. And Modica was apparently another Sicel town, to judge from the chamber tombs there. One can easily

Figure 114 Syracuse Museum, relief from Caltagirone, photograph courtesy of Soprintendenza ai Beni Culturali ed Ambientali, Syracuse

understand how Camarina, when she became at odds with Syracuse in the sixth century, had Sicel allies on her side, and the Sicel corridor running north from Modica to Licodia Eubea remained a consideration in Sicilian politics down to Ducetius' time and beyond.

The Geloan penetration of the interior was in some ways different from that of Syracuse, especially at its beginning. At the site of Butera, on the northwest edge of the Geloan plain, the early tombs (stratum 1) of the necropolis of Piano della Fiera are without trace of Greek contact. They were chamber tombs and are chronologically similar to the first phase of Monte Finocchito. In a second phase the chamber tomb is given up and replaced by inhumations in storage vessels ('enchytrismos') or cremation. Both rites are typical of a Greek necropolis. The pottery, however, is largely Siculo-geometric, dependent on colonial manufactures from Gela as well as on imported pieces. The large storage vessels decorated with checkerboards and wavy lines are typically Geloan, as are similar large pots decorated with the Geloan version of the indigenous 'piumata' design, one case in which the influence of native crafts is evident in a Greek city. But there is imported Corinthian pottery too. The large quantity of bronze and iron objects, chains, pendants, fibulae, reflects Greek manufacture (especially of iron), but the taste for the profusion of ornaments belongs to the Sicel. The protecting of pithos burials under a covering of stone slabs, possibly perpetuating the idea of a chamber in miniature and the practice of separate burial of the skull found at Butera are both very un-Greek. All in all, this necropolis illustrates neither a case of natural development in the native culture nor of replacement by Greek customs, but of the substantial modification of traditional native practices in some ways and their persistence in others. The Geloan expansion, in this case, apparently led to the creation of a hybrid culture, even possibly to the formation of a hybrid population.

There is nothing Sicel about the town at Monte S. Mauro, Caltagirone. This site, and the modern city nearby, is located at the head of the Maroglio Valley leading north from Gela. This is the watershed between the valleys of the south coast and the valley behind the Catania plain, which passes Menaeum before arriving below Caltagirone. Monte San Mauro lies below

the watershed comprising five small hillocks, which mark a ridge extending southward below the pass. The houses of the site, excavated on hill III, are of the Greek 'pastas' type. Prominent among their furnishings are portable terracotta altars, often decorated in relief, sometimes with animals or mythological scenes, and typical of the Greek colonial sites. The pottery of the houses, documenting their occupation in the sixth century, is Greek. The tombs below hill III are Greek trench tombs, covered by tiles, and burials in storage jars.

Monte S. Mauro was also the find place of an early archaic relief in Sicilian limestone which displays two sphinxes back to back, separated by double palmettes, while on a small frieze above them is an animated scene of male dancers, one holding a jug, thus suggesting that the scene is a revel associated with Dionysus (figure 114). Although the surface is damaged, this stele is an accomplished work of art. It may well have been a grave monument combining the protective functions of the sphinx, so frequently employed in the archaic age, with the imagery of the Dionysiac thiasos (retinue) and its suggestions of ecstasy even for the dead. The prototypes of the decoration can all be found on Greek pottery, and there is no reason to think that the relief was not executed on the spot.

The Greek character of the site is further emphasized by the temple or temples of hill I–II documented by the discovery of architectural terracottas, including fragments of architectural sculpture. The roof terracottas are so close to others from the acropolis of Gela that it seems they are products of the same group of craftsmen.

Not all the structures excavated at Monte San Mauro have been considered Greek. Again on hill III Orsi excavated the remains of a rectangular building, divided into two chambers and measuring 8 by 16 meters (26 ft 3 in by 52 ft 6 in) not counting the two small porches at either end. The foundations were robust (1.5 to 2.0 meters or 5 to 6 ft 7 in for the exterior walls) and the whole carefully constructed, despite the narrowing of the foundations along one side. Reasoning from the stratigraphy found with the construction, which showed that the foundations of the walls were associated with mixed Greek archaic and Sicel sherds but that they reached to a depth of some 80 centimeters (2 ft 7 in) below the surface and at some points rested directly on a deposit of the Middle Bronze Age, Orsi felt that the building was not a late-comer in the stratigraphical sequence. Furthermore, he was influenced in his thinking by the massive construction, which included stretches of wall on both long sides built with boulders, like the Late Bronze Age palace ('anaktoron') at Pantalica. Orsi thus cautiously extended the same term to the building at Monte S. Mauro, seeing it as the palace of a chief of a native community.

The stratigraphy, of course, can be interpreted differently and today there is general agreement that the foundations of an archaic building were sunk deeply into the underlying stratum, so deep in fact that they touched the Bronze Age stratum below. The building is now recognized as a Greek sacellum. Its proportions match those of other small temples in the area of Geloan influence in the Himera Valley, notably the sacellum at Monte Saraceno (see p. 94). The fragments of architectural terracottas, including a gorgoneion, now make sense, as does the most unusual find from the building, fragments of a law code inscribed in Greek.[24]

The code was apparently not displayed on the temple walls, since it was inscribed on both the recto and verso of bronze sheets. Possibly it was kept in a chest. It had been brutally and deliberately chopped into pieces, mute testimony to some unknown episode of social revolution in the town. There are insufficient remains of the text to restore any of the elements of the code, but the surviving fragments clearly deal with fines in the case of murder. The language of the inscription is our best clue to the origins of the Greek inhabitants of the town. It is written not in the alphabet of Gela but in the Chalcidian script of cities like Leontini and Catania. The early law code of Charondas was drawn up in Catania and the Monte S. Mauro fragments may well belong to the code of Charondas or to a law code based on it. (The objections that our sources do not mention homicide in connection with Charondas' law or that the penalties do not seem to mirror the supposed severity of his code are mere cavil.) This evidence means that the town at M. San Mauro was not politically Geloan but was connected in its institutions, and probably in its origin, with the Chalcidian cities whose sphere of influence lay on the north side of the Caltagirone watershed.

A few kilometers east of Monte S. Mauro is Terravecchia di Grammichele, the site of the discovery of an important dump of Greek votive and architectural terracottas and of two significant large-scale pieces of archaic Greek art. The first of these is a marble kouros, which we shall examine in respect to the arts under the Deinomenid tyrants of Syracuse. The second is the seated terracotta statue of a goddess, in all probability a cult statue, which is a noble example of mature archaic taste in Sicily and the only example of such terracotta sculpture of the archaic period that can be reconstructed in full (figure 115). There are archaic Greek inhumation graves at the site as well. But before classifying this as a purely Greek town one must take note of the

Figure 115 Syracuse Museum, terracotta goddess from Grammichele. Photo courtesy Soprintendenza ai Beni Culturali ed Ambientali, Syracuse

Sicel chamber tombs with pottery like that of Licodia Eubea, and so belonging to the sixth century. Although the evidence is not abundant, there seem to be grounds for hypothesizing the existence of two distinct elements in the population, one Greek and one Sicel, another variation of the pattern of Greek and native contact.

Three sites north of Caltagirone present similar questions of interaction between Greek and Sicel. At Monte Bubbonia just northwest of Caltagirone and again strategically placed to command the valleys entering the plain of Gela, there is an archaic city. The architectural terracottas originally attributed to an 'anaktoron' were certainly those of a simple Greek-style temple, but this was incorporated into a long warehouse or barracks in the fourth century. Little more is known about the site. Still more meager is the information concerning the settlements at Montagna di Marzo and Monte Navone near Piazza Armerina.

But at a site still further north, crowning the rim of hills to the west of the Catania plain, there is fuller information. This is the archaic settlement of Morgantina located on Monte Cittadella. As we have seen, this site was occupied by an Ausonian settlement during the Iron Age. Oval and oblong huts with native pottery were still in use until the opening of the sixth century. But at this point the site underwent an intensive moment of Hellenization. A number of sacella were built with Greek roof terracottas. Among these there were both the familiar simas of the Sicilian type, with tubular water spouts and a series of antefixes which must have been used without the high sima. Such terracotta heads, female faces, gorgons and felines, are uncommon. The female heads of the Morgantina type are found at only two other sites in Sicily, Caltagirone and Adrano. The antefix is more characteristic of the Italian mainland both in Etruria, Latium and Greek south Italy. Still, it is not necessary to postulate direct importation from these sources. Antefixes were used on small buildings in Greek Sicily of the mature archaic period. There is a series of painted antefixes from Gela. And in the Fusco cemetery at Syracuse there is a pair of antefixes in the form of female heads from a funeral monument. The subsequent misfortunes of archaic Morgantina and its rebuilding, connected with conquests of the Syracusan-Geloan

tyrants of the early fifth century and the wars of Ducetius, have robbed us of the first houses that took the place of the Iron Age huts. But it is certain that the town did not become completely Greek because the tradition of the chamber tomb and lavish collections of burial goods continued into the fifth century. In this way Morgantina and Terravecchia di Grammichele are similar. Possibly these were cities that could, with justice, claim to be either Greek or Sicel, depending on the dominant element of the moment.

Ducetius' capture of Morgantina in 457 BC left a dramatic record on the archaic site. One building fronting on a small piazza had an upper story over a three room basement. To judge from the large quantity of loom weights found, a small weaving factory must have existed here. On the upper floor the owner kept a service of pottery for the symposium, the men's evening drinking party so important in Greek social life. Most of the vessels were plain black glaze cups. But the centerpiece of the service was a crater (wine mixing bowl) imported from Athens. Its rim was decorated with flamboyant palmettes and its neck carried figured scenes, the drawing done by the master vase-painter Euthymides. On one side a symposium was represented. On the other Heracles and the Greeks were shown conquering the Amazons, the mythological warrior women from non-Greek Asia Minor.[25] In the sack of 457 BC the crater was hurled out of an upper window and shattered when it fell into the adjoining alley. It is not difficult to imagine that it belonged to the ruler of the town, a minor Greek tyrant. As he and his friends enjoyed their evening gatherings with the lyre, poetry and talk of politics, after the work of the slavegirl weavers had finished for the day, did they perhaps see Greeks confronting the Sicels in the guise of Heracles policing the barbarian Amazons? What is sure is that this petty tyrant and his treasured crater both met a sad end.

To sum up this discussion, one may say that between the extremes of Greek and Sicel there seems to have existed a middle ground of cities where both elements merged, but merged in different ways in different places. Butera is a case of the Sicel town that modified its culture under Greek pressure. It must have been one of the native communities brought under Geloan domination by force of arms. But the population cannot have been replaced by Greeks. At some sites like Grammichele and Morgantina there may have been at times a true symbiosis of Greek and Sicel, reminding us of the traditions of such a mixed community in the early days of the colony at Leontini. In order to make an estimate of the degree of Hellenization of any site the evidence of house architecture and house cults, documented particularly by Greek portable house altars ('arulae'), as well as traditions of funeral architecture are particulary important, as becomes apparent from examination of the Greek penetration of the Himera Valley.

Along this important valley which reaches far to the north and opens down the valley of the northern Himera a passageway to the north coast, Greek influence proceeded as quickly as in the east.[26] Moving inland from the Greek city at Licata one finds first the town at Monte Saraceno, which in the sixth century was thoroughly Greek in character, in its houses and their house altars, its tombs and sacred architecture. The same may be said of Vassalaggi just west of Caltanissetta.

The fullest evidence for the development of an interior native site comes from Sabucina, which overlooks the gorge of the Himera at modern Caltanissetta. Sabucina, like Morgantina, was a thriving village of the Iron Age, although its traditions are those of the Pantalica-Cassibile rather than those of the Ausonian group. The large oval houses of the town included one which can be interpreted as a temple. This was a large round structure, 7.5 meters (24 ft 7 in) in diameter, which was modified during the seventh century by the addition of a small porch supported by faceted columns. The round temple was then replaced by a rectangular structure of similar size. The interior of this building has a complicated history of benches for votive material and altars. The first offering bench may have been nothing more than the curving socle of the wall of a round hut over which the small temple was built. The later bench was built against two walls of the structure. In the earlier bench votive offerings were made in niches carefully left open for the purpose. The material included pigs' knuckle bones (frequently used like dice in divination), other pig bones, goat skulls, painted native pottery and an ingot of raw bronze, probably an example of the pre-coin monetary metal called by the Latin term

'aes rude'. On the floor there were a Greek wine mixing bowl, an iron knife, shells and fragments of drinking cups.

A similar sacred deposit had been excavated earlier in the original round temple. From it comes one of the most precious documents of the acculturation of native Sicily to Greek art and architecture. The object is a temple model in terracotta made in one piece with its stand and already discussed above. Embodying an interest in and understanding of a foreign architectural tradition, it is almost a model for the transformation of the circular hut into the rectangular temple beside it.

Sabucina developed a townscape of irregularly clustered houses composed of rectangular rooms but without any of the apparent elements of the Greeks' 'pastas' house plan. The inhabitants acquired a taste for Greek figured pottery and Greek terracotta figurines but did not use Greek household altars. It is clear that in the archaic age this was a native city. Since it is west of the Salso River (what the Greeks called the southern Himera), it belongs in the Sican rather than the Sicel territory. Two other sites, Monte Capodarso just across the Himera from Sabucina and Gibil Gabib, a name from the Arab period in Sicily and meaning 'Hill of the Dead', might tell a similar story to that of Sabucina, but they have been less thoroughly explored.

As one moves westward from the Himera Valley, he enters a region where the forces of Greek penetration were weaker and the native Sican population, like the Sicels of the northern mountains, enjoyed relative security. By all odds the most impressive evidence of these native cultures comes from the site of S. Angelo Muxaro, hardly 20 kilometers northwest of Agrigento but belonging to a world of steep hills and deep valleys that gives it a remoteness even today. S. Angelo is a conical hill set in a surrounding ring of heights and overlooking the Platani, the next major river to the west of Acragas. The modern village clings to the peak of the hill. Along its lower flanks there are a series of chamber tombs. They vary from small and simple chambers hardly different from the tombs of the Early Bronze Age in the region to the grandest underground burial chambers of ancient Sicily. The largest of these, the so-called Tomb of the Prince, was approached by a short vestibule and has two chambers, both circular and both conical in shape. The interior and smaller of the two is also distinguished by a stone shelf or couch which was left to receive the burial. The exterior chamber was given a bench against its wall. The funeral couch is a common feature of these tombs and the bench repeats a tradition found already in the Thapsos tombs. Despite the traditional aspects of the S. Angelo tombs, much has been made of their possible connection with the Late Bronze Age tholos tombs of Greece, best known from the largest of them, the so-called Treasury of Atreus at Mycenae and the tholos at Orchomenos in Boeotia. One detail of the S. Angelo tombs does seem appropriate to the tholos. This is the knob-like recess at the apex of the ceiling. This element seems to echo the oculus at the apex of the tholos chamber, which resulted from the technique of corbeled vaulting. A corbel vault was made by projecting each successive course of stone slightly toward the center of the vault and thus building up a vault without any true vaulting (a corbel arch was constructed in the same way). At the top, the opening over the last ring or course was closed by a flat stone. This detail and the general cupola effect of the interior of the S. Angelo tombs might not, in themselves, have suggested that these tombs, rock cut rather than built, much inferior in size to even the average Mycenean tholos, and at least four centuries later in date, were somehow inspired by tombs of the Greek Bronze Age. Legend, however, told of the exploits of the Greek architect Daedalus, not only in the Crete of King Minos but also in Sicily. Fleeing the Cretan King, Daedalus was said to have taken refuge with Kokalos, King of the Sicans, and to have executed various architectural projects, including the king's capital, Camicus. It was here that the Sicilian monarch murdered Minos when the Cretan King came in pursuit of his architect. Much of the Daedalus tale belongs to the realm of fantasy, especially the episode of the escape from Crete by flying on contrived wings, successful for the architect but fatal for his son, Icarus, who climbed too high toward the sun and fell to his death when the wax in his set of wings melted. But the kernel of the story was believed in archaic and early classical times. The Agrigentine tyrant Theron went so far as to seek out the remains of Minos and send them home to Crete. And modern learning has not been slow to grasp at the possible

tie between legend and history, postulating a tradition behind the tholos of S. Angelo deriving from contacts between Bronze Age Sicily and the Aegean. Aside from a certain regularity of execution introduced into the Sicilian chamber tomb in the Thapsos period very possibly as a result of influences from the eastern Mediterranean present in Sicily at the time, there is little direct evidence to support these hypotheses.

The burials at S. Angelo Muxaro must have been splendid. In the nineteenth century four gold bowls decorated in repoussé were found

Figure 116 London, British Museum, gold bowl from S. Angelo Muxaro

in the tombs. One survives today in the British Museum (figure 116). It has four bovines disposed symmetrically around the interior. In a simplified but elegant fashion it is based on similar bowls of Greek workmanship dating to the seventh century, of which a notable example comes from Gela. Two gold finger rings, now in Syracuse, belong to the same tombs. They are of familiar Greek-orientalizing shape and have been claimed as imports from Cyprus or nearby regions. They may also have been made in Sican Sicily. One has the intaglio motive of a cow suckling her calf, also known on Greek gems. The other shows a lion, whose exaggerated claws recall numerous representations of lions in seventh century Greece and in Greek-like decoration in Italy.

The pottery associated with S. Angelo Muxaro also retained an independence of character (figure 117). It is dark surfaced ware decorated with impressed designs in a distinctive and very un-Greek fashion.

The Sican culture responsible for the tholos of S. Angelo Muxaro is also known from sites farther inland, where a variety of painted pottery, Polizzello ware, achieves a bold originality of design. This ware is now well documented from the graves excavated at Marianopoli, which carry its history down to the fifth century. At Polizzello itself there is a cemetery of chamber tombs of the traditional Sicilian type (figure 118). The initial excavations were made by Paolo Orsi, and recent work has added to his discoveries, bringing to light tombs with hundreds of vases accompanying multiple burials. And on the summit above the necropolis a Sican sanctuary is now being uncovered. First reports indicate that it had round sacella like the sanctuary of Sabucina. Far less rebuilding has occurred, however, and the sanctuary therefore exists in its primitive state.

Figure 117 Palermo Museum, vase from S. Angelo Muxaro

Figure 118 Palermo Museum, vase from Polizzello

3

LATE ARCHAIC AND CLASSICAL GREEK SICILY

Sculpture in the Age of the Tyrants and its aftermath

The two decades of Sicilian history between the mid 480s and the mid 460s BC belong to the Deinomenids of Gela and Syracuse and to the Emmenids of Acragas. The leaders of these two families were Gelon and Hieron, tyrants of Syracuse, and Theron, tyrant of Acragas. These years were an age of splendor in both capitals.

Gelon, a descendant of that Telines who had negotiated the end to a secession in the early days of Gela, began his rise to power as a member of the guard of the Geloan tyrant Hippocrates. This leader put together a formidable empire stretching northeast from Gela and Camarina to Catane and Leontini. Gelon became cavalry commander under Hippocrates, and on his death, Gelon found himself guardian of the tyrant's sons. The boys did not survive for long, and at some time after 491 and before 485 BC Gelon became the new tyrant. He was quickly able to add Syracuse, the prize that had escaped his predecessor, to Hippocrates' domains. Class conflict played into his hands. The Gamoroi, the Syracusan aristocrats whom we have met before both as a ruling class of landowners and sitting as a privileged court (reminiscent of the Roman Senate), had been expelled by the lower order of citizens with the support of the disenfranchised and exploited mass called the kyllirioi. The Gamoroi had taken refuge at Casmenae, that inhospitable mountain town on Syracuse's northern frontier. Gelon answered their call for help. He was soon tyrant of Syracuse. His brother Hieron remained as tyrant at Gela.

Usually a Greek tyrant was the leader of a faction of aristocrats backed by a following among the commons. Gelon was different. He was a tyrant brought in by the upper classes. He strengthened his hand by bringing the aristocrats of Megara Hyblaea and Euboia (another city of southeastern Sicily) to Syracuse. He also fattened his coffers by selling the populace of Megara in the slave market. Similarly the whole citizenry of Camarina was brought to Syracuse and the capital's population was further diluted, and the tyrant protected, by a large group of mercenary soldiers from the mountains of the Peloponnesos in Greece. Gelon was thus in command of a metropolis where mixed origins made for few common loyalties except to himself.

On Gelon's death in 478 BC, Hieron succeeded him at Syracuse. Another brother, Polyzalus, took command at Gela and also married Gelon's widow, Damarete. This lady played an important role in Deinomenid politics because she was the daughter of Theron of Acragas. Hieron himself was married in the interests of foreign policy to a daughter of the tyrant of Rhegium and Zancle-Messina, Anaxilas. It was Anaxilas, together with Theron's rebellious governor at Himera, which Acragas had taken over shortly before, who called the Carthaginians into Sicily against Acragas. Gelon had answered Theron's appeal for aid and together Syracuse and Acragas were victorious at the Battle of Himera in 480. Henceforth Anaxilas was bound to defer to the victorious Syracusans, who under Hieron pursued a policy of expansion into the Tyrrhenian.

Hieron presided over one of the most brilliant Greek cities. The poets Pindar and Bacchylides, from Thebes and the island of Ceos respectively, were commissioned to commemorate the tyrant's victories in the great games of the Panhellenic Sanctuaries. Simonides, another Ionian master of lyric poetry, was his confidant and trusted emissary. Gelon had been proclaimed the 'New

Oikist' of Syracuse. Hieron appropriated the same title and honors by refounding Catane as Aetna. Aeschylus came from Athens and produced his play *The Women of Aetna* for the occasion. The same group of poets was favored by Theron of Acragas until his death in 472. Hieron died in 466 BC, and both tyrannies fell within a few years.

The archaeology of Sicily is connected with these rulers in more than one way. Temples erected by them commemorated the victory over Carthage at Acragas, Syracuse and Himera. Their thank offerings for the same victory in the Panhellenic Sanctuaries were famous. Notices

of them from Roman times tell us something about them and about the artists, almost exclusively members of the famous school of Aegina in the Greek homeland, who executed these monuments and others for athletic victories. The bronze charioteer from the group erected by Polyzalus after a success in the four-horse chariot race at the Pythian Games was rediscovered during the excavations at Delphi in 1896 (figure 119).

The favor accorded to poets and artists from mainland Greece by the Deinomenids and Emmenids and their henchmen is symptomatic of patronage at the end of the Archaic Age in western Greece and specifically in Sicily. This snobbish preference for the masters from mainland Greece and Ionia was shared by other aristocrats and accounts for the new character taken both in sculpture and in architecture at this time.

The most apparent instance of importation from the motherland is found in the kouroi in island Greek marble from eastern Sicily belonging

Figure 119 Delphi Museum, bronze charioteer, photograph courtesy of Alison Frantz Archive

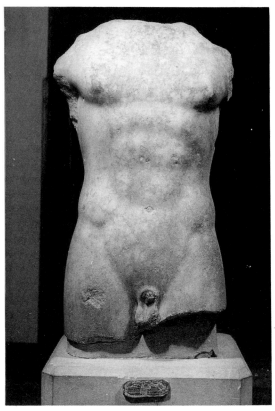

Figure 120 Syracuse Museum, Kouros from Grammichele

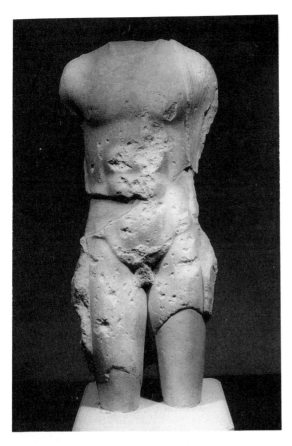

Figure 121 Syracuse Museum, draped kouros

to the opening years of the fifth century. This group includes the life-size but headless kouroi from Leontini and Terravecchia di Grammichele (figure 120). A kouros head long in the Catania Museum may possibly belong to the Leontini torso and legs. From Megara Hyblaea there comes a fragmentary small-scale kouros, only the chest and shoulders preserved. Finally, although not strictly a kouros by modern definitions of the term, the statue in Syracuse posed as a kouros but wearing a short jacket or chlamys also belongs here (figure 121). The group is not large. But the level of work is as fine as anything known in archaic Greek sculpture. These statues are the rivals of the best in Attic work, and as a group they far outshine the usual level of the Ionian kouroi or of the numerous kouroi from the Sanctuary of Apollo at Ptoon in Boeotia. It is as if one or more of the best Greek sculptors had been brought to Sicily and set to work supplying sculpture in imported marble for the

Sicilian aristocrats. This phenomenon deserves close inspection.

Pindar's and Bacchylides' victory odes for Hieron, Theron and their friends were exercises in the poetry of identification of patron and hero. The Emmenids, Deinomenids and other grandees had all established appropriate heroic pedigrees, and the poet's task was to magnify the victor of the games by implicit identification with a hero from his family's past or attached to it by artistic invention. As best we can determine, the late archaic kouroi of eastern Sicily, such as Sambrotides' kouros at Megara a half century earlier, and like many of the finest kouroi in the motherland, were grave markers. All would have been identified, by this period almost surely on their bases, although we may recall that earlier Sambrotides' kouros carried its inscription on its leg. The later kouroi were no more portraits than was the figure over the tomb of the Megarian doctor. Rather, like the victory odes, they provided ideal images to which the individual dead man could be implicitly assimilated. The Greek term is eidolon, signifying a phantom which assumes a meaning that is assigned to it according to its use. The idea of the kouros as tomb marker was not new with these late archaic marble statues.[1] But now, just as poets from the homeland were commissioned for the celebrations of victorious athletes, marble kouroi were employed to decorate aristocratic graves. One of the group comes from Grammichele, a town where, as we have seen, Greek and Sicel mingled. One assumes that the statue was set up over a Greek grave, rather than beside a Sicel family vault. Transporting a marble block inland added to the expense of what was already a costly statue. Could it have been destined for the tomb of a governor of Grammichele if this was one of the 'Sicel' cities of Hippocrates' and then Gelon's empire?

That we are dealing with the work of a small group of sculptors is suggested by the remarkable similarity of the Leontini kouros and the draped figure from Syracuse. As has been emphasized recently in a thorough study of the question, the torsos of these two statues are based on the same set of anatomical conventions (visible especially in the execution of the chest, stomach and groin) and might even be the work of a single artist.[2] The Grammichele torso does not share this same set of anatomical conventions,

Figure 122 Syracuse Museum, head from Megara Hyblaea

Figure 123 Syracuse Museum, head from Megara Hyblaea, profile

but together with the other two figures it is strongly reminiscent of the best Attic work of the time.[3] Like the poets of the Deinomenids and Emmenids it would seem that a group of sculptors were brought to Sicily from Athens to work for the tyrants and their friends. This hypothesis is confirmed by another important piece in marble, a female head from Megara Hyblaea (Syracuse Museum no. 16968, figures 122 and 123). Despite the battered condition of the face, one can recognize two mannerisms which connect this head to the finest Attic sculpture of the early fifth century. The first is the spacing of the wavy lines indicating the hair on the crown of the head so that an opening is left between groups of five lines. The same mannerism was used by the sculptor of the Euthydikos Kore (no. 686) from the Acropolis in Athens to indicate the soft folds of the girl's himation over her right arm.[4] The eyes of the Megara head also answer to Attic examples, for instance another masterpiece of the Acropolis sculpture, the head no. 696, placed by Humfry Payne just before the Euthydikos Kore in the development of Attic sculpture.[5]

The aristocrats of Sicily, and the Deinomenid tyrants foremost among them, were also intent on glorifying themselves and their cities by victories at the Panhellenic contests, especially those of the Olympic Games and their counterparts at Delphi, and by memorials dedicated in these great sanctuaries of the mother country. A forthright claim that private display at the games was an instrument of patriotic service to one's city is to be found in the speech given to Alcibiades, Pericles' nephew, by the historian Thucydides in his account of the debate which decided for the expedition against Sicily in 415 BC. Pindar's victory odes ring with the same sentiments. Some of the tyrants' immediate circle were champion athletes in their own right, like Glaucus of Carystus, the famous boxer and ruler of Camarina under the Deinomenids. But the four-horse chariot competition held a particular appeal for the tyrants and similarly minded aristocrats. Fielding a team (or stable of teams) was a lavish display of wealth and the victorious owner acquired all the prestige of a victory, even though he did not personally drive in the race.

Gelon, Hieron and Polyzalus all won Olympic or Pythian crowns, and left monuments to their glory in the sanctuaries. The Aiginetan sculptors Glaucias and Onatas did chariot groups for Gelon and Hieron at Olympia (and Glaucias a victor's statue for Glaucus of Carystus also in the Olympia sanctuary) which were still to be seen there centuries later. We would be reduced to the most hypothetical reconstructions of these monuments had not the remains of another chariot group, set up by Polyzalus on the terrace above the Temple at Delphi, come to light during the excavations of the sanctuary. The Delphi Charioteer, life-size and in bronze, is justly famous, and knowing the dedicator adds still further to its significance (figure 119). One block of the front side of the base of the group has survived, bearing part of the inscription. Despite the loss of the first part of the two lines of the dedication, one reads clearly '[P]olyzalos set me up [   ] give increase, revered Apollo.' Strange as it may seem, this is not the original text. It has been carved over an earlier version, still faintly visible below the new letters, which reads '[over G]ela he set [me] up ruling.' Putting the two versions together it appears that the bronze group of charioteer, chariot, and page leading the horses (part of a leg of a boy as well as fragments of the horses survive) was dedicated by Polyzalus tyrant of Gela. The inscription was then altered at a later time after the fall of the Deinomenids when cities like Gela preferred to forget the period of the tyrants. Polyzalus became ruler of Gela on the death of Gelon in 478 BC when Hieron took charge at Syracuse. Nothing is known about him thereafter, but various circumstances point to the year 474 as the occasion of his victory in the Pythian Games. The Pythian competition of 470 was won by Hieron. When Hieron died in 466, it was not Polyzalus who inherited his position at Syracuse but the youngest of the four Deinomenid brothers, Thrasyboulus. Had Polyzalus still been alive and the succession functioning as it did on the death of Gelon, one would expect him to have become tyrant at Syracuse. The natural conclusion, therefore, is that he had died by 466. Although it is possible that his Pythian victory was won in 478 immediately after his installation at Gela, 474 seems the more likely date.

The Delphi Charioteer is thus the image of Sicilian aristocracy victorious under the gaze of the god of Delphi. Calm and confident, this image is both heir to the detachment of the archaic eidolon and a step toward the optical verisimilitude that became the object of all Greek painting and sculpture as the classical age progressed. In one sense the exploration of visual impression has its roots in Greek speculative thought and especially in the debate over sense perception and reality. In the archaic age the two were one and the same. In the classical period the representation of transient states of being was to become a ruling interest of the artist. There is a restful geometry in the impersonal structure of the features of the charioteer and in the regular division of the pleats of his long charioteer's robe below the belt into twenty channels, the same number as those of a column of the Ionic order. But the statue is animated. The head turns slightly to one side, as if to acknowledge the applause of the crowd. The arms are extended to hold the reins of the horses. The folds of the upper part of the robe have a naturalistic pattern. Much of the bold, simple style and denial of archaic decorative intricacy is due to the fact that this is a large-scale bronze statue. As far as we know, casting of large-scale bronze statues was not attempted in the Greek world before the later sixth century. The stylistic revolution in Greek sculpture which follows, referred to as the Severe Style, is to a large degree the product of this innovation, which encouraged freedom of pose but at first led sculptors to avoid intricate details which might be difficult to cast since the molten metal cools rapidly as it is entering the mold. The charioteer's hair, done almost as engraving except for curls at the temples, illustrates the desire to eliminate complicated relief. Inlays added to the fascination of these statues. The charioteer's eyes are contrasting white paste and black onyx pupils; his diadem was inlaid with a silver meander.

The surviving texts relating to Greek art are largely of Roman date, and the sources behind them sometimes Hellenistic. None of their authors ever saw Polyzalus' dedication, which was apparently buried in an earthquake, possibly as early as the fourth century. And had the group survived to late antiquity we would never have the Charioteer today because bronze statuary was a prime target for remelting. When later commentators, like Pausanias, the author of a guidebook to Greece written in the second

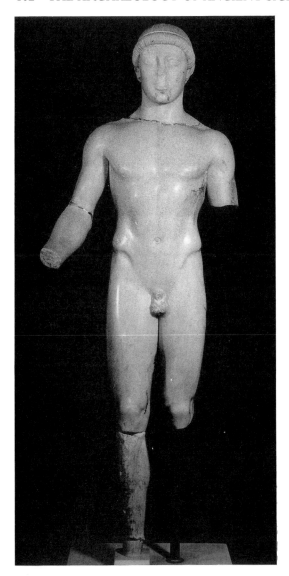

Figure 124 Agrigento Museum, Kouros

therefore, would hardly hinder us from looking on the charioteer and seeing either Polyzalus, ruler of Gela or his charioteer. As to the authorship of the charioteer, we may once more be guided by the testimonia relating to the Deinomenid dedications at Delphi and Olympia. Gelon, Hieron, Glaucus of Carystus and Phormis of Syracuse, another Deinomenid follower, all turned to sculptors from Aigina. Only one commission from the Deinomenid circle went to a non-Aiginetan, the making of the tripod and Victory which Gelon set up at Delphi after the Battle of Himera. Their author was Bion, son of Diodorus, from Miletos. In this case it is less likely that Gelon employed a sculptor working in Ionia than that Bion was a fugitive who had settled in Sicily after the failure of the revolt of the 490s against Persia in his homeland. As a whole, the evidence points to Aiginetan authorship of the Delphi Charioteer.

In the early fifth century bronze quickly became a favored medium for sculpture and the freedom of pose possible in the new medium was quickly imitated in marble work. Such a figure is the late kouros statue from Acragas, which even today keeps the highly polished surface which it was given in imitation of bronzework (figure 124). The torso of a struggling figure from excavations in the vicinity of the Temple of Heracles at Acragas is another major marble piece of the second quarter of the fifth century in which the new dynamism is readily apparent. Ernesto De Miro has suggested that a helmeted head in marble from the same area belongs with the torso.[6] Both may come from the pedimental decoration of a temple.

Sicilian sculpture around 500 BC cannot be appreciated without considering two other media. The first is terracotta. As we have already seen, notable success was achieved in terracotta sculpture for buildings. Large-scale terracotta sculpture not intended for architectural use has a different character, and its best pieces are directly dependent on images in stone and bronze. The life-size terracotta head of a woman in Acragas is such a piece, which derives from a bronze model of the end of the sixth century (figure 125). There are no bronze korai for comparison but the modeling of this head, avoiding sharp transitions with consistently plastic style, is the same as found in the earliest known large-scale Greek bronze, the Apollo from the Peiraeus (Athens).

century AD, did inspect the other Deinomenid chariot dedications, he took one of the charioteers to be a 'portrait' of Gelon. The youthfulness of the Delphi Charioteer has induced most commentators to deny that this figure could ever have been identified with the 'victor' Polyzalus rather than the charioteer who drove for him. But like its archaic predecessors the charioteer is an eidolon too, idealized surely, but for that reason free to be identified as the patron or as whomever the viewer desires. Greek tradition,

Figure 125 Agrigento Museum, terracotta head of a kore

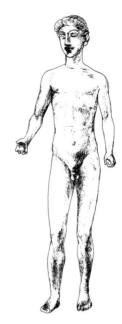

Figure 126 Palermo Museum, bronze kouros from Selinus

Modeled plasticity, to be sure, rather than the stone worker's angularity would be natural to an artist working in clay, but the remarkable fact is that earlier major Sicilian terracottas (aside from the Ionicizing masks of Persephone) tend to be cast in a form reminiscent of stone sculpture. Such, for example, are the major terracottas from the Malophorus Sanctuary at Selinus which recall the heads of the metopes of Temple C. Perhaps the most telling case of the reproduction of stone sculpture in terracotta is the male head from the same votive deposit in the sulphur spring at Palma di Montechiaro from which the three wooden korai were recovered. This head can be compared to the finest Attic kouroi of the later sixth century (the fragmentary head in Boston, no. 34.169 for example) and represents yet another link between Attic sculpture and Sicily at this time.

There is another connection between stone and large-scale terracotta sculpture, but one that is frequently overlooked because the stone sculpture in question is work in soft calcareous materials and has all but vanished because it is easily broken and is easily weathered. However, a few fragmentary pieces are preserved in the Acragas museum, and these show that the style of other large-scale terracotta heads strikingly

resembles the chisel work on soft stone. The history of Sicilian Greek sculpture in what we think of as secondary media is thus a complicated one in which influence from sculpture in wood, soft stone, marble and bronze all played a part.

Recognition of reciprocal influences between media aids in understanding a statue which has long been an enigma. This is the half life-size kouros in bronze from Selinus, apparently a tomb sculpture, which was formerly displayed in the Town Hall of Castelvetrano and is now in Palermo (figure 126). The arms were previously too short, the result of earlier restoration, and this defect has now been rectified. The small kouros, however, is still ungainly. It is as if its maker had miscalculated almost every measurement and every angle by a small amount, no one error too serious in itself (save possibly the exaggerated length of the thighs), but added together enough to ruin the whole. The type is that of the marble Acragas kouros, although the movement of the head and legs is that of a more developed version, possibly of the same date as the Delphi Charioteer. One might imagine, in fact, that this is a bronze statue copying one of the marble pieces in Sicily made under the influence of bronze sculpture. It is the work of a founder who had the technical ability to

Figure 127 Palermo Museum, metope from Temple E, Selinus, photograph courtesy of Soprintendenza ai Beni Culturali ed Ambientali, Palermo

produce a hollowcast bronze but was not an accomplished sculptor. The result was this odd attempt to work backward to something like a bronze by one of the mainland Greek masters.

One splendid monument of architectural sculpture of the decades between 480 and 450 BC in Sicily has survived in large part. This is the decoration of Temple E in the eastern extramural group of sanctuaries at Selinus. The building itself, which is similar in size to the Parthenon on the Acropolis of Athens but was dwarfed by its gigantic neighbor, Temple G, was reerected in the 1950s and will be discussed subsequently. The sculptured metopes were placed on the interior friezes above the columns of the porches at the two ends of the cella (figures 127, 128, 129 and 130). There are four well-preserved metopes and a fifth in poor condition. Together they are almost half of the original number since there would have been six metopes over each porch. The subjects have a common theme: struggle between man and woman. Thus Heracles overcomes an Amazon. Zeus, seated in a rocky peak, grasps Hera's forearm and draws her imperiously toward himself. Artemis watches as Actaeon is mangled by his own dogs. And Athene dispatches a giant. The fifth metope also sets a man against a woman, although their identities are not clear. The program of decoration thus calls on traditions of Greek mythology, beginning with the antithesis of Cronus and Rhea, which carry the encounters and conflicts of the sexes to a level of divine majesty. The figures of Temple E are the contemporaries of the heroes and heroines of Aeschylus, appearing like the protagonists of Attic tragedy in a religious drama. In Sicily love and hate, the passions expressed in these mythological scenes, were employed as conceptual terms for pairs of opposites in the dualist physics of Empedocles of Acragas. But it is more likely that the sculptor of the Temple E metopes and Empedocles, the poet philosopher, drew on the same common traditions than that the metopes of Temple E were planned as an expression of early dualist cosmology.

Figure 128 Palermo Museum, metope from Temple E, photograph courtesy of Soprintendenza ai Beni Culturali ed Ambientali, Palermo

Figure 129 Palermo Museum, metope from Temple E, photograph courtesy of Soprintendenza ai Beni Culturali ed Ambientali, Palermo

Figure 130 Palermo Museum, metope from Temple E, photograph courtesy of Soprintendenza ai Beni Culturali ed Ambientali, Palermo

The style of the metopes, as is natural for relief, is related to graphic work, and the Temple E metopes are closely allied to the so-called 'Mannerist Movement' of the early fifth century, which we also see reflected in Attic red-figure pottery (in which the background is glazed and the figures are shown in the red-orange color of the fired clay). 'Mannerism' perpetuated some of the decorative details of archaic art, noticeable in the Temple E sculptures in the 'swallow-tail' edges of the drapery of Hera and Athene. At the same time it emphasized compositional balance and grace at the expense of kinetic energy. The master of these metopes, however, was very much a sculptor. His Heracles and Actaeon, for example, are based on the same canon of proportions as the Acragas kouros, and his 'mannerism' was probably derived as much from the current style of Selinuntine relief, shown by fragments of an Ionic frieze and a fragmentary grave stele from Selinus, as by direct imitation of graphic sources. He was, moreover, an artist who felt and expressed the passion and power of his subjects. If one compares his vision of Artemis and Actaeon with the equally famous representation of the scene by the Attic ceramicist known as the 'Pan Painter' in Boston, the vigor of the Selinuntine metope is obvious. The 'Pan Painter', a true 'mannerist', draws dogs that could hardly inflict a scratch. The Selinus dogs are vicious hounds, their ears back and their teeth bared. Small details reveal his attitude toward his subject perhaps even more clearly. No ancient visitor to the temple could have seen the expression of dominant impatience on Zeus' face or the muscular tension drawing back the corners of his mouth and revealing his teeth; these aspects of his countenance are apparent only if the head is seen in frontal view. Heracles not only seizes the Amazon's headdress but also tramples her foot. These are scenes created by a passionate nature, which found a congenial task in carrying out a program of sculptures which dwelt on the cruel and tragic, but universal and fundamental, struggles between the male and female components of the world.

The sculpture is executed in a mixed technique. The material is local limestone, but the women's heads, feet, arms and hands are made separately in marble and inserted. In addition to the heads belonging to the preserved metopes at least three other similar marble pieces are known. The six heads testify to an extraordinary subtlety of surface modulation (figure 131). From any dis-

Figure 131 Palermo Museum, head of metope of Temple E, photograph courtesy of Alison Frantz Archive

tance they seem to belong to the rigidly balanced formula of facial composition introduced by the bronze-casters of the early fifth century and typified by the head of the Delphi Charioteer. Closer inspection reveals that the surface swells and falls away over the cheeks and lower face in a way that imparts both delicacy and vitality to these images.

The richness of the sculptural material from Selinus over the century and more that separate Temples E and C allows one to follow the development of a school of sculpture at this Sicilian city. A startling addition was made to

this material in 1979 when an over-life-size statue in marble of a young male figure dressed in a long robe and girdle over it was excavated at Motya (figures 132 and 133). Despite the distortion of the anatomy (especially in the groin) and the fluidity of the pose which goes beyond what one expects at the time, there is no question that this is a great work of early classical art near in time to the metopes of Temple E. The head is a translation into marble of the limestone head of Heracles from the metopes, and the fine channels of the light garment of the figure are developed in the same way as the dress of Hera or Athene of the metopes. The sculpture is therefore surely of Selinuntine workmanship. The identification of the subject remains a matter of debate. Vincenzo Tusa, its discoverer, and other scholars identify the figure as a Punic subject and believe the statue was commissioned from a Greek sculptor for the Punic city. Still others believe he is a Greek charioteer (though surely heroic or divine considering the scale, Apollo perhaps) or, according to the suggestion of Sandro Stucchi, based on examination of what this scholar identifies as the stubs for the attachment of bronze wings on the back, Daedalos, the mythical artist-architect who escaped from Crete to Sicily on improvised wings. In the view of this school of thought the statue would have come to Motya as war booty after the sack of Selinus by the Carthaginian general Hannibal (the ancestor of Rome's great opponent) in 409.[7]

In the summer of 1988 another colossal statue, 2.46 meters (7 ft 6 in) in height, went on display at the J. Paul Getty Museum in Malibu, California (figure 134). This is a female figure composed of a limestone body covered with the swirling drapery which is first found in the work of the school of Phidias on the pediments of the Parthenon in Athens and a marble head, inset like the marble heads of the Temple E metopes. (The other exposed extremities were in marble as well and of these an arm and foot are preserved). The similarity between the female heads of Temple E and the head of the Getty statue is extraordinary. It is almost as if this figure were the work of a member of the Selinus school twenty years or so after the Temple E commission was completed. Since styles may be perpetuated, the date may be later still, even reaching the early fourth century. The provenance of the statue has been

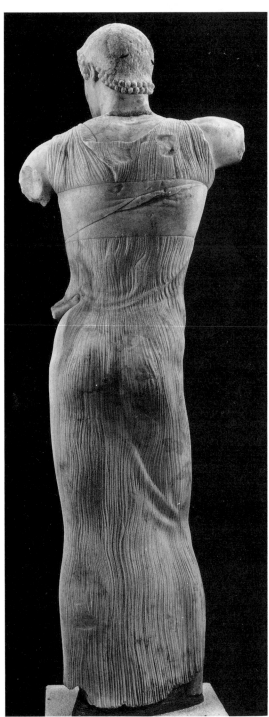

Figure 132 Marsala Museum, youth from Motya, photograph courtesy of V. Tusa

Figure 133 Marsala Museum, youth from Motya, photograph courtesy of V. Tusa

said to be Sicily, a supposition which therefore seems fully credible.[8]

The character of mid-fifth century Sicilian bronze sculpture is reflected at small scale in the 'Adrano Boy', a bronze statuette in Syracuse (figure 135). A posture similar to that of the

Figure 134 Malibu, J. Paul Getty Museum, statue of a Goddess, 425–350 B.C., limestone and marble, photograph courtesy of J. Paul Getty Museum

Figure 135 Syracuse Museum, bronze statuette ('The Adrano Boy'), photograph courtesy of Soprintendenza ai Beni Culturali ed Ambientali, Syracuse

'Adrano Boy' is found in two over-life-size bronze statues, which though they were not found in Sicily may, nevertheless, be Sicilian in origin. They are the so-called 'Heroes of Riace', which were recovered from the sea only 200 meters (656 ft) off the beach on the eastern coast of Calabria in 1972 (figure 136 and137). Again these are figures of the Early Classical period around 450 BC. Hero B, who originally wore a helmet now missing, seems stylistically the

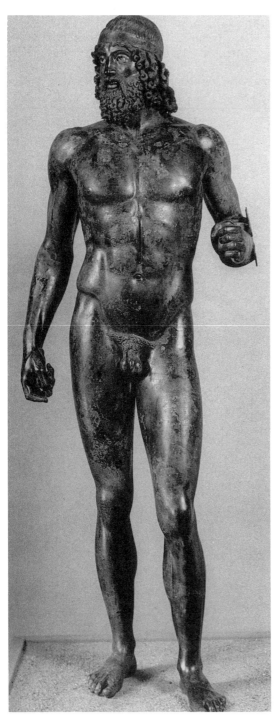 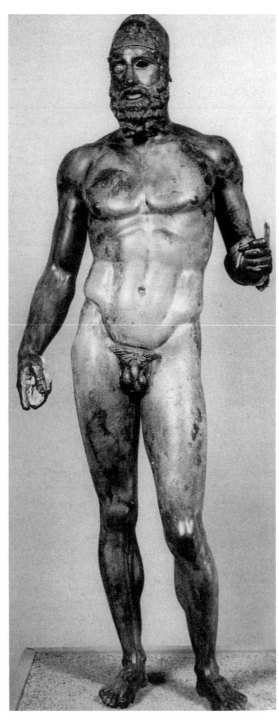

Figure 136 Reggio Calabria Museum, bronze statue from Riace ('Hero A'), photograph courtesy of Soprintendenza Archeologica, Reggio Calabria

Figure 137 Reggio Calabria Museum, bronze statue from Riace ('Hero B'), photograph courtesy of Soprintendenza Archeologica, Reggio Calabria

more advanced of the two. There is a distinct curvature through the trunk of the statue, which suggests, though it does not carry out, the rotation of the body in an easily moving posture which we associate with the sculptor Polykleitos of Argos working principally after 450 BC. The side view, however, shows that there is no real rotation of the torso and in fact this view of Hero B corresponds rather closely with the profile of Hero A. Seen from the back the two figures have a striking similarity as well. The difference between them consists largely in the heads and the more conservative posture of Hero A, whose pelvis is only slightly inclined toward his advanced left leg. The two heads are given different characterizations. Hero A's is turned more decisively to the side. Hero A has abundant locks and a curling beard; Hero B of course wore a helmet and the hair of his beard is combed out, curling only at the ends. But the manner of working the hair is the same in both cases; the mass of the locks is subdivided by shallow engraved channels on their surface. The moustaches, in particular, are identical. Details of the structure of the two bodies are the same, the way the chest projects from the line of the shoulders and is defined by a depression separating the two, the detailed veins shown on the arms, hands and feet of both figures and on the pelvis of Hero B. Although critics have been inclined to date the statues differently, making Hero A older than B by a decade or more, or to make them contemporary but by different artists, the observations just outlined lead me to feel that the apparent difference in frontal view may be a calculated variation of style on the part of the sculptor rather than a matter of authorship or date. In any case, I see no reason why the two figures cannot have been made at the same date for the same monument. That date must have been at a time when the pose of the later Severe Style given to Hero A was still current together with the greater displacement, but still not Polykleitan pose of Hero B. That date would have been the mid-fifth century, slightly before 450 BC. But where was the monument?

The circumstances of the find are peculiar. The statues were found in 5 meters (16 ft 4 in) of water but close to shore. They were lying on a sandy bottom but in the curve of a reef which forms a submerged landmark. There was no real trace of a wreck, despite wide-ranging efforts to find one. An iron grappling anchor, perhaps modern, was found 56 meters (184 ft) away. A fragment of wooden keel, even if ancient, had no closer relation to the statues. The only other find, and one made reasonably close to the findspot of the statues, consisted of a group of lead rings, possibly sail grommets. In themselves, they hardly document a wreck. The best face that has been put on the mystery is to suppose that the statues had been jettisoned from a vessel that found herself in danger close to shore during a storm. The vessel either survived or was carried farther along the coast before she sank.

There is a suspicion, however, that the shoreline of Riace had not been the first resting place of the statues. Rumors have circulated to the effect that the statues were not discovered for the first time at Riace but had been found by scuba divers off the coast of Sicily. Their appearance in the waters off Riace would have been involved with the murky dealings by which the initial discoverers sought to sell them abroad. Apparently the first stage of export had been completed when something interrupted the voyage and the statues were secreted beside the reef off Riace, which would have served admirably as the landmark for their eventual recovery. But as luck would have it, before that could happen another, and more scrupulous, scuba diver saw the bronze arm projecting from the sand and reported it to the authorities.

Up to now commentators have assumed that the two heroes were taken by the Romans from one of the Panhellenic sanctuaries. The possibility that the statues were found off Sicily, however, changes the situation notably. And to appreciate it we must recall some of the history of art as booty in antiquity.

The Greeks, as a rule, did not prize statues as trophies of war. Alexander's restoration of art works, such as the Tyrannicides of Antenor to Athens, was the return of one's own from barbarian captivity. The Greeks, in fact, could be brutally indifferent to the fate of art works in a captured city. Another Calabrian find, the bronze statuary from the wreck of Porticello, just north of the Straits of Messina, illustrates the point very well. In this case there is ample material from the wreck to date it with great precision to the opening years of the fourth century. I have no doubt that the statuary on board came from the sack of Rhegium by Dionysius I in 387 BC. The bronzes had been hacked to pieces and were obviously being treated as scrap metal. If the artistic merit of conquered art work had had any appeal to the victorious Syracusans, they certainly would have spared the portrait of a bearded philosopher, which is one of the surprising masterpieces of Greek sculpture of the fifth century. It may well be an imaginary portrait of the early law-giver Charondas, who may be identified as the bearded figure represented on the coins of Rhegium.

The Romans, on the other hand, gloried in the artistic trophies they brought home to embellish their triumphs and adorn the city. But when the Romans came to fight in Sicily in the First and Second Punic Wars, how much art of the fifth century, we may ask, was left for them to carry home? The fate of the Sicilian cities in earlier centuries is all too well known. Those that were not sacked by the Carthaginians were razed by the Greeks, and often more than once. Only Syracuse escaped pillage, until Marcellus took the city in 211 BC. So elsewhere in Sicily the Greeks would have destroyed their own art. The Carthaginians behaved like the Romans. They despoiled, and they also shipped art home, and even to Tyre the mother city of Carthage, as trophies of victory. The Motya figure can be interpreted as such a trophy from Selinus and the practice is recorded by Diodorus for each of the cities the Carthaginians captured in the campaign of 406–405 BC, Acragas, Gela and Camarina.

If the Riace Heroes did come from a wreck in Sicilian waters it is only likely to have been a Roman wreck if the statues were taken from Syracuse in 211 BC. There is, however, a consideration that argues against this possibility: the nature of the dedication from which the Heroes might have come. Up to now, we have become accustomed to having the Heroes discussed as if they were two statues from a multi-figured dedication in one of the Panhellenic sanctuaries. But why hold to this when it appears equally possible that the statues came originally from a Greek city in Sicily? That they are a pair of figures who belong together is equally clear. And, therefore, they correspond perfectly to those pairs of oikists found in several of the Sicilian cities, notably Acragas (Aristonous and Pystilus), Gela (Antiphemus and Entimus), and

Camarina (Dascon and Menecolus), but not Syracuse. With Syracuse thus excluded, I have no hesitation in suggesting that the Riace Warriors represent a pair of Sicilian oikists and that they were shipped away as spoils of war on a Carthaginian vessel after the sack of Acragas, Gela or Camarina in 406–405 BC. The Carthaginian ship foundered off Sicily. The discovery of the statues and their voyage to Calabria came only in the twentieth century AD.

Classical architecture

From the historian Diodorus Siculus we learn that a temple was erected on the site of the Battle of Himera following the Greek victory over the Carthaginians in 480 BC. On the strip of land between the city and the sea a peripteral temple of the early fifth century was long known to exist, hidden by the large farmstead built over it. The temple was laid bare in two years of excavation in 1929 and 1930. This must be the temple mentioned by Diodorus. Its dimensions are similar to those of the Temple of Apollo at Syracuse and are almost those of Temple C at Selinus (being only some 9.15 meters or 30 ft shorter, figure 138). But the character of the architecture is very different from that of Sicilian temple design up to that time. The Himera Temple is no longer distinctively Sicilian but is copying contemporary temple architecture of the motherland. The exterior is the crystallized Greek mainland Doric of the opening of the fifth century, typified by the Temple of Aphaia on the island of Aigina. Although the building at Himera is not preserved above its lowest column drums and the entablature cannot be reconstructed fully from the surviving fragments, there is no problem in visualizing its order. This is because the Temple of Athene in Syracuse, today incorporated in the city's cathedral, is its twin (figure 139). Thus while Himera received the memorial of Theron of Acragas, Gelon of Syracuse erected his temple at home. If we recall that work on the Ionic temple nearby was apparently halted when the new temple was built, we can appreciate even more the effect of Gelon's project. He was not only rejecting the Ionianism, but also rejecting the past of Sicilian architecture. In this new Sicilian Doric, the columns are made shorter in respect to their lower diameters than

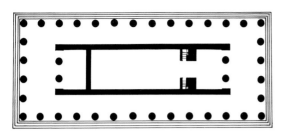

Figure 138 Himera, Temple

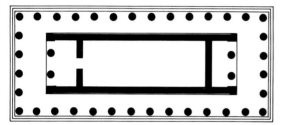

Figure 139 Syracuse, Temple of Athene

Figure 140 Palermo Museum, lion's head spout from Temple at Himera

was normal in late archaic Sicilian work. The capitals have the firm outline adopted by mainland Doric at the time. The precise simplicity of the traditional elements of the Doric frieze could be mistaken for elements from a temple in the homeland, although the Sicilian entablatures remained slightly taller in respect to the columns than was the case in the homeland. Imported marble from the Aegean was employed for the sima.[9]

Returning to Himera, we find another stone sima. A magnificent set of lion's head spouts, comparable to the best Greek work of the day, the spouts of the Temple of Zeus at Olympia of about 460 BC (as well as the spouts of the Temple of Athene in Syracuse and the series from the Temple of Demeter at Acragas), can be seen today in the Museum of Palermo (figure 140). At the time of their discovery some of the sections still had their original painted decoration. The lions' manes were blue, their mouths and ears red. They were framed by a lotus and palmette decoration, also in red and blue. The moldings above, ending in a simple Doric

hawksbeak, as at Syracuse, carried further patterns in the same colors.

The ground plans of the two temples show peristyles of six columns on the fronts and fourteen on the flanks, close to the canonical six by thirteen plan of the mainland. Gone are the old spacious colonnades of the flanks and deep porches once common in Sicily. And the additional inner chambers so often found earlier in Sicilian temples have been suppressed. The rear porch or opisthodomos of the mainland appears, with two columns in antis, mirroring the arrangement of the entrance.

Fragments of sculpture from the site suggest that the temple at Himera had both sculptured metopes and stone sculpture in its pediments. The pediments must have had mythological scenes, no doubt battles, with groups of figures. There is a possible instance of terracotta pedimental sculpture earlier at Himera, but in this way too the new temples probably look to the

Greek motherland where stone pedimental sculpture was already common.

These temples show the same taste as that which was responsible for the late archaic marble kouroi of Sicily and encouraged the patronage of poets and dramatists from the home country. It was a sense of cultural provincialism turning against the individuality of sixth-century Sicilian Doric. It preferred the Doric style of mainland Greek architecture. Most of fifth-century Sicilian temple architecture followed the trend established by the twin temples at Syracuse and Himera, although there is one conspicuous exception, the Temple of Olympian Zeus at Acragas.

Before turning to these buildings, we must examine one development of Doric design of the fifth century in which the Sicilians played a leading role. This is the so-called problem of angle contraction (figure 141). Back in the seventh century when the Doric peristyle came into being, the columns and entablatures above them were wood. The wooden beams spanning the intervals from column to column were capable of bearing heavy loads and thus the columns of the peristyle could be spaced at relatively wide intervals. Under these conditions, the decoration of the frieze, placing a triglyph over the center of each column and over the center of each inter-columniation, could be made so that the triglyphs centered over the corner columns were wide enough to reach to the very end of the frieze. In these early Doric entablatures there was no thought of leaving a blank edge beyond the final triglyph (centered over the last column of a row) and the corner of the frieze. In practical terms this meant that the triglyphs had to be almost as wide as the abacus, the topmost element, of the capitals (they could be slightly shorter only because the capital was permitted to project somewhat beyond the entablature resting on it). Thus the Doric frieze came into being with no apparent contradictions in its design but with a firm convention regarding the placement of the triglyphs in relation to the columns below and an equally firm notion that a Doric frieze could not have a blank space beyond the triglyphs at the corners.

The translation of the Doric order into stone produced a problem in the arrangement of the frieze which defied a rational solution and necessitated a long series of compromises. The weight of the stone architrave and stone frieze above

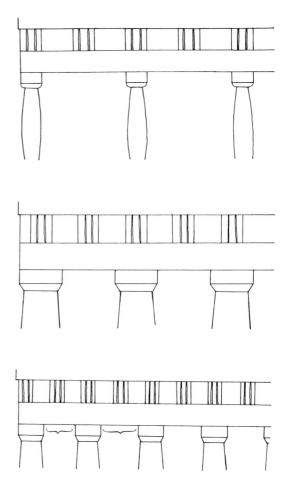

Figure 141 The corner metope problem: (top) the Doric order of the primitive wooden entablature, (middle) the Doric order in stone without angle contraction, (bottom) the Doric order in stone with angle contraction; note the smaller interval between the final two columns

it was a matter of great concern for the Greek architects, even when these elements were still only partly stone. More than that, stone does not have the compression strength of wood and internal flaws can propagate into dangerous cracks. The timidity of Greek builders working with limestone and marble must have been based on a history of dangerous and expensive failures of stone peristyles. The earliest peristyle still preserved, that of the Temple of Apollo at Syracuse, shows the measures taken as result. The columns were made thicker and the intervals between them were drastically reduced in order to compensate for increased weight and possible structural weakness above. The columns of the Temple of Apollo are spaced so closely that they are less than the arm span of a single person apart.

The new stone temples met engineering requirements but complicated the design of the frieze. Under the new conditions triglyphs approaching the width of the column capitals were impossible. Because of the thick columns and close spacing, there was simply not enough room on the frieze to fit one over each column and over each intercolumniation. However, reducing the width of the triglyphs immediately produced the unpleasant result of a blank space at the end of the frieze. The job of the architectural designer was now to give the impression that the old distribution of triglyphs was maintained when in fact subterfuge was necessary to produce the desired visual result. First of all, the triglyphs had to be made thinner if there were to be any metopes at all. Next, the blank space at the end of the frieze was eliminated by moving the triglyphs slightly away from their proper positions and in the direction of the end of the frieze. This displacement had to be carried out toward both ends of the frieze working outward from the center, or from some point down the line but still far enough away from the end of the frieze so that the displacement was not obvious. The result was the Doric frieze as we know it on all stone Doric temples, a frieze which appears to obey the conventions developed for the wooden buildings but actually has adjusted the relation of triglyphs and columns to fit new conditions.

During the sixth century another kind of modification was introduced in the battle with the corner triglyph problem. It occurred to architects that reducing the final intercolumniation of each of the four sides of the peristyle would also help to eliminate the blank space at the end of the frieze. When this device, known as angle contraction, was employed, the need to modify the spacing of the triglyphs was reduced, and consequently the visual deception achieved by the frieze became more convincing. Angle contraction is first found in Sicily in the Temple of Heracles at Acragas of 490–480 BC.

The twin Sicilian temples at Himera and Syracuse took this solution one step farther. In their ground plans the final two intercolumniations on each side of the peristyle are diminished, leading to what is known as 'double angle contraction'. This refinement in dealing with the corner triglyph problem was never imitated in the Greek homeland, and it suggests that however much these temples look as if they were mainland Greek creations, their architect was working with creative ingenuity even though his patrons demanded a design of non-Sicilian character. The temple at Himera, although not the building at Syracuse, included another characteristically western feature. Just behind the entrance porch there are stairways leading to the attic of the temple. It is uncertain whether these stairs, also found at Selinus and Acragas, were intended purely to facilitate service access to the upper parts of the temple or whether they were needed for cult purposes.[10]

Finally, the Athene Temple in Syracuse is one of the few such buildings for which we possess a description of its furnishing, if not in the days of its greatest glory, at least while it was a respected monument and home of a living cult. The passage comes from Cicero's prosecution of the rapacious Roman governor of Sicily, Gaius Verres. Cicero expatiates on the magnificence of the doors of the temple embellished with gold and ivory decoration which the Roman governor stripped off. From the interior of the temple he removed twenty-seven historical paintings, including one showing the tyrant Agathocles (317–289) in a cavalry engagement, very likely a painting of the kind reproduced by the famous Alexander Mosaic from the House of the Faun in Pompeii. Finally, we hear from the anecdotist Athenaeus that the pediment of the temple was ornamented with a gilded shield which in the rays of the rising sun was visible far out to sea. Some of this decoration, if not all of it, was added after Gelon's time, but Cicero's description eloquently suggests the splendor of a rich Greek temple.

Selinuntine architecture was less radical in its adoption of the standards of mainland Greek Doric. Temple F in the eastern group of temples had a stone entablature at the end of the sixth century. About 460 BC a new Temple E (the third on the spot) was erected beside it (figures 142 and 143). The overall dimensions of this temple were slightly larger than those of F, and we gain some perspective on the grandiosity of Sicilian temple building if we recall that Temple E is as long as the Parthenon on the Acropolis

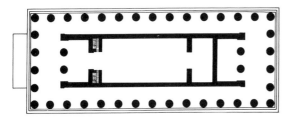

Figure 142 Selinus, Temple E

Figure 143 Selinus, Temple E, photograph courtesy of Fototeca Unione presso l'Accademia Americana neg. 7688

peristyle and although there are porches with the in antis arrangement of columns, the temple retains an inner room or adyton. The same approach to the ground plan can be seen in two temples erected in the fifth century on the acropolis in the neighborhood of Temple C: Temple A and Temple O. Near them is the small Temple B. It is a building with a cella preceded by a colonnaded porch. The order is mixed Doric and Ionic, Ionic columns carrying a Doric frieze. The same mixture of orders is found in the fourth-century temple of Megara Hyblaea, a building related to the Ionic temple at Taormina. We have already noted another, and later, example of mixed Ionic and Doric on the so-called Tomb of Theron at Acragas. To the east of Temple A there is a large T-shaped structure which was adorned with Doric columns. It has been restored as a gateway and as an altar.

Two temples on the ridge marking the southern boundary of Acragas belong to the conventionalizing current in Sicilian architecture. They are the so-called Temple of Concord of about 430 BC and its neighbor the temple conventionally designated the Temple of Hera of about 450 BC. The Temple of Concord is one of the best-

Figure 144 Agrigento, Temple of Concord

of Athens, though slightly less wide. Together with F, the new building was the neighbor of G, one of the largest temples ever built by the Greeks, which was still under construction as late as the end of the fifth century. The plan of Temple E is six columns on the fronts and fifteen on the flanks. By comparison with those of the Parthenon they are heavy and squat. The building's entablature is about half again as high as that of the Parthenon, thus perpetuating a Sicilian taste for an imposing roofline, which the Sicilians shared with the Dorian Peloponnesos. The sima was of the simpler variety we have already encountered at Syracuse and Himera. The roof was sumptuously done with bronze roof tiles, and, as we have already seen, there were sculptured metopes over the two porches. The cella is also raised above the level of the

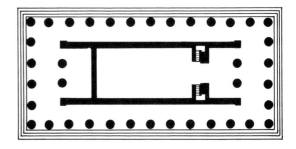

Figure 145 Agrigento, Temple of Concord

preserved Greek temples, having been transformed, like the Hephaisteion in Athens, into a church (Figures 144 and 145). With a width of only 16.77 meters (55 ft) and a length of 39.34 meters (129 ft), it is not a large temple, and although a visitor from Athens would have found the entablature somewhat heavy, it is a graceful building. The Temple of Hera is completely destroyed above its lower column drums. At some time in its later history a broad flight of steps was added on the east side leading up to the temple from its altar.[11] The poorly documented temple of Hephaestus closes out the group of Agrigentine temples of the later fifth century.

Although the Greek temple was the house of the god, the heart of cults of the Olympian divinities (as distinct from those related to the underworld) was the altar before the temple on which the inedible parts of animal sacrifices were burnt for the consumption of the gods. Such altars were massive platforms, in width often matching the temples they served, or even exceeding them, as we have seen in the case of the altar in the Malophorus Sanctuary at Selinus. Their parapets were often decorated, as demonstrated by the surviving elements from the sixth century at Megara Hyblaea, Syracuse and Selinus, to cite only the most conspicuous examples. The altars still in place, however, have lost their decoration, but notwithstanding their sorry state of preservation it is important to remember that the ancient cult was served by both temple and altar.

In the same decade that witnessed the construction of the twin temples of Himera and Syracuse in commemoration of the victory over Carthage, there was under construction at Acragas another temple, which is the very antithesis of the conventionalizing current in Sicilian temple architecture of the fifth century. This building is the Temple of Olympian Zeus. Today the building is covered by a mountain of gigantic wall blocks thrown down by earthquake, and then partly plundered in the eighteenth century for the stone to build the jetties at Porto Empedocle, modern Agrigento's harbor (figures 146 and 147). But once again the History of Diodorus Siculus (XIII, 82, 3–4) comes to our assistance by giving a brief description of the temple.

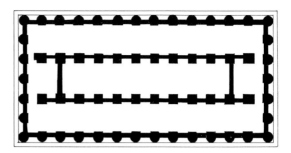

Figure 146 Agrigento, Temple of Zeus

The temple is three hundred forty feet long and sixty feet wide.[a] Its height is one hundred twenty feet above the foundations. It might well be judged to be the greatest of the temples of Sicily or of those outside Sicily because of the size of its ground plan. And if the [Carthaginian] invasion had not put a stop to construction, the choice would be obvious. Other temples are built to a certain height with simple walling, others have colonnades. But this temple combines both forms, because the columns form part of the walls. On the exterior they are round, toward the interior they are rectangular. Their exterior circumference is twenty feet, and in each of the flutings it would be possible to place a human figure. On the interior they measure twelve feet. The length and height of the pediments ('stoai') is extraordinary. The east pediment has a sculptured battle of gods and giants. The west pediment shows the fall of Troy. Each hero is carefully worked so as to be distinguishable from what is at either side.

[a]The measurements of the temple show that Diodorus should have given 160 ft for the width.

This colossal temple was the rival in size of Temple G at Selinus, and far more revolutionary in design. There was in fact no peristyle but rather Doric half columns were simulated as if attached to the exterior walls, seven across the fronts of the building, fourteen along its flanks. A molding, more than a man's height, ran along the base of the wall and half columns. The form of the molding approximates the base of Ionic columns from Ionia, a convex member surmounting two concave elements. The Doric

Figure 147 Agrigento Museum, restored model of the Temple of Zeus, photograph courtesy of German Archaeological Institute, Rome, inst. neg. 63.2225

entablature was of the normal variety, but between the columns gigantic male figures (telamones) seemed to assist the columns in supporting the roof. Like the columns the telamones (each 7.65 meters or 25 ft high) were part of the walling. There is some disagreement about the exact height at which they were placed on the wall (as there is about the total height of the order) and about their accessory framing. There is no question, however, about their general placement. Above the simulated architrave and the frieze the sima is finished off with a hawksbeak molding compatible with the tastes of conventionalizing architecture.

The most recent studies suggest that the 'cella' of the temple was unroofed, while the corridors between the exterior and 'cella' walls were roofed. The weight of these roofs on the 'cella' was borne by a series of pillars lining the long walls of the 'cella' and projecting into it. The building was entered through two doors placed symmetrically between the columns of the facade.

If we trust Diodorus' figures (as emended) the building was planned as a 1,000 ft temple, the sum produced by adding the lengths of both fronts and both sides. Archaic Greek temples as early as the seventh century were planned with 100 ft lengths, from which the term hekatompedon derives. A 1,000 foot temple would be a kind of super hekatompedon, although the proper term chiliopedon is not attested. There is some dispute over this issue, due to difference of opinion as to the length of foot employed at Acragas.[12]

Unusual though it is in planning and detail, the Olympieion is not a Sicilian adaptation of a Punic or oriental temple, celebrating the victory of Himera by usurping an architectural type, although this is an interpretation which was seriously entertained in the past. In fact one architectural historian argues that the plan of the Olympieion develops naturally from that of a neighboring temple, the so-called Temple of Heracles, which dates possibly to the decade before 480 BC (figure 148).[13] Although the space between the cella and outer wall or colonnade is greater in the Olympieion than in its predecessor, the cella (without the spur walls of the Olympieion) is similarly proportioned and is placed at the same distance from the facades. The Olympieion, however, has carried the Sicilian notion of the peristyle as an enclosure around the cella to its logical conclusion, one also suggested by the partitions between the columns of Temple F at Selinus.

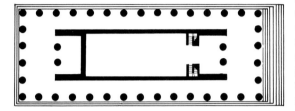

Figure 148 Agrigento, Temple of Heracles

The idea of the telamones of the exterior need not be traced to oriental genii or slaves. Greek decorative arts of the archaic age show numerous instance of male figures used in supporting postures, whether as pitcher handles or as the handles of paterae (open bowls). In this case, as in so many others, the composition of the early Selinuntine metopes for example, the minor arts seem to have been the sources exploited readily in the west. The engaged columns of the exterior were not invented by the architect. He was familar with them from the engaged columns used in the interiors of Sicilian sarcophagi. Half-columns had already been employed to terminate the 'antae' of Temple D at Selinus. Another example of their use in fifth century Acragas is the 'Temple of Aesclepius' situated outside the walls to the south of the city. The walls of the small temple are still standing. It had a cella preceded by a porch with Doric columns in antis. The two engaged columns are found on the rear wall creating the impression of a second porch. And finally, the molding at the base of the exterior wall was used for Ionic columns made at Acragas.[14] These considerations show the genesis of the plan and decoration of the Olympieion. But the elements were put together through the genius of its creator, all the more remarkable because he worked at a time when the conventionalizing current was running strongly in Sicilian architecture.

One of the latest Sicilian temples of the fifth century is also the most dramatic in its setting. This is the Temple of Segesta which faces the city it served from a small eminence backed by the majesty of Mt Bernardo (figures 149 and 150). If any temple may be said to gain from its setting, it is Segesta. The Elymnians of Segesta, furthermore, were the only non-Greek peoples who made the Greek temple so much their own,

Figure 149 Segesta Temple, photograph courtesy of Fototeca Unione presso l'Accademia Americana, neg. 7844

Figure 150 Segesta, Temple, photograph courtesy of Alison Frantz Archive

both here and at the world-famous but now vanished Temple of Aphrodite on the mountain of Eryx.[15]

The Temple of Segesta is unfinished. Its columns were never fluted and the lifting bosses were never removed from many of the foundation blocks. The foundation platform is actually incomplete, some of the blocks of its upper parts between the columns never having been set. Only the peristyle was ever built, and it was long thought that there was never intended to be a cella. But recent work has shown that there are cuttings for the cella walls in the bedrock showing that a cella was planned. The building has six columns on the front and fourteen along the flanks. It was given double angle contraction. It is close in size to the twin temples of Syracuse and Himera. At Segesta Greek architecture became a proclamation of the cultural self-image of a people who considered themselves fugitive Trojans and thus partners in the heroic heritage of the Greeks. Although the interpretation of architectural meaning in the Greek cities is more subtle, Gelon's choice of conventional mainland Doric was a not dissimilar enunciation of cultural association.

4 COINAGE

The coins of Greek Sicily are the most splendid productions in the history of medallic art. Beginning with the crystalline images found on the coinages of the cities of the Deinomenid Empire, they mature, after the end of the era of the tyrants, in the sumptuous issues of the later fifth century. The Carthaginian disaster at the end of the century interrupted most of the Sicilian coinages, the exception being the long and glorious series of Syracuse. During the preceding century the Sicilians had replaced merely competent die engraving with the work of master engravers. The fame of these artists, particularly the group active at the end of the fifth century, was such that they were encouraged to sign their work. The cities thus took pride in the authorship of the coin designs as well as the art.

Sicilian coins, however, were still money. Coins, which had begun their life only in the seventh century BC, among the Greeks of Asia Minor or their immediate neighbors inland, the Lydians, marked an enormous advance in the use of metals as media of exchange and repositories of value. Issued by city governments, a coin became a public instrument. By serving to pay the obligations of the city and excluding other forms of payment for fines and taxes, the coin strengthened the control of the city over economic life. It also quantified, and thus clarified, dealings between individuals. Thus, in the view of some scholars, there was an intimate relation between the development of coinage and the growth of political equality among the citizens of the Greek city.

The earliest coins, minted in the seventh century, were probably not issued by governments. They are more likely to have been an initiative taken by temple administrations (temples were the first ancient banks) to meet a particular monetary problem in Asia Minor. The medium of exchange in this region was electrum, the

naturally occurring alloy of silver and gold. But in electrum the ratio of gold and silver can vary widely. Once refining processes were developed which could separate the two elements, it became all too clear that equal weights of unrefined electrum could have significantly different values. The problem for monetary circulation was to create a stable value, and this was done by announcing ownership of individual lumps of the metal by marking them with the owner's seal. The owner thus agreed to take back the piece so marked without questioning its composition.

Mainland Greece and the Aegean islands, where silver rather than electrum was the medium of exchange, faced a different problem but one that was also helped by the new invention. As happens in any market, the raw silver lumps used in exchange tended to disappear from circulation. This was especially true of major markets involving foreign merchants who would leave for home with the proceeds of their commerce, thus reducing the supply of silver in local circulation. The coin, however, now issued by the city, announced where it would be accepted without question, and this innovation tended to attract silver back to its home city. It was not very long before the cities realized the advantages of defining legal tender, especially where the payment of fines and taxes was concerned.

It was formerly thought that coinage was introduced to the cities of Sicily and southern Italy somewhat later than it became common in the mother country. Now there seems little reason to maintain this belief. Early issues of Sybaris in Calabria have been found in a hoard (the Sambiase Hoard) with some of the earliest coins of Corinth. Indeed, it is far more likely that the Sicilian coinages were born when silver first began arriving there in the form of coined money, as early as the mid-sixth century. It is of some importance to remember that Sicily has no silver deposits (and save for meager traces in Calabria, this is true of the entire area of Greek colonization in Italy as well). Sicily's needs for silver were met, according to another long-held theory, by the importation of ingots, from Greece and possibly even from Spain. No doubt silver did reach the island in this form. But a recent discovery points to coined silver from Greece as an even more important source of metal to be reissued as coin by the Sicilians.

The find in question is a hoard of coins from the area of Selinus which was found about 1984 and reached the international antiquities market through the usual channels.[1] It contained raw silver: fragments of three ingots and one other complete ingot of the round or 'bun' shape. The ingots are marked with small punch stamps, a female head, a simple cross and a turtle, as well as letters scratched on the surfaces. Raw silver is often found in early Greek coin hoards, for example in the large hoard found at Taranto early in this century and in the hoards of archaic Greek coins from Egypt and the Near East. What is extraordinary about the new hoard is its approximately 250 silver coins apparently representing the very first phases of coinage in the Greek west. Once again, there are early issues of Corinth (thirty-nine coins). But with them are coins of Aegina (eighty-one coins), the other major mint of mid sixth-century Greece. There is also an early coin from Abdera, one of the Greek cities in Thrace having access to the silver mines of the region and producing large mintings of coins which found their way throughout the Greek world and into the Near East and Egypt. It has even been supposed that cities like Abdera intentionally marketed their silver in the form of coin. In the hoard are coins from three major Greek cities in southern Italy, Metapontum (two coins), Sybaris (five coins) and Poseidonia (one coin). Two Sicilian cities are represented: Selinus, where the hoard is said to have been found (thirty-five coins), and Himera on the north coast (one coin). Never before has the presence of early Greek coins in Sicily been documented so extensively, and the evidence of this hoard can be joined to the indications offered by the two recorded cases of early Sicilian coins clearly overstruck on imported pieces, both of them Selinus over Corinth. Although Corinthian coins were somewhat below the normal weight standard of Selinuntine issues, Selinus evidently made do with overstrikes on Corinthian coins. If well done, overstriking obliterates all traces of the undertype and so any case in which the undertype can be read points to a liberal reuse of existing coins for a new issue. The surprise of the new Selinus hoard, however, is that Aiginetan and Abderite coins, struck on their own individual weight standards, were coming to Sicily. To be reused such pieces would have had to be remelted, and we now see that the abundant coinage of Aegina, drawing on the silver mines of the Aegean and those of the Thracian cities, with the mines of Mt Pangaeus at their back, were important sources of silver for Sicilian coinage.

The arrival of these Greek silver coins in Sicily also means that something of equivalent value was leaving the island in exchange. From the appeal made by the Greeks of the mother country to Gelon of Syracuse in the face of the Persian threat of 480, we know that Sicily had grain to export (Rome may have been receiving Sicilian grain about this time), and Sicily was no further from Greece than the coasts of the Black Sea from which the Greeks were already importing cereals. But if coinage is to be taken as an indication of income in the form of silver from the sale of grain, this does not seem to have been the initial impetus for coinage in the island, because the natural exporters of grain, Catane and Leontini on the east coast and Gela, Camarina and Acragas on the south coast, did not begin their coinages until somewhat later.

The first group of cities to make coins in Sicily was composed of Naxos and Zankle (Messina) in the northeast, Himera along the north coast of the island, and Selinus in the far west.[2] The first three of these were Chalcidian colonies, primary or secondary settlements of these leaders in overseas adventuring. Naxos, the first Greek settlement in Sicily, was the natural landfall to voyagers reaching the tip of Calabria. Zankle (Messina) had the best harbor on the gateway through the Straits of Messina. And Himera was situated along the north coast facing north on the Tyrrhenian. None of these cities had as important agricultural territories as other Greek cities on the island. But together they issued what appear to be the earliest Sicilian coins. Their resources must have lain at least in part in timber from the slopes of Mt Aetna and the mountains of the north coast and from their position as way stations, Naxos to southern and eastern Sicily, Zankle (Messina) to the Tyrrhenian Sea and Himera to Carthaginian Sardinia and Spain.

The coins of Naxos present a gracefully archaic head of the god Dionysus on their obverse face; the reverse shows a heavy bunch of grapes with leaves hanging from its tendrils and below the legend, 'Of the Naxians' (figure 151). Whatever

Figure 151 Coin of Naxos, Syracuse Museum, ex Gagliardi collection

Figure 152 Coin of Zankle-Messina, Syracuse Museum, ex Gagliardi collection

Figure 153 Coin of Himera, American Numismatic Society, New York, photograph courtesy of ANS

their local significance, the types clearly refer to the Aegean island of Naxos which gave its name to the colony, and presumably a delegation of settlers as well, though under Chalcidian

leadership. This is not the only evidence of Sicilian Naxos' maintaining such ties.[3] Naxos issued a larger coin, usually described as a drachm, at a maximum weight of 5.7 gm and a fractional piece of about 0.8 gm.

At Zankle the principal type of the coinage is decidedly local in reference (figure 152). The type is a dolphin, a symbol not only of the sea but also of good luck since dolphins have often guided drowning sailors to shore. 'Zankle' meant sickle in the Sicel language, a name which describes the shape of the city's famous harbor. The sickle-shaped harbor is shown on the coins, and on some of them warehouses can be seen along its curve. The die of the reverse side had the form of the punch mark found widely on early Greek coins (called the incuse square or incuse). Here it has the shallow, Corinthian form, with a shell added in the central compartment. Zankle's drachms were on the same standard as those of Naxos.

Himera had no need of an inscription on her coins because the type, a cock, the bird who announces the day, immediately implies 'hemera', Greek for 'day' (figure 153). This is an example of what is called in French a 'type parlant', that is a type that suggests a word. This is also called a 'punning type', although there is no humor involved. The reverse is again an incuse. The weight standard was that of Naxos and Zankle, and two denominations were issued. The surprising aspect of the coinage of Himera is its volume. This is studied not through the number of surviving coins but the number of dies represented among them.[4] From about 550 BC to the end of the century Himera employed 122 obverse dies for its drachms. This is twice as many as Zankle and about six times as many as Naxos, where, however, there were larger issues of fractions. Furthermore, at the end of the period, the Himeran mint was working intensively and using two obverse dies at the same time.[5]

The final early mint of the island was Selinus (figure 154). The type was simplicity itself, a single leaf of the selinon plant, the 'type parlant' of the city. The reverse is an incuse. Selinus' coinage did not belong to the area of circulation represented by the three Chalcidian mints of the east and north coasts. Her standard approached 9 gm for the larger denomination. The coinage must have been an extensive one, although it has not been fully studied.

Figure 154 Coin of Selinus, Syracuse Museum

The four cities that introduced coinage to Sicily were all points of transit. For Naxos and Himera this fact needs no emphasis. Himera and Selinus were both on the frontier of the Greek world, but open to commerce with the Etruscans, the Carthaginians and lands further west. It would be incorrect to say that the commerce of these cities demanded coinage. Commerce was carried on for millennia in the Near East without coins, as the Carthaginians continued to do until they began employing Greek mercenary soldiers who demanded their pay in coin. Rather, the use of coins was taken up by the Greeks of Sicily, as it was in the motherland, in order to attract the silver so marked back to its home market place and for the evident advantages of city state control over the means of payments. The significance of this development in Sicily is less that some cities began to coin immediately than that others did not. In other words, even important places like Acragas, Gela, Syracuse and Catane did not have sufficient silver for a coinage. The usual quantities of raw silver that we must imagine reaching the Greek colonies of Sicily from the time of their foundation were simply not sufficient to permit any city to establish a coinage. It was the influx of coined silver that made coinage possible in Sicily, and the flow of coined silver into the island was stronger on the northern coast than in the south and east. It was from the north coast that the coins in the new hoard appear to have reached Selinus, making possible the early coinage of that city.

When they do begin, the coinages of Acragas, Gela and Syracuse seem to owe their existence to a new source of silver and possibly new purposes for coinage. The coins of these cities of the southern and eastern part of the island are struck on the standard of the coinage of Athens and of certain coinages of the silver-producing regions of northern Greece. By the last quarter of the sixth century the Athenians, already drawing silver from the mines of Laurium, were striking four-drachmai pieces, the tetradrachm, each weighing 17.6 gm as well as two-drachmai pieces, the didrachm of 8.8 gm, and other small denominations. A hoard found in 1956 at Gela, which when recovered by the authorities numbered 870 coins but originally seems to have contained over twice that number, shows that Athenian silver coins were common in Sicily in the early fifth century. The hoard was buried around 485 BC and in the parcel that was recovered had 166 Athenian tetradrachms, and 2 coins of Acanthus (in northern Greece) on the Attic standard. Another hoard, found at Monte Bubbonia 25 kilometers north of Gela in 1910 and buried about 470 BC, also contained tetradrachms of Athens and Acanthus, though in relatively smaller proportion to the whole (7 out of 338 coins). Apparently the arrival of Athenian and north Greek silver coins on the Athenian standard toward the end of the sixth century provided the metal for the second group of Sicilian mints.

At Acragas the types of the coinage are perfectly simple (figure 155). On the obverse is an eagle, the symbol of Zeus, but also, as shown by a later Agrigentine type, chosen as a sign of

Figure 155 Coin of Acragas, Syracuse Museum, ex Gagliardi collection

good omen. On the reverse is the Agrigentine crab, a 'type parlant' (crab, 'karkinos') to identify the city. The largest denomination at Acragas was the Attic didrachm weighing only slightly more than the heaviest coins issued by the Chalcidian cities and by Selinus.

At Syracuse, however, the coinage begins with innovation. The largest denomination is a tetradrachm, often directly overstruck, one may presume, on Athenian owls or on coins of Acanthus or other Attic weight coinages from northern Greece (figure 156). The obverse type has both a literal significance and quite likely a metaphorical one as well. The literal significance

Figure 156 Coin of Syracuse, American Numismatic Society, New York, photograph courtesy of ANS

becomes apparent when one looks at the type of the didrachm, a youth mounted and leading a second horse: two horses, two drachmai. The type of the tetradrachm is a four-horse chariot, the quadriga. The type is thus a numeral. The Syracusans clearly intended to make distinctions of denominations through the coin types. When small fractions were struck immediately after the opening issues of the coinage, both the fifth of the drachm (the litra) and the sixth of the drachm (the obol) were issued. The litra was identified by a wheel, the obol by a sepia (cuttlefish). The chariot of the tetradrachm also makes reference to the competitions of the Panhellenic games. It may thus have been intended to convey an idea of victory, and thus of good omen, not unlike the Agrigentine eagle. The first tetradrachm of Syracuse had only a punch mark on the reverse. Soon, however, the reverse is no longer a simple flat incuse, but in its center there is a small circle carrying a profile female head. This is the first appearance of the lady who was destined to adorn the great series of the Syracusan coinage. (These small heads on the large surface of the coin resemble the punch marks on a silver ingot, such as the profile female head mark found on an ingot of the Selinus hoard discussed above. Their appearance shows how much large archaic coins were still thought of as bullion.)

The striking of a tetradrachm implies the need to make larger payments and thus the need for coins of greater value than the pieces of under 10 gm generally struck in Sicily. The reason was

probably not so much the cost of public works but military expenses, and very likely the pay of mercenaries. Mercenaries had been used in Sicily at least since the time of Phalaris (about 550 BC), and under Gelon and his brother tyrants they were to become a scourge of the island. It is very likely that the Syracusan oligarchs (the gamoroi) of the late sixth century, whom we know faced opposition from the mass of citizens, were resorting to mercenary troops and paying them with tetradrachms.

At Gela the military overtones seen in the first Syracusan issue become still more insistent. The principal denomination in the first years of the Geloan coinage is the didrachm (figure 157). The reverse is a powerfully archaic forepart of

Figure 157 Coin of Gela, Syracuse Museum, ex Gagliardi collection

a man-headed bull. But the obverse is an unusual type, a horseman brandishing a lance. In every case examined up to this point the major Sicilian coin types have been images suggesting verbal equivalents or have belonged to the realm of accepted religious symbolism or omens of good fortune. Even the quadriga at Syracuse and the youthful horseman of the Syracusan didrachms refer to the games carried on as part of religious festivals. The Geloan horseman is heroic, because he is shown nude, or at most wearing a Thracian helmet. But, as has been long recognized, he is also a reference to the power of the Geloan cavalry of the day. In another way, the type is aggressively contemporary in reference. At the time when the Geloan series began in the late 490s, Gela was ruled by the tyrant Hippocrates, who prepared the way for the creation of the Deinomenid Empire ruled by Gelon, Hieron and Polyzalus in the 480s. In Greek his name means 'Horse Powerful'. It is a fine aristocratic Greek name, but it is also echoed by the mounted warrior Hippocrates put on the Geloan coins.

The act perhaps exposed Hippocrates to accusations of excessive pride. But it also exploited the resources of the 'type parlant', though not for the city, but for its ruler.

The profile head comes into its own on a noble group of reverses for tetradrachms of Syracuse which introduce the female head as a major type (figure 158). She is surrounded by

Figure 158 Coin of Syracuse, Syracuse Museum, ex Gagliardi collection

the legend, 'Of the Syracusans' and circling dolphins. One group of these reverses presents a large head whose beaded hair serves to set off the delicately angular line of a pure archaic profile. These dies have been identified as the work of a single artist, 'The Master of the Large Arethusa Head'. The work of two other master die-engravers of the same period has also been recognized. On the obverse the message of the racing team is made more explicit by the addition of a small figure of Victory who flies overhead to crown the team.

Soon, however, the character of the Syracusan tetradrachms changed radically. The monumental quality of the dies of the 'Master of the Large Arethusa Head' and his colleagues is abandoned, and in its place appears a series of heads, far less majestic and symptomatic of the work of competent but less ambitious and possibly hurried die cutters. The number of dies in this group is overwhelming. No fewer than 142 obverse dies were employed in a series of issues which were analyzed in a die study by Erich Boehringer in 1929.[6] If all this output of coinage took place in the five years between Gelon's seizure of power at Syracuse, about 485 BC, and the Carthaginian invasion of 480, as Boehringer concluded, the scale of production was indeed colossal. Boehringer assumed that there was no Syracusan coinage produced during the five

years following the victory. But even allowing the mass coinage to occupy this void or to extend to fifteen years' duration, it would represent a ten times greater consumption of obverse dies per year than that of any other period of Syracusan coinage before the end of the fifth century.

The linch pin of Boehringer's chronology, as it has been for Sicilian coinage as a whole, was the Damareteion, a fifty-litra coin reputed to have been struck in the name of Gelon's wife Damarete, daughter of Theron, tyrant of Acragas. The tradition is given in its fullest form in the world history of Diodorus Siculus,

> Having thus saved themselves unexpectedly, the Carthaginians undertook to carry out Gelon's terms, and more than that, they promised to give a gold crown to Damarete, Gelon's wife, who at their request had been of the greatest assistance in the conclusion of the peace. Rewarded with a crown of one hundred talents gold, she caused a coin to be struck which was called after her the Damareteion. The coin weighed ten Attic drachmai, and among the Sicilians it passed as a fifty-litra piece on account of its weight.[7]

Diodorus' source gave detailed information about the Damareteion. But in one particular, the information is contradictory. If the coin weighed ten Attic drachmai, i.e. 44 gm, and was of gold, it would have been worth some 600 litra at the least (with gold to silver at 12 to 1). But if the coin were silver, it would indeed have been a fifty-litra piece. Such a silver coin is known, a Syracusan dekadrachm close to the issues of the 'mass coinage', but infinitely finer in style, and this coin was already identified by the Duc de Luynes before 1850 as the Damareteion referred to by Diodorus (figure 159). The Damareteion is accompanied by tetradrachms that share with it two unmistakable characteristics. The first is the lion found below the ground line of the obverse (in the exergue, to use the proper numismatic term). The second is the circle within which the female head of the reverse is engraved. The two heads, furthermore, are clearly the work of a single engraver of marked individualism, who is known as the Damareteion Master.

Two arguments have been advanced in recent years to suggest that the Damareteion has been

incorrectly identified. Both arguments concern the mass coinage, which more than one numismatist has felt was compressed into too short a span in Boehringer's original scheme. Colin Kraay pointed out that in one Sicilian hoard (Passo di Piazza, again from the area north of Gela) only the initial dies of the mass coinage were represented but with them was a coin of Messina which must date after 484 BC (figure 160).[8] This coin displays a two-horse chariot

and the coin in the Monte Bubbonia Hoard comes mid-way through the second of the two groups into which the series can be divided.[10] Such evidence, according to Kraay, pointed to the continuation of the mass coinage after 480. If so, the early dekadrachm could not be the Damareteion of history, but was issued for another reason and at another time, even as late as the end of the 460s, the date to which Kraay felt the mass coinage could be extended.

Figure 160 Coin of Messina, Syracuse Museum, ex Gagliardi collection

(biga) drawn by mules. Anaxilas, tyrant of Rhegium and Messina, won a victory in the mule team race at the Olympic games in 484 or 480, and we have it on the authority of Aristotle that to celebrate the victory Anaxilas had coins minted showing a chariot drawn by mules.[9] The Syracusan coins in a second hoard (the Monte Bubbonia Hoard already mentioned above) extend almost to the end of the mass coinage. This hoard had one of Anaxilas' mule biga coins and also one of the coins struck with both the type of Himera, the cock, and the type of Acragas, the crab (figure 161). These coins are attributed to Himera during the period of Agrigentine control that began shortly before the Carthaginian invasion (the date 483 BC is generally given). These issues lasted until 472

Figure 161 Coin of Himera, Syracuse Museum, ex Gagliardi collection

New evidence next appeared with the discovery of a hitherto unknown tetradrachm of Aetna (figure 162). This was the name by which Catane was known after 474 BC when the population was replaced by Hieron, now tyrant of Syracuse, with new settlers from Greece and a draft of Syracusans. The obverse of the Aetna coin has a quadriga which can be paralelled in

Figure 162 Coin of Aetna, private collection

the late phases of the mass coinage, that is somewhat before the generally assumed place of the Damareteion. As interpreted by Christoph Boehringer, this would mean that the Damareteion belonged at the end of the 470s.[11]

It has been objected, however, that the author of the Aetna issue may have looked back somewhat in the Syracusan coinage for his prototype. Furthermore, the hoard evidence cannot be made to exclude even the traditional dating of the mass coinage and so the traditional dating of the dekadrachm. A solution which permitted the mass coinage to continue into the early 470s would, in fact, be in comfortable agreement with the hoard evidence and reduce the distance between the Aetna coin and its Syracusan prototype to a few years at most. Remembering that although related to the mass coinage, the Damareteion group is not die linked in any way to it, it is possible to adopt this view and maintain the identification of the dekadrachm as Damarete's coin.

This does not mean that we understand why the dekadrachm was struck. A coin of this kind should represent some kind of extraordinary expenditure, or the desire to make the expenditure in an extraordinary form. The later dekadrachms of Syracuse, issued by the tyrant Dionysius I, are now agreed to have been minted to pay mercenaries. The Athenian dekadrachm, once thought to have commemorated the victories over the Persians at Marathon or Salamis, now, in light of a recent hoard from Asia Minor which more than doubled the number of known specimens, appears to be a coin minted by some princeling or satrap within the Persian Empire to pay mercenaries. The coins acquired credibility by seeming to be Athenian, just as in the fourth century 'Athenian' tetradrachms were minted in Egypt because Athen's owls were the coin of international preference. We would not be far wrong if we see the Damareteion as another impressive coin minted to pay mercenary soldiers, on whom the tyrants of Syracuse placed great reliance.

The name, however, is still a problem. Why was the dekadrachm Damarete's coin? The lion in the exergue gives a clue. Damarete's family, the Emmenid tyrants of Acragas, claimed descent from Polyneices, son of Oedipus. Polyneices' shield device, in one account at least, was the forepart of a lion, and the pedigree-conscious

Emmenids will have been aware of what the lion meant to them.

We may proceed further by asking yet a further question. When did Damarete and Gelon marry? Diplomacy was surely the reason for the match. But Gelon did not rule a city until he emerged as Hippocrates' successor at Gela in the early 480s and he was not ruler of Syracuse until about 485 BC. If we assume that Damarete married the tyrant of Syracuse to seal the alliance between Syracuse and Acragas made to meet the pending Carthaginian attack, the union was not made until the eve of the war of 480. There is no reason to assume that her dowry, which would have been a handsome one, was spent on the single campaign that overcame the Carthaginians. If Bentley's emendation of the ancient commentary to Pindar's Second Pythian Ode (line 152) is correct, the tripod dedicated by Gelon at Delphi as a thank offering for victory was offered, 'From Damarete's gold'.[12] If the dekadrachm was minted about the same time and from the same funds, then the mercenaries were paid off with dekadrachms bearing the Emmenid lion. The symbol was discreet, but it told them where the funds came from, and so the soldier in the ranks and the man in the street nicknamed the dekadrachm 'A Damarete'.[13]

The Damareteion Master also made at least one die for Leontini, where under Deinomenid rule a coinage was initiated. The tetradrachms were originally struck with the quadriga obverse that became almost synonymous with the coinages of the Deinomenid realm. Beside Syracuse and Leontini, Gela now issued tetradrachms with the same type. The artistic distinction of the Leontini series was achieved after the downfall of the Deinomenid state after 466 BC (figure 163). At

Figure 163 Coin of Leontini, Syracuse Museum, ex Gagliardi collection

this time a lion's head, an appropriate punning type, appears on the obverse. Our example shows the wiry vitality of this vision of youthful god and beast. The lion head owes much to the lion's head water spouts that became popular together with stone simas on Greek temples. The Apollo head might have come from the hand of one of the graphic masters of the red-figure style of vase painting in Athens of the 470s, the Pan Painter for example.

The most remarkable dies of this era of Sicilian coinage are those of the engraver known as the Aetna Master. His title comes from the only other known tetradrachm of Aetna, the unique coin in Brussels struck, like the tetradrachm we have discussed in relation to the Damareteion problem, for Hieron's new city at Catane, which

The reverse presents the god of the mountain, Zeus Aetnaeus. A feathery thunderbolt is held in his left hand and his eagle is perched serenely on a small mountain pine. Zeus is seated on a stool, rather than on a throne, and over it a feline skin has been spread. The stool has been given legs with cutout moldings typical of the best Greek furniture work of the day. The god's right hand grasps what may be a slender, gnarled staff or the top of a growing stalk.

The Aetna tetradrachm was probably struck within a few years after the foundation of Aetna in 474 BC. The second masterpiece of the Aetna Master belongs to the end of the next decade

Figure 164 Coin of Aetna, Brussels, Bibliothèque royale, photograph courtesy of collection Bibliothèque royale

Figure 165 Coin of Naxos, Syracuse Museum, ex Gagliardi collection

was given a new population and renamed Aetna in 474 BC (figure 164). Few coins approach the boldness and strength of the Aetna Master's name piece. The obverse is a satyr's head that almost bursts the tondo of the coin. This is graphic work turned into high relief. The vision of the satyr has little in common with that other Sicilian masterpiece of the subject, the satyr of the terracotta antefixes from Gela, but it is perfectly in tune with Greek painting, and one can find satyrs with the bold simplicity of this head in the work of several of the leading Athenian vase painters of the waning archaic age, the Kleophrades Painter and the Berlin Painter among them. A hallmark of the Aetna Master's style is the precise strands of hair and beard. A less obvious characteristic is his modelling of the neck muscles above the curving cut line of the neck of the bust. Around the head is the inscription, 'Of the Aetneans', and below the head is a beetle, a symbol of good luck taken over by the Greeks from the Egyptians. The satyr is crowned with ivy as befits a companion of Dionysus.

and was created for the Naxians (figure 165). The citizens of Naxos had also been involved in Hieron's reshuffling of populations because, together with the Catanians, they had been deported to Leontini by the tyrant. But after the fall of the Deinomenid tyranny they reclaimed their old city and for the occasion they apparently ordered dies for a tetradrachm from the Aetna Master. The obverse of the coin has Dionysus, but how the god has changed from the archaic head used in the city's first coinage. Dionysus is a distinguished figure of almost Periclean stamp, whose slightly rumpled hairknot behind the head emphasizes the humanity of this conception of the god. His beard, however, is very much the Aetna Master's own, and the question of authorship is settled by the undulating cut line of the neck and the structure of the muscles above it.

On the reverse there is another satyr seated, his legs splayed apart; he is raising a wine cup to his lips. His pose has been rightly compared to the seated groom from the East Pediment of the Temple of Zeus at Olympia, which was completed shortly before 456 BC. This is the graphic version, based more probably on a painting than sculpture. The satyr has all the taut anatomical detail of a Signorelli painting reflecting a paramount interest of artists both in Early Classical Greece and in fifteenth-century Italy. But his head, like those of many satyrs of the day, still owes much to the mask-like concept of the archaic age.

The Naxos tetradrachm of the Aetna Master typifies an era of elegance in the coinages of eastern Sicily. Following the mass coinage, Syracuse began a series of tetradrachms characterized by a sea serpent in the exergue of the

Figure 166 Coin of Syracuse, Syracuse Museum, ex Gagliardi collection

obverse (figure 166). The gallery of the goddesses who accompany the perennial quadriga on the obverses of these coins moves with style and strength through ceaseless small variations on the design. The series of Catane and Leontini are no less distinguished; Catane in particular issued a group of noble heads of Apollo in the third quarter of the fifth century. And the series of bigas at Messina prolonged the old type with charming variations. Coinage of the Greek pattern was also issued by the non-Greek city of Segesta

Figure 167 Coin of Segesta, Syracuse Museum

in western Sicily (figure 167). The distinctive type of the city is a hunting dog. The reverse is the head of a goddess or nymph.

None of these coinages, however, prepares one to expect the flowering of coin design that occurred in the final two decades of the century. At the mint of Syracuse the period of coinage known as the era of the 'Signing Masters' begins with a series of tetradrachms marked with the name Eumenes. It is difficult to date the beginning of the signed series precisely. The Carthaginian invasions of the last decade of the century and Syracusan reprisals of the same years, between 409 and 403, led to the virtual abandonment of a number of Greek cities and to the reduction of others to mere villages, certainly without important silver coinages. There was no recovery until after the peace between Syracuse and the Carthaginians in 387 BC or, as more commonly believed, until the 340s. The Carthaginian invasions thus mark a break in the numismatic history of Sicily. Only Syracuse and Messina, of the major Greek cities, escaped this fate. Hoards containing the last issue of cities such as Naxos and Catane also include Syracusan coins representing almost all of the period of the 'Signing Masters'. We can therefore be sure that the major part of these coins was struck before 404 BC.

The dies marked with Eumenes' name, both obverses and reverses, are hardly more distinguished than those that preceded them. Eumenes' quadrigas, though enlivened by prancing horses, are in some ways less accomplished than the walking quadrigas they replaced. Eumenes' heads, too, run to a frizzy hairstyle that is more animated, but less engaging, than the elegant heads they replace. It is hard to believe that Eumenes was signaled out as an artist of distinction. But the appearance of his name is important, because it opened the door to the signatures of a group of unequalled master engravers. The first of these was Euainetos. His career possibly began at Catane, and he was also to execute dies for Cam-arina. He appears at Syracuse in company with Eumenes, executing an obverse chariot die (figure 168). At one stroke Euainetos transformed Eum-enes' awkwardly animated image into breath-taking verisimilitude. No longer is the charioteer disproportionately tall in respect to the team. Both wheels of the chariot are shown in con-vincing perspective. And the horses leap forward at full speed. Their gait is perhaps wrong, but the raised forehooves and the springing of the team off the ground

Figure 168 Coin of Syracuse, Syracuse Museum, ex Gagliardi collection

line achieve their visual purposes dramatically well. A Victory gently hovers above bearing a wreath and a placard with the name Euainetos.

In Victorian times there would have been no hesitation in awarding the gold medal of art to Euainetos. But even an age that no longer considers academic representationalism the pinnacle of artistic success can still appreciate this conquest of space. Such imitation of the visual field was the end to which Greek art had striven over much of the fifth century and succeeded in achieving even in the small dimensions of coin relief.

Eumenes and Euainetos signed dies differently. Euainetos' signature, like those of the other artists who soon provided dies for Syracuse, is in miniature. Many of these signatures are almost hidden, placed on the goddess' hairband or on the belly of one of the dolphins around her head. On the other hand, Eumenes' inscriptions are unmistakable. In one case his name occupies the exergue space below the quadriga of the obverse.

The issues of the 'Signing Masters' Period were gathered in a die study early in the twentieth century, and this work, as later revised, shows that there are two long die-linked chains among these issues.[14] Beside the die links, the coins of each chain are distinguished by common symbols in the exergue of their quadriga dies.[15] The linked group in which Eumenes and Euainetos appear is distinguished by two dolphins in the exergue of the quadriga die. The second major group is distinguished by a grain ear in the same position. It is a reasonable deduction that the two series are the output of two distinct ateliers. At this time the Syracusan coinage, evidently,

was not produced by a state mint but was struck on contract by independent contractors. The system may have been new with Eumenes, who was authorized or required to mark his coins. He should be seen as the owner of a workshop rather than as an artist. A second contract was soon awarded to the grain ear atelier. It was the owner of this workshop who set out to outshine the work from Eumenes' establishment and for the purpose gathered a cluster of master engravers. Eukleides was one of them and to him is due a double innovation, the substitution of Athene for the frequently non-specific goddess of the tetradrachms, and the execution of the first dies

Figure 169 Coin of Syracuse, Syracuse Museum, ex Gagliardi collection

with a facing head (figure 169). Eumenes' reply to this artistic challenge was to commission dies from Euainetos. Soon Euainetos may have taken over the 'Double Dolphin' contract, while another major artistic personality, Kimon, emerged as the leader of the 'Grain Ear' workshop.

Eukleides' Athene head shows the influence, if only the distant influence, of the Athene Parthenos cult statue by Phidias in the Parthenon at Athens. This gold and ivory vision of the goddess also wore a triple crested helmet, enlivened by colored glass elements playing the part of precious stones, as we know from the debris excavated in the workshop of Phidias' other monumental cult image, the Zeus at Olympia. The florid style of the coin image, the waving plumes and abundant hair also belong to the currents of Athenian art at the end of Phidias' career. Such observations raise the question of the origin of Eukleides and the artists who created this era of artistic eminence in Sicilian medallic art. Athenians had established the red-figured pottery industry of southern Italy in the 440s. Declining Athenian fortunes in the Peloponnesian war sent numerous other artists, including sculptors who were trained on the Parthenon, to find work overseas. But Eukleides signs his name with a Doric genitive. Despite the knowledge of Athenian styles and a passion for Athenian culture, not unlike the love for Athenian poetry that saved the life of more than one Athenian captive capable of reciting Euripides' lyrics when the Athenian army met disaster before Syracuse in 413 BC, there is no reason to hold that any of the master engravers of Syracusan coins was not a Sicilian.

Kimon's Arethusa is the masterpiece of facing images on coins. The goddess of the earlier tetradrachms was indefinite. Only if she were literally associated with the quadriga could one hold, with Erich Boehringer, that she is an Artemis of the Horses whose cult is attested at Syracuse. When grain ears appear in her hair, as they do in some dies of the sea monster group, and in dies of Kimon's contemporaries as well, she is Persephone. But Kimon's goddess is Arethusa, the nymph of the freshwater spring on Ortygia, the island of Syracuse, who, legend told, had been the nymph of a stream in northern Greece flowing toward the Ionian Sea (figure

Figure 170 Coin of Syracuse, Syracuse Museum, ex Pennisi collection

170). Pursued by the river god Acheloos, Arethusa fled beneath the sea until she emerged on Ortygia. The nymph's name is written above her head, just outside the row of dots that makes the border of the die. Kimon's signature is on the hairband just above her forehead. The slight inclination of the nymph's head imparts a graceful and human qaulity to the image. The dolphins are now lost in the flowing locks of hair, that have been compared, unnecessarily I think, to the effect of an underwater scene. Kimon's two Arethusa dies were delicate work and were set in the anvil as obverses to protect them from the damage they might have suffered in the mobile reverse position. The danger is seen in

one of Eukleides' Athene head dies which developed a major crack during use.

One Sicilian city quickly followed the innovations of another, and the facing heads of Apollo done by Herakleides for Catane were the most luxuriant images of this group. There is beauty but also uneasy mystery in these images of a God both master of prophecy and dealer of destruction (figure 171).

Figure 171 Coin of Catane, Syracuse Museum

Of the other artistic personalities active at Syracuse, the most distinctive is possibly Phrygillos. We see one of his long-necked goddesses, wearing the grain ear of Persephone, a poppy from the grain field tangled in it and resting on her forehead, on a die that was used in one of the three strikings of the period done outside the two major ateliers (figure 172). This

Figure 172 Coin of Syracuse, Syracuse Museum, ex Gagliardi collection

issue came from the workshop of Euth . . ., who used the abbreviation of his name together with a Scylla, the monster, part snake, part dog and part woman, who preyed on mariners in western waters and who shows her marine associations through the trident resting on her shoulder and the small fish swimming in front of her. The chariot is driven by Eros, shown as a nude and winged youth. There are cosmic dimensions to Eros as well as his amorous personality, but the exact significance of this specific coin type is not easy to establish.

There are distinguished series of tetradrachms elsewhere in Sicily at this time. The obverse of the coinage of Camarina was a Heracles head dressed in an impressive lion's skin (figure 173).

Figure 173 Coin of Camarina, Syracuse Museum, ex Pennisi collection

The ever-present chariot accompanies it on the reverse. The charioteer is Athene, the principal goddess of Camarina. At Selinus there are also chariots, a biga, the two-horse chariot, carrying Apollo, identified by his bow, and his sister Artemis (figure 174). On the reverse we find

Figure 174 Coin of Selinus, Syracuse Museum

a view of a youthful god sacrificing in a sanctuary. He is pouring a liquid offering over an altar on which a fire has already been kindled. There is a cock, a favorite sacrificial victim, in front of the altar. At some distance away we see the statue of a charging bull on a pedestal. The young god holds a tree branch (a normal sign of purification) and in the field there is a selinon leaf. The young god is probably the spirit of the river Selinus, and as at Gela, the bull is also an image of the river.

At the end of the 'Signing Masters' Period the coinage of Syracuse was still in the hands of the two major ateliers, but these are dominated almost completely by Euainetos and Kimon. This juncture is the beginning of the grand series of Syracusan dekadrachms signed by these two masters. The types are so well known that they are generally identified by the name of their respective authors, the 'Kimon type' and the 'Euainetos type' (figures 175 and 176). The reverses are almost identical, the familiar quadriga crowned by Victory. In the exergue there is a a full suit of armor, helmet, breastplate and greaves, occasionally accompanied by the legend 'athla', 'prizes'. It was once thought that the 'prizes' were given at games celebrating the defeat of the Athenian invasion of 415–413 BC. But these dekadrachms were issued over an extended period of time, the later ones repeating the Euainetos type but probably not from dies made by the master. They must belong, at least in part, to the period of Dionysius I, tyrant of Syracuse from 405 to 367. Dionysius came to power as Greek Sicily was crumbling before the onslaught of Carthage. He saved Syracuse, though

Figure 175 Coin of Syracuse (dekadrachm of the Kimonian type), Syracuse Museum, ex Gagliardi collection

Figure 176 Coin of Syracuse (dekadrachm of the Euainetos type), Syracuse Museum, ex Gagliardi collection

at the price of sacrificing the other Greek cities, and at the high-water mark of his first counter-offensive in 397 BC, following the successful siege of the Carthaginian island city of Motya, he had practically succeeded in driving the Carthaginians from the island. The peace of 387 BC, however, essentially divided the island between the two powers. Dionysius was a great employer of mercenaries and so, once more, there is reason to associate the dekadrachm and mercenary pay. For the mercenaries the prize shown in the exergue, a new fighting kit, would have been only too welcome.

The two reverse types of Kimon's and Euainetos' dekadrachms are the most familiar images from the repertoire of Sicilian coinage. The Euainetos type (figure 176) may depict another Syracusan goddess, the nymph Cyane, if the stalks intertwined in her hair are those of water plants, as has been recently suggested.[16] Kimon's goddess is radiant with a hairnet that we can imagine made of gold thread. The influence of these coins was enormous. Down to the third century Euainetos's Cyane was being

recalled by new coin types and was being used by silversmiths as a model for the centerpieces of silver cups, and by potters for modest imitations of the same in black glazed wares.

Much as the Syracusan dekadrachms have excited admiration and imitation, they are no more splendid than another dekadrachm whose issue was cut short when the Carthaginian invaders took Acragas in 406 (figure 177). Only seven specimens of this coin exist today. The reverse proves that the traditional eagle type of the city was intended as a omen because in this version it illustrates precisely the omen given to the Greek host waiting for a favorable wind for Troy, according to the famous passage of the *Agamemnon* of Aeschylus (lines 114 ff.): two eagles devouring a pregnant hare. The pair of eagles, one screaming triumphantly, the other spreading his wings as he perches on the prey, is a coin design with few equals. The rocky ground is indicated below the hare, and to the right a cicada adds another hint of good omen. On the obverse of the same coin the sun god drives his plunging team across the heavens. An

Figure 177 Coin of Acragas Syracuse Museum, ex Pennisi collection

eagle clutching a serpent, the familiar Agrigentine type, flies above, and the crab lies earthbound below. Learned commentators on the Agrigentine tetradrachm frequently cite the victory of one Exainetos of Acragas in the quadriga race at Olympia in 412 BC as the event commemorated by this coin. Although Exainetos received a splendid welcome home, one may wonder why the city would have struck a dekadrachm for this one Olympic victor. Mercenary pay and the tragic threat of the Carthaginian invasion is a somber motive for such a radiant coin, but probably closer to the truth.

The difficult years of the end of the fifth century also brought coinage in gold. A gold coinage in a Greek city is an unmistakable sign of financial crisis, as when the Athenians were forced to turn to their gold reserves (which in part formed the drapery of the great cult statue of Athene Parthenos) at the end of the Peloponnesian War. The Sicilian gold issues are generally so rare as to be almost ephemeral but again, as with the extended issues of dekadrachms, one senses a change in the character of Syracusan money, because there are also large issues of gold from the workshops of Kimon and Euainetos (figure 178). These fifty- and one-hundred-litra

Figure 178 Coin of Syracuse, American Numismatic Society, New York, photograph courtesy of ANS

pieces must also have been issued under the tyranny of Dionysius I and played a part in a completely new concept of money and state finance prefiguring the monarchies of the Hellenistic Age that arose following the conquests of Alexander the Great. Part of the scheme of finance was the use of bronze coinage, which was an invention of the Sicilian Greeks.

The first bronze coins look more like weights than coins. They are cast and were made at Acragas and Selinus, probably around the middle of the fifth century, though the date is conjectural (figure 179). The Selinus pieces show a rough approximation of the selinon leaf and the Agrigentine pieces bear an eagle and crab. But

Figure 179 Coins of Selinus, Syracuse Museum

at Acragas the coins are lozenge-shaped, and the small denominations at Selinus are roughly triangular. These bronzes carry dots of value in a recognizable duodecimal system, reinforced at Selinus by a variety of types accompanying the selinon leaf.

The first bronzes that imitate silver fractions were made at Syracuse. Once again the date is uncertain. The types are a female head obverse, and the polyp for the reverse, accompanied by marks of value in the form of pellets. These coins repeat the types previously used for the litra (one-fifth drachm) in silver, and they were certainly intended as fractions of the litra, again on a twelve-part scale. If a group of these fractions with the value of a litra (say four one-quarter pieces) were weighed, they would together be only about 16 gm of bronze. Since silver was about 120 times as valuable as bronze, the true weight corresponding to a litra of silver (0.85 gm) would be slightly more than 100 gm The Syracusan coins were definitely overvalued by a factor of about six.

The overvalued coin could not have existed in the Greek world without the revolution in Greek thought of the fifth century known as the sophistic movement. Sophism was born in the law courts of Sicily after the fall of the Deinomenid Empire when the claims for restitution on the part of returning exiled citizens met the assertion of rights by the new settlers whose grants had been made by Gelon and Hieron. The sophist argued these cases by defining words like justice to the advantage of his clients. Meaning, it now became clear, was not an inherent property of words but the result of definition, and to paraphrase a remark of Protagoras, the sophist who became the intimate of Pericles, 'Things are to me as they appear to me, and things are to you as they appear to you.' It is true that there had been an element of the conventional in Greek coinage since the first Ionian banker put his seal on a lump of electrum, but without the sophistic revolution no Greek would have been prepared to accept 16 gm of bronze as the equivalent of a litra of silver. The 16 gm of bronze was now a litra because it was officially defined as such.

It was Dionysius I who extended the use of overvalued bronze. One of the commonest series of Syracusan bronze coins is composed of two denominations. The larger is a heavy bronze coin that approaches the limits practical for striking

But what was their value? Under the pressure of the Carthaginian danger after 409, Syracuse halved the fictitious bronze litra from about 16 to about 8 gm. So much is clear from the bronze series containing dies signed by some of the 'Signing Masters' that must come between the first 'polyp' bronzes and the 'heavy' Athene head series. If the fictitious bronze litra represented by these coins was 8 gm, a fictitious bronze drachm would have been five times that weight or 40 gm. This drachm is the Athene head/star and dolphins coin; the Athene head/hippocamp

Figure 180 Coin of Syracuse, Syracuse Museum

(figure 180). The coin weighs 40 gm or more. The obverse has a helmeted head of Athene modeled on the Athene head of the staters (didrachms) of Corinth. The reverse has two dolphins flanking a star. The smaller denomination has the same obverse head and on the reverse a hippocamp (a sea monster with the forepart of a winged horse). The smaller coin seems to be one-fifth of the larger piece. The older manuals of numismatics attributed these coins to the period of Dionysius I, but in 1927 E. Gabrici argued that these coins and those of other, generally inland Sicilian towns which are similar and frequently overstruck on the Athene/ Star and Dolphin bronzes all belong to the period of redevelopment in Sicily which followed the arrival of Timoleon from Corinth in 344 BC, the suppression of a new generation of tyrants in the island, a new defeat of the Carthaginians and the repopulating of the old Greek and inland cities.[17] In recent excavations, however, the hippocamp bronzes have been found at Naxos in strata belonging to the fall of the city in 405 and at Motya in a context of the siege of 397. There can be no question now that these coins are the money of Dionysius I.

of 8 gm would be a fictitious bronze litra. The very abundance of these coins shows that they were issued over a long period of time, and it is therefore likely that they were minted from 405 at least until the end of the reign of Dionysius I in 367 BC.

The Athene head of these coins, as already noted, was copied from the silver staters of Corinth. The Corinthian stater was no stranger in Sicily. In fact, the Corinthian stater is by far the commonest ancient silver coin in Sicilian hoards. One hoard alone, discovered in the eighteenth century, contained 7,400 Corinthian staters, which from the winged horse of their obverse were known as 'pegasi'. Not all were direct products of the Corinthian mint. Many come from the Corinthian colonies in northwest Greece, the area of Acarnania, Epirus and the nearby islands, which minted coins distinguishable from those of the mother city only by symbol or legend. Most numismatists and historians attribute the phenomenal influx of Corinthian coinage to the period of Timoleon's revival of Greek Sicily in the 340s and after (see Appendix). And in fact many of these 'pegasi' are from the later fourth century. But in the hoards there is a good representation of 'pegasi' minted before 350 BC. They might have arrived with the later issues, or they may have circulated during the time of Dionysius I. The latter hypothesis is attractive for several reasons. First, the noble series of Syracusan tetradrachms runs out soon after the types represented in the hoards of about 405 BC. Dionysius clearly put an end to coining tetradrachms. The place of the major silver denomination could have been filled by nothing else than the Corinthian staters. Second, Dionysius' bronze drachm and litra imitate the Corinthian Athene heads and so may well have been intended to circulate alongside of them.

Dionysius' coinage thus appears to have worked as follows: gold and silver dekadrachms to meet major state expenses, especially the pay of the mercenaries, Corinthian staters providing the largest freely circulating silver coin, and bronze issues for the drachm and smaller fractions.

One may ask with some justification how the tyrant could count on a ready supply of Corinthian coins. The answer is evident. Sicilian coinage could never have existed without coins from the Greek motherland to melt down or overstrike. Dionysius simply authorized the circulation of some of this foreign coinage as official Syracusan money. It wasn't Syracusan, but for a sophist financier it was the definition that counted; and that could be altered to suit one's convenience.

Dionysius' fiscal imagination did not stop with adopting Corinthian coins for Syracuse. Something in the early fourth century was leading to the hoarding of the old Syracusan tetradrachms and the tetradrachms which were still being minted in the Carthaginian zone of Sicily but found their way into the Syracusan part of the island. That something, I believe, was another financial manipulation of Dionysius. According to this theory the tyrant decreed that the Corinthian stater weighing 8.5 gm was a tetradrachm (which should have weighed 17.6 gm). He simply substituted the Corinthian coin for the old Syracusan tetradrachm, whose issue he suspended. An anecdote preserved in the pseudo-Aristotelian *Economicus* says that Dionysius doubled the value of coinage by fiat, taking loans at the old standard and paying back the same coins as if they were worth twice as much.[18] In fact, just as the anecdote recorded it, the tyrant effectively doubled the value of coins by fiat. A maneuver of the sort immediately drove the existing tetradrachms into hiding, while the overvalued Corinthian coins remained in circulation.[19]

Naturally this revaluation would have affected all the denominations of the Syracusan monetary system. Therefore during most of the reign the bronze drachm would have been a didrachm and the bronze litra would have become a dilitron.

The Sicilian tetradrachm was far from dead, however. The Carthaginians of Panormus (Palermo), Solus, Eryx, the city known to them as Rsmlqrt and the mint signing its work 'The Camp' ('mchnt' or variants of this and 'The People of the Camp', 'shm mchnt'), produced an ample coinage not only of tetradrachm weight but for the most part with types copied directly from Greek issues and intended for use by Greeks, principally Greek mercenaries engaged by the Carthaginians.[20] So we find it on an issue

Figure 181 Siculo-Punic coin, Syracuse Museum

which reproduces the types of Syracuse but with a Punic legend in the exergue of the reverse (figure 181). The die cutting of the Siculo-Punic issues, as they are called, is often superb but also reveals occasions when the work was entrusted to engravers who were not at home with the style of the prototypes. The coinage has moments of originality, as for example the splendid tetra-

Figure 182 Siculo-Punic coin, Syracuse Museum

drachms presenting a female head wearing an oriental tiara accompanied on its reverse by a prowling lion before a palm tree (figure 182). The female head has been identified romantically as Dido, the Phoenician Queen who fled to the west and founded Carthage in the ninth century. Other commentators view the head as a variation on the supreme Carthaginian goddess Tanit. More recently, identification has been proposed with Astarte-Aphrodite of Eryx, the ancient Elymnian divinity seen in Phoenician garb as protectress of the Carthaginian province of Sicily. The palm, found regularly on Carthaginian issues, had a meaning for the Greeks whose word for the tree was 'phoinix', the same as 'Phoenician'. And on such coins as this the lion may be thought of as maintaining his oriental connotations of majesty and power.

At Syracuse the years between the death of Dionysius I in 367 BC and the coming of the Corinthian Timoleon in 344 are politically confused and difficult to see clearly in the numismatic

Figure 183 Coin of Syracuse, Syracuse Museum

record. The 'pegasi' minted at Syracuse with the Syracusan legend may belong to these years (figure 183), and there is a notable series of bronze coins. A leading type is the head of Zeus matched, in this case, with a thunderbolt and

eagle on the reverse (figure 184). Zeus had a special meaning for the Syracusans as Zeus the Liberator, to whom the citizens had dedicated a famous statue after the overthrow of the Deinomenid dynasty. The type of the free horse, also prominent in this issue, is another slogan type with the same significance. The problem is that it is difficult to distinguish the propaganda of one contending faction from that of the other. Except for Dionysius II, who ruled briefly after his father's death, all the contenders would have flown the banner of 'liberty'.

The cities of the interior now regained their independence and celebrated it by issuing their own bronze coinages, liberally overstruck on the heavy bronze of Dionysius.

Order returns to our picture of Sicilian numismatics only after 320, when a new strong man emerged at Syracuse. His name was Agathocles and his reign over Syracuse and leadership of Greek Sicily lasted until 289. Agathocles is thus the first Sicilian monarch of the Hellenistic Age, the beginning of which is generally placed at the death of Alexander the Great in 323 BC. Agathocles was very much a Hellenistic king. He contracted marriage alliances with the Ptolemies of Egypt and with Pyrrhus of Epirus. And for the first time in the history of the Carthaginian wars he carried the Greek attack into Africa, narrowly failing to capture Carthage itself.

In 304, together with the successors who had carved up Alexander's empire, Agathocles took the title 'king'. One series of his silver tetradrachms has a reverse type also used by the Seleucids, whose dominions covered much of the Near East. It is a figure of Victory erecting a military trophy. Seleucus used his own portrait as the obverse type with this image. But Agathocles preferred a Sicilian type of wide appeal to Greeks

Figure 184 Coin of Syracuse, Syracuse Museum

Figure 185 Coin of Agathocles, Syracuse Museum

and non-Greek alike, the head of Kore (Persephone) plainly labelled on the die (figure 185). Agathocles' somewhat conservative outlook is also shown in his series of tetradrachms which revive the hallowed Syracusan type of female head and quadriga, as well as by his extensive issues of electrum, we may assume for paying mercenaries, with the head of Apollo accompanied on the reverse by the Delphic tripod.

For two years, 278–276, Sicily became a battleground for the adventurous Epirote king Pyrrhus. Having fought brilliant battles against the Romans at Heraclea and Asculum on behalf of the south Italian Greeks, Pyrrhus, like Hannibal after him, was faced with a stalemate in Italy. Hoping for decisive victories and a western kingdom, Pyrrhus came to face the Carthaginians in Sicily, but abandoned this enterprise too. The majority of his coins seem to have been struck in Sicily, from metal collected from the Sicilian Greeks. His most common silver issue picks up Agathocles' head of Kore and unites it with a fighting Athene of archaistic style that was used

Figure 187 Coin of Pyrrhus, Syracuse Museum

Syracuse by 269 and died in 215) was a period of cultural brilliance. His coinage was both conventional and modestly personal. The major silver series bore the portrait of his queen, Philistis, modeled on the portraits of the Ptolemaic queens in Egypt. With her there was shown a quadriga

Figure 188 Coin of Philistis, Syracuse Museum

Figure 186 Coin of Pyrrhus, Syracuse Museum

by other monarchs, both the Macedonian royal house and those transplanted Macedonians in Egypt, the Ptolemies (figure 186). Pyrrhus's gold is one of the masterpieces of Hellenistic coinage. It too was probably struck at Syracuse, and the memory of Agathocles, at one time Pyrrhus' father-in-law, is once again present. We find a Victory and a trophy, but now the Victory sweeps forward carrying the trophy on her shoulder (figure 187). The head of Athene, not unlike the Athene heads of the gold coinage of Alexander the Great, serves as the obverse type.

Eastern Sicily became a stable Hellenistic kingdom under Hieron II of Syracuse. Hieron allied himself to the Romans during the first Punic War (264–241) and by doing so gained a kingdom encompassing southeastern Sicily. His long rule (he was already in control of

driven by Victory, but moving quietly at a walking pace (figure 188). Hieron's own portrait appeared on the bronze.

The Second Punic War beginning in 218 and ending in Sicily in 211 when the Romans sacked Syracuse, which had imprudently joined Carthage after Hieron's death, marks the end of independent Greek Sicily. The war in Sicily was not without numismatic importance. The Roman denarius was put into circulation during the war, and the date of the first denarius was established with certainty only as a result of discoveries in the stratified contexts in the excavations at Morgantina, the inland city which threw off Roman control and was recaptured on two occasions during the war. The coinage of Hieron's grandson, Hieronymus, who reigned for a short thirteen months in 215–214, is a mine of information concerning the organization of the production of Syracusan coinage in the third century.

Following the war there were still local bronze coinages, of increasingly irregular character and indifferent artistic quality. But these come to an end after the reign of the first Roman emperor, Augustus.

Appendix Numismatic evidence and the Timoleontic recovery of Sicily in the fourth century BC

The history of Sicily in the fourth century BC seems studded with villains. The most prominent are Dionysius I and Agathocles, the tyrants of Syracuse of the first half and of the closing years of the century respectively. But a score of less well-known figures at Syracuse and among the tyrants who exercised control of the large majority of the Sicilian cities of the day seem hardly less black of heart. This image, it is easy to see, is due less to the sins of the Sicilian tyrants and demagogues than to the writing of history as personal vendetta, a genre in which Greek authors of the time excelled.

One historical figure of fourth-century Sicily alone remained untainted by such attacks. This was the Corinthian Timoleon, leader of the expedition sent by his city to Sicily in 345 in answer to an appeal from Syracuse for help against Dionysius II, son of the old tyrant, who after losing control of the city had regained his position. Successful at Syracuse, Timoleon moved against the tyrants of other cities, and finally, when the Carthaginians joined the tyrants against him in 341, won a stunning victory over their numerically superior army. Timoleon established a new constitution at Syracuse and extended his reforms to the cities of Greek Sicily. New colonists recruited from the motherland restored the shrinking Greek population and brought an era of prosperity to the island.

The excavations at Gela and at sites in the Salso Valley in the 1950s seem to give vivid archaeological illustration of the effects of the Timoleontic revival. At Gela private houses on the acropolis encroached on the old sanctuaries

and a series of terraces were levelled to make room for additional living space. At the same time whole new quarters grew up at the western end of the city. In the interior a site, such as Monte Navone near Piazza Armerina, which does not manifest a phase of well-being at this time is the exception. Other coastal cities reflect the new vigor; Camarina for example, which also received a draft of Timoleontic colonists, expanded in much the same fashion as Gela. Farmhouses of the period have been identified in the area of Gela (Manfria and Butera) and in the country near Camarina. The establishment at Manfria was also the site of a flourishing potter's shop producing vases decorated in the red-figure style imitating Attic and south Italian prototypes.[21]

There is, however, a flaw in the reasoning behind this reconstruction of the Timoleontic revival. The most eloquent evidence pointing to a date in the third quarter of the fourth century for the strata of the 'reconstruction' period at Gela and for the revival of the interior sites was that of coins, especially the heavy Syracusan bronze (obverse, head of Athene, reverse, star with dolphins and the fractional piece obverse, head of Athene, reverse, sea horse). The accepted dating of these coins in the 1950s and 1960s was to the Timoleontic period. But as we have seen above, new excavational evidence at Motya and Naxos makes it clear that these are issues of the time of Dionysius I in the first half of the fourth century. This is not to say that this abundant coinage did not remain in circulation after Dionysius' death in 367. Indeed much of the pottery from the excavations in Gela suggests independently dates in the second half of the fourth century, although pottery, especially utilitarian pottery, is often not precisely dated. The cautionary point should be made, however, that the revival of Sicily under Timoleon was less the resuscitation of deserted towns and recovery of a deserted landscape than the strengthening of Greek Sicily.

5

LATER GREEK, PUNIC AND ROMAN SICILY

Military architecture

The last decade of the fifth century saw a revolution in siege warfare in Sicily. In 415-413 BC Athens had launched a grand expedition to Sicily. The successes of the Athenian army and navy in the north and center of the island were conspicuous but the enterprise failed in its main objective, the capture of Syracuse. In Thucydides' account of the siege and the struggle that slowly broke the Athenian hold on the besieged city and ended in the destruction of the Athenian army, what is striking is the undeveloped state of siegecraft. The attackers establish their lines around their objective and trust to starvation or treachery to achieve their ends. The besieged spend their efforts in outworks calculated to break the encirclement. The action consists mainly of pitched battles around the outworks or engagements between the opposing fleets in the Great Harbor. Never is there a mention of a siege tower being advanced to the walls by the attackers, never a mention of rock- or dart-throwing artillery (catapults or ballistas).

All this changed in 409, when the Carthaginian general Hannibal (namesake of Rome's fearful antagonist of two centuries later) disembarked in Sicily and advanced on Selinus. Hannibal brought siege engines and artillery with him. He took Selinus by assault, and moved on to overcome Acragas, Himera, Gela and Camarina. Five of the greatest Greek cities of Sicily lay ruined and almost deserted. Syracuse survived, and under the tyrant thrown up in the wake of the danger, Dionysius I, there began a furious campaign of work on the fortifications of the city and the production of every kind of armament. We shall come back to Dionysius' fortifications at Syracuse later. First let us follow

him on the counter-attack in which he swept across the island in 397. Dionysius was aided by the plague at Carthage. Greek and Sicel both rose joyfully to join him. The Syracusans and their allies rolled on toward the last Carthaginian stronghold, Motya.

Motya is an island situated in a shallow bay on the western edge of Sicily. In more recent times the island was the property of the Whitakers of Palermo, an English family whose fortune was based on the trade in Marsala wine. Joseph I.S. Whitaker began excavations there a century ago, and in more recent years work has been pursued by the Sicilian authorities in collaboration with university archaeologists both Italian and English. Motya was never again a city after its capture by Dionysius I in 397. The Carthaginians built a new city at Lilybaeum, the modern Marsala. Because of its securely dated destruction, Motya is a notable archaeological site, and it is even more notable for the drama of its last days.

Motya was connected to the mainland across the shallow lagoon by a causeway which is still visible in air photographs. On the approach of the Greek army the defenders opened a breach in the causeway. The interruption was easily repaired however, and having thwarted reinforcement efforts by sea, the Greeks moved against the walls, which ringed the entire island.

The excavators have been able to give us a precise notion of the defenses protecting the city (figure 189). The Greeks were faced with a city wall the earliest phases of which went back to the seventh century. Over two hundred years of use, sections had been gradually rebuilt as necessary. There were towers projecting from the wall at least by the early sixth century. The structure was sun-dried mud brick and rubble walling above a socle of boulders. The total

Figure 189 Motya, city wall, after B. Ennison in *Motya I*

height of the wall is not known, but Dionysius overtopped the wall with siege towers as high as a six-story building. The reconstruction made by the most recent English excavators suggests a wall approximately half that height. It was a stout wall, as much as 6 meters (19 ft 8 in) thick in its final phase. Although protected by towers, the gates were not recessed or otherwise strengthened. One gate was a water gate for warships leading into a small artificial basin or cothon, more like a submarine pen than a harbor.

Such a defense was no match for the armament of Dionysius and his men. The siege towers were placed on shallow-draft vessels. The catapults mounted on them drove the defenders from the parapet, and the battering rams broke down the defenses. Bitter fighting continued street by street, the defenders protecting themselves by barricades while their wives and children pelted the attackers from nearby roofs. But there was no hope, and the Greeks set about matching the outrages their people had suffered from Hannibal. To climax his victory Dionysius crucified the Greek mercenaries whom he captured among the defenders.

The walls of Megara Hyblaea before 480 BC are an example of the best Greek defense works of the archaic age. The wall, 2.8 meters (9 ft 2 in) thick on the average, was built with an inner and outer facing. The outer facing is composed of dressed, although not perfectly rectangular, blocks and was given an inward batter. The fill between the faces was rubble. Round towers projected from the wall at irregular intervals. One gateway is known, and this was set back at the end of an alley opening obliquely from the line of the defenses. To the protection thus afforded the gate was added a tower beside the entrance to the alley. The fortification was preceded by a ditch.

Without exception, the Greek and Hellenized towns of the interior were sited on hilltops, often with very steep slopes. The common form of defensive wall consisted of a roughly built outer wall behind which an earth fill was mounded up, a type of construction commonly referred to by its Latin name, 'agger'. But defenses with two curtain walls and a rubble fill are also found, especially on more level terrain. The walls at Sabucina have round towers like those of Megara Hyblaea, and at Vassalaggi the wall facing the gentlest approach to the town was strengthened with a line of rectangular towers. In several cases, notably at Monte Desusino and at Monte Bubbonia, these walls remained in use into the fourth century, when their gates were provided with flanking towers. Occasionally dressed masonry is encountered, for example in the walls of Monte Saraceno. One Sicel site in the region of Mt Aetna, the town at modern Mendolito (near Adrano), was protected by walls built of lava boulders. The gate of the town, over which an inscription in the Sicel language was displayed, was flanked by towers in the Greek manner. Lava boulders also were used in the walls of the Greek colony of Naxos, where the walls of the sixth century have been uncovered for a length of over 200 meters (656 ft).

The best preserved of such fortifications are to be seen surrounding the town at Mt Adranone (Sambuca di Sicilia) northwest of Acragas (figure 190). The circuit of the walls can be followed for some 700 meters (approximately half a mile). The full circuit would have been 5 kilometers (over 3 miles). They are built of roughly dressed stone. The original circuit was built in the sixth to fifth centuries. It was repaired at a later date and much rebuilt at the time of the first Punic War in the third century when a bastion and outwork were added on the side of easiest approach. There are occasional bulges along its line

tween them where a gate was situated. There are two lines of fortification on the hillside. The earlier, and largely destroyed wall, is possibly to be dated to the sixth century. Slightly uphill from it is the circuit of the fifth century built of handsome ashlar masonry.

The walls of Camarina of the sixth and fifth centuries are also preserved for a considerable distance along the eastern side of the city. The construction is rubble interspersed with sections in squared blocks. The degree to which this wall preserves its original appearance is uncertain because the fortifications were pulled down, at least in part, by the Carthaginians after taking the city in 405 and were hastily rebuilt, some sections in mud brick, later in the fourth century. On the west side of the circuit toward the harbor a tower was discovered, its upper portions also in mud brick, containing a supply of barley. This

Figure 190 Monte Adranone, city wall

that served as towers. Today at some points the wall is preserved to a height of 6 meters (19 ft 8 in). Seen from the approaches to the town, it remains much as it must have appeared to friend and foe in antiquity.

Little is known of Leontini, Syracuse's neighbor to the north. The walls of Leontini, however, have been exposed, skirting the flank of one of the two hills on which the ancient city stood and crossing the head of the narrow valley be-

evidence suggests the use of irrigation in the marshes which flanked Camarina on the west.

Mud brick construction is also found in the walls of Heraclea Minoa, the city situated at the mouth of the Belice River between Selinus and Acragas. The walls were strengthened by towers. The first period of construction, of the fifth century, was in sedimentary stone. In the fourth century mud brick superstructure was employed. The full circuit of the walls is 6 kilometers (3.7

miles) long. In the second century a hastily built wall was constructed around a small part of the original city.

One of the most remarkably preserved Greek fortifications known is the wall of Capo Soprano at Gela (figure 191). This structure is mud brick (strengthened in part with fired brick) seated on a lower section in stone carefully worked with recessed edges around the blocks. It comprises the salient of the western end of the fortifications of the city in the fourth century. The date of its building, in the third quarter of the century, is given by three votive deposits, consisting each of a small silver coin, a 'pyxis' (in this case a two-handled container with lid), and in two cases a clay lamp as well. The votive deposits were found along the outside of the wall below the level of its foundation footing and under the layer of stone chips from the dressing of its stonework.

The stonework of the wall is 3.4 meters (11 ft 2 in) high (lower on the interior). The original mud brick added another 2 meters (6 ft 8 in) of height (not counting the merlons providing the archery openings: the parapet of the wall was waist high, but the merlons raised it as much again). As the sand encroached on the foundations the mud brick top of the walls was raised twice, resulting in a total height of 8.25 meters (27 ft). But the sand moved higher and at some time in the first half of the third century the walls disappeared from view. It was the bombardment during the Allied landings at Gela in 1943 that first revealed this uniquely preserved example of ancient mud brick fortification.

The walls of Capo Soprano can be followed for over 300 meters (almost 1,000 ft). There is one postern gate, which was bricked up, evidently at some time when the town was under attack. The closing of the postern and the initial height-

Figure 191 Gela, Capo Soprano, city wall

The walls at Capo Soprano were visible for no more than a century after their construction. Sand from the shifting dunes which form this end of the long hill of Gela began mounding up against the wall soon after its construction.

ening of the wall have been associated with the defense of Gela against the Carthaginians made by the Syracusan tyrant Agathocles at the end of the fourth century. The original construction is attributed to the resettlement of the city after the reestablishment of the democracy at Syracuse by the Corinthian Timoleon in the 440s and the successes of the same leader against the Carthaginians. There is a small tower beside the postern, and another at the southwest corner of the circuit, where two sections of construction come together. Toward the end of their useful life an outwork was made where the wall comes to an end at the southeast.

Mud brick construction was economical, especially on a site like Gela where stone could not be quarried on the spot. It also absorbed the impact of the stone missiles hurled by ballistas better than stone. The builders of the Capo Soprano defenses realized that siege towers could not easily be rolled forward over the sandy ground, and this circumstance may explain why the Gela walls were not protected by a regular system of towers. The same consideration was probably responsible for the simple circuits which were built, as at Tyndaris, an impressive circuit

The new state of siege warfare is visible in the two most elaborate fortresses of Greek Sicily, the acropolis of Selinus and the Castle Euryalos of Syracuse. The dates of the successive phases of both of these defense works have long been a matter of discussion, and, therefore, it will be best to inspect the remains of each of the sites without regard to chronology.

The original fortification of the Euryalos on the high ground north of Syracuse (the Epipolai) was the work of Dionysius I (figure 192). The narrowest point of the ridge, 3 kilometers (1.8 miles) beyond the city, where the easiest access to the plateau could be had from the hills further north and west, was a weak point where the greatest defensive efforts had to be concentrated. The entire plateau was enclosed with a wall, and the Euryalos salient, where there was a narrow level approach, was turned into an independent fortress. Its two courtyards are walled off from the interior of the circuit. At the furthest edge

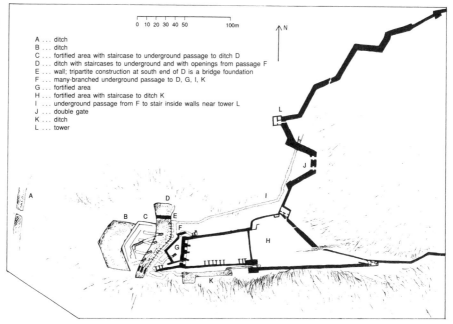

Figure 192
Syracuse, Euryalus fortification

A ... ditch
B ... ditch
C ... fortified area with staircase to underground passage to ditch D
D ... ditch with staircases to underground and with openings from passage F
E ... wall; tripartite construction at south end of D is a bridge foundation
F ... many-branched underground passage to D, G, I, K
G ... fortified area
H ... fortified area with staircase to ditch K
I ... underground passage from F to stair inside walls near tower L
J ... double gate
K ... ditch
L ... tower

0 10 20 30 40 50   100m

N

as yet unstudied, during the fourth century where steep ground impeded the use of towers by the enemy. Certainly, after the overwhelming victories of Hannibal and Dionysius I, no city could trust a simple fortification wall where the ground gave an easy approach.

there were five mighty towers, which originally supported heavy stone-throwing artillery. The ballista towers are preceded by an angular outwork that reaches to the edge of the first of three moats cut across the level approach. This moat, measuring 15.6 meters (51 ft 2 in) across at its widest point, 9 meters (29 ft 6 in) deep and some 80 meters (262 ft) long, is one of the world's most impressive pieces of defensive quarrying. The moat was never completely cut through the level approach to the fortress. It remained closed on the west. On the east it opened on to the sloping ground of the hillside but was then closed by a transverse wall inside its mouth. From the bottom of the moat below the artillery battery a series of passages open into an underground corridor which runs parallel to the moat. Three stairways lead up to inside and just outside the outwork above, while long communication passages connect the passage with another dry moat along the west side of the fortress and the gate into the Epipolai below the fortress to the east. This was a double gateway at the base of a funnel-shaped recess in the walls. In front of it three separate outworks were built at various times.

The outwork above the dry moat was extended up to its edge on the west side by a construction carrying a walkway, which then continued over

the moat on a bridge to reach a second, but smaller artillery emplacement beyond. Since the inner pier of the bridge blocked one of the doorways to the hidden corridor behind the moat, it is clear that this is an addition to the original scheme. Stairways cut through the rock from this outer bastion gave access from it to the dry moat.

A second dry moat was placed in front of the smaller artillery battery. It remained in an unfinished state, as is shown by the bank of rock remaining unremoved in one corner of the moat. Nevertheless, it may never have been intended to bisect the level approach to the fortress serving, however, as a formidable obstacle to any siege engine. Finally, before the Euryalos was abandoned forever, a third moat was begun still farther to the north.

The fortifications at the north end of the acropolis of Selinus, representing a time when most of the pre-409 city was abandoned, have much in common with the Castle Euryalos (figure 193). They too protect against an advance

Figure 193
Selinus, acropolis
fortification

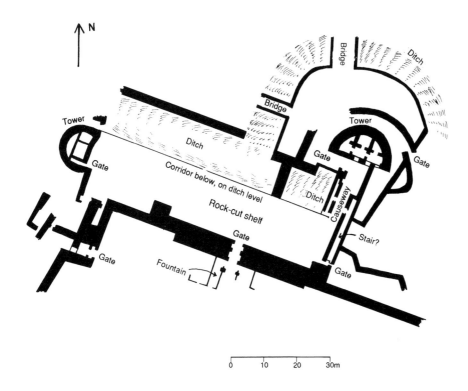

along the level ground immediately beyond. Again there is a dry moat and an outwork provided with a tower for an artillery battery. There is a causeway leading to the battery, which is also protected by a ditch beyond its apron. Between the moat and the circuit walls of the city there is a wide terrace, which has been cut down in the bedrock. One end is protected by a round tower; at the other end beyond the causeway there is a meandering outwork below the main circuit wall. Alongside the moat and below the terrace there is a corridor cut in the rock with openings on to the moat.

Both the Castle Euryalos and the northern fortifications of the acropolis of Selinus have one purpose: to keep siege towers away from the circuit walls. This is the purpose of both the artillery and the deep dry moats. The underground passages opening off the moats were possibly intended for sallies of the defenders under the protection of the walls and outworks, but more probably they were installed to allow the defenders to remove the rubble which the attackers would dump in the moat in an attempt to fill it up. Both Selinus and Syracuse have the artillery batteries, dry moat (and concealed corridors) and outworks. At Syracuse, however, the main battery is on a loftier position and the dry moat has been doubled, and was being tripled at the end of the life of the fortifications.

Dionysius I's haste to throw fortifications up at the Euryalos is recorded by Diodorus Siculus. In twenty days the tyrant succeeded, with the help of all available manpower, in readying a line of defenses. Very little, if anything, of Dionysius' fortification can be identified in the existing defenses at the Euryalos. The development of the defenses may have followed the sequence proposed by Frederick E. Winter.[1] In this reconstruction the gateway to the east of the fortress belongs to the third quarter of the fourth century, as does the inner dry moat and associated tunnels, save the long tunnel leading to the gateway which was installed at a later time. The five great ballista towers could belong to the end of the fourth century or the following century. It was not until the later third century or even the Second Punic War that the small outer battery and second moat were made. At the same time the long tunnel from the first moat to the gateway was installed and the wall closing the eastern end of the inner moat was erected.

At Selinus much of the fortification circuit belongs to the fifth century. Parts belong to the sixth century. The most impressive of these early walls is the stepped wall below the temenos of Temple C overlooking what was the eastern harbor of Selinus. Recent and largely unpublished researches are reported to indicate that the fortress at the north end of the acropolis originated with the Syracusan Hermocrates who attempted to revive Selinus after the Carthaginian sack of 409.[2] Clearly the Selinuntine fortress and the defenses of the Euryalos are closely related, the Syracusan castle representing only a more elaborate version of the other. Therefore, the publication of the results of the work at Selinus may cause a revision of the chronology just outlined for Syracuse and place the major phases of the Euryalos as well as the northern defenses of Selinus within the early fourth century.

The Greek Classical and Hellenistic house

In the archaic period, as has already been observed earlier, the Greek city house developed from the single-room shelters of the first colonists to a courtyard house, which was to remain a constant of Greek domestic architecture. It was a farmhouse, the courtyard serving the many purposes of agricultural life. In the country of the classical age, Greek farms retained their large courtyards surrounded by barns, stables and housing. Few of these Greek farmsteads have been investigated but one, Capodicasa near Camarina, is known in detail. Here we find a large complex, some 25 meters (82 ft) square, the buildings enclosing a courtyard. There was an oil press in one wing and at another corner there was a tower where the family could find a modicum of safety in troubled times. Several other large courtyard farms are known in the area of Gela. This building type is eternal. A Sicilian farmer of any of the centuries before the advent of mechanization after the Second World War would have found them familiar and comfortable. In the city simple houses consisting of a line of rooms facing on a courtyard continued to be built into the later fourth century. At Camarina they belong to the refoundation of the city in this period. Such houses recall the first courtyard houses of Megara Hyblaea in the seventh century and like them they seem to have belonged to farmers or to families that practiced various crafts from a base in the city. Where the crowding was intense and no regular street plan was established, as in the case of the town at Sabucina near Caltanissetta, a townscape of cramped and cluttered houses persisted in the fifth century. Two other nearby sites, Vassallaggi and Monte Saraceno, enjoyed modest versions of rectangular street plans laid out in the fifth century and courtyard houses. The origin of these plans is to be sought in the coastal cities, like Acragas, where, however, the houses excavated up to now belong largely to the Roman period, and Gela, where several blocks of the fourth-century town have been revealed.

Space determined the development of the courtyard house in the city. Under the most cramped conditions the court was reduced to little more than a lightwell. Where space and resources permitted, it became the heart of large houses and the forecourt of the ample rooms for entertaining that fronted on it. In the fourth and third centuries domestic luxury is reflected in the peristyles (porticoes around courts or gardens) that are now common in the grander dwellings. Always, however, the Greek house looked inward, on its court or its peristyle garden.

The houses of Himera in the city that existed between the laying out of the new street plan about 470 and the Carthaginian sack of 409 provide a revealing picture of Greek private life in the fifth century. These houses are more significant for what they lacked than for what they possessed. The building lots of the new city were sizeable. Each block was divided into house sites, each 16 meters (52 ft 6 in) square. A small alley divided the blocks down their long axis. The archaeological remains, however, show that the original lots were subdivided and reshuffled as time went by. Thus despite the standard lots, there is no standard Himeran house. The courtyards of the larger houses were impressively large as were the main rooms of the ground floor opening on to them. However, there were no colonnades or, apparently, balconies giving on rooms of an upper story. Paving, even in the courtyards, was almost nonexistent. In the rooms the flooring was pounded dirt with a chalky material added to it. There were drains to the streets made of inverted roof tiles. But these can only have been to carry off excessive rain water;

traces of any sanitary arrangements are absent. And similarly the residents of Himera in the fifth century had no permanent kitchens. The comfort and elegance of the houses of the Greek city of Olynthos, destroyed by Philip of Macedon in 348 BC, are singularly lacking. The difference is certainly not due to the poverty of Himera but to the rise in domestic comfort after the fifth century.

To find the developed Sicilian house we must move forward to the third century. Excavations on the site of Monte Iato (Ietas) in the Elymnian area of western Sicily have brought to light an especially well preserved example of a courtyard city house in which the open center has been transformed into an ornamental peristyle. The rooms of the ground floor give on to the peristyle, with the exception of one corner dining-room, which was approached through an open vestibule emphasized by two columns where it is entered from the peristyle. The building had two stories and the two orders of the peristyle were Doric below and ornamental Ionic above (figure 194). The peristyle at Monte Iato has much in common with the so-called atrium of Roman houses of the Republican and Early Imperial age known at Pompeii and Herculaneum and it should be counted among their Hellenistic predecessors. In its later phases it had fresco decoration of simple panels of solid colors and imitation marbling referred to as the first Pompeian Style. Central court city houses of similar date (their earlier phases belonging to the fourth century) and with more than one story are known at Heraclea Minoa. The excavations at this site have also brought to light smaller houses in which space for the court has been reduced to provide for the living area.

The culmination of the Hellenistic house in Sicily is found in the houses of Morgantina, many of which suffered in the sacks of the city during the Second Punic War at the end of the third century, some of which belong to the second century. The fine houses of Morgantina which were built on the crests to east and west of the city's agora were single or double peristyle buildings. They had mosaic floors. The figured mosaics in the central panels of these were almost all removed for the Roman art market after the town fell into abandonment in the first centuryAD. One damaged figured mosaic panel was not worth the trouble to lift and repair and

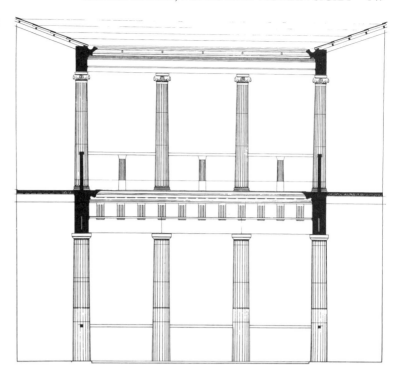

Figure 194 Monte Iato, peristyle house, reconstruction, courtesy of H. P. Isler

Figure 195 Morgantina, House of Ganymede, mosaic, photograph courtesy of Morgantina Excavation Archive, Princeton University

so survived. This is a scene of the young Ganymede borne aloft by Zeus's eagle (figure 195.) The design is carried out in miniature tesserae, filled out with larger sections of marble and other colored stone. The whole is surrounded by a perspective meander border. The art of mosaic working was at least as old as the late fourth century in Sicily. There is a meander border of that date in mosaic from Gela, which is thought to antedate the transfer of the Geloans to the new city called Phintias in 282. The comfort of the Morgantina villas may also be judged from the pressurized distribution system which carried water in lead pipes up to the second stories of the houses.[3] The pressure came from the difference in elevation between the residential quarters and the site of the reservoirs at a higher level in another part of the city.

The Morgantina villas also embody the kind of house which became known to the Romans as the 'Greek type'. This form of house is described in detail by Vitruvius, the architectural writer of the time of Augustus (VI, 7). The Romans were referring, however, not to houses in Greece or the Greek Near East but to the houses of Hellenistic Sicily.[4] Vitruvius' description runs as follows:

The Greeks, having no use for atriums, do not build them, but make passage-ways for people entering from the front door, not very wide, with stables on one side and doorkeeper's rooms on the other, and shut off by doors at the inner side. This place between the two doors is termed in Greek 'Thuroreion'. From it one enters the peristyle. This peristyle has colonnades on three sides, and on the side facing the south it has two antae, a considerable distance apart, carrying an architrave, with a recess for a distance one third less than the space between the antae. This space is called by some writers 'prostas', by others 'pastas'.

Hereabouts, toward the inner side, are the large rooms in which mistresses of houses sit with their wool-spinners. To the right and left of the prostas there are chambers, one of which is called the 'thalamos:', the other the 'amphithalamos'. All around the colonnades are dining rooms for everyday use, chambers, and rooms for the slaves. This part of the house is termed 'gynaeconitis'.

In connection with these there are ampler sets of apartments with more sumptuous peristyles, surrounded by four colonnades of equal height, or else the one which faces the south has higher columns than the others. A peristyle that has one such higher colonnade is called a Rhodian peristyle. Such apartments have fine entrance courts with imposing front doors of their own; the colonnades of the peristyles are decorated with polished stucco in relief and plain, and with coffered ceilings of wood-work; off the colonnades that face the north they have Cyzicene dining rooms and picture galleries; to the east, libraries; exedrae to the west; and to the south, large square rooms of such generous dimensions that four sets of dining couches can easily be arranged in them, with plenty of room for serving and for the amusements.

Men's dinner parties are held in these large rooms; for it was not the practice, according to Greek custom, for the mistress of the house to be present. On the contrary, such peristyles are called the men's apartments, since in them the men can stay without interruption from the women.

(tr. M.H. Morgan)

Let us examine one of the Morgantina houses, The House of the Official, with Vitruvius in mind (figure 196). The house is oriented north–south on its long axis. It is entered through a small door on the long side which leads into an antechamber, the 'thuroreion', fitted with a bench (room 1). To the left would be the porter's lodge (room 2). To the right (room 3 – divided only in a second phase of the house's history) there is ample room for the stable. Beyond the 'thuroreion' one has the choice of turning left or right to reach the two peristyles of the house. Let us turn north, or right. The peristyle (room 4) is disposed just as Vitruvius prescribes. On one side the architrave runs between antae the full width of the peristyle ('a considerable distance'). The architrave is supported by columns of greater diameter than the others composing the peristyle. Although the passageway behind this architrave and its columns, the 'prostas', is shallower than Vitruvius specifies, it faces in the required direction, south. At either end of the 'prostas' there are two small chambers, the 'thalamos' and the 'amphithalamos' (rooms 5 and 6). This part of the house is thus the 'gynaeconitis' or family quarters.

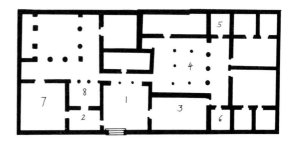

Figure 196 Morgantina, House of the Official

The southern section of the house must therefore be the men's apartments. One of the rooms of this peristyle is clearly a dining room (room 7) in which ledges for the dining couches are still in place. The vestibule with two columns in antis (room 8) reminds one of the arrangement at Monte Iato, although it does not give directly on to the dining room. A house excavated at Morgantina in the 1880s, the so-called Pappalardo House, is another example of such a double courtyard house.[5]

Houses of the Hellenistic Age are also known at Solunto. In its final state the residential quarter uncovered at Acragas belongs to late Roman Imperial times. The origin of the houses, however, is earlier, in some cases Hellenistic. A similar situation exists at Tyndaris on the north coast.

Theaters

At the time of the great Attic playwrights, in the fifth century, Greek theater was produced with almost no permanent buildings. A hillside provided the seating (experiments had been made with wooden stands, but at Athens, at least, an accidental collapse made people wary of them). The scene building was a tent, serving both as backdrop and green room. The major

ancient Greek theaters that exist today were all built after the time of Alexander the Great.

The development of the stage building follows a well-defined typology. The first permanent backdrop was the 'parascenium' theater. The stage building in this form consists of two towers joined by a wall, which provided the backdrop (figures 197 and 198). The stage, if any, was only slightly raised above the level of the orchestra (the level floor within the curved seating of the cavea where the chorus had originally performed). The towers could be used by the actors and behind the wall a crane could be installed for the airborne appearances 'ex machina'. Subsequently the 'proscenium' theater building was introduced. There was now a high stage backed by the stage building and supported by a colonnade. The columns of this portico were usually made so that movable scenery panels could be inserted between them. In the Roman theater the stage was lowered and the colonnade eliminated.

In southern Italy and Sicily the history of the stage is complicated by the low wooden stages known to have existed in the fifth and fourth centuries. Such stages are depicted on vases, especially Campanian vases representing scenes from popular farces. The theater at Heraclea Minoa shows an early phase of the development

Figure 197 Typical Greek theater, parascenium scene building

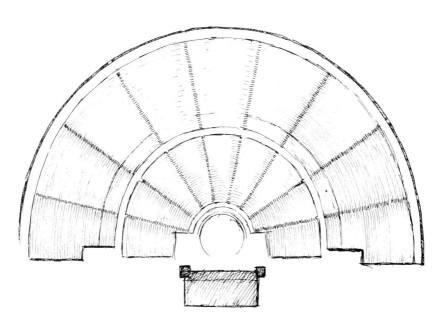

Figure 198 Typical Greek theater, parascenium scene building with stage

of the scene building. The cavea of this theater, which was built at the end of the fourth century BC, was fully developed; its seats were cut into the soft rock of the hillside; and the auditorium (cavea) was given the horseshoe shape around the orchestra characteristic of Greek theaters. But there was no permanent scene building. Post holes, however, suggest some kind of wooden structure or backdrop.

The successive phases of the theater at Morgantina can be dated with some accuracy. When the hillside of the agora of this city was first used for dramatic productions, an orchestra was created by means of a low terrace wall, which lies below the later scene building. This simple stage arrangement, like the wooden post construction at Heraclea Minoa, was probably contemporary with the building of the cavea of the theater, although before a fill against the hillside supported by heavy walls was made to obtain a curved auditorium, straight rows of seats were used. The retaining walls for the curved cavea were planned with buttresses for further strength but these were never built above their foundations. The result proved the wisdom of the design because the northern retaining wall collapsed and had to be rebuilt while the theater was in use. An inscription on the face of one of the middle rows of the seventeen tiers of seats gives the name of the dedicator, Archias the son of Eucleides, and specifies that the theater is for the god Dionysus. Coins and pottery from the original working trenches alongside the retaining

walls show that the cavea was constructed at the end of the fourth century.

The first permanent scene building at Morgantina consisted of two rectanglar units separated by a passageway. Subsequently a proscenium stage building was erected. To each side of it there is the foundation for an extension beyond the end of the stage and these constructions, a form of reduced parascenium, were very possibly connected to the main stage building by vaulted passageways. The proscenium phase of the Morgantina theater belongs to the time of Hieron II of Syracuse when much of the building in the agora of the city took place.

At Monte Iato the theater building was also begun in the late fourth century and modified in the third. It was originally a parascenium theater and, as at Morgantina, was subsequently given a proscenium stage. But both phases had a low stage which was made wider during the second period. Just as at Morgantina there were lateral constructions at the sides. In the final stage of the theater the entrances between the cavea and the scene building were covered. The antefixes from the roofs of both periods are preserved (satyr and maenad masks). Figures of telamones inspired by the giants of the Temple of Zeus at Acragas decorated the facade of the first period. The Monte Iato figures have shaggy heads and wear short fleece skirts (figure 199). They alternated with female caryatids also shown with bent head and raised hands in the same supporting attitude (figure 200).

Figure 199 Monte Iato, theater, telamon, photograph courtesy of H.P. Isler

Figure 200 Monte Iato, theater, caryatid, photograph courtesy of H.P. Isler

Tyndaris and Segesta (figure 201) each had proscenium theaters. The Segestan scene building is probably the earlier; the scene building at Tyndaris, which is restored with full third-story facade, was probably built later in the third century. A still later proscenium stage building is known at Acrae. The theater at Acrae is un-

usual because the cavea is a perfect semicircle, rather than having the normal horseshoe shape.

The theater at Syracuse is not only the largest of the Sicilian theaters, but also the most difficult to interpret. The area of the scene building is a perplexing network of foundations and cuttings. Bernabò Brea has concluded from his detailed

Figure 201 Segesta, theater, photograph courtesy of German Archaeological Institute, Rome, inst. neg. 72.2199

study of the remains that the theater had two periods, both as a proscenium theater, in the third and second century.[6] But earlier phases of the theater have been distinguished by Anti and Polacco, who believe that there are the post holes for a primitive scene arrangement in wood and that the seats of the first cavea cut into the hillside were not arranged in an oval or circular shape but along three straight axes, one at the base of the cavea, the other two diagonally at either side.[7] A third interpretation would provide the theater with a low stage in wood before the erection of the stage building in two successive phases of the late fourth and third century.[8] Seats at the center of the cavea also bear inscriptions, of King Hieron II and his family. During his reign the scene building had telamones and caryatids of the same types employed at Monte Iato.

There are remains of two other Greek theaters in Sicily, at Elorus and Catania respectively. Sicily's most picturesque theater is at Taormina. This was a Greek theater in origin but today appears as transformed into a Roman theater. Much of its scene building is preserved, and its architecture shows the influence of Roman theater building in Asia Minor. Taormina also has a small covered theater (odeum) of the Roman period, as does Catania. Under the Roman Empire modifications were carried out in a number of theaters to fit them for gladiatorial shows and entertainments with wild beasts. The lower rows of seats were cut away to protect the spectators and arrangements were introduced to close off the arenas thus created.

Punic Sicily

How early the western voyages of mariners from the Phoenician coast of Syria and Lebanon brought them to Sicily is uncertain, but it would be difficult to imagine Sicily's eastern contacts of the Late Bronze Age without Phoenicians' playing some part in them. Was the town at Thapsos and its warehouses possibly one of the 'Phoenician' trading stations that Thucydides' informants told him had existed on promontories and islands around Sicily before the Greek colonies were founded? What is certain is that Phoenician Carthage was established at the same time or just before the Greek settlements in Sicily, and that the Phoenician colony on Motya was planted at the end of the eighth or at the beginning of the seventh century.

As has been frequently pointed out, Motya was a site of the kind often preferred by the Phoenicians. It is an island just offshore in a shallow bay, resembling other Phoenician cities, Sidon for example, which was a peninsula, but in very much the same situation as the Sicilian town. When the fortifications were constructed in the sixth century (discussed on pp. 141–2) and the cemetery of the town was transferred to the mainland, a causeway was built across the shallow lagoon between the two. The causeway, which still exists, was always slightly underwater but the depth over it was kept shallow enough so that carts could pass over it.

Gradually excavation is revealing more and more of the city destroyed by Dionysius. Just inside the north gate where the causeway from the mainland reached the island there was a typically Punic sanctuary surrounded by an enclosure wall. Straddling the wall there is a temple with three long rooms side by side and a 'porch' crossing them. The 'porch' is inside the enclosure wall; the three other rooms project beyond it. The enclosure wall belongs to the sixth century but there were already small cult buildings and a well connected with the cult on the site. In front of the temple there is still in place a foundation intended to carry three upright pillars, the 'bet el' of the sanctuary.

Nearby and contiguous to the city wall was an industrial area in which the discovery of masses of mollusk shells points to the existence of a dye works, possibly manufacturing the famous Tyrian purple cloth. The earlier necropolis

of the city was cut through in this area by the city wall.

Farther along the wall Joseph I.S. Whitaker discovered the 'tophet' of Motya. Meaning 'the place of burning', the 'tophet' was the place where the Phoenicians sacrificed their firstborn sons. At Motya what has been found (not accepted by all scholars as a sacrifical 'tophet') is a burial ground of infants who were cremated and their ashes placed in small jars. Beside the urns there were placed terracotta statuettes and terracotta masks, both female heads and one male grotesque. The inscriptions of the stone markers identify the divinity so honored as Bàal Hammon. There are more than one thousand grave markers from Motya; they are often decorated with simple relief figures. The burials begin in the seventh century.

Clearly life did not cease on Motya with the sack of 397 and the foundation of the new Carthaginian port of Lilybaeum. Houses on Motya of a later date have been excavated, there was continued activity in the industrial quarter, and burial in the 'tophet' continued into the third century .

In its artistic tastes Motya, like all of Punic Sicily, was thoroughly Hellenized. From the seventh century on the town used Greek pottery or pottery based on Greek models. In the sixth century the Motyans erected a stone pedimental decoration in the form of lions attacking a bull, such as is found on several temples in mainland Greece. Another building was decorated with a grand gorgon mask after the Sicilian temple pediment type. The large figure of Cypriote type in black stone from Motya has long been known. The marble youth of the mid-fifth century, discussed on p. 107, is a recent discovery. The Phoenician sculpture of Sicily is completed by the two marble anthropoid sarcophagi from Cannita near Palermo of the type more commonly found in ancient cities of Phoenicia. Such sarcophagi were inspired by Egyptian mummy cases, but the features of the image are worked in the style of Greek high classical sculpture. The peristyle house with a pebble mosaic of battling animals excavated by Whitaker is generally ascribed to a date following the sack of 397. But it has been remarked that any reoccupation of the island would have been limited and probably would not have led to the building of such pretentious houses.[9] A redating to the late fifth century would make the Motya mosaic a forerunner of the pebble mosaics of the fourth century (conspicuously those of Pella in Macedonia) and would make the Motya house a very early example of the peristyle type. A group of grave monuments in the form of miniature gabled shrines with painted decoration including scenes of the dead shown as a banqueter come principally from Lilybaeum.

Thucydides mentions three Phoenician settlements in particular, Motya, Palermo, and Soluntum. From Punic Palermo there are only tombs. Soluntum, situated dramatically on the heights of Monte Catalfano a few miles to the east of Palermo, is a town of the second century. Its cult places, however, have nothing architecturally in common with Greek and Roman religious architecture of the day, and are interpreted as Punic in inspiration. At one spot along the main avenue of the town there was a base with three 'bet el'. Greek inscriptions from the site also testify to the worship of Zeus.

At Marsala, the ancient Lilybaeum, the fortifications enclosing the Phoenician town in a square are being brought to light. In the harbor remains of two Punic ships have been discovered. The larger vessel was some 35 meters long and seems to have been a small warship of the first Punic War (264–241) between Rome and Carthage, which was fought largely in Sicily and was marked by a series of great naval battles in Sicilian waters.[10] And on the breathtaking height of Eryx, site of the Elymnian sanctuary of Aphrodite, other vestiges of the fortifications of the Punic period can be seen.

The transformation of Selinus from a Greek metropolis into a Punic town after the calamity of 409 is apparent from the houses that invaded the old sanctuaries of the acropolis, occasionally with a Tanit charm as a good luck symbol

Figure 202 Selinus, Tanit sign

(figure 202) worked in marble cubes into the red flooring made by mixing ground-up pottery into the cement. (This became the commonest form of Sicilian house paving after the fourth century.) Such a pavement in the pronaos of Temple A, with the symbol of Tanit and the bull's head of the sun, shows the continuing use of this building as a cult place. The Punic settlers also transformed the Malophorus sanctuary and evidently modified its cult.

Like Selinus, the nameless ancient city at Monte Adranone (some miles to the northeast) also became Punic in the fourth century. In this period an earlier Greek sanctuary just outside the main gate of the town was surrounded with a large enclosure including rooms backing on the perimeter wall. As at the Malophorus Sanctuary a cult continued to exist on the spot. A Punic temple has been identified on the acropolis of the town. The temple was rectangular; the main room, whose roof was supported by two columns in its center, was entered on its long side; there were other chambers at both ends of the building. On a lower terrace of the town, near a large cistern, there was another sanctuary building of the more usual Greek cella and anteroom type. Investigation of the houses of the site is continuing.

Hellenistic and Roman cities

The aspirations of Greek city planners during the two centuries which began with the reign of Alexander the Great are nowhere better revealed than in the Sicilian city of Morgantina in the third century. This inland community had been important during the sixth and fifth centuries. In the mid-fifth century it had been part of Ducetius' short-lived Sicel empire. Subsequently Morgantina enjoyed a notable period of expansion. The old site on the eastern end of the long ridge now known as Serra Orlando was largely abandoned and a new city was laid out on the center and western extremity of the ridge. The new Morgantina was conceived on a vast scale; the city was 1.5 kilometers (almost 1 mile) by 0.5 kilometers (about one-third of a mile) at its widest part. A rectangular street plan was established which crossed the rises and dips along the ridge with little heed to topography. The realization of the planners' scheme was another matter, and more than a century elapsed before the city grew into its layout.

We have already seen something of the houses which were built on the two hills flanking the agora, the market-place and political center of the town (figure 203). Like the houses, the buildings of the market are the result of the prosperity of the third century, when Morgantina was part of the Syracusan state ruled for over fifty years by the monarch Hieron II. Hieron's domain was a Hellenistic kingdom poised uncertainly between the two rival powers Rome and Carthage. The kingdom survived the first Punic War (264–240), which was largely fought in Sicily and on the sea surrounding it, and as a result of her Roman alliance Syracuse prospered. But the Second Punic War, which began in 218, brought the downfall of Hieron's kingdom. The old monarch remained faithful to the Roman cause through the black days of Hannibal's march over the Alps and the Carthaginian's early victories in Italy, but the king died in 215 and his grandson and successor, Hieronymus, was wooed into a Carthaginian alliance. The Romans took Syracuse in 211. Morgantina's fortunes mirrored those of the capital. During the war the city twice changed hands and allegiance. Finally recaptured by the Romans in 211, it was turned over to a company of Spanish mercenaries and began its slow decline.

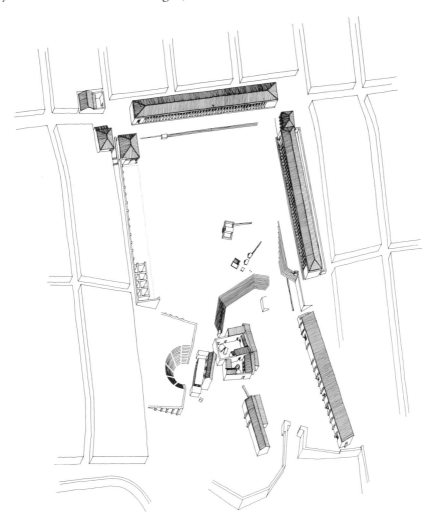

Figure 203 Morgantina, reconstruction of agora, courtesy of M. Bell

The showpiece of the agora of Morgantina is the stairway that leads up from the southern and lower area of the market-place, where one entered from the main city gate, to the main area of the agora at a high level (figure 204). There are three banks of stairs set at an open angle to each other. The eastern bank was never finished, but a retaining wall shows its intended length. This would have left space for a ramp to descend along the flank of the market-place. A smaller set of steps is found on the far side of the ramp forming a terrace before one of the two porticoes (stoas) which frame the upper area. Between the western and central bank of steps a large drain served to carry water away from the high ground to the north. The usual Greek approach to planning an agora for a city situated on sloping ground is illustrated by the agora of Solunto. There the main street enters the market-place on the level, traversing the long axis of the market. There is no problem of changes in elevation in the market, while the upper and lower parts of the city can be reached by the transverse streets, these turned into staircases if necessary, but hidden from view in the level market-place. The design problem at Morgantina was different and the solution marked by originality. The architect broke free of the traditional Greek preference for building in rectangles and made the shape of the stairs serve the pedestrian traffic pattern of the market. Thus in addition to the main axis leading from the city gate to the upper level, there was a secondary axis leading to the western part of the market, and especially to the theater, which shared the orientation of this bank of the steps. The theater of Morgantina was discussed on p. 152. Like it, the steps were built during the third century, in two phases, separated, it seems, by only a few years.

It has been suggested that the stairs at Morgantina also served as a political assembly place (ecclasiasterion) and a low foundation near their eastern end has been interpreted as the speaker's rostrum (bema). Those gathering for any such meetings would have had to remain standing

Figure 204 Morgantina, agora steps, photograph courtesy of Morgantina Excavation Archive, Princeton University

Figure 205 Acragas ecclesiasterion, photograph courtesy of Soprintendenza ai Beni Culturali ed Ambientali, Agrigento

because of the narrow width of the steps. And the Morgantina assembly place would have contrasted sharply with the ecclesiasterion of Acragas where benches were cut out of the soft native rock in a semicircular auditorium around the speaker's platform (figure 205). Beside the ecclesiasterion at Acragas there is a Roman podium temple (the Oratory of Phalaris).

However, the visitor to the Hellenistic agora of Morgantina would have found something to remind him of the previous phases of the market-place. Most prominent was the sanctuary of Demeter and Persephone situated just east of the theater, encroaching on the plaza at the foot of the steps. This was a typical 'house shrine', its altars, both round and oblong, enclosed in courtyards around which there were also a series of rooms, some of them intended for banqueting couches. The nocturnal character of some of the ceremonies of the cult is shown by the thousands of lamps excavated within the sanctuary. Lead tablets found on the spot were inscribed to Earth, Hermes, the Underground Divinities and Pluto. The power of the gods was evoked for both personal welfare and the discomfort of enemies. One tablet is a curse. There were two small cult places, dating from pre-Hellenistic times, in the main upper agora. One was simply an altar, the other a modest sacellum with three altars before it.[11]

Flanking the lower area from the city gate to the great stairs at each side was a granary. The eastern granary is well preserved, the western

one less so. The building of these two public storehouses in the third century should be related to the taxation system of Hieron II, which was based on the painstaking survey of crops before harvest and the subsequent collection of taxes from the producers by tax farmers who bid for the tax contracts on the basis of the crop estimates. This was the so-called lex Hieronica, which remained in vigor under the Romans.

As planned, the upper agora was to be dominated by two porticoes, one to the east (figure 206), one to the west. A further portico closed off the area on the north. The eastern stoa corresponds to the normal Greek stoa of the day. It incorporated a peristyle with dining-rooms, probably for town officials, at one end. The western stoa was to have been a grander affair, but it was never completed. Behind the colonnade there were to be a line of shops consisting of an outer and inner room. It is quite possible that a second story was planned. The finished building would have been much like the Stoa of Attalos in the Athenian Agora, which has been reconstructed to house the museum of the excavations of the American School of Classical Studies in Athens. In Athens the Stoa of Attalos housed shops for luxury goods on its first floor and the expectation may well have been the same for the western stoa at Morgantina.

At the northwest corner of the market-place the city's senate chamber or bouleuterion has been discovered. From a small courtyard one passed through a portico into the chamber where

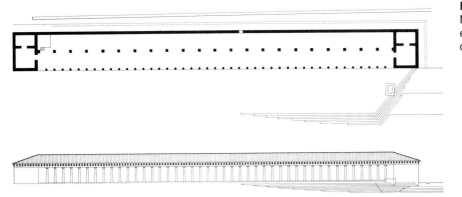

Figure 206
Morgantina,
east stoa, courtesy
of M. Bell.

the seats for the senators were grouped in an ascending semicirular auditorium. A comparable building has recently been excavated at Acragas. Others are known at Solunto, Monte Iato and Acrae.

Finally, at the opposite (northeast), corner of the agora recent excavation has brought to light a fountain house of the third century, consisting of a portico fronting on an inner and outer basin (figure 207). The reconstruction of the facade assumes a Doric order in wood. The fountain house passed through various rebuildings during the decline of the city before it was finally totally abandoned during the first century AD. At one time, there was a smaller roofed area and a stone entablature.

During the second century a meat market was built in the center of the upper agora (figure 208). This building has the typical plan of such a facility in the Roman world (the macellum) including the round structure in its interior court. The macellum at Morgantina is the earliest known Roman meat market.

In the agora of Morgantina we have seen almost all the amenities of a Greco-Roman city save one, the bath. Bath buildings came early to Sicily. One is known at Gela in the fourth century, fitted with sitzbaths, such as remained popular throughout the Hellenistic period, for example in the baths excavated at Megara Hyblaea. These tubs had no drains. The water must have been sponged out by attendants.

Figure 207
Morgantina,
Fountain House,
courtesy of M. Bell

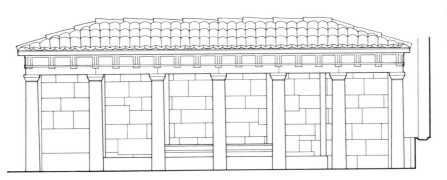

Figure 208
Morgantina, agora,
courtesy of M. Bell

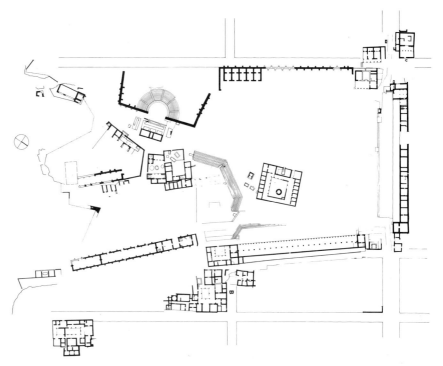

A complex of buildings in the western part of Morgantina, excavated in the early 1970s, has been interpreted as a bath connected to a sanctuary of Aphrodite. Two large buildings were brought to light, separated by a street and both having circular halls which have been reconstructed with domes. Structurally the domes would have relied on terracotta tubes for lightness and strength. One of the chambers had fresco decoration, although it is not known whether the frescoes were original or added later in the history of the structure. Even though the purposes of these buildings have not been established with certainty, this discovery has great significance for the history of domed architecture in the ancient world.

What is known of Hellenistic and Roman towns in Sicily outside Morgantina is not extensive. Grid plans were universal. Solunto, the Hellenized Punic city of the third to first centuries, was planned under the influence of cities of the fourth century in Asia Minor, notably Priene. Tyndaris on the north coast has a grid plan of the early fourth century. This city provides one architectural enigma, a vaulted structure covering a street-width passageway, with another street-size ramp leading up an incline beside it. As it stands the building defies explanation. It may be part of an unfinished project. The date is uncertain, but the rusticated masonry would be at home in the mid-first century AD.

The urban landscape of Syracuse, the queen of Sicily, is becoming better known as the result of excavations on the mainland where the city expanded from its nucleus on the island of Ortygia. Near the agora, where a few columns of the Roman period are still to be found, there is an elegantly fitted-out Roman cult place possibly dedicated to the worship of the Egyptian gods Isis and Serapis or to the Syrian goddess Atargatis. Behind the podium temple there is a small theater, with stage and auditorium. The whole is enclosed by porticoes. It was built in the second century AD. A general rectangular street pattern has now emerged extending to the Greek theater and the Roman amphitheater (of the Augustan period), one of three in Sicily, the others at Catane and Termini (the successor of Himera). The same section of the city is bordered by vast and picturesque quarries that show the scale of Syracusan building. The quarries served as prisoner-of-war pens for the captured Athenians of 413. In other days they housed the workshops of ropemakers, and today the quarries near the Greek theater have been transformed into magnificent gardens. Not far away is the great altar of Hieron II. This grandiose monument was cut from the native rock to form a platform almost 200 meters (656 ft) in length and 22.6 meters (74 ft 1 in) wide. It was here that the monarch had a sacrifice of 100 bulls performed. The altar fronted on a garden surrounded on its other three sides by porticoes. There was a fountain in its center, and trees were planted in pits set out in rows across the open space. The limestone cliffs above the theater and extending along the side of the Epipolae, the high ground protected by Dionysius I's fortifications, are dotted at intervals with rock-cut prehistoric tombs and the sarcophagus-size cuttings of historical times. There are also the niches of small shrines cut in the rock, especially for the Great Mother of the Gods, the divinity of Asia Minor whose cult flourished in Hieron II's kingdom. The image of the divinity seated on a throne supported by lions appears in relief. Other similar shrines of the same cult with figures of Hermes, Attis and the Dioscuri as well as the Great Mother herself can be seen at Acrae. A Roman bath has been excavated at Syracuse. Others are known from Catania and Tyndaris.

Not far away a fountain house facing on a street originally constructed in the fifth century has been excavated in Piazza della Vittoria. Nearby the votive deposit of an important cult center of Demeter and Persephone, worshipped in association with Artemis, has been unearthed. The foundations of the temple to which it belongs have also been excavated. Like the fountain house, this cult place came into being when the city expanded into what had previously been a cemetery.

The terracotta statuettes from the deposit in Piazza della Vittoria begin in the fourth century and belong largely to the Hellenistic age. They are one of the most important such groups to have been excavated in Sicily. The deposit is well illustrated by the material exhibited in the new archaeology museum of Syracuse. The most typically Sicilian terracottas of this age are the busts of goddesses which take the place of the masks of archaic times, and begin to be made in the fourth, perhaps even in the fifth century (figures 209 and 210). The figurines, many in scale really small statues, are related to similar work of the Greek motherland (figure 211). The Sicilian production is distinctive and rich. In the absence of detailed publications from centers like

Figure 209 Syracuse Museum, terracotta bust from Grammichele, photograph courtesy of Soprintendenza ai Beni Culturali ed Ambientali, Syracuse

Figure 210 Aidone Museum, terracotta bust from Morgantina, photograph courtesy Morgantina Excavation Archive, Princeton University and M.Bell

Figure 211 Aidone Museum, terracotta figurine from Morgantina, photograph courtesy Morgantina Excavation Archive, Princeton University and M. Bell

Cupid envisaged as a winged young man). These busts are related to a distinctively Sicilian variety of pottery, which was made at Centuripe, near the western slopes of Mt Aetna. The vases of the Centuripe type come both from burials and sanctuaries. They are large and were painted gaudily with the gilding and confectioner's palette also found on the contemporary female busts. Some of the decoration – leaves and rosettes – was made separately in molds and applied to the surface. The importance of these pieces lies in the decoration, again groups of women, often suggesting the dressing of a bride. This iconography would have been appropriate both for the tombs of unmarried girls, who were thus accompanied by what they had been denied in life, and for Persephone, the bride of Hades *par excellence*. Dionysiac scenes are also known. Dionysus, of course, was also a god of transformation and salvation, typified iconographically by his union with Ariadne, in a funeral setting suggesting the soul swept into eternal union with the divinity. An especially vivid instance of Dionysiac iconography in the tomb is given by the numerous figures of actors from the graves of the fourth century on Lipari. The figures are precious documents for a knowledge of the figures of Middle Comedy, in the period between Aristophanes and Menander, which is known otherwise only in fragments of the plays. Dionysus, god of the theater, was present with the dead through his company of actors and their masks. The figure of the slave (figure 212) is an easily recognizable one, as is the mask of the chief slave (figure 213). Other figurines and masks represent further members of the Middle Comedy company of actor types, for example the experienced hetaira (courtesan, figure 214) and the flatterer (figure 215).

We have one important bronze statue, often ignored in studies of Hellenistic art; the life-size figure of a ram from Syracuse now in Palermo. The statue was originally one of a pair, perhaps the decoration of a fountain.

The mosaic from the House of Ganymede at Morgantina is also an important remnant of Hellenistic graphic art. The Sicilians of the third century held an important place as mosaic workers. Their skill was displayed, for example, in the decoration of the yacht 'Syracosia' that Hieron II gave as a present to King Ptolemy of Egypt. The vessel, of course, has perished,

Syracuse and Acragas one may best see the panorama of the Sicilian Hellenistic terracotta figurines in the material from Morgantina, largely from the house sanctuaries of Demeter and Persephone.[12]

The large busts of the two goddesses, well represented at Morgantina and belonging to a tradition which apparently begins in the later fifth century, were elegantly gilded and painted, predominantly in white, pink and blue. They often have figured decoration on their dress. The scenes are groups of women; with them there can be a winged Victory or Eros (the early Greek

Figure 212 Lipari Museum, terracotta figurine

but a lengthy description of the decoration has been preserved by Athenaeus.

Cicero and Verres

In 70 BC Gaius Verres, praetor (next to the consul the highest office in the government of Rome) and then Roman governor of the Province of Sicily, was brought to trial. The charge was extortion and abuse of power, the motivation of the charges political. Verres was an adherent of the optimate party headed, before his death, by Sulla. His opponents were from the party that had gathered around Pompey the Great.

Figure 213 Lipari Museum, terracotta mask, photograph courtesy of L. Bernabò Brea

Figure 214 Lipari Museum, terracotta mask, photograph courtesy of L. Bernabò Brea

Cicero was the prosecuting attorney, and even though the case never came to trial, Cicero published four speeches he had ready to use. The fact that Verres went into voluntary exile and the power of Cicero's brief have led the world to judge the praetor severely, as he may deserve. But whatever Verres' guilt, Cicero's speeches open a window on collecting and dealing in art in the early first century in Sicily.

Figure 215 Lipari Museum, terracotta mask, photograph courtesy of L. Bernabò Brea

In the Fourth Verrine Cicero sets forth in detail Verres' alleged thefts of art. There are two categories: statuary and metal vessels. It seems that Verres had set up a factory in Syracuse to produce silver plate and other decorative metal-work, including pieces such as candelabra and incense burners. But the work was modern only in part. The principal decorative elements were antique pieces presented in the new settings. Among them were the medallions, often in high relief and usually silver, that were placed in the center of cups or platters as well as pieces of open work. Cicero claimed that Verres acquired these elements largely by extortion. Verres maintained that he paid for them, and this was probably the truth more often than not because even Cicero admits that adverse circumstances had forced some Sicilians to sell their plate. To supply Roman demand for elegant silver and other decorative metal-work Verres must have been operating much like the entrepreneurs who removed the figured medallions of mosaic pavements at Morgantina for shipment and resetting as the center pieces of new pavements elsewhere.

Verres' methods for collecting statuary, if Cicero can be trusted, verged on the barbaric. Sanctuaries and temples were raided by gangs of toughs employed for the purpose. And no shrine was too venerable to escape. The temples of Ceres (Demeter) and Persephone at Enna, Ceres' temple at Catania, and others at Assoros, Segesta and Syracuse all gave up images to the plunderers. And even when the hue and cry prevented them from seizing the principal image, the vandals got away with smaller figures. The doors of the temple of Athene at Syracuse were stripped of their ivory paneling and gold fittings. Intimidation was not unknown. In midwinter a venerable city magistrate at Tyndaris was bound astride a bronze equestrian statue to endure exposure and the chill of the metal until his fellow officials handed over a statue of Hermes to Verres. The subsequent history of this sculpture suggests that Verres' acquisitions were not all intended for his private enjoyment but were gathered to be sold on the Roman art market. The Hermes went to one of the Marcelli.

At other times mere unscrupulousness sufficed. When an Antiochos of the family of the Greek rulers of Syria stopped at Syracuse on his way to Rome, Verres politely asked if his metalsmiths might examine a gem-studded incense burner that Antiochos was bringing as a gift to Jupiter Optimus Maximus. Needless to say, the incense burner was never restored to its owner.

The Hermes from Tyndaris may have been a prize sculpture of the fifth century, since it was one of the pieces restored to the Sicilians by Scipio Africanus from the trophies of war ceded by the Carthaginians. Another piece returned from Carthage was an Artemis at Segesta also acquired by Verres. Still other statues returned by Scipio had belonged to Himera and Gela. Acragas, finally, had received back the bull of Phalaris which the Carthaginians had taken away in 405 BC.

Other statuary collected by Verres had more questionable credentials. The group acquired from C. Heius at Messina comprised three figures, one said to be by Praxiteles, one by Myron and one by Polyclitus. Praxiteles, who worked in the fourth century, was a perennial favorite with the Romans. Myron and Polyclitus, active in the fifth century, were two of the most celebrated Greek masters. It is doubtful whether any of the three sculptors worked in Sicily, and Cicero's remarks on the Eros from Messina leave open the possibility that it was actually a copy of Praxiteles' Eros at Thespiae in Greece. So too may have been the other statues. The 'Apollo of Myron' at Acragas is just as suspect, because a signature in silver letters inlaid on the bronze, as Cicero describes the inscription on the piece, is not in keeping with fifth-century practice.

The Sicily we meet in Cicero's oration is the island as it survived the Punic Wars and slave rebellions of the later second century. The cities of the north and east coast are flourishing, as are Segesta and the old Punic cities of the west. In the interior, there is little change among cities along the corridor from Catania to Himera via Enna, Centuripe, Assoros, Agirium, Herbita. But the south coast has lost many of its old Greek cities, Camarina, Gela and Selinus. And in other parts of the interior city life was giving way to large agricultural estates, the latifundia and woodlands that were to provide hunting grounds for the Roman magnates of later centuries.

6

THE VILLA AT PIAZZA ARMERINA

Thinking of inland Sicily, the first image that comes to my mind is a treeless hillside, green with wheat, speckled here and there by the red dots of poppies in late winter and spring, then brown and desolate through the heat of the summer and fall. This image, of course, is no longer accurate. Today wheat is not the backbone of Sicilian agriculture. In many areas vineyards are rapidly taking the place of wheat fields; in others the fields lie uncultivated. Even the famous orchards of oranges and lemons of the north and east coasts and the Catania Plain are feeling the pressure of foreign imports.

There is another image of Sicily in the summer and early fall that is no less characteristic of the island in the distant and more recent past. This is the hunter in pursuit of small game. Indeed not only Sicilian landlords like the Prince of Giuseppe di Lampedusa's *Leopard* but sportsmen from northern Italy came to hunt over the fields and limestone hills of the island. The area around Enna, the geographical center of Sicily, was particularly favored by hunters. And from time to time the hunters would encounter a small valley where the water from a spring made a sheltered oasis in the parched landscape.

One of the most pleasant of these valleys is situated a mile or so south of the town of Piazza Armerina. The spring feeds a small stream, and the valley is shaded by oaks and thick stands of alder. The air, even in summer, is refreshing. It is perhaps not surprising that this spot was chosen by a magnate of the Roman Empire as the site for a villa.

During the Roman Empire, town life in the interior of the island declined to a low ebb. But Sicilian grain and Sicilian pasture were as important as ever and the senatorial families who controlled immense estates in Sicily grew rich from the proceeds. The villa at Piazza Armerina, no doubt, was connected with one of these vast holdings. The location was also close to the road from Roman Catania to Agrigentum and near the village of Philosophiana, which grew up as a post station for couriers and travelers along the highway.

The villa is not a residence of the High Empire such as we know from the magnificent villas around the Bay of Naples and the grandest of all Roman villas, the retreat of the Emperor Hadrian at Tivoli. The villa at Piazza Armerina belongs rather to the fourth century AD, to the Empire of Constantine the Great, when the initial barbarian invasions and civil war had already shaken the foundations of the Empire but there still remained protected and peaceful regions such as Sicily was to be until the invasions of the Vandals in the next century (AD 440).

The fame of this residence comes from its mosaic pavements. They cover some 3,500 square meters (approximately 32,000 square feet) and more than half of them are mosaics with figured decoration executed in the vibrant colors of this branch of graphic art. The walls of the villa were decorated too, with marble incrustation or with fresco painting. But these elements have perished almost entirely. The statuary and decorative marble work that would have added to the luxury of the building has also vanished, except for some fragments including a head of Hercules and the torso of a marble statue of Apollo based on an original by the Greek sculptor of the fourth century BC, Praxiteles. There is nothing remarkable in this, however, considering that the villa was occupied, in one way or another, into the period of the Norman Kingdom, which began in the eleventh century AD.

The villa is in every way a monument of the

cosmopolitan empire surrounding it. Rome, the capital city, was never far from the thoughts of the magnates of the empire, and William Mac-Donald has pointed out how the architectural masses of the building mimic the cityscape of Rome where basilicas (the vast halls which served as both courtrooms and commercial exchanges), porticoes, monumental arches and baths shouldered against each other in the monumental center.[1]

In the plan of the villa the formal symmetry that we instinctively consider one of the fundamental attributes of classical architecture has been replaced with visual harmony (figure 216). The architects of the villa were perfectly at home with geometric regularity such as they gave the bath wing of the building (figure 216: 1). But they were also willing to permit the central portico of the villa (figure 216: 2) to depart from the normal rectangular. One reason for oblique

Figure 216
Piazza Armerina,
Late Roman Villa

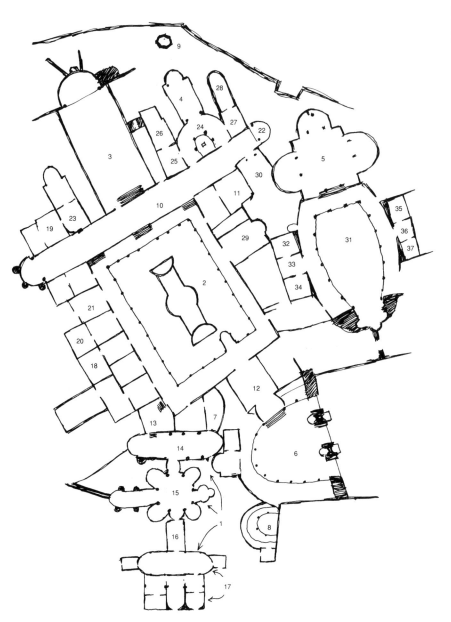

planning was a desire to avoid unobstructed views along an interior axis, for example across the main peristyle from the entrance to the villa to the apse of the great triclinium, a view that might have been possible if absolute rectangular planning had been followed.[2] Instead, the view from the entrance to the peristyle is immediately blocked by a small shrine. And in no other case is there an unobstructed line of sight from one point into the successive architectural element.

The building was made up foremost of great halls (figure 216: 3, 4, 5) all apsidal, and one (figure 216: 5) trilobate. These are the auditoria or triclinia of Roman villas and palaces, halls for formal audiences or banquets. In each case these are preceded by peristyles or courtyards. The passage from the main peristyle (figure 216: 2) to the great triclinium (figure 216: 3) requires mounting two sets of stairs, thus emphasizing the dignity of the triclinium itself. The length of the open area of the peristyle is exactly the same as that of the triclinium, a balancing of spaces that prepares the visitor for the interior chamber. The approach to the smaller triclinium (figure 216: 4) and its suite situated beside the great triclinium is less formal. Here a small horse-shoe-shaped portico leads to the triclinium. The important trilobate hall, on the other hand, is preceded by a deep oval portico. The entrance to this complex is not on axis but through a passage that opens on to the portico very near the doorway to the hall. However, the visitor was once again prepared for the space of the hall since the length of the portico is the same as the width of the hall across the two lateral apses. Similar angular entrances are made from the entrance court (figure 216: 6) to the main peristyle (figure 216: 2) and from the peristyle to the baths (figure 216: 1). The open space of the main peristyle was emphasized by a splendid fountain. It made use of water brought to the villa by its own aqueduct. Finally, the main approach to the villa was emphasized by an archway.

Sanitation was provided by three latrines, one at the entrance to the baths (figure 216: 7), one facing on what is possibly a large yard beside the entrance court (figure 216: 8) and one behind the great hall and apartments facing on the portico of the Great Hunt (figure 216: 9). Like many Roman latrines, these were hand-somely installed with columns and marble work, but in these splendid surroundings the Romans joined each other on a single stone bench, per-forated at intervals and placed over a drain flushed by continuously running water.

The internal porticoes are flanked by individual rooms, the cubicula, which certainly included bedrooms. The villa does not seem to have had an upper story.

Most of the service dependencies of the villa have not been excavated. The kitchens, the storerooms, the stables, the servants' quarters should all be added to our mental image of the establishment. What has been exposed, and is now protected under the steel and glass covering that suggests something of the architectural mass of the original building, is thus largely the public core of the villa. The questions that immediately arise concerning the villa are its ownership and date, and the significance of its vast mosaic decoration.

Although the existence of the villa was known since the nineteenth century, no large-scale excavations were made before 1950–4. Excavation beneath the floor level of the villa to recover material from the original building fill in order to date the construction of the building was carried out in 1970. The coins from these deposits, like those found earlier below some of the mosaics, belong to the third century AD. The pottery, related closely to material from North African sites, is generally no later than the first quarter of the fourth century AD. Therefore it seems that the building should be dated in the years before AD 330. This evidence confirmed the opinion of those scholars who maintained that the mosaics belonged to the period of Constantine the Great (Emperor, AD 312-336) or the later part of the reorganized government instituted by Diocletian in AD 289 and shared by that emperor with three colleagues in a four-way division of imperial responsibility (the Tetrarchy).

The mosaics, to be sure, show the return to a style of limited visual depth that is one of the hallmarks of late antique style. The dress of men and women shown in them is also characteristic of the times. Several important figures in the Great Hunt mosaic of the long portico (figure 216: 10) wear a 'pillbox' cap that became fash-ionable under the Tetrarchy. The tunics worn by men show the decorative roundels that were sewn on to linen garments, many of which have been preserved in burials from late antique Egypt. The evidence of fashion, however, was insufficient to limit the date of the mosaics to the early years of the fourth century, and in the period immediately following the excavations of the 1950s attempts were made to place the mosaics toward the end of the century. The evidence of the stratigraphic excavations makes these suggestions improbable.[3] It also suggests that the villa was built all at one time and that the mosiac decoration was also carried out as a single job. The sole exception is the mosaic of the girl athletes (who became famous in the 1950s as the 'Bikini Girls'). This paving was laid over an earlier geometric floor (figure 216: 11). There are repairs to the mosaics, most noticeable in the case of the Great Hunt (figure 216: 10), carried out during a later stage of the long life of the villa.

The very magnificence of the building and of its decoration prompted the same scholars who had correctly dated the building to the early years of the fourth century to assume that this was an imperial villa. Although none of the attempts to identify imperial personages from the gallery of the Tetrarchs and their families was fruitful (and, as H.P. L'Orange once said pithily, 'One would never walk on an imperial portrait'), the iconography of some of the mosaics seemed to favor this hypothesis. It is the threateningly powerful vision of the labors of Hercules in the trilobate hall that seemed to proclaim the importance of this hero and his triumphs for the *patronus* of the villa. Since Maximian, the partner of Diocletian, and his son Maxentius adopted the title 'Herculean', as Diocletian claimed the title 'Jovian', the villa, it was argued, might well have been a retreat of one or the other of these two imperial personages.

Recent discoveries, however, make it clear that the villa at Piazza Armerina was not unique but was one of a number of sumptuous Sicilian villas of the late Empire.[4] Both the villa at Patti in the Province of Messina (on the north coast of the island) and the villa at Tellaro south of Syracuse are of the same scale as the villa at Piazza Armerina. Both have central peristyles and great apsidal halls. The hunt mosaic from the villa at Tellaro, of which photographs have appeared in preliminary reports, is of greater complexity than its counterparts at Piazza Armerina. (The mosaics of the villa at Patti are apparently much

less well preserved than in the other two buildings). The existence of two comparable residences of the same period makes it more likely that the villa of Piazza Armerina was built by one of the Senatorial magnates of the period.[5]

Only half the Piazza Armerina mosaics are representational scenes. It is not clear that this implies a hierarchy of rooms. For example, half the rooms along the north side of the main peristyle have geometric pavements. These include both rooms giving directly on the peristyle and rooms behind. And the same is true of the rooms with pavements done with figured scenes. Brick pavements were used, but sparingly, in open courtyards.

The subject matter for the mosaics was deliberately chosen. The entrance hall between the forecourt and the main peristyle (figure 216: 12) has a mosaic of a scene of greeting, unfortunately much destroyed but clearly composed of a group of men, some wearing wreath crowns and carrying green sprigs while their attendants hold torches. Passing to the portico of the main peristyle (figure 216: 2) we find a long series of medallions each representing the head of a wild animal enclosed in a wreath. In this way images of game from the hills surrounding the villa were put on display.

The bath, entered from the main peristyle, was given a rich mosaic decoration. The vestibule (figure 216: 13) shows a family group on the way to the bath, a lady with her two children and two maids, one carrying a brazier, the other a chest with fresh clothes. The next room (figure 216: 14) shows the villa mimicking the metropolis. The form of the chamber, a long rectangle with apsidal ends, is transformed into a miniature of the Circus Maximus at Rome by the mosaicist. Chariots at full gallop sweep around the island (or spina) in the center of the racecourse. One has overturned, while beyond the spina the race comes to an end; a trumpeter announces the winner and a magistrate prepares to award the palm of victory. The winner belongs to the Red Faction, as shown by the horses' trappings. On the racecourse we see a structure with the seven 'eggs', which were lowered successively to mark the completion of each lap of the race. Beside it there is a small loggia (or *phala*) that was used at certain times by spectators. There are *sparsores* ready to sprinkle water on the racecourse. A mounted official of the games is on the race

Figure 217 Piazza
Armerina, Late
Roman
Villa, Mosaic

course. The representation of the spina is detailed. In addition to the obelisk and the three upright turning markers at each end, there is statuary, including a Victory on a column, small loggias, baldachinos, and another lap recorder. Three temples appear on the skyline at one end of the Circus, with the starting gates and attendants below. At the other end we see the Arch of Titus which stood in the Circus. Above it, spectators fill the stands. We may imagine that those entering the bath looked at the circus mosaic with the interest always shown by persons confronting the model of a building, machine, ship or scene from elsewhere indoors. The conversation piece and the architectural conceit thus led the way to the bath.

The next room was the *frigidarium* or cold bath (figure 216: 15), an hexagonal chamber surrounded by niches, defined by columns, one of which opened into the bathing pool proper. Appropriately the floor mosaic of the *frigidarium*

is a seascape enlivened at the center by fishing cupids and encircled by a company of marine deities mounted on sea-horses or other aquatic mounts. This mosaic was restored several times during the life of the villa. The niches contain further scenes of preparation for the bath or the enjoyment of waiting for fresh clothes, offered by one's valets, while wrapped in a comfortable white bath robe.

Beyond the *frigidarium* is a vestibule (figure 216: 16) leading to the warm baths. The mosaic is a scene of the bather receiving a rubdown. Two of the attendant slaves are named, the only persons so distinguished in the whole villa. They are Titus and Cassius.

The warm rooms of the bath (figure 216: 17) have lost their floors, which, as commonly in Roman baths, were suspended on masonry piers so that warm air could be kept circulating for the comfort of the bathers.

Returning to the main peristyle, one finds the

Figure 218
Piazza Armerina,
Late Roman
Villa, Mosaic

next suite of rooms along the peristyle's north side. The rooms with the figured mosaics are in the center of the group. One (figure 216: 18) has the Rape of the Sabine Women rep-resented by youths and young women in contemporary dress. There is little even faintly erotic art among the mosaics of the villa. The Rape of the Sabines was a modest theme con-

Figure 219
Piazza Armerina,
Late Roman
Villa, Mosaic

sidering its noble associations with the early years of Rome. A small medallion in the center of the geometric mosaics of room 19 (figure 216) of a youth and a largely undraped girl is the only other even mildly erotic scene. A second room of the group on the north side of the main peristyle contains a geometric mosaic including medallions of the Seasons and of fish and fowl. The fishing cupids return in a third room (figure 216: 20; figure 217). The sea and the cupids' net are full of life. One of the cupids sports with a dolphin. At the top of the mosaic there is the facade of a seaside villa.

The final mosaic of this group is one of the most charming of the entire decoration of the villa. It is called the Little Hunt (figure 216: 21). In its lower center one finds a scene of the culmination of the chase (figure 218). Beneath an awning suspended from trees the hunters, reclining on cushions, enjoy the freshly cooked game. One feeds a hound some of the scraps. Horses are tethered nearby. Servants are busy with wine that has been brought in carboys and more food from a wicker hamper. Above the feast there is a scene of sacrifice by a huntsman at a rustic shrine of Diana, goddess of the wild. Grooms stand by with horses and dogs. Two huntsmen approach with a wild boar, another holds a hare he has caught. Around the central elements there are other scenes: huntsmen with dogs, fowling, deer driven by horsemen into a net, the slaying of the wild boar, a mounted

hunter and hare. The charm of these pictures comes partly from their disconnected, vignette-like quality, partly from the richly varied trees and vegetation and partly from the gay tunics of the huntsmen.

The Great Hunt (figure 216: 10) which occupies the corridor separating the main peristyle from the great hall and other apartments above on the east side of the villa is not the hunting of local game but the collection of noble and exotic animals for display in the amphitheaters of Rome (figure 219). The mosaic is 59.6 meters in length (195 ft 5 in). It represents a typically Late Antique spatial projection embracing Africa, Asia and Italy. Italy is in the center, where the animals destined for the amphitheater are being unloaded from two ships. Immediately beyond this, two other ships are loading game. One, toward the northern scenes of the mosaic, is taking on animals apparently from North Africa, ostriches and antelope, while other prey are brought to the vessel by cart or in boxes or litters borne on the shoulders of huntsmen. Scenes of capture occupy the further parts of the mosaic. A ring of huntsmen armed with spear and shield surround a board on which the body of a kid has been nailed to attract a leopard. Hunting in the mountains by mounted huntsmen takes place in a somewhat damaged part of the scene followed by images of a lion, leopards and antelope in the wild. The backdrop of this activity, along the upper border of the mosaic, are

Figure 220
Piazza Armerina,
Late Roman
Villa, Mosaic

the villas of North Africa. A much-damaged allegorical figure in the apse of the far end may represent Mauritania.

In the southern wing of the mosaic an elephant is being taken aboard ship. There are a camel and tiger in the background and an aurochs followed by two rhinoceroses come behind. Despite the Asian tiger, this scene certainly borders on equatorial Africa. Lions and tigers dominate the fauna of the subsequent scenes. A change of geographical setting seems to be indicated by a ship, again loading captured animals. Two vignettes of some interest are a tiger decoyed by its own reflection in a mirror and the scene of a griffin guarding a man in a wooden cage – surely a distorted reference to the notion of the Scythians and their treasure guarded by griffins. The allegorical figure of the apse at this end of the mosaic is perfectly preserved (figure 216: 22). It is a female figure holding an elephant tusk and flanked by an elephant and a tiger. She

may be India, thus completing the geographical sweep of the mosaic from western North Africa to furthest Asia.

This prominent representation of the collection of animals for the games is also found in several North African villas of the same period in which local dignitaries celebrated their munificence in providing animal shows for their cities. It is probable that the owner of the villa at Piazza Armerina had also staged games at Rome during his career and thus celebrated the scale and splendor of his undertaking. The owner's portrait has been sought among the figures of the mosaic, usually in the figure of the elderly man with two younger companions placed in the midst of the hunt in the south wing of the mosaic (figure 220). But the identification is mere speculation.

Returning to the north end of the corridor, we find a small suite of rooms largely with geometric mosaics save for one which is the only scene with a Sicilian subject in the entire villa (figure 216: 23). We see the cave of the Cyclops and Odysseus offering Polyphemus the bowl of wine which by intoxicating the giant will win freedom for Odysseus and his crew. Polyphemus appears not one-eyed but with an added 'single eye' placed in his forehead.

The Great Hall, which is entered from the corridor on the axis of the main peristyle, has lost its marble pavement. To the south, however, there is a suite of rooms with elaborately decorated pavements. The entrance (figure 216: 24) is a curved vestibule in the form of a small portico. The fishing cupids make yet another appearance here against the familiar background of seaside villas. Immediately behind the portico is an apsidal hall (figure 216: 4). Once more the subject of the mosaic floor is familiar, the marine thiasos (gathering of divinities), but presided over by the mythical poet Arion, whose music was known to have tamed the the deep (figure 221). Indeed, the sea nymphs and their companion tritons and cupids in the scene are mounted on horses, lions, and tigers whose hindquarters like those of the hippocamp (sea-horse) end in a fish's tail. There is even a centaur with fishy hindquarters in the group. In the apse there was a large head of Oceanus, now much damaged.

To left and right of this hall and its forecourt there are rooms where the decoration is given over to scenes of children (figure 216: 25, 26, 27, 28). One of the antechambers has a parody

Figure 221
Piazza Armerina,
Late Roman
Villa, Mosaic

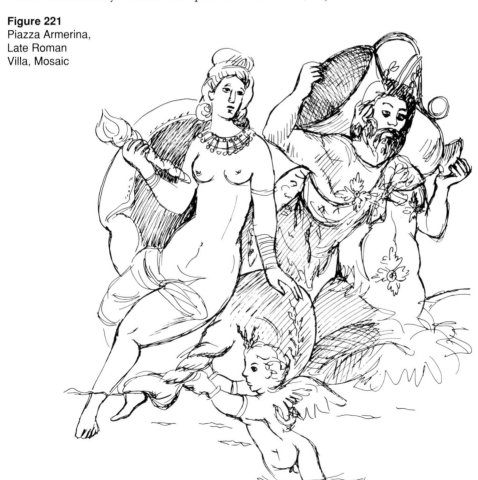

circus scene, children driving chariots pulled by birds (figure 216: 27). The four circus factions, green, blue, red, and white, are represented. The opposite antechamber shows a wrestling match between Cupid and Pan, the half-goat divinity of the wilds (figure 216: 25) There is a referee. Children are cheering for Cupid; adult figures (Hermes, two maenads – followers of Dionysus or Bacchus) are on Pan's side. Behind there is a table with palm branches of victory displayed in decorated bowls. Prizes of money in sacks are placed below the table. The mythological significance of this scene is far from clear.

The room behind the pavement with the scene of Cupid and Pan is divided into an inner and outer part (figure 216: 26). The floor of the outer part has a hunting scene. Young boys pursue hares, ducks, cocks, a goat and a peacock in a fruit garden. The inner scene is also a garden, where young girls are busy picking fruit. Between the two there is the scene of a boy carrying away the harvest.

The chamber behind the room with the circus scene pavement has to do with competitions (figure 216: 28). It is again a two-part room and in the opening to the apsidal inner area there is shown a table with prizes. Two sacks of money are placed on the table and between them are two baskets each containing a crown decked with branches. The crowns also carry small discs on sticks which were inserted into the crown. These discs appear to be decorated with spirals but the crowns of the lower scenes have discs marked with letters. In the apse itself there is a scene of two girls seated on upturned baskets in the act of making these crowns. Baskets of fruit stand beside them. In the main part of the chamber there is a mosaic with three registers. The upper register is a musical competition. The lower two registers are damaged, but here too there is a lyre player in the scene. In the center the only fully preserved figure is a child wearing mesh tights under his tunic and holding a whip while he stands on tiptoe. The precise implications of these scenes are not yet fully understood.

Only one further chamber opening off the main peristyle has its original figured mosaic floor. It is on the south side of the peristyle, and the room, large and apse-ended, was probably a dining-room (figure 216: 29). The scene is Orpheus, the magical poet and master of beasts and birds. All the exotic animals of the Great Hunt are gathered around him (including the griffin) as well as common fauna and small creatures down to the hedgehog, turtle and lizard.

The girl athletes in another room on the south side of the main peristyle (figure 216: 11) were added after the original pavements. These images of women athletes are not parodies of their male counterparts but refer to actual competitions practiced in late antiquity.

The marine and hunting scenes of the mosaics in the rooms around the main peristyle and of the baths are well attested subjects in the repertoire of late antique floor mosaics. The scenes of children in the mosaics of the apartments off the long corridor are more unusual. The grand mosaics of the trilobate hall (figure 216: 5) are the most unusual of the entire complex and are some of the most haunting scenes to have reached us from all of ancient art.

The trilobate hall, almost certainly used as a dining room, is hidden from the main body of the villa. It can be approached only through a doorway at the south end of the long corridor (figure 216: 30) and then through another small doorway that gives access to the oval portico situated before the hall itself (figure 216: 31). The entrance is quietly oblique, at the near end of the portico beside the steps leading up to the hall. Clearly the portico was not intended as the formal approach to the hall, such as the main peristyle was intended to be for the great hall above the long corridor (figure 216: 3). Rather, it was built to provide a view for the diners inside the trilobate hall outward into a planned architectural vista. This purpose was admirably served by the tapering lines of the oval portico which ended in an apsidal structure containing three niches for large sculptures.

The mosaics surrounding the oval portico repeat the animal protomes (heads and shoulders) from the portico of the main peristyle. Here however, the protomes are set in a continuous pattern of leafy ovals. The mosaics of the rooms opening off of the portico (figure 216: 32–7) are populated with cupids and children. On the south side of the portico, the two surviving pavements are both scenes of cupids fishing, familiar from the mosaics of the main wing of the villa. On the opposite side of the portico one room has a floor with a medallion of Hercules in the center of a design of cupids gathering the grapes. The neighboring room is another autumn scene in which children bring home the grapes and set to work trampling out the vintage in front of a country house.

The mosaics of the trilobate hall have a style of visual imagination and narrative brutality that we have not encountered up to now in the decoration of the villa. On entering the hall the wide pavement immediately before us is covered with the defeated adversaries of Hercules. It is as if the labors of the hero had been transformed into a nightmare in which each opponent suddenly looms up and then recedes in confusion among the other victims. The figures themselves are twisted in ways that have no precedents in classical art. A bull charges in the traditional butting position yet the head is not turned toward the viewer but is strangely hidden as it faces away. Desperate riders cling to their careening or fallen horses (figure 222). The monstrous Lernean water snake, now human-headed, shrinks miserably in size. The giant corpse of the lion sprawls across the scene in death.

The shock of the central floor is little relieved by the scene of the main apse above it. Here there are five of the giants, men with snakes for legs, who attempted to invade the home of the gods on Mt Olympus. All have been hit by divine arrows and writhe in agony as they die. Hercules joined the gods to repulse them.

The lateral apses show us Hercules in triumph to the left and to the right the Thracian king Lycurgus, foiled in his attempt on the nymph Ambrosia, who, seeking the protection of the earth, is already being transformed into a grape vine. The evil king's ax is raised but to the rescue comes the troop of the god Bacchus (Dionysus), including three maenads and a faithful panther. The figure of Bacchus is largely obliterated. Below, cupids gather the grapes.

Other scenes of transformations, drawing on the ever-popular *Metamorphoses* of Ovid, are shown at small scale on the thresholds of the three apses. The preserved sections give us Andromeda (or Hesione), Endymion, Daphne and Cyparissus.

The mosaicists who carried out the work at Piazza Armerina belong to the school that also worked in North Africa, especially in Tunisia. This is made evident not only by general comparisons of the more conventional mosaics of the main part of the villa with similar scenes in North Africa but also from small details of style such as the convention of indicating the folds of the forehead with a 'v' shape.

The program of the mosaics at Piazza Armerina, however, was by no means the transfer of an African scheme to Sicily. As already suggested, the mosaic decoration of the villa can be divided into three units: first, the main peristyle and

Figure 222
Piazza Armerina,
Late Roman
Villa, Mosaic

adjoining rooms including the bath, second, the rooms with the 'children's' mosaics, and third, the trilobate hall and the rooms off its portico. The first group represents standard themes of the Sicilian-North African mosaicists, hunts and marine compositions of sea divinities and cupids. Of course, there is variety and originality. The collection of animals for the amphitheater in the long corridor was clearly devised for this villa, and it seems to reflect the pride of the owner in games he had given at Rome. The circus and chariot racing appears as an architectural conceit in the baths and the vignettes of bathers and their attendants are happy touches invented for the occasion. The scene of the Rape of the Sabines is unusual. However, by and large the mosaics have a clearly functional and non-symbolic purpose: they suggest alternatively the adventure of the hunt – to be found in the vicinity of the villa – and the coolness of water to rest the returning hunter. Being inland the owner of the villa could not emulate his contemporaries with seaside villas who lay in their pools and simultaneously watched ships on the sea and hunters in the forest.[6] But his guests could be refreshed by the suggestion of cool waters after the exertions of the hunt.

The decoration of the private apartments of the villa, including the 'children's suite', is more difficult to interpret. There must be hidden conceits in the mosaics of the children. These may not be the children's apartments, but the decoration must have had a meaning for the family that we cannot understand. The trilobate triclinium and its court also present an originality of decoration and of artistic vision behind it which, together with the clearly private position of this suite, suggests that we have to do with the personality and beliefs of the master and mistress of the house. The decoration of the trilobate hall and of the rooms off the oval peristyle is directed to two divinities, Hercules and Bacchus. To pagan thought in the Late Empire, eager for security and a new order, these two divinities, harbingers of triumph and transformation, the Gloria Novi Saeculi (Glory of a New Era) and Nova Spes (New Hope) of contemporary coin types, were especially congenial. And in the intellectual climate of the age one must seriously consider to what extent the mosaics, particularly in this part of the villa, were intended to have a moral implication as well. Salvatore Settis has done this, arguing that not only in this suite, but also throughout the villa victory over nature is to be seen as a moral victory over one's baser self.[7] The same interpretation can be given to the hunts and the fishing scenes. It is applicable also to the circus scenes in which Late Antiquity equated the four factions with the four seasons, thus making possible an equation of victory in the circus with victory over time. In this view it would be a mistake to see cupids as merely playful figures; they are part of the Bacchic retinue (as when they harvest the grapes) and carry this association with them. The children's scenes may also be not merely parodies in the comic sense of the word but serious parodies with hidden meanings. In essence Hercules and Bacchus project a vision of victory and felicity. And for Late Antiquity theirs would be a triumph won not by force alone but by moral strength (virtus).

This interpretation, in my opinion, holds true for the visionary mosaics of the trilobate hall. Just as the lord of the villa glorified the organization of the games in the mosaics of the long corridor, here he commissioned an expression of the faith he shared with his age in the figure of Hercules as savior and preceptor, together with Bacchus, god of transformation and hope. Whether a similar outlook was intended for the decorated pavements elsewhere in the villa is a question on which opinions will differ.

NOTES

1 Prehistoric Sicily

1 About 6 million years ago the Mediterranean was dry during the so-called Messenian Event (K.J. Hsü (1983) *The Mediterranean was a Desert,* Princeton, NJ). But this is somewhat early for the arrival of tool-using hominids. I owe this reference to Prof. John Imbrie.

2 A. Leroi-Gourhan (1968) *Treasures of Prehistoric Art,* New York. For a critical appraisal see A. Sieveking (1989) *The Cave Artists,* London.

3 G. Navarra (1984) *E le 'Pietre Strane' Raccontano Ancora,* Bologna.

4 M. Gimbutas (1974) *Gods and Goddesses of Old Europe,* London.

5 C. Malone (1985) 'Pots, prestige and ritual in Neolithic Southern Italy', *Papers in Italian Archaeology* IV, pt ii, Oxford British Archaeological Reports International Series 244: 118-51.

6 The expression is that of A. Sherratt (1976) 'Resources, technology, and trade: an essay in Early European metallurgy', in G. de Sieveking *et al.* (eds) *Problems in Economic and Social Archaeology,* Boulder, Col., pp. 557-81.

7 B. Malinowski (1932) *The Argonauts of the Western Pacific,* London.

8 T. Veblen (1899) *The Theory of the Leisure Class,* New York.

9 D. Trump (1972) *Malta: An Archaeological Guide,* London. There is an additional temple known at Ta Raddiena.

10 C. Renfrew (1973) *Before Civilization,* London.

11 L. Maniscalco (1989) 'Ocher containers and trade in the Central Mediterranean Copper Age', *American Journal of Archaeology,* 93: 537-52.

12 B. E. McConnell (1985) *San Cono-Piano Notaro-Grotta Zubbia Ceramics in Sicilian Prehistory,* diss., Brown University. John Evans suspected such a relationship but revealed his suspicions only in a passing phrase of his (1959) *Malta,* London, p.161.

13 K.G. Ponting (1966) *The Wool Trade,* Manchester p. 2.

14 J. Gledhil and M. Larsen (1982)'The Polanyi paradigm and a dynamic analysis of archaic states', in C. Renfrew, M.J. Rowlands and B.A. Seagraves (eds) *Theory and Explanation in Archaeology,* Southampton Conference, New York, pp. 197-230.

15 G. Pettinato (1979) 'Il commercio internazionale di Ebla: economia statale e privata', in E. Lipinski (ed.) *State and Temple Economy in the Ancient Near East,* Orientalia Lovaniensia Analecta 5, Louvain, pp. 171-234.

16 No argument against McConnell's thesis based on the supposed small burden of Early Bronze Age vessels should be entertained. The sketch of a ship scratched onto a block of the Tarxien Temple is reminiscent of the longboats of the Aegean, but, as a recent study has shown these are not normal vessels but traditional craft maintained for ceremonies; C. Broodbank (1989) 'The longboat and society in the Cyclades in the Keros-Syros Culture', *American Journal of Archaeology* 93: 319-38.

17 For the development of the Sicilian chamber tomb see B. E. McConnell (1988) 'Indagini preistoriche nel territorio di Ribera (AG); Le tombe dell' età del rame in Contrada Castello ed a Cozzo Mastrogiovanni', *Sicilia Archeologica* 21: 101-12.

18 G. Sluga Messina (1983) *Analisi dei motivi decorativi della ceramica di Castelluccio di Noto,* Rome.

19 Bernabò Brea (1985) *Gli Eoli e l'inizio dell' età del bronzo nelle isole Eolie e nell' Italia meridionale,* Naples.

20 R.J. Harrison (1980) *The Beaker Folk,* London; S. Tusa (1987) 'The bell beaker in Sicily', in W.H. Waldren and R.C. Kennard (eds) *Bell Beakers of the Western Mediterranean,* Oxford, pp. 523-50.

21 The 'Mycenean' sherds reported from Morgantina appear dubious, cf. R. Leighton (1984) 'Mycenean pottery at Morgantina', *American Journal of Archaeology* 88: 389-91.

22 F. Lo Schiavo, E. Macnamara and L. Vagnetti (1985) 'Late Cypriote imports to Italy and their influence on local bronze work', *Papers of The British School at Rome* 53: 1-71.

23 Ten Mycenean sherds are now reported from the settlement, but the exact phase of Mycenean pottery and the relation of the sherds to any building is not stated; R.A. Wilson (1987–8), *Archaeological Reports:* 113.

24 G. Bass (1967) *Cape Gelidonya: A Bronze Age Shipwreck*, Transactions of the American Philosophical Society, vol. 57, pt 8; J.D. Muhly, T.S. Wheeler and R. Maddin (1977) 'The Cape Gelidonya shipwreck and the bronze age trade in metals in the eastern Mediterranean', *Journal of Field Archaeology* 4: 353–65; G. Bass (1986) 'A Bronze Age shipwreck at Ulu Burun (Kas)', *American Journal of Archaeology* 90: 269–96; subsequent reports in the same journal by C. Pulak (1988) 92: 1–37 and G. Bass (1989) 93: 1–30.

25 The legend of the Trojan War, as known from the tradition of epic verse enshrined in the Iliad and Odyssey, should not be confused with the history of the Late Bronze Age. In the present author's opinion the roots of the Troy story have to do with retribution meted out to the perpetrators of the sack of a sanctuary in the third millennium. In the 2,000 years between that time and the composition of Homer's poetry, the tale became inextricably intertwined with folktale, fiction and saga. The persistent efforts to make Homer's Troy and Homer's Greece into literal history are a sad commentary on the entrenched myopia with which these questions are viewed. The author's view is argued in R.R. Holloway (1981) *Italy and the Aegean: 3000–700 BC*, Archaeologia Transatlantica, vol. 1, Providence, RI, and Louvain.

26 Summarized in L. Bernabò Brea (1957) *Sicily before the Greeks*, London.

27 L. Maniscalco (1985–6) 'Tipologia funeraria nella Sicilia del tardo bronzo, Pantalica, Dessueri, Caltagirone', *Archivio Storico per la Sicilia Orientale* 81–2: 241–65.

28 A.M. Bietti-Sestieri (1979) 'I processi storici nella Sicilia orientale fra la tarda Età del Bronzo e gli inizi dell' Età del Ferro sulla base dei dati archeologici', in Istituto Italiano di Preistoria e Protostoria, Atti della XXI Riunione Scientifica, Il Bronzo Finale in Italia, Florence, pp.599–630.

2 Early Greek Sicily

1 G. Voza (1978) 'La necropoli della valle del Marcellino presso Villasmundo', in *Insediamenti Coloniali Greci nell' VIII e VII Secolo a.C.*, Cronache di Archeologia 17: 104–10.

2 Recent finds of Thapsos cups and similar material in southeastern Sicily are reported by P. Pelagatti (1978) 'Materiali tardo geometrico dal retroterra di Siracusa', ibid., pp. 111–12.

3 The designations by which the temples of Selinus are known are a combination of the systems of J.I. Hittorff and L. Zanth (1870) *Architecture antique de la Sicile: Recueil des monuments de Ségeste et de Sélinonte*, Paris, and that of R. Koldewey and O. Puchstein (1899) *Die griechischen Tempel in Unteritalien und Sicilien*, Berlin.

4 For Temple ER see Chapter 3. The quarries of Selinus are an impressive testimony to the building activity of the city. For them see A. Peschlow-Bindokat (1990) *Die Steinbrüche von Selinunte*, Mainz.

5 G. Navarra (1964) *Città sicane, sicule e greche nella zona di Gela;* (1975) 'E Gela e Katagela', *Römische Mitteilungen* 82: 21–82

6 A. De Miro (1962) 'La fondazione di Agrigento e l'ellenizzazione del territorio fra il Salso e il Platani', *Kokalos* 8: 122–52.

7 A. De Miro (1986) 'Il santuario greco di località Casalicchio presso Licata', in *Atti della seconda giornata di studi sull' archeologia licatese e della zona della bassa valle dell 'Himera*, pp. 97–124.

8 Inscriptiones Graecae 14, 256.

9 P. Orsi (1900) 'L'Heroon di Antifemo?', in *Notizie degli Scavi*, pp. 272–7.

10 B. Pace (1949) *Arte e Civiltà nella Sicilia Antica*, Milan, vol. 1, 2nd edn, p.188.

11 P. Orsi (1900) in *Notizie degli Scavi*, pp. 280–1; G.V. Gentili (1964) in *Epigrafica* 8: 11–18.

12 E. De Miro and G. Fiorentini (1978) 'Gela nell' VIII e VII, secolo a. C., in *Insediamenti coloniali greci in Sicilia nell 'VIII e VII secolo a. C.* (Atti della 2a riunione scientifica della Scuola di Perfezionamento in Archeologia Classica dell' Università di Catania) pp. 90–9.

13 See the summary by Anna Siracusano (1983) *Il santuario rupestre di Agrigento*, Rome.

14 See also the remarks of T.J. Dunabin (1948) *The Western Greeks*, pp. 324–5.

15 The following treatment depends heavily on P. Pelagatti and G. Vallet (1980) 'Le necropoli', *La Sicilia Antica*, Palermo, 1, 2: 355–96

16 E. De Miro (1983) 'Lastra di piombo con scena dionisiaca dal territorio di Piazza Armerina', in *Aparchai, nuove ricerche e studi Paolo Enrico Arias*, Pisa, pp. 179–83.

17 The fact that Greece, including Greek Sicily, did not have a money economy until the second half of the sixth century, is of little consequence. Payment was made in other ways.

18 M. Guarducci (1983) 'Ancora sull'epigrafe del tempio di Apollo a Siracusa', *Accademia nazionale dei Lincei, Classe di scienze morali, storiche e filologiche Rendiconti* 8, 32: 13–20.

19 V. Tusa (1983) *La scultura in pietra di Selinunte*, Palermo.

20 The purpose of such series was to suggest sexual congress, an idea present in all the troops of satyrs and women on Dionysiac vases and one spelled out by the scene of coitus on a painted antefix from a small sanctuary at Gela.

21 Below the cloak and peplos the goddess' feet emerge as is traditional in the earliest Greek female statues. The lower body of such a figure is known from Megara, a tube of stone with the feet exposed under a low arch of the hem.

22 An early kouros head in limestone in a style not unlike that of the cult statue head from Temple E at Selinus comes from Acragas. The body is unfortunately lost. Only if it were preserved could one compare its style with that of the Sambrotides kouros.

23 The hypogea of Megara Hyblaea and at Monte Adranone (Sambuca di Sicilia), which were built in masonry, are not to be confused with the rock-cut chamber tombs of the Sicels.

24 F. Cordano (1986) 'Le leggi calcidesi di Monte San Mauro di Caltagirone', *Decima Miscellanea Greca e Romana, Rome*, pp. 33–60.

25 The vase is illustrated in *American Journal of Archaeology* 1959, 63, pls 43 and 44.

26 Exploration of the hinterland of Himera and the contact of this city with the native populations is only in a preliminary phase of development. One site in this region which has produced interesting results is Terravecchia di Cuti. At this site, possibly a sub-colony or dependency of Himera, evidence of sanctuaries with Greek terracotta masks and figurines and fragments of five large-scale statues in terracotta has been brought to light.

3   Late Archaic and Classical Greek Sicily

1   In addition to the Sambrotides kouros there are two early archaic stone kouros heads from Acragas.

2   B. Barletta (1987) 'The Draped Kouros and the workshop of the Syracusan youth', *American Journal of Archaeology* 91: 233–46.

3   Barletta argues that the Sicilian kouroi are more slender than their Attic counterparts. However, she is comparing them, I think, with the Attic kouroi of the end of the sixth century, rather than the pieces such as Acropolis no. 692 that belong to the very end of the series in the early fifth century. Despite her careful analysis and wide collection of comparative material for the draped kouros in Syracuse, I believe her reconstruction of an enterprising atelier of Sicilian sculptors, whose relations with the marble quarries on Paros would have brought it into a milieu from which it acquired both skill at working marble and the style of Aegean artists, to be both

cumbersome and unrealistic. These kouroi are masterpieces of artists with long training in an eminent school of marble working, not quick transplants of rapidly acquired technique. I therefore prefer to maintain the opinion originally expressed in my (1975) *Influences and Styles in the Late Archaic and Early Classical Greek Sculpture of Sicily and Magna Graecia*, Louvain, p. 32–3.

4   The mannerism is descended from sculpture in Ionia, G.M.A. Richter (1968), *Korai*, London, nos. 37 and 38.

5   H. Payne (1936) *Archaic Marble Sculpture from the Athenian Acropolis*, London, pp. 39–40.

6   E. De Miro (1968) 'Il guerriero di Agrigento e la scultura di stile severo in Sicilia', *Chronache di Archeologia e di Storia d'Arte* 7: 143–56.

7   Joint authors (1988) *La Statua Marmorea di Mozia, Atti della Giornata di Studio, Marsala, 1986*, Rome (Studi e Materiali dell'Istituto di Archeologia dell' Università di Palermo, vol. 8, 1988).

8   The debate concerning the origin of this statue and its possibly illegal export from Italy may be followed most easily in the Italian press, especially *Corriere della Sera* for 5, 10 and 14 August 1988 and notably the issue of 4 August quoting a statement by Prof. Graziella Fiorentini, Superintendent of Cultural Property at Agrigento, whose jurisdiction (as of 1988) has been particularly concerned with the affair.

9   The opinion of authorities on this point is not unanimous. H. Berve and G. Gruben (1976) *Greek Temples, Theaters and Shrines*, New York, p. 421 remark, 'The hitherto eccentrically withdrawn architecture of the West became receptive to the now mature achievement of classical architecture of the ancient homeland.' But D. Mertens (1984) *Der Tempel von Segesta und die dorische Tempelbaukunst des Griechischen Westens in Klassischer Zeit*, Mainz, p. 195, suggests (in translation), 'One may observe that the Syracusan temple in its weaker plasticity of its single elements despite their size holds to a tendency toward a more extensive rationalization of the groundplan fully in the western Greek tradition. Influence from the motherland can only have arrived in fragmentary form'.

10   Selinus, Temples A, O and E, Acragas, Temple of Heracles, Hera, Concord and Aesclepius. For the suggestion of cult practices using upper parts of temples see M. Miles' summary of communication to the annual meeting of the Archaeological Institute of America (1985) *American Journal of Archaeology* 89: 341.

11   The early nineteenth-century restoration on a temple podium in the so-called Sanctuary of the Chthonian divinities contains elements of an entablature characterized by a cyma reversa

molding decorated with boldly modeled leaves below the mutules. Fragments of similar moldings are known from the inland city of Morgantina, where they were found reused in the theater.

12 M. Bell (1980) 'Stylobate and roof in the Olympieion at Akragas', *American Journal of Archaeology*, 84: 359–72; J. de Waele (1980) 'Der Entwurf der dorischen tempel von Akragas', *Archäologischer Anzeiger*, pp. 216–22; I. Caretto Castigliano and M. Savio (1983) 'Considerazioni sulla metrologia e sulla genesi concettuale del tempio di Giunone ad Agrigento', *Bollettino d'árte* 68: 35.

13 de Waele, op. cit.

14 B. Barletta (1983) *Ionic Influence in Archaic Sicily: The Monumental Art*, Gothenburg, p. 134.

15 Remains of an extramural sanctuary at Segesta have been excavated in Contrada Mango. There are remains of temples of the Doric order of both the fifth and sixth centuries. The material is unpublished.

4 Coinage

1 C. Arnold-Bucchi, L. Beer-Tobey and N.M. Waggoner (1988) 'A Greek archaic silver hoard from Selinus', *American Numismatic Society Museum Notes* 33: 1–36.

2 It has been alleged that the use of the city's name in its full form, as it appears on the earliest coins of Naxos and Zankle (Messina) means that these coins cannot be earlier than the adoption of a similarly full form of inscription, rather than a single letter or an abbreviation, by the cities of old Greece. But evidently, in this case, the Sicilians were the leaders.

3 See p.49.

4 Any extensive collection of a coinage will contain coins sharing common dies; it is, therefore, the number of dies in use that is the true indication of the size of the coinage. The obverse die (in Roman and later coinages usually the side bearing a bust – and thus our 'heads') was fixed in an anvil. The reverse die (our 'tails') was held above the flan of metal to be struck. Reverses consequently were subject to greater wear than obverses, and frequently replaced, even more than once, during the life of a single obverse. Frequently one of the new reverses had not been totally consumed when the obverse was replaced, and this phenomenon gives rise to the cross connection between dies referred to as die linkage. It is often possible to reconstruct the sequence in which the coins comprising an individual series were issued and, given any chronological fixed points, to arrive at surprisingly precise dates for individual pieces. The chronology of early Greek series are naturally somewhat elastic, except where individual pieces may be connected with historical events.

5 As shown by the pattern of die linkage.

6 E. Boehringer (1929) *Die Münzen von Syrakus*, Berlin.

7 11:26:3.

8 C. Kraay (1969) *Greek Coins and History*, London.

9 The victory must have been won after the expulsion of the Samians from Messina in the early 480s, and before Anaxilas' death in 476 BC. While in control of Messina, the Samian adventurers who had come there fleeing the débâcle of the Ionian revolt against the Persian Empire issued a coinage recalling that of their homeland, a lion's pelt on the obverse and the prow of a galley on the reverse. The coins have no legends but are marked with a series of letters apparently indicating the year of issue. The chronological problems posed by these issues are difficult. For one solution see R.R. Holloway (1978) *Art and Coinage in Magna Graecia*, Bellinzona, pp. 40–6.

10 J.K. Jenkins (1971) 'Himera: the coins of the Akragantine type', *La Monetazione arcaica di Himera fino al 472 a.C.*, Naples, pp. 21–36.

11 C. Boehringer (1968) 'Hieron's Aetna und das Hieroneion', *Jahrbuch für Numismatik und Geldgeschichte*, 18: 69–98.

12 The emendation made on the basis of the variant version of the epigram of the dedication given in a Byzantine lexicon (the *Suda*).

13 For this theory see R.R. Holloway (1964) 'Damarete's Lion', *American Numismatic Society, Museum Notes* 11: 1–11. I believe that the tale of a Carthaginian gift to Damarete is simply learned but unsubstantiated speculation of later historians. Other versions of the story, repeated in Pollux, *Onomasticon* 9:85 and in Hesychios, *ad verb.*, to the effect that Damarete made a collection of jewelry among the women of Syracuse for the war effort, or contributed her own jewelry, may possibly contain a distorted reference to the dowry. The reasons for the dramatic increase in coinage at Syracuse seen in the 'mass coinage' are related to the fiscal policies of the tyrants, see R.R. Holloway (in press) 'Coinage production in sixth and fifth century Sicily', in Centre National de la Recherche Scientifique – Monnaie de Paris, *Colloques, Rhythmes de la Production Monetaire*.

14 L.O. Tudeer (1913), 'Die tetradrachmenprägung von Syrakus', *Zeitschrift für Numismatik* 30, revised by R.R. Holloway (1977) 'La struttura delle emissioni di Siracusa nel periodo dei "Signierende Kunstler"', *Annali dell' istituto*

italiano di Numismatica 23: 33–38.

15 Since in some of the issues of the 'Signing Masters' Period the female head becomes the obverse die, it is not possible to identify the two types as the obverse or reverse die.

16 D. White (1986) 'The Morris Coin', *Expedition* 28: 13–21.

17 E. Gabrici (1927) *La monetazione del bronzo nella Sicilia antica*, Palermo.

18 *Economicus* 2.

19 A few 'pegasi' were subsequently minted in Sicily, by Syracuse, Leontini and Eryx.

20 The coinage of Motya, largely of didrachms, was brought to an end in 397 BC.

21 For the red-figure pottery of Sicily see A.D. Trendall (1989) *Red-Figure Vases of South Italy and Sicily*, New York.

5   Later Greek, Punic and Roman Sicily

1 F.E. Winter (1979) 'The Chronology of the Euryalos Fortress at Syracuse', *American Journal of Archaeology* 67: 363–87; cf. A.W. Lawrence (1979) *Greek Aims in Fortification*, pp. 290–9.

2 V. Tusa (1986) *La Fortification dans l'histoire du monde grec*, Paris, pp. 111–20.

3 Personal observations of the author while a member of the Morgantina Excavation staff between 1958 and 1962, House of the Arched Cistern. The lead piping of this building, including the joints and preserved lengths of pipe running up to the second story, was subsequently robbed from the site.

4 The following comparison of Vitruvius' 'Greek' house and the dwellings at Morgantina is based on the memorial lecture delivered by the late Prof. Richard Stillwell, co-director of the Morgantina Excavations, in honor of his Princeton classmate Prof. Charles Alexander Robinson, Jr, at Brown University in 1966. The lecture was unfortunately never published.

5 Attempts to discover the basis for Vitruvius' Greek house in present-day Greece and Turkey have been made but are far from convincing, see for example K. Reber (1988) 'Aedificia Graecorum, zu Vitruvius Beschreibung des griechischen Hauses', *Archäologischer Anzeiger*, pp. 645–66 and F. Pesando (1988) *La Casa dei Greci*, Milan, which, however, takes up the evidence from Morgantina.

6 L. Bernabò Brea (1967) 'Studi sul teatro greco di Siracusa', *Palladio* 16: 97–152.

7 C. Anti and L. Polacco (1981) *Il Teatro Antico di Siracusa*, Rimini.

8 C. Courtois (1989) *Le Bâtiment de scène des théâtres d'Italie de Sicile*, Louvain, p. 26–30.

9 F. Coarelli and M. Torelli (1989) *Sicilia* (Guide archeologiche Laterza), Bari, p. 65.

10 H. Frost *et al.* (1976) 'Lilybaeum. The Punic ship', *Notizie degli Scavi*, ser. 8, supp. to vol. 30.

11 Several other house sanctuaries have been discovered throughout the city. In the North and South Demeter Sanctuaries in particular, excavation recovered an abundance of votive offerings, large terracotta busts of the goddesses, terracotta figurines, pottery, coins, and jewelry including a silver diadem. The fury of the destruction which was visited on these shrines during the Second Punic War suggests that in some way they may have been connected with political associations, D.H. White (1964) 'Demeter's Sicilian cult as a political instrument', *Greek, Roman and Byzantine Studies* 5: 261–79.

12 M. Bell (1981) *The Terracottas*, Morgantina Studies, vol. 1, Princeton, NJ.

6   The villa at Piazza Armerina

1 W.L. MacDonald (1983) *The Architecture of the Roman Empire*, vol. 2, New Haven, Conn., pp. 277–9.

2 As has been pointed out by R.J.A. Wilson (1983) *Piazza Armerina*, Austin, Tex.

3 The representation of the Circus Maximus in Rome on the mosaic of the bath was interpreted by A. Ragona (1966) *L'obelisco di Constanzo II e la datazione dei mosaici di Piazza Armerina, Caltagirone*, to support a date for the mosaic after AD 357 when Constantius II erected an obelisk in the Circus Maximus and had a flame-like finial such as is represented on the obelisk as shown on the Piazza Armerina mosaic attached to it. It is not certain, however, that this must be the obelisk of Constantius II because Augustus himself had erected an obelisk in the Circus which remained there, although eventually fallen and broken, until it was recovered and moved to the Piazza del Popolo in 1589. Rather than assuming that the Augustan obelisk was somehow moved out of the way, it would now seem better to identify the Piazza Armerina representation with the obelisk of Augustus, also sporting, evidently, a metal cap. See also now J. Humphrey (1986) *Roman Circuses*, Berkeley, Calif., pp. 223–33.

4 See G. Voza, 'Le ville romane del Tellaro e di Patti in Sicilia e il problema dei rapporti con l'Africa', *150-Jahr-Feier Deutsches Archäologisches Institut Rom* (Mitteilungen des Deutschen Archäologischen Instituts, Römische Abteilung, Ergänzungsheft 25, 1982), pp. 202–9. There are some other notable examples of Roman villas in Sicily. The villa at Castroreale Terme dates to the

first century AD, as does the villa at Dussueli (Realmonte) with important mosaics (one a marine scene with Poseidon). The Roman house of the High Imperial Age discovered at Villa Bonanno in Palermo contained the important mosaics, Orpheus, the Seasons, now in the Palermo museum. There is significant mosaic decoration in houses at Acragas, especially the House of the Gazelle and the House of the Abstract Master. At Marsala (Lilybaeum) there are remains of houses of the third century AD. Finally, a villa with a history extending far into Late Antique times is under excavation at Favara.

5   This question was debated at the Congress organized by the Scuola di Perfezionamento in Archeologia Classica of the University of Catania at Piazza Armerina in 1983 and published as *La Villa Romana del Casale di Piazza Armerina* (Cronache di Archeologia, vol. 23, 1984). A. Carandini has made a case for Proculus Populonius in A Carandini, A. Ricci and M. de Vos (1982) *Filosofiana, The Villa of Piazza Armerina,* Palermo.

6   Gerontius, *Vita Sanctae Melaniae*, 18, 'Cum igitur lavaret in natatoria, videbat et naves transeuntes et venationes in silva'.

7   S. Settis (1975) 'Per l'interpretazione di Piazza Armerina', *Mélanges de l'école française de Rome. Antiquité* 87: 921–94.

BIBLIOGRAPHY (1980–9)

Since the 1960s English readers have turned to two admirable works for knowledge of Sicilian archaeology, T.J. Dunbabin's (1948, repr. 1964) *The Western Greeks, The History of Sicily and South Italy from the Foundation of the Greek Colonies to 480 B.C,* Oxford, and L. Bernabò Brea's (1957) *Sicily before the Greeks,* London. Both, however, have aged. More recent books in English concerned with Greek Sicily have brought the treatment of *The Western Greeks* up to date only in part. Among these one may mention A.G. Woodhead (1962), *The Greeks in the West,* London; M.I. Finley (1968), *A History of Ancient Sicily to the Arab Conquest,* London; E. Sjöqvist (1973), *Sicily and the Greeks,* The Jerome Lectures, Ann Arbor, Mich., and J. Boardman (1980), *The Greeks Overseas,* 2nd edn, London. For prehistory Bernabò Brea's treatment has found no successor outside Italy, although Sicilian prehistory and Greek colonization were placed in a wider context by R.R. Holloway (1981), *Italy and the Aegean: 3000–700 BC,* Archaeologia Transatlantica, vol. 1, Providence, RI, and Louvain. A collection of photographs by Max Hirmer with commentary was published by E. Langlotz (1965), *Ancient Greek Sculpture of South Italy and Sicily,* New York, while a thorough collection of sculpture in stone and bronze from the same region was published by R.R. Holloway (1975), *Influences and Styles in the Late Archaic and Early Classical Greek Sculpture of Sicily and Magna Graecia,* Louvain.

The bibliography in Italian is understandably richer. B. Pace's (1935) *Arte e Civiltà nella Sicilia Antica,* Milan, (4 vols, 2nd edn of vol. 1, Milan, 1949, is still basic. More recent is the work by a team of authors under the editorship of E. Gabba and G. Vallet (1980), *La Sicilia Antica,* Palermo, 2 vols in 5 parts. A similar, and magnificently illustrated, volume, edited by G. Pugliesi Carratelli (1985) *Sikanie, storia e civiltà della Sicilia greca,* Milan, has been sponsored by the Credito Italiano; a companion volume dealing with the indigenous people of Sicily and Italy has been announced. A detailed summary of Sicilian prehistory is given by S. Tusa (1983), *La Sicilia nella preistoria,* Palermo.

An important bibliographical tool is now being produced under the editorship of G. Nenci and G. Vallet (1977 ff.), *Bibliografia Topografica della Colonizzazione Greca in Italia e nelle Isole Tirreniche,* Pisa and Rome. Vol. 5 (1987) carries the bibliography of individual sites through 'Crotone'. A noteworthy addition to general bibliographies is G.A.M. Arena (1985) *Bibliografia Generale delle Isole Eolie,* Biblioteca dell' Archivio Storico Messinese, vol. 3. There are two older works with excellent topographical coverage. The first is *Enciclopedia dell' Arte Antica* (1958–73) in seven volumes with supplement and atlas, Rome. A further supplement is in preparation. The second is R. Stillwell (ed.) (1976) *The Princeton Encyclopedia of Classical Sites,* Princeton, NJ. A detailed bibliography for the preceding years was published by P.G. Guzzo and R. Paris in (1983) *Bollettino d'arte* pp. 99–135 and as a supplement to the same periodical (1985) pp. 5–59. Otherwise the basic bibliographic source is the annual *Archäologische Bibliographie* of the German Archaeological Institute.

Reports of current work are to be found in *Sicilia Archeologica,* Trapani, in *Kokalos,* Palermo, especially in the volumes of *Kokalos* devoted to the successive congresses of Sicilian archaeology, the Proceedings of the Fifth Congress in (1980–1) vols 26–7 and of the Sixth Congress in (1984–5) vols 30–1. Reports published at intervals and in each case covering several years' work are found in *Archaeological Reports* (Society for the Promotion of Hellenic Studies) and *Archäologischer Anzeiger* (German Archaeological Institute).

There are two excellent and recent archaeological guidebooks for Sicily. The guide of F. Coarelli and M. Torelli (1984), *Sicilia,* Guide archeologiche Laterza, covers the entire island. The guide by V. Tusa and E. De Miro (1983), *Sicilia occidentale,* Itinerari archeologici, Newton Compton, covers central Sicily as well as the west. Both have extensive bibliographies.

The titles grouped in the following bibliography include only works published after 1980. Some of the greatest names of Sicilian archaeology are therefore absent. First and foremost among them is Paolo

185

Orsi, who shaped almost every branch of Sicilian archaeology during his long working life on the island between 1888 and 1936. The monographs and papers of Orsi and the other distinguished figures of his generation and of its successor, to whom the notable advances of the immediate postwar period are due, are readily at hand for those who pursue the sources cited above. Our bibliography is also selective. Studies of individual objects or classes of objects have generally not been included, except in the case of coins. No attempt has been made to gather the bibliography of Sicilian epigraphy or history.

Prehistory

Amore, G. (1981) 'Nuove acquisizioni sul neolitico nel territorio di Caltagirone', *Kokalos* 25: 3–24.

Amoroso, D. (1981) 'Insediamenti castellucciani nel territorio di Caltagirone: indagine topografica', *Kokalos* 25: 25–53.

—— (1983) 'Un corredo tombale e la fase di Thapsos nel territorio calatino', *Archivio Storico per la Sicilia Orientale* 79: 259–77.

Barfield, L.H. (1984) 'The Bell Beaker Culture in Italy', in *L'Age du cuivre européen*, Paris, pp. 129–34.

Bernabò Brea, L. (1980) 'Sardiniens Beziehungen zu Malta Sizilien und zu den Aeolischen Inseln', in *Kunst und Kultur Sardiniens vom Neolithicum bis zum Ende der Nuragenzeit*, Karlsruhe, pp. 192–200.

—— (1985) *Gli Eoli e l'inizio dell'età del bronzo nelle isole Eolie e nell'Italia meridionale. Archeologia e leggende*, Naples.

—— (1987) 'L'età del rame nell' Italia insulare, Sicilia, e le isole Eolie', in D. Cocchi (ed.), *L'età del rame in Europa*, Rassegna di Archeologia, Viareggio, vol. 7, pp. 469–508.

Bernabò Brea, L. and Cavalier, M. (1980) *Meligunìs Lipára, 4. L'acropoli di Lipari nella preistoria*, Palermo.

Bietti Sestieri, A.M. (1980–1) 'La Sicilia e le isole eolie e i loro rapporti con le regioni tirreniche dell'Italia continentale dal neolitico alla colonizzazione greca', *Kokalos* 26–7: 8–66.

—— (1988) 'The "Mycenean Connection" and its impact on the central Mediterranean societies', *Dialoghi di Archeologia* 3, 6: 23–51.

Bloedow, E.F. (1987) 'Aspects of ancient trade in the Mediterranean: Obsidian', *Studi Micenei ed Egeo-Anatolici* 26: 187–98.

Borgognini Tarli, S. and Repetto, E. (1985) 'Diet, dental features and oral pathology in the Mesolithic samples from Uzzo and Molara caves (Sicily)', *Papers in Italian Archaeology*, Oxford, 4, 2: 87–100.

Castellana, G. (1984) 'Tre indagini sulla cultura indigena in Sicilia', in *Studi di antichità in onore di G. Maetzke*, Rome, pp. 211–27.

—— (1984–5) 'Ricerche nel territorio di Palma di Montechiaro e nel territorio di Favara', *Kokalos* 30–1: 521–7.

—— (1985–6) 'Il villaggio neolitico di Piano Vento presso di Palma di Montechiaro', in *Quaderni dell'Istituto di archeologia della Facoltà di lettere e filosofia dell'Università di Messina*, vol. 1, pp. 19–29.

—— (1986) 'Il villaggio neolitico di Piano Vento nel territorio di Palma di Montechiaro. Rapporto preliminare', in *Atti della seconda giornata di studi sull'archeologia Licatese e della zona della bassa valle dell'Himera, 19 gennaio 1985*, Licata, pp. 9–67.

—— (1987) 'Capanne della cultura di San Cono-Piano Notaro-Grotta Zubbia di Palma di Montechiaro', in D. Cocchi (ed.), *L'età del rame in Europa*, Rassegna di Archeologia, Viareggio, vol. 7, pp. 546–7.

—— (1987) 'Il villaggio neolitico di Piano Vento nel territorio di Palma di Montechiaro (Agrigento)', in *Atti della XXVI riunione scientifica dell'Istituto italiano di preistoria e protostoria, Firenze, 7–10 Novembre 1985*, Florence, pp. 793–800.

—— (1987) 'L'insediamento eneolitico di Piano Vento presso Palma di Montechiaro e l'annessa necropoli', in D. Cocchi (ed.), *L'età del rame in Europa*, Rassegna di Archeologia, Viareggio, vol. 7, pp. 544–5.

—— (1987) 'Ricerche nella piana di Gaffe nel territorio di Licata', *La preistoria in Sicilia* 1: 123–52.

Cavalier, M. (1981) 'Villaggio preistorico di S. Vincenzo', *Sicilia archeologica*, Trapani, 15: 46–7.

—— (1984) 'Materiali Micenei vecchi e nuovi dall'acropoli di Lipari', *Studi Micenei ed egeo-anatolici* 25: 143–54.

—— (1985–6) 'Nuovi rinvenimenti sul castello di Lipari', *Rivista di Scienze Preistoriche* 40: 225–54.

Cavalier, M. and Vagnetti, L. (1983) 'Frammenti di ceramica "matt-painted" policroma da Filicudi (Isole Eolie)', *Mélanges de l'école française de Rome* 95: 335–44.

—— (1984) 'Materiali micenei vecchi e nuovi dall' acropoli di Lipari', *Studi Micenei ed egeo-anatolici* 25: 143–54.

—— (1986) 'Arcipelago eoliano', in *Traffici Micenei nel Mediterraneo*, Taranto, pp. 141–6.

Ciabatti, E. (1985) 'Note conclusive concernenti lo scavo di un relitto dell'età del bronzo nella Baia di Lipari', in *Arqueologia submarina*, pp. 303–11.

Cultraro, M. (1987) 'Distribuzione dell' eneolitico nella fascia etnea meridionale e sue margini della Piana di Catania', in D. Cocchi (ed.), *L'età del rame in Europa*, Rassegna di Archeologia, Viareggio, vol. 7, pp. 550–1.

D'Agata, A.L. (1986) 'Considerazioni su alcune spade siciliane della media e tarda età del Bronzo', in *Traffici Micenei nel Mediterraneo*, Taranto, pp. 105–10.

— (1987) 'Un tipo vascolare della cultura di Thapsos: Il bacino con ansa a piastra bifida', *Studi Micenei ed egeo-anatolici* 26: 187–98.

Di Stefano, G. (1983) *Cava Ispica, Recenti scavi e scoperte*, Modica.

— (1984) *Piccola guida delle stazioni preistoriche degli Iblei*, Ragusa.

Egg, M. (1983) 'Ein eisenzeitliche Weihefund aus Sizilien', in *Jahrbuch des Römisch- Germanische Zentralmuseums (Mainz)*, vol. 30, pp. 195–205.

Frasca, M. (1983) 'Una nuova capanna sicula a Siracusa, in Ortigia. Tipologie dei materiali', *Mélanges d'archéologie et d'histoire de l'ecole française de Rome. Antiquité* 95: 565–98.

Giardino, C. (1986) 'Sicilia e Sardegna fra la tarda età del Bronzo e la prima età del Ferro. Aspetti e contatti nel Mediterraneo Centro-Occidentale nell' ambito della metallurgia', in *Atti del 2° Convegno di studi 'Un millennio di relazioni fra la Sardegna e i Paesi del Mediterraneo'*, Cagliari, pp. 419–29.

Gnesotto, F. (1982) 'Il sito preistorico di Casalicchio-Agnone in territorio di Licata (Agrigento)', in *Studi in onore di F. Rittatore Von Willer, 1. Preistoria e protostoria*, Florence, pp. 195–220.

Guzzardi, L. (1980) 'Un ipogeo preistorico a Calaforno e il suo contesto topografico', *Sicilia archeologica* 13: 67–94.

Holloway, R.R. (1983) 'Primi saggi di scavi a 'La Muculufa (Butera)', *Sicilia archeologica* 16, 52–3: 33–44.

— (1984) 'Synoicism in Bronze Age Sicily', *Papers in Italian Archaeology*, Oxford, 4, 3: 389–98.

— (1984–5) 'Scavi archeologici del periodo castellucciano a "La Muculufa" (Butera)', *Kokalos* 30–1: 483–8.

— (1986) 'Scavi archeologici alla Muculufa e premesse per lo studio della cultura Castellucciana', in *Atti della seconda giornata di studi sull'archeologia Licatese e della zona della bassa valle dell'Himera, 19 gennaio 1985*, Licata, pp. 69–90.

Holloway, R.R., Joukowsky, M.S. and Lukesh, S.S. (1988) 'Mining La Muculufa', *Archaeology* 41, 1: 40–7.

Infrance, G.C. (1981) 'I "Sesi" di Pantelleria', *Sicilia archeologica* 15: 46–97.

Joint authors (1986) *Traffici Micenei nel Mediterraneo: problemi storici e documentazione archeologica. Atti del Convegno di Palermo, 11–12 maggio e 3–6 dicembre 1984*, Taranto.

Joukowsky, M.S. (1987) 'L'industrie de la pierre et du matériel de broyage au début de l'âge du bronze à la Muculufa, en Sicile', *L'Anthropologie* 91, 1: 273–82.

La Rosa, V. (1980–1) 'La media e tarda età del bronzo nel territorio di Milena. Rapporto preliminare sulle ricerche degli anni 1978 e 1979', *Kokalos* 26–7: 642–8.

— (1984–5) 'L'insediamento preistorico di Serra del Palco in territorio de Milena', *Kokalos* 30–1: 475–82.

— (1985) 'Sopravvivenze Egee nella Sikania', *Quaderni della Ricerca Scientifica, Consiglio Nazionale delle Ricerche* 112, 2: 167–79.

— (1986) 'Nuovi ritrovamenti e sopravvivenze egee nella Sicilia meridionale', in *Traffici Micenei nel Mediterraneo*, Taranto, pp. 79–92.

Leighton, R. (1981) 'Strainer-spouted jugs and the problem of the earliest Phoenician influence in Sicily', *Journal of Mediterranean Archaeology and Anthropology* 1: 280–91.

— (1984) 'Evidence, extent and effects of Mycenaean contacts with south east Sicily during the Late Bronze Age', *Papers in Italian Archaeology*, Oxford, 4, 3: 399–412.

— (1984) 'Mycenean pottery at Morgantina', *American Journal of Archaeology* 88: 389–91.

Leonard Jr., A. (1980) 'A Bronze Age settlement on Monte Castellazzo, Sicily', *Muse. Annual of the Museum of Art and Archaeology, University of Missouri* 14: 19–23.

Lo Schiavo, F., Macnamara, E. and Vagnetti, L. (1985) 'Late Cypriote imports to Italy and their influence on local bronze work', *Papers of the British School at Rome* 53: 1–71.

McConnell, B.E. (1985) *San Cono-Piano Notaro-Grotta Zubbia Ceramics in Sicilian Prehistory*, diss., Brown University.

— (1987) 'La necropoli di Contrada Castello (Ribera, Agrigento) e lo sviluppo della tomba a grotticella con pozzetto', in D. Cocchi (ed.), *L'età del rame in Europa*, Rassegna di Archeologia, Viareggio, vol. 7, pp. 548–9.

— (1988) 'Indagini preistoriche nel territorio di Ribera (AG): Le tombe dell' età del rame in Contrada Castello ed a Cozzo Mastrogiovanni', *Sicilia Archeologica* 21: 101–12.

Malone, C. (1984) 'Pots, prestige and ritual in Neolithic southern Italy', *Papers in Italian Archaeology*, Oxford, 4, 2: 118–51.

Mambella, R. (1987) 'La problematica dei sacelli circolari del santuario sicano di Polizzello (CL)', *Rivista di Archeologia* 11: 13–24.

Maniscalco, L. (1985–6) 'Tipologie funerarie nella Sicilia del tardo bronzo: Pantalica, Dessueri, Caltagirone', *Archivio Storico per la Sicilia Orientale*, 81–2: 241–65.

— (1989) 'Ocher containers and trade in the Central Mediterranean Copper Age', *American Journal of Archaeology* 93: 537–42.

Mannino, G. (1982) 'Il villaggio dei Faraglioni di Ustica. Notizie preliminari', in *Studi in Onore di Ferrante Rittatore Von Willer*, Florence, pp. 279–98.

— (1987) 'Il Monte Finestrelle di Gibellina', *La preistoria in Sicilia* 1: 111–21.

Marazzi, M. and Tusa, S. (1987) 'Selinunte e il suo territorio. Analisi storica e progetto di ricognizione', *La preistoria in Sicilia*, 1: 39–109.

Matthäus, H. (1988) 'Heirloom or tradition? Bronze stands of the second and first millennium B.C. in Cyprus, Greece, and Italy', in *Problems in Greek Prehistory*, Bristol, pp. 285–93.

Moscetta, M.P. (1988) 'Il ripostiglio di Lipari, nuove considerazioni per un inquadramento cronologico e culturale', *Dialoghi di Archeologia* 3, 6: 53–78.

Navarra, G. (1984) *E Le 'Pietre Strane' Raccontano Ancora*, Bologna.

Pacci, M. (1982) 'Lo stile "protocastucciano" di Naro', *Rivista di scienze preistoriche* 37: 187–216.

— (1987) 'Nota su alcuni vasi protocastellucciani dalla Sicilia occidentale conservati all'Ashmolean Museum di Oxford', *La preistoria in Sicilia*, Trapani, 1: 7–37.

Palermo, D. (1981) 'Polizzello', *Cronache di Archeologia e Storia dell'Arte* 20: 103–50.

Panvini-di Stefano, R. (1986) 'La necropoli preistorica di contrada Anguilla di Ribera', in *Traffici Micenei nel Mediterraneo*, Taranto, pp.113–22.

Parker, G.S. (1985) 'The Early Bronze Age chamber tombs at La Muculufa', *Revue des Archéologues et Historiens d'art de Louvain* 18: 33.

Pelagatti, P. (1980) 'Materiali tardo geometrico dal retroterra di Siracusa', *Insediamenti Coloniali Greci nell VIII e VII Secolo a. C. Cronache di Archeologia* 17: 111–12.

Piperno, M. (1985) 'Some C^{14} dates for the palaeoeconomic evidence from the Holocene levels of Uzzo cave, Sicily', *Papers in Italian Archaeology*, Oxford, 4, 2: 83–6.

Pottino, G. (1981) 'Monumenti funerari della prima e media età del bronzo nella Sicilia centro meridionale', *Sicilia archeologica* 46–7: 73–86.

Sluga Messina, G. (1982) 'Due nuovi insediamenti preistorici nel bacino meridionale del Simeto: Coste di Palagonia e contrada Grotta S. Giorgio', in *Aparchai. Nuove ricerche e studi sulla Magna Grecia e la Sicilia antica in onore di P.E. Arias*, Pisa, pp. 45-50.

— (1983) *Analisi dei motivi decorativi della ceramica da Castelluccio di Noto (Siracusa)*, Rome.

— (1988) 'Villasmundo (Siracusa): Tomba neolitica presso il villaggio preistorico del Petraro', *Sicilia Archeologica* 21: 81–6.

Smith, T.R. (1987) *Mycenaean Trade and Interaction in the West Central Mediterranean, 1600–1000 B.C.*, British Archaeological Reports, International Series, Oxford.

Tomasello, F. (1984) 'L'architettura funeraria in Sicilia tra la media e tarda età del Bronzo. Le tombe a camera del tipo a tholos', in *Traffici Micenei nel Mediterraneo*, Taranto, pp. 93–100.

Tusa, S. (1985) 'The beginning of farming communities in Sicily. The evidence of Uzzo cave', *Papers in Italian Archaeology*, Oxford, 4, 2: 61–82.

— (1986) 'Dinamiche storiche nel territorio selinuntino nel II millennio alla luce delle recenti ricerche in contrada Marcita (Castelvetrano)', in *Traffici Micenei nel Mediterraneo*, Taranto, pp. 133–7.

— (1987) 'L'insediamento di Roccazzo (Mazara del Vallo, Trapani), nuovi elementi di inquadramento ed interpretazione dell'Eneolitico Siciliano', in D. Cocchi (ed.), *L'età del rame in Europa*, Rassegna di Archeologia, Viareggio, vol. 7, pp. 553–4.

Tusa, S., Piperno, M., Valente, I. and Durante, S. (1980) 'Campagne di scavo 1977 e 1978 alla Grotta dell'Uzzo', *Sicilia archeologica* 13: 49–66.

Tusa, V. (1985) 'La cultura degli Elimi nella Sicilia occidentale', in *Le littoral thrace et son rôle dans le monde ancien*, Jambol, pp. 307–42.

Vagnetti, L. (1982) *Magna Grecia e Mondo Miceneo*, Taranto.

— (1983) 'I Miceni in Occidente. Dati acquisiti e prospettive future', in *Modes de contacts et processus de transformation dans les sociétés anciennes*, Paris, pp. 165–81.

— (1986) 'Cypriote elements beyond the Aegean in the Bronze Age', in *Acts of the International Archaeological Symposium 'Cyprus between the Orient and the Occident'*, Nicosia, pp. 201–16.

Valente, I. (1986) 'Indizi di presenza micenea nella Sicilia occidentale durante la media età del Bronzo', in *Traffici Micenei nel Mediterraneo*, Taranto, pp. 123–6.

Villari, P. (1980) 'L'evoluzione della situla in Sicilia e Calabria', in *Klearchos. Bollettino dell'Associazione Amici del Museo nazionale di Reggio Calabria*, vol. 22, pp. 5–13.

Voza, G. (1980) 'La necropoli della valle del Marcellino presso Villasmundo', *Insediamenti Coloniali Greci in Sicilia nell VIII e VII Secolo a.C. Cronache di Archeologia* 17: 104–10.

— (1980–1) 'L'attività della Soprintendenza alle Antichità della Sicilia orientale', *Kokalos* 26–7: 675–80.

Topography

Adamesteanu, D. (1986) 'Quadro storico delle fortificazioni greche della Sicilia e della Magna Grecia', in *La Fortification dans l'histoire du monde grec*, Paris, pp. 105–10.

Agnello, S.L. (1980) 'Osservazioni sul primo impianto urbano di Siracusa', *Insediamenti Coloniali Greci in Sicilia nell VIII. e VII. secolo a.C. Cronache di Archeologia* 17: 152–58.

Allen, H.L. (1985) 'I luoghi sacri di Morgantina', *Cronache di archeologia e di storia dell'arte* 16: 132–9.

Ampolo, C. (1984) 'Le ricchezze dei Selinuntini. Tucidide VI 20, 4 e l'iscrizione del tempio G di Selinunte', *La parola del passato* 39: 81–9.

Aoyagi, M. (1980–1) 'Ripresa degli scavi nella villa

romana di Realmonte', *Kokalos* 26–7: 668–73.

Arias, P.E. (1980; 1983) 'Studi italioti e sicelioti', *La Parola del Passato* 35: 289–320 and 38: 208–40.

Asheri, D. (1982–3) 'Le città della Sicilia fra il III e IV secolo d.C.', *Kokalos* 28–9: 461–76.

Bacci, G.M. (1980–1) 'Ricerche a Taormina negli anni 1977–1980', *Kokalos* 26–7: 737–48.

Bakhuizen, S.C. (1981) 'Le nom de Chalcis et la colonisation chalcidienne', in *Nouvelle contribution à l'étude de la société et de la colonisation Eubéennes*, Naples, pp. 163–74.

Basile, B. (1988) 'A Roman wreck with a cargo of marble in the Bay of Giardini, Naxos (Sicily)', *Nautical Archaeology* 17: 133–43.

Bejor, G. (1982) 'L'abitato e le fortificazioni di Rocca Nadore presso Sciacca. Una notizia preliminare', in *Aparchai. Nuove ricerche e studi sulla Magna Grecia e la Sicilia antica in onore di P.E. Arias*, Pisa, pp. 445–58.

— (1983) 'Aspetti della romanizzazione della Sicilia', in *Modes de contacts et processus de transformation dans les sociétés anciennes*, Paris, pp. 345–75.

— (1986), 'Gli insediamenti della Sicilia romana', in *Società Romana e Impero Tardoantica*, Bari, pp. 463–519.

Bejor, G., Canzanella, M.G., Corretti, A., Giangiulio, M., Lombardo, M., Nenci, G. and Parra, M. (1986) 'Entella. Ricognizioni topografiche e scavi, 1983–1986', *Annali della Scuola Normale Superiore di Pisa, classe di lettere e filosofia* 3, 16: 1075–104.

Bell, M., III (1984–5) 'Recenti scavi nell'agora di Morgantina', *Kokalos* 30–1: 501–20.

Belvedere, O. (1980) 'Himera. Campagne di scavo 1976–1979', *Beni culturali e ambientali, Sicilia* 1: 65–9.

— (1980) 'Nuovi aspetti del problema di Himera arcaica', *Insediamenti Coloniali Greci in Sicilia nell'VIII. e VII. Secolo a.C., Cronache di Archeologia* 17: 75–89.

— (1981) 'I santuari urbani sicelioti: preliminari per un'analisi strutturale', *Archeologia Classica* 33: 122–42.

— (1982) 'Termini Imerese. Saggi di scavo in piazza Vittorio Emanuele', *Sicilia archeologica* 15, 48: 37–44.

— (1982–3) 'Osservazioni sulla topografia storica di Thermae Himerenses', *Kokalos* 28–9: 71–86.

— (1986) 'Il ruolo dell'Imera settentrionale e dell'Imera meridionale nel quadro della colonizzazione greca', in *Atti della Seconda Giornata di studi sull'archeologia licatese e della zona della Bassa Valle dell'Himera*, Licata, pp. 91–5.

— (1987) 'Himera, Naxos e Camarina. Tre casi di urbanistica coloniale', *Xenia* 14: 5–20.

Belvedere, O. and others (1988) *Himera III. Prospezione archeologica nel territorio*, Rome.

Bernabò Brea, L. (1980–1) 'Attività archeologica nelle isole Eolie (1976–1980)', *Kokalos* 26–7: 749–55.

— (1987) 'Le fortificazioni greche di Lipari', *Saggi in onore di G. De Angelis d'Ossat*, Rome, pp. 19–24.

Bernabò Brea, L. and Albanese Procelli, R.M. (1982) 'Calascibetta (Enna). La necropoli di Cozzo S. Giuseppe in contrada Realmese', *Notizie degli scavi di antichità* 36: 425–632.

Bérard, C. (1983) 'Urbanisation à Mégara Nisaea et urbanisme a Mégara Hyblaea', *Mélanges d'archéologie et d'histoire de l'école française de Rome. Antiquité* 95: 634–40.

Bivona, P. and Di Maria, F. (1982) 'Palermo. Testimonianze archeologiche lungo l'Eleutero', *Sicilia archeologica* 15, 49–50: 107–8.

Bonacasa, N. (1980–1) 'Cantieri di scavo dell'Istituto di Archeologia dell'Università di Palermo: Himera, Cefalù, Caltavuturo, Terravecchia di Cuti (1976–1979)', *Kokalos* 26–7: 853–61.

— (1981) 'Il problema archeologico di Himera', *Annuario della Scuola Archeologica di Atene e delle Missioni Italiane in Oriente* 43: 319–41.

— (1983) 'Himera 1963–1983, bilancio e programmi dopo un ventennio di ricerche', *Beni culturali e ambientali, Sicilia* 4: 159–64.

— (1984–5) 'Attività dell' Istituto di Archeologia dell' Università di Palermo nel quadrennio 1980–1984', *Kokalos* 30–1: 621–2.

Bonacasa Carra, R.M. (1980) 'Ipotesi sulla fortificazione di Himera', *Beni culturali e ambientali, Sicilia* 1: 71–2.

Bottini, A. (1986) 'Necropoli punico-romana di Palermo', *Annali della Scuola Normale Superiore di Pisa, classe di lettere e filosofia*, 3, 16: 977–1,074.

Bouffier, S.C. (1987) 'L'alimentation en eau de la colonie grecque de Syracuse', *Mélanges d'archéologie et d'histoire de l'école française de Rome. Antiquité* 99: 661–91.

Bound, M. (1989), 'The Dattilo Wreck (Panarea, Aeolian Islands): first season report', *Nautical Archaeology* 18: 203–19.

Broise, H., Gras, M. and Treziny, H. (1983) 'Mégara Hyblaea: bilan des fouilles récentes sur le plateau sud (1977–1982)', *Mélanges d'archéologie et d'histoire de l'école française de Rome. Antiquité* 95: 647–50.

Calderone, A. (1980–1) 'Monte Saraceno. Scavo dell'abitato nel biennio 1978–1979', *Kokalos* 26–7: 601–12.

— (1984-1985) 'Monte Saraceno di Ravanusa. Abitato del terrazzo inferiore', *Kokalos* 30–1: 535–38.

Camerata-Scovazzo, R., Agosta, G. and Vassallo, S. (1984–5) 'Himera. Scavo nella città bassa', *Kokalos* 30–1: 629–36.

Cantarelli, F. (1987) 'Le possibilità insediative e produttive dell'isola di Pantelleria dalla preistoria alla romanizzazione. Aspetti storici e proposte per il riconoscimento di una "limitatio"', in *Studi di antichità in memoria di Clementina Gatti*, Milan, pp. 47–65.

Castellana, G. (1980) 'Indigeni ad Himera?', *Sicilia archeologica* 13, 44: 71–6.

— (1982) 'Nuove ricognizioni nel territorio di Palma di Montechiaro (Agrigento)', *Sicilia archeologica* 15, 49–50: 81–102.

— (1983) 'Nuove ricognizioni nel territorio di Palma di Montechiaro (Agrigento), 2', *Sicilia archeologica* 16, 52–3: 119–46.

— (1984) 'La Neapolis nella chora acragantina e la colonizzazione dionisiana della Sicilia. Proposta di identificazione di una città antica con nota sul sito di Caltafaraci presso Agrigento', *La parola del passato* 39: 375–83.

— (1984) 'Tre indagini sulla cultura indigena di Sicilia', in *Studi di antichità in onore di G. Maetzke*, Rome, pp. 211–27.

— (1984–5) 'Ricerche nel territorio di Palma di Montechiaro e nel territorio di Favara', *Kokalos* 30–1: 521–7.

Cavalier, M. (1981) 'Stromboli. Villaggio preistorico di S. Vincenzo', *Sicilia archeologica*, 14, 46–7: 27–54.

— (1984–5) 'Attività archeologica nelle isole Eolie (1980–1984)', *Kokalos* 30–1: 695–710.

Ciancio, S. (1980) *Siracusa e provincia. Topografia storica e archeologica*, Syracuse.

Ciasca, A. (1980) 'Scavi alle mura di Mozia, 1975–1979', *Beni culturali e ambientali, Sicilia* 1: 95–7.

— (1980-1) 'Scavi alle fortificazioni di Mozia, 1976–1979', *Kokalos* 26–7: 862–9.

— 1982-3) 'Mozia', *Kokalos* 28–9: 150–5.

— (1986) 'Fortificazioni di Mozia (Sicilia). Dati tecnici e proposta preliminare de periodizzazione', *La Fortification dans l'histoire du monde grec*, Paris, pp. 221–7.

Ciasca, A. and Guzzo, P.G. (1980) 'Mozia 1979. Scavi alle mura, campagna 1979', *Revista di studi fenici* 8: 237–52.

Cilia, E. (1980–1) 'Cozzo Matrice-Scavi 1979. Aspetti e problemi di una ricerca su un centro indigeno ellenizzato', *Kokalos* 26–7: 613–19.

Cintas, P. and Jully, J.J. (1980) 'Onze sépultures de la nécropole archaïque de Motyé', *Cuadernos de trabajos de la escuela española de historia y arqueologia en Roma* 14: 31–52.

Clemente, G. (1980–1) 'Considerazioni sulla Sicilia nell'impero romano (III sec. a.C. – V sec. d.C.)', *Kokalos* 26–7: 192–248.

Coarelli, F. (1981) 'La Sicilia tra la fine della guerra annibalica e Cicerone', *Società romana e produzione schiavistica* 1: 1–18.

Coarelli, F. and Torelli, M. (1984) *Sicilia*, Rome.

Colonna, G. (1980–1) 'La Sicilia e il Tirreno nel V e IV secolo', *Kokalos* 26–7: 157–83.

Cordano, F. (1982) 'Note per la storia di Gela', in *Ottava miscellanea greca e romana*, Rome, pp. 45–56.

— (1984) 'Camarina, 7. Alcuni documenti iscritti importanti per la storia della città', *Bollettino d'arte* 69, 26: 31–56.

— (1986) *Antiche fondazioni greche. Sicilia e Italia*

meridionale, Palermo.

— (1986) 'Le leggi calcidesi di Monte San Mauro di Caltagirone', in *Decima Miscellanea Greca e Romana*, Rome, pp. 33–60.

— (1988) 'Gruppi gentilizi presso i nassii di Sicilia', *Bollettino d'arte* 73: 18–22.

Cracco Ruggini, L. (1982–3) 'Sicilia, III/IV secolo. Il volto della non-città', *Kokalos* 28–9: 477–515.

Crouch, D.P. (1984) 'The Hellenistic water system of Morgantina, Sicily. Contributions to the history of urbanization', *American Journal of Archaeology* 88: 353–65.

Cuomo di Caprio, N. (1981) 'Annotazioni technice in margine al cosidetto "Luogo di Arsione" di Mozia', *Sicilia archeologica* 14, 45: 7–14.

De Miro, A. (1986) 'Il santuario greco di località Casalicchio presso Licata. Prime ricerche e risultati', in *Atti della Seconda Giornata di studi sull'archeologia licatese e della zona della bassa valle dell'Himera*, Licata, pp. 97–124.

De Miro, E. (1977) 'Nuovi santuari ad Agrigento e a Sabucina', *Cronache di archeologia e di storia dell'arte* 16: 94–104.

— (1980) 'Agrigento paleocristiana e bizantina', *Felix Ravenna*, 119–20: 131–71.

— (1980) 'Influenze cretesi nei santuari ctonî dell'area geloo-agrigentina', *Antichità cretesi. Studi in onore di D. Levi*, Catania, 2: 202–7.

— (1980–1) 'Ricerche archeologiche nella Sicilia centro-meridionale', *Kokalos* 26–7: 561–80.

— (1983) 'Forme di contatto e processi di trasformazione nelle società antiche. Esempio da Sabucina', in *Modes de contacts et processus de transformation dans les sociétés anciennes*, Paris, pp. 335–42.

— (1984–5) 'L'attività della Soprintendenza archeologica di Agrigento (Anni 1980–1984)', *Kokalos* 30–1: 453–66.

— (1985) 'Nuovi santuari ad Agrigento e Sabucina', in *Il tempio greco in Sicilia. Architettura e culto, Cronache di Archeologia* 16: 94–104.

— (1988) 'Akragas, città e necropoli nei recenti scavi', in *–Veder Greco – Le necropoli di Agrigento*, Rome, pp. 235–52.

de la Genière, J. (1980) 'A propos de deux sondages extra-muros de l'acropole de Sélinonte', in *Philias Charin, Miscellanea di studi classici in onore di E. Manni*, Rome, vol. 4, pp. 1,293–9.

— (1981) 'Nuove ricerche sulla topografia di Selinunte', *Rendiconti dell'Accademia dei Lincei, classe di scienze morali, storiche e filologiche* 8, 36: 211–17.

— (1982) 'Sélinonte: recherches sur la topographie urbaine, (1975–1981)', *Annali della Scuola Normale Superiore di Pisa, classe di lettere e filosofia*, 3, 12: 469–79.

— (1983) 'Mégara Nisaea, Mégara Hyblaea et Sélinonte', *Dialogues d'histoire ancienne* 9: 319–36.

— (1984–5) 'Sulla pianta di Selinunte', *Kokalos* 30–1, 1: 160–3.

— (1988) 'Alla ricerca di Segesta arcaica', *Annali della Scuola Normale Superiore di Pisa, classe di lettere e filosofia* 3, 18: 287–316.

de la Genière, J. and Rouget, J. (1985) 'Recherches sur la topographie de Sélinonte. Campagne 1985', *Atti dell'Accademia nazionale dei Lincei, Rendiconti* 40: 289–97.

de la Genière, J. and Theodorescu, D. (1980–1) 'Contribution à l'histoire urbanistique de Sélinonte', *Kokalos* 26–7: 973–96.

de Waele, J.A. (1980) 'Agrigento. Gli scavi sulla Rupe Antenea, 1970–1975', *Notizie degli scavi di antichità* 34: 395–452.

— (1980) 'La popolazione di Akragas antica', in *Philias Charin. Miscellanea di studi in onore di E. Manni*, Rome, vol. 3, pp. 747–60.

Denti, A. (1980–1) 'Monte Saraceno di Ravanusa. Necropoli–Scavi nella necropoli occidentale (anni 1978 e 1979)', *Kokalos* 26–7: 620–41.

— (1984–5) 'Monte Saraceno di Ravanusa (Ag.). Scavi 1981 e 1982 nella necropoli occidentale', *Kokalos* 30–1: 529–34.

Dewailly, M. (1983) 'La divinità femminile con polos a Selinunte', *Sicilia archeologica* 16, 52–3: 5–12.

Di Stefano, C.A. (1980) 'Lilibeo alle luce delle nuove scoperte archeologiche', *Sicilia archeologica* 13: 7–20.

— (1980) 'Testimonianze archeologiche lilibetane del IV sec. a.C.', in *Philias Charin. Miscellanea di studi classici in onore di E. Manni*, Rome, vol. 2, pp.785–800.

— (1980–1) 'Marsala: ricerche archeologiche dell'ultimo quadriennio', *Kokalos* 26–7: 870–6.

— (1981) 'Marsala. Interventi nella zona archeologica di Lilibeo', *Beni culturali e ambientali, Sicilia* 2, 1–2: 121–6.

— (1982–3) 'La documentazione archeologica del III e IV sec. d.C. nella provincia di Trapani', *Kokalos* 28–9: 350–67.

— (1982–3) 'Lilibeo', *Kokalos* 28–9: 156–64.

— (1982–3) 'Appunti per la carta archeologica della regione camarinese in età romana', *Kokalos* 28–9: 332–40.

— (1987) 'Camarina, 8. L'emporio greco arcaico di contrada Maestro sull'Irminio', *Bollettino d'arte* 72: 129–40.

Di Stefano, G. (1980–1) 'Ricerche nella provincia di Ragusa (1977–1980)', *Kokalos* 26–7: 756–63.

Di Vita, A. (1980) 'Contributi per una storia urbanistica di Selinunte', in *Philias Charin. Miscellanea di studi classici in onore di E. Manni*, Rome, vol. 4, pp. 801–29.

— (1981) 'L'urbanistica più antica delle colonie di Magna Grecia e di Sicilia. Problemi e reflessioni', *Annuario della Scuola Archeologica di Atene e delle Missioni Italiane in Oriente* 43: 63–79.

— (1983) *Camarina 1958. Documenti e note*, *Bollettino d'arte* 68, 17: 31–44.

Epifanio, E. and Vassallo, S. (1984–5) 'Terravecchia di Cuti. Scavi nel santuario extraurbano in contrada Cuti (1980 e 1982)', *Kokalos* 30–1: 651–3.

Falsone, G. (1980) 'I nuovi scavi di Mozia', *Beni culturali e ambientali, Sicilia* 1: 99–103.

— (1980) 'Per salvare Entella', *Sicilia archeologica* 13, 43: 23–44.

— (1981) *Struttura e origine orientale dei forni da vasaio di Mozia*, Palermo.

Falsone, G., Leonard Jr, A. and Fresina, A. (1980–1) 'Quattro campagne di scavo a Castellazzo di Poggioreale', *Kokalos* 26–7: 931–72.

Falsone, G., Spatafora, F. and Giammellaro Spanò, A. (1980–1) 'Gli scavi della "zona K" a Mozia e il caso stratigrafico del locus 5615', *Kokalos* 26–7: 877–930.

Fiorentini, G. (1980–1) 'Ricerche archeologiche nella Sicilia centro-meridionale', *Kokalos* 26–7: 581–600.

— (1982–3) 'Monte Adranone nell'età tra i due Dionisi', *Kokalos* 28–9: 180–4.

— (1983) 'Gela protoarcaica. Dati topografici, archeologici e cronologici', *Annuario della Scuola Archeologica di Atene e delle Missioni Italiane in Oriente* 45: 53–73.

— (1984–5) 'La necropoli indigena di età greca di Valle Oscura (Marianopoli)', *Quaderni dell'istituto di archeologia della facoltà di lettere e filosofia dell' Università di Messina* 1: 31–54.

— (1984–5) 'Recenti scavi a Marianopoli', *Kokalos* 30–1: 467–74.

Fourmont, M.H. (1981) 'Sélinonte. Fouille dans la région nord-ouest de la rue F.', *Sicilia archeologica* 14, 46–7: 5–26.

Frasca, M. (1981) 'La necropoli di Monte Finocchito', *Cronache di archeologia e storia dell'arte* 20: 13–102.

Giammallaro-Spano, A. and Spatafora, F. (1982) 'Necropoli di Selinunte, un'ipotesi di ricerca', *Sicilia archeologica* 15, 48: 85–92.

Giardino, C. (1987) 'Il ripostiglio di Polizzello', *Sicilia archeologica* 20, 65: 39–55.

Gibbons, D. J. (1989) 'The Roman Wreck of ca. AD 200 at Plemmirio near Siracusa, Sicily', *Nautical Archaeology*, l8: 1-26.

Gibbons, D.J. and Parker, A. J. (1986) 'The Roman Wreck at Plemmirio near Siracusa (Sicily). Interim Report', *Nautical Archaeology*, 15: 267-304.

Giustolisi, V. (1979) *Topografia storia e archeologia di Monte Pellegrino (Palermo)*, Palermo.

— (1981) *Camico, Triocala, Caltabellotta Sicilia archeologica che scompare*, vol. 6, Palermo.

— (1983) *Il vescovo e il drago. Archeologia, storia e leggenda nel sito dell'antica Triocala oggi Caltabellotta*, Palermo.

— (1985) *Nakone ed Entella alla luce degli antichi decreti recentemente apparsi e di un nuovo decreto inedito*, Palermo.

Goldsberry, M.A.S. (1980) *Sicily and its Cities in Hellenistic and Roman Times*, diss., University of North Carolina.

Gras, M. (1980–1) 'La Sicile et l'Italie centrale au VIIe siècle et dans la première moitié du VIe siècle avant J.C.', *Kokalos* 26–7: 99–156.

Guarducci, M. (1985) 'Una nuova dea a Naxos in Sicilia e gli antichi legami fra la Naxos siceliota e l'omonima isola delle Cicladi', *Mélanges d'archéologie et d'histoire de l'école française de Rome. Antiquité* 97: 7–34.

Guidice, F. (1979) 'La stipe di Persefone a Camarina', *Monumenti antichi* 49: 277–354.

Habermann, W. (1987) 'IG3 386/387 'Sizilische Häute und die atenische-sizilischen Handelsbeziehungen im 5 Jahr. v. Chr.', *Münstersche Beiträge zur antiken Handelsgeschichte* 6: 89–113.

Isler, H. P. (various dates) Monte Iato annual reports of excavations, in *Sicilia archeologica* from 1969 and in *Antike Kunst* from 1972.

—— (1980–1) 'Iaitas. Scavi della missione archeologica M. Iato dell'Università di Zurigo (1977–1980)', *Kokalos* 26–7: 997–1,008.

—— (1984–5) 'Iaitas. Scavi della missione archeologica M. Iato dell'Università di Zurigo (1981-1984)', *Kokalos* 30–1: 611–20.

Isler, H.P. and Isler-Kerényi, C. (1984) *Studia Ietina, 2. Der Tempel der Aphrodite. La ceramica proveniente dall'insediamento medievale. Cenni e osservazioni preliminari*, Zurich.

Isserlin, B.S.J. (1982) 'Motya, urban features', in *Phönizier im Westen. Die Beiträge des Internationalen Symposiums über 'Die phönizische Expansion im Westlichen Mittelmeerraum' in Köln vom 24. bis 27. April 1979*, Mainz, pp. 113–27.

Italia, A. and Lima, D. (1987) 'Solunto. Struttura urbana e tipologia residenziale. Evoluzione e trasformazione di un sito archeologico', *Sicilia archeologica* 20, 65: 57–72.

Joint authors (1979) 'Afrodite a Monte Jato?', *Kokalos* 25: 259–355.

Joint authors (1980–1) 'Atti del 5. Congresso internazionale di studi sulla Sicilia antica', *Kokalos* 26–7.

Joint authors (1981–3) 'Grecia, Italia e Sicilia nell'VIII e VII secolo a.C.', *Annuario della Scuola Archeologica di Atene e delle Missioni Italiane in Oriente* 59–60.

Joint authors (1982) *Secondo Quaderno Imerese*, Rome.

Joint authors (1982–3) 'Città e contado in Sicilia fra il III ed il IV sec. d.C. Colloquio, 2–4 dicembre 1982', *Kokalos* 28–9: 319–540.

Joint authors (1984) *Lilibeo, Testimonianze archeologiche dal IV sec. a. C. al V sec. d.C.* (Catalogo della mostra), Palermo.

Joint authors (1984–5) 'Atti del 6. Congresso internazionale di studi sulla Sicilia antica', *Kokalos* 30–1.

Joint authors (1985) *Greci e Indigeni nella Valle dell'Himera. Scavi a Monte Saraceno di Ravanusa*, Mostra, Università di Messina, Messina.

Joint authors (1985) *Archeologia subacquea, 2. Isole Eolie*, Rome.

Joint authors (1986) *Atti della seconda giornata di studi sull'archeologia Licatese e della zona della bassa valle dell'Himera, 19 gennaio 1985*, Licata.

Joint authors (1986) *Himera. Zona archeologica e Antiquarium*, Palermo.

Joint authors (1987) *Un trentennio di indagini nel territorio di Lentini antica. Atti dell'Incontro di studi su Alfio Sgalambro. Un impegno per i beni culturali*, Lentini.

Joint authors (1988) *–Veder Greco – Le Necropoli di Agrigento*, Mostra Internazionale, Rome.

La Barbera, S. (1982) 'Catania. Museo di Castello Ursino', *Sicilia archeologica* 15, 49–50: 37–44.

Lagona, S. (1980) 'La Sicilia tardo-antica e bizantina', *Felix Ravenna* 119–20: 111–30.

—— (1984–5) 'Un fortalizio greco a Monte S. Basilio, presso Scordia', *Kokalos* 30–1: 805–8.

Lentini, M.C. (1983) 'Camarina VI', *Bollettino d'arte* 68, 25: 5–30.

Levi, M.A. (1988) 'La lezione di Mozia', *Acme* 41: 5–10.

Linington, R.E. (1983) 'La prospezione geofisica eseguita nel 1980 a Camarina', *Bollettino d'arte* 68, 25: 45–8.

Lombardo, M. (1982) 'Il sinecismo di Entella', *Annali della Scuola Normale Superiore di Pisa, classe di lettere e filosofia* 3, 12, 3: 849–86.

Lyons, C.L. (1983) *The Archaic Necropolis of Morgantina, Sicily*, diss., Bryn Mawr College.

Malkin, I. (1984–5) 'Dieux et colons dans la Sicile archaïque', *Kokalos* 30–1, 1: 155–9.

—— (1986) 'Apollo Archegetes and Sicily', *Annali della Scuola Normale Superiore di Pisa, classe di lettere e filosofia*, 3, 16: 959–72.

—— (1987) 'La place des dieux dans la cité des hommes, Le découpage des aires sacrées dans les colonies grecques', *Revue de l'histoire des religions* 204: 331–52.

—— (1987) *Religion and Colonization in Ancient Greece*, Leiden.

Manbella, R. (1987) 'La problematica dei sacelli circolari del santuario sicano di Polizzello', *Rivista di archeologia* 11: 13–24.

Manganaro, G. (1985) 'Per la storia dei culti nella Sicilia greca', *Cronache di archeologia e di storia dell'arte* 16: 148–64.

Mannino, G. (1981) 'Ustica. Due nuove tombe ipogeiche', *Sicilia archeologica* 14, 45: 55–60.

—— (1982) 'Il pozzo di Piazza Edison', *Sicilia archeologia* 15, 49–50: 103–6.

Martin, R. (1980–1) 'Recherches sur l'acropole de Sélinonte', *Kokalos* 26–7: 1,009–16.

—— (1981) 'Selinonte. L'acropole et le processus d'urbanisation de la ville', *Beni culturali e ambientali, Sicilia* 2, 1–2: 11–14.

—— (1982) 'Sélinonte. Résultats et problèmes de la première phase de recherches, 1973–1979', *Annuario della Scuola archeologica di Atene e delle Missioni italiane in Oriente* 44: 183–8.

— (1983) 'L'éspace civique, religieux et profane dans les cités grecques de l'archaïsme à l'époque hellénistique', *Architecture et Société de l'archaïsme grec à la fin de la Republique romaine*, Paris, pp. 9–42.

Martorana, G. (1980–1) 'Religioni', *Kokalos* 26–7: 359–82.

Mazza, M. (1980–1) 'Economia e società nella Sicilia romana', *Kokalos* 26–7: 292–358.

Meier-Welcker, H. (1980) *Himera und die Geschichte des griechischen Sizilien*, Boppard am Rhein.

Migliore, M. S. (1981) *Sabucina*, Caltanissetta.

Morel, J.P. (1980) 'La Sicile dans les courants commerciaux de la Méditerranée sud-occidentale, d'après la céramique à vernis noir', in *Philias Carin. Miscellanea di studi classici in onore di E. Manni*, Rome, vol. 5, pp. 1,561–82.

Muller, A. (1983) 'De Nisée à Mégara. Les siècles de formation de la métropole megarienne', *Mélanges d'archéologie et d'histoire de l'école française de Rome. Antiquité* 95: 619–28.

Munn, M.L.Z. (1983) *Corinthian Trade with the West in the Classical Period*, diss., Bryn Mawr College.

Musti, D. (1980–1) 'La storiografia sulla Sicilia antica', *Kokalos* 26–7: 249–62.

Nenci, G. (1982) 'Considerazioni sui decreti di Entella', *Annali della Scuola Normale Superiore di Pisa, classe di lettere e filosofia* 3, 11: 1069–80.

— (1985) 'Nuove considerazioni sui decreti di Entella', *Annali della Scuola Normale Superiore di Pisa, classe di lettere e filosofia* 3, 13: 997–1,001.

— (1986) 'Entella. Ricognizioni topografiche e scavi 1983–1986', *Annali della Scuola Normale Superiore di Pisa, classe di lettere e filosofia* 3, 16: 1,075–104.

— (1987) 'Un nuovo decreto entellino (IX)', *Annali della Scuola Normale Superiore di Pisa, classe di lettere e filosofia* 3, 17: 119–28.

Palermo, D. (1983) 'Polizzello', *Cronache di Archeologia* 20: 103–48.

Pancucci, D. (1980) 'I temenoi [sic] del santuario delle divinità ad Agrigento', in *Philias Charin. Miscellanea di studi classici in onore di E. Manni* Rome, vol. 5, pp. 1,663–76.

— (1980–1) 'Recenti scavi sull'acropoli di Monte Bubbonia (1976–1980)', *Kokalos* 26–7: 649–55.

— (1984–5) 'Scavi nella necropoli di Monte Riparato (Caltavuturo)', *Kokalos* 30–1: 637–40.

Patanè, R. (1988) 'Ricerche e problemi di archeologia centuripina', *Sicilia Archeologica* 21: 93–100.

Pelagatti, P. (1980) 'Siracusa. Elementi dell'abitato de Ortigia nell'8. e nel 7. secolo a.C., *Insediamenti Coloniali Greci in Sicilia nell'VIII. e VII. secolo a.C., Cronache di Archeologia* 17: 119–33.

— (1980) 'Naxos nell'8. e nel 7. secolo a.C.', *Insediamenti Coloniali Greci in Sicilia nell'VIII. e VII. Secolo a.C. Cronache di Archeologia* 17: 136–41.

— (1980–1) 'L'attività della Soprintendenza alle Antichità della Sicilia Orientale, II', *Kokalos* 26–7: 694–736.

— (1981) 'Bilancio degli scavi di Naxos per l'VIII e il VII sec. a.C.', *Annuario della Scuola archeologica di Atene e delle Missioni italiane in Oriente* 43: 291–311.

— (1982) 'Siracusa: le ultime ricerche in Ortigia', *Annuario della Scuola Archeologica di Atene e delle Missioni Italiane in Oriente* 44: 117–63.

— (1984) 'Prime importazioni euboiche in Sicilia. La situazione di Naxos. L'impianto urbano di Naxos', *Gli Eubei in Occidente*, pp. 151–6.

Pelagatti, P. and others (1983) 'Camarina V', *Bollettino d'arte*, 64: 29–56.

Polacco, L. (1986) 'I culti di Demetra e Kore a Siracusa', *Numismatica e Antichità Classiche, Quaderni Ticinesi* 15: 21–41.

Pottino, G. (1987) *Rapporto su Erice*, Palermo.

Presicce Parisi, C.C. (1984) 'La funzione delle aree sacre nell' organizzazione urbanistica primitiva delle colonie greche alla luce della scoperta di un nuovo santuario periferico di Selinunte', *Archeologia classica* 36: 19–132.

Procelli, E., (1988) 'La montagna di Ramacca, scavi 1984, 1985, e 1986: Nota preliminare', *Sicilia Archeologica* 21: 73–80.

Rallo, A. (1982–3) 'L'abitato di Selinunte. Il quartiere punico e la sua necropoli', *Kokalos* 28–9: 169–74.

Rizza, G. (1980) 'Leontini nell'8. e nel'7. secolo a.C.', *Insediamenti Coloniali Greci in Sicilia nell'VIII. e VII. secolo a.C. Cronache di Archeologia* 17: 26–37.

— (1980–1) 'Attività dell'Istituto di archeologia dell'Università di Catania. Scavi e ricerche in Sicilia negli anni 1976–1979', *Kokalos* 26–7: 764–70.

— (1981) 'Leontini e Katane nell'VIII e nel VII secolo a.C.', *Annuario della Scuola archeologica di Atene e delle Missioni italiane in Oriente* 43: 313–17.

— (1984–5) 'La necropoli di Butera e i rapporti fra Sicilia e Creta in età protoarcaica', *Kokalos* 30–1, 1: 65–70.

— (1984–5) 'Università di Catania. Istituto di Archeologia. Scavi e ricerche in Sicilia dal 1980 al 1984', *Kokalos* 30–1: 847–54.

Scibona, G. (1980) 'Fonti per una storia della viabilità di Sicilia. 1. La Tabula Peutingeriana', *Archivio Storico Messinese* 31: 391–410.

— (1980) 'Troina 1: 1974–1977. Nuovi dati sulla fortificazione ellenistica e la topografia del centro antico', *Archivio Storico Messinese* 31: 349–89.

— (1984–5) 'Messina: notizia preliminare sulla necropoli romana e sul giacimento preistorico del torrente Boccetta', *Kokalos* 30–1: 855–63.

Scurria, C.F. (1981) 'Problemi della ellenizzazione del retroterra zancleo. La questione di Agathyrno', *Rivista storica dell' antichità* 11: 53–68.

Seibert, J. (1982–3) 'Die Bevölkerungsfluktuation in den Griechenstädten Siziliens', *Ancient Society* 13–14:

33–65.

Spatafora, F. and Calascibetta, A.M. (1986) 'Monte Maranfusa (Pa), La prima campagna di scavo', *Annali della Scuola Normale Superiore di Pisa, classe di lettere e filosofia* 3, 16: 1,105–16.

— (1986) 'Monte Maranfusa. Un insediamento nella media valle del Belice', *Sicilia archeologica* 19, 62: 13–27.

Spigo, U. (1980–1) 'Ricerche a Monte S. Mauro, Francavilla di Sicilia, Acireale, Adrano, Lentini, Solarino', *Kokalos* 26–7: 771–95.

— (1984–5) 'Ricerche e rinvenimenti a Brucoli, Valsavoia, nel territorio di Caltagirone, ad Adrano e Francavilla di Sicilia', *Kokalos* 30–1: 863–904.

— (1986), 'L'anonimo centro greco di monte S. Mauro nel quadro dell' arcaismo siceliota: prospettive di ricerca', *Decima Miscellanea Greca e Romana*, Rome, pp. 1–32.

— (1987) 'L'attività della Soprintendenza archeologica a Lentini negli anni 1977–1985', *Un trentennio di indagini nel territorio di Lentini antica*, Lentini, pp. 23–38.

Steures, D.C. (1980) *Monte Finocchito Revisited. 1. The Evidence*, Amsterdam.

Svenbro, J. (1982) 'A Mégara Hyblaea. Le corps géomètre', *Annales. Economies, sociétés, civilisation* 37: 953–64.

Tamburello, I. (1980) 'Palermo dopo la conquista romana', *Sicilia archeologica* 13: 67–74.

— (1983) 'Palermo punico-romana. La ricostruzione archeologica', in *Atti del I Congresso internazionale di studi fenici e punici, Roma 1979*, Rome, pp. 271–7.

Tullio, A. (1980) 'Architettura "povera" nell'antichità: gli epitymbia di Cefalù', *Ricerche di Storia dell'Arte* 11: 45–8.

— (1980) 'La necropoli ellenistico-romana di Cefalù. Scavi 1976–1979', *Beni culturali e ambientali, Sicilia*, 1: 83–8.

— (1984) *Cefalù antica*, Cefalù.

— (1984–5) 'Scavi e ricerche a Cefalù (1980–1984)', *Kokalos* 30–1: 641–50.

Tusa, S. (1984) 'Sulla "Missione Malophoros". Nuovi rinvenimenti nell'area del santuario della Malophoros a Selinunte', *Sicilia archeologica* 17, 54–5: 5–15.

Tusa, S. *et al.* (1984, 1986) 'Selinunte, Malophoros. Rapporto preliminare sulla prima campagna di scavi, 1982', *Sicilia archeologica* 1984, 17, 54–5: 17–58; 1986, 19, 60–1: 13–88.

— (1981) 'Segesta', *Sicilia archeologica* 14, 46–7, 135–144.

— (1981) 'Selinunte', *Sicilia archeologica* 14, 45: 61–72.

— (1982) 'Ricerche e scavi nelle necropoli selinuntine', *Annuario della Scuola archeologica di Atene e delle Missioni italiane in Oriente* 44: 189–202.

— (1983) 'Greci e Non Greci in Sicilia', in *Modes de contacts et processus de transformation dans les sociétés anciennes*, Paris, pp. 299-314.

— (1983) 'Mozia ed altre località della Sicilia occidentale', *Annuario della Scuola archeologica di Atene e delle Missioni italiane in Oriente* 45: 347–56.

— (1983) 'Presenza di strutture religiose e forme anelleniche di culto in contesti urbanistici greci nella Sicilia occidentale', in *Architecture et société de l'archaïsme grec à la fin de la République romaine*, Paris, pp. 501–13.

— (1985) 'Nuovi rinvenimenti nell'area del santuario della Malophoros a Selinunte', *Cronache di archeologia e di storia dell'arte* 16: 115–18.

— (1986) 'Cinta muraria dell'Acropoli di Selinunte', in *La fortification dans l'histoire du monde grec (Actes du colloque, Valbonne, 1982)*.

— (1986) 'Selinunte. La cinta muraria dell'Acropoli', in *La fortification dans l'histoire du monde grec*, Paris, pp. 111–19.

Uggeri, G. (1982–3) 'La viabilità romana in Sicilia con particolare reguardo al III e al IV secolo', *Kokalos* 28–9: 424–60.

Vallet, G. (1980) 'Problemi di urbanistica nella Megara arcaica', *Insediamenti Coloniali Greci in Sicilia nell'VIII. e VII. secolo a.C., Cronache di Archeologia*, 17: 23–5.

— (1980–1) 'Travaux et recherches à Mégara Hyblaea', *Kokalos*, 26–7: 796–804.

— (1981) 'Megara Iblea. Bilancio e programmi (1981–1982)', *Beni culturali e ambientali, Sicilia* 2, 3–4: 55–61.

— (1982) 'Bilan des recherches à Mégara Hyblaea', *Annuario della Scuola Archeologica di Atene e delle Missioni Italiane in Oriente* 44: 173–82.

— (1983) 'Topographie historique de Mégara Hyblaea et problèmes d'urbanisme colonial', *Mélanges de l'école française de Rome, Antiquité* 95: 645–7.

— (1983) *Urbanisation et organisation de la chora coloniale grecque en Grande Grèce et en Sicile*, in *Modes de contacts et processus de transformation dans les sociétés anciennes*, Paris, pp. 937–56.

— (1984) 'Les cités chalcidiennes du Détroit et de Sicile', in *Gli Eubei in Occidente*, Naples, pp. 83–143.

— (1984–5) 'Megara Hyblaea', *Kokalos* 30–1: 905–12.

Vallet, G., Villard, F. and Auberson, P. (1983) *Mégara Hyblaea 3. Guide des fouilles*, Rome.

Vassallo, S. (1985) 'Pizzo Nicolosi', *Sicilia archeologica* 18, 57–8: 115–48.

— (1987) 'Pizzo di Casa', *Sicilia archeologica* 20, 65: 25–32.

Voza, G. (1980) 'Eloro in età protoarcaica', *Insediamenti Coloniali greci in Sicilia nell'VIII. e VII. secolo a.C., Cronache di Archeologia* 17: 134–5.

— (1980–1) 'L'attività della Soprintendenza alle Antichità della Sicilia Orientale, I', *Kokalos* 26–7: 674–93.

— (1982) 'Bilancio degli scavi a Siracusa sulla terraferma', *Annuario della Scuola archeologica di Atene e delle Missioni italiane in Oriente* 44: 165–7.

— (1982) 'Evidenze archeologiche di VIII e VII secolo

a.C. nel territorio di Siracusa. La necropoli di Villasmundo, nella valle del Marcellino', *Annuario della Scuola archeologica di Atene e delle Missioni italiane in Oriente* 44: 169–71.

— (1984–5) 'Attività nel territorio della Soprintendenza alle Antichità di Siracusa nel quadriennio 1980– 1984', *Kokalos* 30–1: 657–78.

Wilson, R.J.A. (1980) 'The Hinterland of Heraclea Minoa (Sicily) in Classical Antiquity', in *Archaeology and Italian Society. Prehistoric, Roman and Medieval Studies*, Oxford, pp. 249–60.

— (1980–1) 'Eraclea Minoa. Ricerche nel territorio', *Kokalos* 26–7: 656–67.

— (1984) 'Changes in the pattern of urban settlement in Roman, Byzantine and Arab Sicily', *The Human Landscape*, Oxford, pp. 313–34.

Architecture

Auberson, P. (in press) 'Il tempio ionico di Siracusa' *Bollettino d'arte,* 'Monograph' I.

Barletta, B.A. (1983) *Ionic Influence in Archaic Sicily. The Monumental Art*, Gothenburg.

— (1985) 'An Ionic Porch at Gela', *Mitteilungen des Deutschen Archäologischen Instituts, Römische Abteilung*, 92: 9–17.

Bell, M., III (1980) 'Stylobate and roof in the Olympieion at Akragas', *American Journal of Archaeology* 84: 359–72.

— (1986–7) 'La Fontana Ellenistica di Morgantina', *Quaderni dell'Istituto di Archeologia della Facoltà di Lettere e filosofia della Università di Messina* 2: 111–24.

Belson, J.D. (1981) *The Gorgoneion in Greek Architecture*, diss., Bryn Mawr College.

Belvedere, O. (1982) 'L'anfiteatro di Termini Imerese riscoperto' in *Aparchai. Nuove ricerche e studi sulla Magna Grecia e la Sicilia antica in onore di P.E. Arias*, Pisa, pp. 647–60.

— (1986) *L'acquedotto Cornelio di Termini Imeresi*, Studi e Materiale dell' Istituto di archeologia dell' Università di Palermo, Rome, vol. 7.

— (1988) 'Opere pubbliche ed edifici per lo spettacolo nella Sicilia di età imperiale', *Aufstieg und Niedergang der Römischen Welt. Teil II: Principat*, Berlin, 11: 346–413.

Bernabò Brea, L. (1986) *Il Tempio di Afrodite di Akrai*, Naples.

Billig, E. (1980) 'Die Bühne mit austauschbaren Kulissen. Eine verkannte Bühne des Frühhellenismus?', in *Skifter Utgivna av Svenska Institutet i Athen,* series in quarto vol. 27, *Opuscula atheniensia*, vol. 13, pp. 35–83.

Bloesch, H. (1985) 'Tempio e culti a Iaitas', *Cronache di archeologia e di storia dell'arte* 16: 183–6.

Bonacasa, N. (1980) 'Dèi e culti di Himera', in *Philias*

Charin. Miscellanea di studi classici in onore di E. Manni, Rome, vol. 1, pp. 257–69.

— (1985) 'Il tempio D di Himera', *Cronache di archeologia e di storia dell'arte* 16: 125–31.

Brommer, F. (1985) 'Zu den Metopen des Tempels E in Selinunt', in *Archäologischer Anzeiger*, pp. 15–20.

Carandini, A., Ricci, A., and de Vos, M. (1982) *Filosofiana. La villa di Piazza Armerina*, 2 vols, Palermo.

Castellana, G. (1983) 'Il tempietto votivo fittile di Sabucina e la sua decorazione figurata', *Rivista di archeologia* 7: 5–11.

Castellana, G., and McConnell, B.E. (1986) 'Notizia preliminare sullo scavo della villa romana in contrada Saraceno nel territorio di Agrigento', *Sicilia archeologica* 19, 60–1: 97–108.

Ceretto Castigliano, I., and Savio, C. (1983) 'Considerazioni sulla metrologia e sulla genesi concettuale del tempio di Giunone ad Agrigento', *Bollettino d'arte* 68: 35–48.

Ciasca, A. (1980) 'Note sull'architettura religiosa', in *Philias Charin. Miscellanea di studi classici in onore di E. Manni,* Rome, vol. 2, pp. 501–13.

Ciurcina, C. (1985) 'Nuovi rivestimenti fittili da Naxos e da altri centri della Sicilia orientale', *Cronache di archeologia e di storia dell'arte* 16: 66–81.

Courtois, C. (1986) 'Étude architecturale du bâtiment de scène des théâtres de l'Italie et de la Sicile antiques, en relation avec la littérature théâtrale', *Revue des archéologues et historiens d'art de Louvain* 19: 50–74.

— (1989) *Le Bâtiment de scène des théâtres d'Italie et de Sicile*, Archaeologia Transatlantica, Louvain and Providence, RI, vol. 8.

De Miro, E. (1980) 'La casa greca in Sicilia. Testimonianze nella Sicilia centrale dal 6 al 3 sec. a.C.', in *Philias Charin. Miscellanea di studi classici in onore di E. Manni,* Rome, vol. 2, pp. 707–37.

— (1985–6) 'Il Bouleuterion di Agrigento. Aspetti topografici, archeologici e storici', *Quaderni dell'istituto di archeologia della Facoltà di Lettere e filosofia della Università di Messina* 1: 7–12.

de Weale, J.A. (1980) 'Der Entwurf der dorischen Tempel von Akragas', *Archäologischer Anzeiger*, pp. 180–241.

— (1982) 'Der Entwurf des Heraion von Olympia', *Bulletin antieke beschaving* 57: 27–37.

— (1982) 'I frontoni dell'Olympion agrigentino', in *Aparchai. Nuove ricerche e studi sulla Magna Grecia in onore di P.E. Arias*, Pisa, pp. 271–8.

— (1982) 'La progettazione dei templi dorici di Himera, Segesta e Siracusa', in *Secondo quaderno imerese*, Rome, pp. 1–25.

Epifanio, E. (1985) 'Nuovi rivestimenti fittili di Himera', *Cronache di archeologia e di storia dell'arte* 16: 165–73.

Fiorentini, G. (1985) 'Sacelli sull'Acropoli di Gela e a Monte Adranone nella valle del Belice', *Cronache di archeologia e di storia dell'arte* 16: 105–14.

Förtsch, R. (1987) 'Ein Fassadenzitat aus dem Theater von Syrakus', *Mitteilungen des Deutschen Archaeologischen Instituts. Römische Abteilung* 94: 309–24.

Fusaro, D. (1982) 'Note di architettura domestica greca nella periodo tardo-geometrico e arcaico', *Dialoghi di archeologia* 4, 1: 5–30.

Griffo, P. (1982) 'Note sul tempio di Zeus Olimpico di Agrigento (con particolare riguardo al problema dei Telamoni)', in *Aparchai. Nuove ricerche e studi sulla Magna Grecia e la Sicilia antica in onore di P.E. Arias*, Pisa, pp. 253–70.

Guarducci, M. (1982) 'Ancora sull'epigrafe del tempio di Apollo a Siracusa', *Rendiconti dell' Accademia Nazionale dei Lincei* 37: 13–20.

— (1987) 'Il tempio arcaico di Apollo a Siracusa. Riflessioni nuove', in *Saggi in onore di G. De Angelis d'Ossat*, Rome, pp. 43–5.

Gullini, G. (1980) 'Il tempio E 1 e l'architettura protoarcaica di Selinunte', *Insediamenti Coloniali Greci in Sicilia nell'VIII e VII secolo a. C.*, *Cronache di Archeologia* 17: 52–61.

— (1981) 'Origini dell'architettura greca in Occidente', *Annuario della Scuola Archeologica di Atene e delle Missioni Italiane in Oriente* 59, 43: 97–126.

— (1985) 'L'architettura templare greca in Sicilia dal primo arcaismo alla fine del V secolo', *Il Tempio Greco in Sicilia. Architettura e Culti*, *Cronache di Archeologia* 16: 21–43.

Holloway, R.R. (1984) 'Le programme de la décoration sculpturale du temple "C" de Sélinonte', *Revue des archéologues et historiens d'art de Louvain* 17: 7–15.

— (1988) 'Early Greek architectural decoration as functional art', *American Journal of Archaeology* 92: 177–83.

Höcker, C. (1985–6) 'Die klassischen Ringhallentempel von Agrigent. Überlegungen zu Bauplanung und Arbeitsorganisation bei der Errichtung dorischer Tempel im Bauwesen Westgriechenlands im 5. Jh. v. Chr.', *Hephaistos. Kritische Zeitschrift zur Theorie und Praxis der Archäologie und angrenzender Wissenschaften* 7–8: 233–47.

Isler, H.P. (1981) 'Contributi per una storia del teatro antico. Il teatro greco di Iaitas e il teatro di Segesta', *Numismatica e Antichità Classiche, Quaderni Ticinesi* 10: 131–64.

Joint authors (1983) 'Fra archeologia e storia sociale. La villa di Piazza Armerina. Seminario dell'Istituto Gramsci, Roma 1982', *Opus. Rivista internazionale per la storia economica e sociale dell'antichità* 2: 535–602.

Joint authors (1984) *La Villa Romana del Casale di Piazza Armerina* (Cronache di Archeologia e storia dell' arte, vol. 23).

Joint authors (1985) *Il Tempio greco in Sicilia, architettura e culti*, Atti della riunione scientifica della scuola di perfezionamento in archeologia classica dell'

Università di Catania, *Cronache di Archeologia* 16, papers on Naxos, Monte San Mauro, Camarina, Agrigento, Sabucina, Gela, Monte Adranone, Selinus, Monte Bubbonia, Himera, Morgantina.

Lauter-Bufe, H. (1987) *Die Geschichte des sikeliotischen korinthischen Kapitells*, Mainz.

MacDonald, W.L. (1986) *The Architecture of the Roman Empire*, New Haven, Conn., vol. 2.

Manganaro, G. (1982) 'Die Villa von Piazza Armerina, Residenz des kaiserlichen Prokurators, und ein mit ihr verbundenes Emporium von Henna', in *Palast und Hütte. Beiträge zum Bauen und Wohnen im Altertum von Archäologen, Vor- und Frühgeschichtlern. Tagungsbeiträge eines Symposiums der Alexander von Humboldt-Stiftung Bonn-Bad Godesberg Veranstaltet vom 25.-30. November 1979 in Berlin*, Mainz, pp. 493–513.

Martin, R. (1982) 'L'architecture de Sélinonte. Témoignage sur la vie politique et sociale d'un cité coloniale', in *Un trentennio di collaborazione italo-francese nel campo dell'archeologia italiana*, Rome, pp. 31–8.

Masseria, C. (1978–80) 'Ipotesi sul "tempio M" di Selinunte', *Annali della Facoltà di lettere e filosofia, Università degli studi di Perugia* 16–17: 61–88.

Mertens, D. (1984) *Der Tempel von Segesta und die dorische Tempelbaukunst des griechischen Westens in klassischer Zeit*, Mainz.

— (1985) 'Nuove ricerche sul tempio di Segesta' in *Cronache di archeologia e di storia dell'arte* 16: 187–93.

Mertens-Horn, M. (1988) 'Die Löwenkopf-Wasserspeier des griechischen Westens im 6. und 5. Jahrhunderts v. Christus', *Mitteilungen des Deutschen Archaeologischen Instituts, Römische Abteilung*, Ergänzungsheft 28.

Mitens, K. (1988) *Teatri greci e Teatri ispirati all'architettura greca in Sicilia e nell' Italia meridionale, c. 350-50 a.C.*, Analecta Romana Instituti Danici, Supplementum 13.

Musti, D. (1985) 'L'iscrizione del tempio G di Selinunte', *Rivista di filologia e d'istruzione classica* 113: 134–57, 443–5.

Østby, E. (1982) 'An Early Sicilian relief-metope in Copenhagen', *Acta ad archaeologiam et artium historiam pertinentia* 2: 1–53.

— (1987) 'Riflessioni sulle metope di Selinunte', *La parola del passato* 233: 123–53.

Palmeri, C. (1983) 'L' "opus signinum" in Sicilia', *Beni culturali e ambientali, Sicilia* 4: 171–6.

Pancucci, D. (1980) 'I Temenoi del santuario delle divinità ctonie ad Agrigento', in *Philias Charin. Miscellanea di studi classici in onore di E. Manni*, Rome, pp. 1,663–76.

— (1985) 'Precisazioni sul sacello di Monte Bubbonia', *Cronache di archeologia e di storia dell'arte* 16: 119–24.

Pelagatti, P. (1985) 'Sacelli e nuovi materiali architettonici a Naxos, Monte San Mauro e Camarina', *Cronache di archeologia e di storia dell'arte* 16: 43–65.

Peschlow-Bindokat, A. (1990) *Die Steinbrücke von Selinunte*, Mainz.

Pesando, F. (1989) *La Casa dei Greci*, Milan.

Polacco, L. (1982) 'La posizione del teatro di Siracusa nel quadro dell'architettura teatrale greca in Sicilia', in *Aparchai. Nuove ricerche e studi sulla Magna Grecia e la Sicilia in onore di P.E. Arias*, Pisa, pp. 431–43.

— (1984) 'Le asimmetrie del teatro antico di Siracusa', *Numismatica e Antichità classiche, Quaderni Ticinesi* 13: 85–93.

Polacco, L., and Anti, C. (1981) *Il teatro antico di Siracusa*, Rimini.

Polacco, L., Trojani, M., and Scolari, A.C. (1982–3) 'Teatro antico di Siracusa. Campagna 1982. La terrazza superiore. Note preliminare', *Atti dell' Istituto veneto di scienze, lettere ed arti* 141: 135–49.

— (1983–4) 'Teatro antico di Siracusa. Campagna 1983. La terrazza superiore. Note preliminare', *Atti dell' Istituto veneto di scienze, lettere ed arti* 142: 165–7.

— (1984–5) 'Teatro antico di Siracusa. Santuario rupestre "in summis." Campagna 1984. Relazione preliminare', *Atti dell'Istituto veneto di scienze, lettere ed arti* 143: 91–106.

— (1985–6) 'Teatro antico di Siracusa. Il santuario in summis. Campagna 1985, relazione preliminare', *Atti dell' Istituto veneto di scienze, lettere ed arti* 144: 23–36.

Pugliese Carratelli, G. (1982) 'Sull'epigrafe del tempio G di Selinunte', in *Aparchai. Nuove ricerche e studi sulla Magna Grecia e la Sicilia antica in onore di P.E. Arias*, Pisa, pp. 191–4.

Riotto, M. (1985) 'Il santuario della Malophoros a Selinunte. Spunti per una discussione storico-religiosa', *Sicilia archeologica*, 18, 59: 25–51.

Settis, S. (1982) 'Neue Forschungen und Untersuchungen zur villa von Piazza Armerina', in *Palast und Hütte. Beiträge zum Bauen und Wohnen im Altertum von Archäologen, Vor und Frühgeschichtlern. Tagungsbeiträge eines Symposiums der Alexander von Humboldt-Stiftung Bonn-Bad Godesberg Veranstaltet vom 25–30. November 1979 in Berlin*, Mainz, pp. 515–34.

Siracusano, A. (1983) *Il santuario rupestre di Agrigento in località S. Biagio*, Rome.

Spigo, U. (1982–3) 'Note preliminari sugli insediamenti di età imperiale romana nei territorio di Lentini, Carlentini, Ramacca, Caltagirone, Grammichele', *Kokalos* 28–9: 341–4.

— (1985) 'Resti di edifici templari a Monte S. Mauro di Caltagirone', *Cronache di archeologia e di storia dell'arte* 16: 91–3.

Szeliga, G.N. (1981) *The Dioscuri on the Roof: Archaic and Classical Equestrian Acroteria in Sicily and Southern Italy*, diss., Bryn Mawr College.

Thalmann, S.K. (1976) *The Adyton in the Greek Temples of Southern Italy and Sicily*, diss., University of California at Berkeley.

Tsakirgis, B. (1984) *The Domestic Architecture of Morgantina in the Hellenistic and Roman Periods*, diss., Princeton University, NJ.

— (1989) 'The decorated pavements of Morgantina I: The mosaics', *American Journal of Archaeology* 93: 395–416.

Tusa, V. (1981) 'Sulla ricostruzione del tempio di Zeus a Selinunte', *Beni culturali e ambientali, Sicilia* 2, 1–2: 17–20.

— (1986) 'Selinunte: la Cinta Muraria dell' Acropoli', in *La Fortification dans l'histoire du monde grec*, Paris, pp. 111–20.

Vaccarello, P. (1986) 'Rilievo del tempietto di Zeus Meilichios a Selinunte', *Sicilia archeologica*, 19, 60-1: 89–96.

Vallet, G. (1987) 'Innovations et tradition. Urbanisme et architecture dans une colonie grecque d'Occident', in *Saggi in onore di G. De Angelis d'Ossat*, Rome, pp. 81–4.

Villari, L. (1985) *Sui siti delle Ible di Sicilia. Ibla Geleata od Erea, la villa romana di Piazza Armerina*, Rome.

— (1987) *Ibla Geleata, la villa romana di Piazza Armerina*, Rome.

Von Sydow, W. (1984) 'Die hellenistischen Gebälke in Sizilien', in *Mitteilungen des Deutschen Archäologischen Instituts, Römische Abteilung* 91: 239–358.

Voza, G. (1982) 'Le ville romane del Tellaro e di Patti in Sicilia e il problema dei rapporti con l'Africa', in *150-Jahr-Feier Deutsches Archäologisches Institut Rom*, (*Mitteilungen des Deutschen Archäologischen Instituts, Römische Abteilung, Ergänzungsheft* 25), pp. 202–9.

Wikander, C. (1986) 'Sicilian architectural terracottas. A reappraisal', in *Skifter Utgivner av Svenska Institutet I Rom* in octavo, vol. 15.

Wilson, R.J.A. (1980) 'On the date of the Roman Amphitheatre at Syracuse', in *Philias Charin. Miscellanea di studi classici in onore di E. Manni*, Rome, vol. 6, pp. 2,217–30.

— (1982) 'Una villa romana a Montallegro, Agrigento', *Sicilia archeologica* 15, 48: 7–20.

— (1983) 'Luxury retreat, fourth-century style. A millionaire aristocrat in Late Roman Sicily', *Opus. Rivista internazionale per la storia economica e sociale dell'antichità* 2: 537–52.

— (1983) *Piazza Armerina*, Austin, Tex.

Yacoub, M. (1983) 'Etude comparative du cadre architectural dans les mosaïques de cirque de Piazza Armerina et de Gafsa', in *III Colloquio internazionale sul mosaico antico, Ravenna 1980*, Ravenna, pp. 263–76.

Art

Allegro, N. (1982) 'Louteria a rilievo da Himera', in *Secondo quaderno imerese*, Rome, pp. 115–66.

Baccio Spigo, G.M. (1984) 'Coppa vitrea ed oreficerie da sepolture di età ellenistica e romana a Naxos', *Bollettino d'arte* 69: 59–68.

Barletta, B. (1987) 'The draped Kouros and the workshop of the Syracusan youth', *American Journal of Archaeology* 91: 233–46.

Bell, M. III (1981) *The Terracottas*, Morgantina Studies, vol. I, Princeton, NJ.

Belvedere, O. (1984) 'Il ruolo dell'artigianato nel V secolo a.C.', in *I Mestieri. Atti del II Congresso internazionale di studi antropologici siciliani, 26-29 marzo 1980*, pp. 3–13.

Bernabò Brea, L. (1981) *Menandro e il teatro greco nelle terracotte liparesi*, Genova.

Boeselager, D. v. (1983) *Antike Mosaiken in Sizilien. Hellenismus und römische Kaiserzeit, 3. Jahrhundert v. Chr.-3. Jahrhundert n. Chr.,* Rome.

Bonacasa, N. (1982) 'Ipotesi sulle sculture del tempio della Vittoria a Himera', in *Aparchai. Nuove ricerche e studi sulla Magna Grecia e la Sicilia antica in onore di P.E. Arias*, Pisa, pp. 291–304.

— (1988) 'Le arti figurative nella Sicilia romana imperiale', in *Aufstieg und Niedergang der Römischen Welt. Teil II: Principat*, Berlin, vol. 11, pp. 306–45.

Canciani, F. (1984) 'Le terrecotte di Lipari e recenti studi sul teatro antico', *Xenia* 7: 43–8.

Carruba, A.M. (1983) 'Der Ephebe von Selinunt, Untersuchungen und Betrachtungen anlässlich seiner letzten Restaurierung', *Boreas* 6: 44–60.

Castellana, G. (1985) 'Statuetta femminile fittile di Himera e problemi di identificazione', *Rivista di Archeologia* 9: 26–9.

Coarelli, F. (1982) 'La "pugna equestris" di Agatocle nell'Athenaion di Siracusa', in *Aparchai. Nuove ricerche e studi sulla Magna Grecia e la Sicilia antica in onore di P.E. Arias*, Pisa, pp. 547–57.

Coldstream, J.N. (1982) 'Some problems of eighth-century pottery in the west seen from the Greek angle', in *La Céramique grecque ou de tradition grecque au VIII siècle en Italie centrale et méridionale,* Naples, pp. 21–37.

D'Agostino, B. (1982) 'La ceramica greca o di tradizione greca nell'VIII sec. in Italia meridionale', in *La Céramique grecque ou de tradition grecque au VIII siècle en Italie centrale et méridionale,* Naples, pp. 55–67.

De Miro, E. (1982) 'Lastra di piombo con scena dionisiaca dal territorio di Piazza Armerina', in *Aparchai. Nuove ricerche e studi sulla Magna Grecia e la Sicilia antica in onore di P.E. Arias,* Pisa, pp. 179–83.

Dehl, C. (1984) *Die Korinthische Keramik des 8 und frühen 7 Jahrhunderts v. Chr. in Italien (Mitteilungen des Deutschen Archäologischen Instituts Athenische Abteilung,*11 Beiheft).

Di Stefano, C.A. (1984) 'Un manico d'osso dalla necropoli di Lilibeo', in *Alessandria e il mondo ellenistico-romano. Studi in onore di A. Adriani,* Rome, vol. 1, pp. 391–395.

Di Vita, A. (1984–5) 'La scultura a Selinunte, le terracotte figurate, Piazza Armerina. Un aggiornamento bibliografico sull'arte della Sicilia antica (1980–1984)', *Kokalos* 30–1, 1: 417–31.

Falsone, G. (1987) 'La statue de Motyé. Aurige ou prêtre de Melqart?', in *Mélanges offerts à J. Labarbe,* Brussels, pp. 407–27.

Fanara, G. (1984) 'Frammento di kourotrophos da Selinunte', *Sicilia archeologica* 17, 54–5: 59–61.

Frel, J. (1985) 'L'auriga di Mozia. Un'opera di Pitagora di Reggio', *La parola del passato* 40: 64–8.

Ghisellini, E. (1982) 'Il bassorilievo con sfingi da Monte San Mauro', *Xenia* 4: 3–14.

Griffo, P. (1987) *Il Museo archeologico regionale di Agrigento,* Milan.

Guidice, F. (1985) 'Stipi votive da Camarina', *Cronache di archeologia e di storia dell'arte* 16: 82–6.

Heldring, B. (1981) *Sicilian Plastic Vases,* diss., Rijksuniversiteit te Utrecht.

Holloway, R.R. (1986) 'Selected antiquities from the Navarra Collection', *Revue des archéologues et historiens d'art de Louvain* 19: 11–49.

— (1988) 'Gli eroi di Riace sono siciliani?', *Sicilia Archeologica* 21: 23–30.

— (1988) 'The severe style, new evidence and old problems', *Numismatica e Antichità classiche, Quaderni Ticinesi* 17: 55–79.

Joint authors (1982) *La céramique grecque ou de la tradition grecque au VIII siècle en Italie centrale et meridionale,* Naples.

Joint authors (1984) *Il Museo Archeologico di Palermo,* Palermo.

Joint authors (1987) *Da Eschilo a Menandro. Due secoli di teatro greco attraverso i reperti archeologici liparesi* (Mostra; Lipari, 1987), Lipari.

Joint authors (1988) *La Statua Marmorea di Mozia,* Studi e Materiali dell'Istituto di Archeologia dell' Università di Palermo, Rome, vol. 8.

Joly, E. (1980) 'Teorie vecchie e nuove sulla ceramica policroma di Centuripe', in *Philias Charin. Miscellanea di studi classici in onore di E. Manni,* Rome, vol. 4, pp. 1,241–54.

Kapitän, G. (1980) 'Three terracotta braziers from the Sea of Sicily', *International Journal of Nautical Archaeology* 9: 127–31.

La Rocca, E. (1985) 'Il giovane di Mozia come auriga. Una testimonianza a favore', *La parola del passato* 40: 452–63.

Lee, H.M. (1984) 'Athletics and the bikini girls from Piazza Armerina', in *Stadion. Zeitschrift für Geschichte des Sports und der Körperkultur,* vol. 10, pp. 45–76.

Mandruzzato, A. (1988) 'La sigillata italica in Sicilia. Importazione, distribuzione, produzione locale', in *Aufstieg und Niedergang der Römischen Welt. Teil II: Principat*, Berlin, vol. 11, pp. 414–49.

Mansuelli, G.A. (1982) 'Pagine di storia artistica della

Sicilia: osservazioni al "de signis" ciceroniano', in *Aparchai. Nuove ricerche e studi sulla Magna Grecia e la Sicilia antica in onore di P.E. Arias*, Pisa, pp. 619–22.

Mayo, M. (ed.) (1982) *The Art of South Italy: Vases from Magna Graecia*, Richmond.

Neeft, C.W. (1982) 'Corinthian hemispherical kotylai, Thapsos panel-cups and the west', in *La Céramique grecque ou de tradition grecque au VIII siècle en Italie centrale et méridionale*, Naples, pp. 39–43.

Paoletti, M. (1983) 'Sicilia e Campania costiera. I sarcofagi nelle chiese cattedrali durante l'età normanna, angioina e aragonese', in *Marburger Winckelmann-Programm*, pp. 229–44.

Papadopoulos, J. (1981) 'Una terracotta dedalica da Caltabellotta', *Xenia* 2: 8–12.

Pelagatti, P. (1982) 'I più antichi materiali di importazione a Siracusa, a Naxos e in altri siti della Sicilia orientale', in *La Céramique grecque ou de tradition grecque au VIII siècle en Italie centrale et méridionale*, Naples, pp. 113–80.

Polacco, L. (1985–6) 'Due rilievi rupestri inediti nell'area del teatro antico di Siracusa', in *Atti. Istituto veneto di scienze, lettere ed arti*, vol. 144, pp. 1–21.

Rebourg, A. (1988) 'Le nouveau Musée archéologique de Syracuse', *Archeologia. Trésors des âges* 234: 12–19.

Sguaitamatti, M. (1984) *L'Offrante de porcelet dans la coroplathie géléenne*, Mainz.

Spanò Giammellaro, A. (1985) 'Eine Marmorstatue aus Mozia (Sizilien)', *Antike Welt. Zeitschrift für Archäologie und Kulturgeschichte* 16, 4: 16–22.

Spigo, U. (1979) 'Nuovo cratere siceliota a figure rosse da Siracusa', *Bollettino d'arte* 54: 59–64.

— (1980–1) 'Ricerche a Monte S. Mauro, Francavilla di Sicilia, Acireale, Adrano, Lentini, Solarino', *Kokalos* 26–7: 771–95.

— (1987) 'La ceramica siceliota a figure rosse. Variazioni sul tema', *Bollettino d'arte* 72: 1–24.

Stone, S.C. III (1981) *Roman Pottery from Morgantina in Sicily*, diss., Princeton University, NJ.

— (1987) 'Presigillata from Morgantina', *American Journal of Archaeology* 91: 85–104.

Szeliga, G. (1983) 'A representation of an Archaic Greek saddle-cloth from Sicily', *American Journal of Archaeology* 87: 545–7.

Tamburello, I. (1979) 'Palermo. Terrecotte figurate dalla necropoli', *Kokalos* 25: 54–63.

Trendall, A.D. (1983) 'The red-figured vases of Lucania, Campania and Sicily – Third supplement (consolidated)', *Bulletin of the Institute of Classical Studies of the University of London*, supplement 41.

— (1989) *The Greek Vases of South Italy and Sicily*, New York.

Trendall, A.D. and Woodford, S. (1980) 'Adrastos on a Sicilian Calyx-Krater from Lipari', *Philias Charin. Miscellanea di studi classici in onore di E. Manni*, Rome, vol. 6, pp. 2,101–10.

Tusa, V. (1983) 'La statua di Mozia', *La parola del passato* 38: 445–56.

— (1983) *La scultura in pietra a Selinunte*, Palermo.

— (1986) 'Il Giovane di Mozia', *Archaische und klassische griechische Plastik* 2: 1–11.

— 'La Statua di Mozia (il Giovane di Mozia)', *Sicilia Archeologica* 21: 15–22.

Uhlenbrock, J.E. (1978) *The Protomai from Gela: History, Chronology, Style*, diss., New York University.

Villard, F. (1981) 'La céramique polychrome du VIIe siècle en Grèce, en Italie du sud et en Sicile et sa situation par rapport à la céramique proto-corinthienne', *Annuario della Scuola Archeologica di Atene e delle Missioni Italiane in Oriente* 49: 133–8.

— (1982) 'La céramique géométrique importée de Mégara Hyblaea', *La Céramique grecque ou de tradition grecque au VIII siècle en Italie centrale et méridionale*, Naples, pp. 181–5.

Voza, G. (1980–1) 'Aspetti e problemi dei nuovi monumenti d'arte musiva in Sicilia', in *III Colloquio internazionale sul mosaico antico, Ravenna 1980*, Ravenna, pp. 5–18.

Wegner, M. (1982) 'Terrakotten einer Frau mit einem Ferkel' in *Aparchai. Nuove ricerche e studi sulla Magna Grecia e la Sicilia antica in onore di P.E. Arias*, Pisa, pp. 201–19.

Wescoat, B. (1989) *Syracuse, The Fairest Greek City, Ancient Art from the Museo Archeologico Regionale Paolo Orsi* (exhibition Emory University, Atlanta, Georgia), Atlanta.

Wielen-van Ommeren, F. van der (1985) 'Polychrome vases and terracottas from southern Italy in the J. Paul Getty Museum', in *Greek Vases in the J. Paul Getty Museum*, vol. 2, pp. 171–82.

Wilson, R.J.A. (1982) 'Roman mosaics in Sicily. The African connection', *American Journal of Archaeology* 86: 413–28.

Coins

Arnold-Biucchi, C. (1983) 'Appunti sulla Zecca di Messana dal 480 al 450 a.C.', *Numismatica e Antichità classiche, Quaderni Ticinesi* 12: 49–64.

— (1988) 'La Monetazione d'argento di Himera classica. I tetradrammi', *Numismatica e Antichità classiche, Quaderni Ticinesi* 17: 85–100.

Arnold-Biucchi, C., Beer-Tobey, L. and Waggoner, N.M. (1988) 'A Greek archaic silver hoard from Selinus', *American Numismatic Society Museum Notes* 33: 1–36.

Baldus, H.R. (1982) 'Unerkannte Reflexe der römischen Nordafrika-Expedition von 256/255 v. Chr. in der karthagischen Münzprägung', *Chiron* 12: 163–90.

Bérend, D. (1988) *Sylloge Nummorum Graecorum, The Collection of the American Numismatic Society, part 5,*

Sicily III: Syracuse-Siceliotes, New York.
— (1989) 'Histoire de poulpes', in *Kraay-Mørkholm Essays*, Louvain, pp. 23–8.
Boehringer, C. (1981) 'Herbita', *Numismatica e Antichità Classiche, Quaderni Ticinesi* 10: 95–114.
— (1982) 'Katanische Probleme. Silberne Kleinmünzen', *Proceedings of the 9. International Congress of Numismatics, Berne, 1979*, Berne, 1: 71-83.
— (1985) 'Der sizilische Stempelschneider SIKA', in *Numismatica e Antichità classiche, Quaderni Ticinesi* 14: 85–91.
— (1985) 'Dokumentation des Schatzfundes von Pachino', *Schweizerische Numismatische Rundschau* 64: 43–8.
Boehringer, C., and Pennisi di Floristella, O. (1984) 'Syrakusanischer Münzstempel der Epoche des Agathokles', in *Festschrift für L. Mildenberg*, Wetteren, pp. 31–42.
Burnett, A.M. (1983) 'The Enna Hoard and the silver coinage of the Syracusan democracy', *Schweizerische Numismatische Rundschau* 62: 5–26.
Buttrey, T.V. (1980) 'A siculo-punic bronze hoard from Cínsi (PA), Sicily', *Numismatica e Antichità classiche, Quaderni Ticinesi* 9: 137–43.
— (1983) 'A siculo-punic control mark at Syracuse', *Numismatica e Antichità classiche, Quaderni Ticinesi* 12: 135–9.
Buttrey, T.V., Erim, K.T., Groves, T.D. and Holloway, R.R. (1989) *The Coins*, Morgantina studies, vol. 2, Princeton, NJ.
Caccamo Caltabiano, M. (1986–7) 'Le prime emissioni anassilaiche a Rhegion e a Messene', *Quaderni dell' Istituto di Archeologia della Facoltà di Lettere e filosofia della Università di Messina* 2: 5–24.
— (1987) 'I decadrammi di Evainetos e Kimon per una spedizione navale in oriente', *Studi per Laura Breglia*, Supplemento al *Bollettino di Numismatica*, 4, 1: 119–37.
Cahn, H.A., Mildenberg, L., Russo, R. and Voegtli, H. (1988) *Antikenmuseum Basel und Sammlung Ludwig, Griechische Münzen aus Grossgriechenland und Siziliens*, Basel.
Calciati, R. (1983) *Corpus nummorum siculorum. La monetazione di bronzo*, Mortara, vol. 1.
— (1986) *Corpus nummorum siculorum. La monetazione di bronzo*, Mortara, vol. 2.
— (1988) 'Monete puniche anepigrafiche di bronzo cirolanti in Sicilia', *Notizie del chiostro del monastero maggiore* 41–2: 9–26.
Cammarata, E. (1984) *Da Dionisio a Timoleonte*, Sciacca.
Cancio, L. (1980) 'Se acuñaron en Sicilia las decadracmas cartaginesas?', *Gaceta numismática* 56: 25–35.
Carbè, A. (1986) 'Note sulla monetazione di Selinunte. Contributo della numismatica alla storia e al patrimonio religioso della città', *Rivista Italiana di numismatica* 88: 3–20.

Clain-Steffanelli, E.E. (1987) 'On some fractional silver coinages of Sicily and Magna Graecia during the fifth century B.C.', *Revue belge de numismatique* 133: 39–65.
Coscarella, A. (1983) 'Variante su una moneta della zecca di Catania', *Archivio storico per la Sicilia orientale* 79: 279–84.
Crawford, M.H. (1985) *Coinage and Money under the Roman Republic. Italy and the Mediterranean Economy*, Berkeley, Calif.
— (1987) 'Sicily', in *The Coinage of the Roman World in the Late Republic*, Oxford, pp. 43–51.
Dembski, G. (1981) 'Phrygillos', *Numismatische Zeitschrift* 95: 5–9.
— (1982) 'Eine neue Gemme des Phrygillos (Gemmen- und Münzstempelschneider in Grossgriechenland)', in *Pro arte antica. Festschrift für H. Kenner*, Vienna, vol. 1, pp. 62–5.
Evans, J.D. (1987) 'The Sicilian coinage of Sextus Pompeius', *Museum Notes. The American Numismatic Society* 32: 97–157.
Gandolfo, L. (1984) 'Emissioni puniche di Sicilia a leggenda sys', *Sicilia archeologica* 17: 75–87.
Garraffo, S. (1978) 'Storia e monetazione di Entella nel quarto secolo a.C. Cronologia e significato delle emissioni dei Kampanoi', *Annali. Istituto italiano di numismatica* 25: 23–44.
— (1981) 'Su alcuni rinvenimenti monetari nell'area cimiteriale della ex Vigna Cassia a Siracusa', *Rivista di archeologia cristiana* 57: 283–324.
— (1984) *Le riconiazioni in Magna Grecia e in Sicilia. Emissioni argentee dal VI al IV secolo a. C*, Catania.
— (1987) 'Nota sulla monetazione siracusana dal 344 al 318 a.C.', *Numismatica e Antichità classiche, Quaderni Ticinesi* 16: 119–29.
Gorini, G. (1985) *La collezione di monete greche di Paolo Orsi. Catalogo*, Mostra organizzata dai Musei civici di Rovereto nella sede della Cassa di Risparmio di Trento e Rovereto, Rovereto.
Hans, L.M. (1987) 'Die Göttin mit der Tiara', *Schweizerische Numismatische Rundschau* 66: 47–58.
Holloway, R.R. (1982) 'Il problema dei "pegasi" in Sicilia', *Numismatica e Antichità classiche, Quaderni Ticinesi* ll: 129–36.
— (1989) *Ripostigli del Museo Archeologico di Siracusa*, Naples.
Kraay, C.M. (1984) *The Archaic Coinage of Himera*, Naples.
Lacroix, L. (1982) 'Acragas ou Hélios sur les décadrachmes d'Agrigente', in *Studia Paulo Naster oblata, 1. Numismatica antiqua*, Louvain, pp. 13–20.
Lange, O. (1986) 'Bemerkungen zu einer seltenen Kleinbronze von Syrakus', *Schweizer Münzblätter*, 36: 30–4.
Lehmann, C.M. (1981) 'The Striding God of Zancle-Messana', *Revue belge de numismatique* 127: 19–32.
Macaluso, R. (1980) 'Monete a leggenda Kainon', in *Philias Charin. Miscellanea di studi classici in onore di E.*

Manni, Rome, vol. 4, pp. 1,363–74.

Manfredi, L.I. (1985) 'RSMLQT, R'SMLQRT, Nota sulla numismatica punica di Sicilia', *Rivista Italiana di Numismatica* 87: 3–8.

Manganaro, G. (1981–2) 'Un ripostiglio siciliano del 214–211 a.C. e la datazione del denarius', *Jahrbuch für Numismatik und Geldgeschicte* 31–2. 37–54.

— (1983) 'Ancora sulle rivolte "servili" in Sicilia', *Chiron* 13: 405–9.

Martini, R. (1983) 'Contromarca inedita della zecca di Panormus con aratro e globetti di Valore', *Notizie dal Chiostro del Monastero maggiore. Rassegna di studi del Civico museo archeologico e del Civico gabinetto numismatico di Milano* 31–2: 35–52.

Molinari, M.C. (1984) 'Relazioni fra metalli monetari nell'età di Agatocle', *Rivista Italiana di Numismatica* 86: 9–16.

— (1986) 'Considerazioni sulle emissioni frazionarie di Imera in età arcaica', *Rivista Italiana di Numismatica* 88: 21–6.

Naster, P. (1988) 'Les revers à carré creux des monnaies de Zancle-Messana', *Rivista Italiana di Numismatica* 90: 3–14.

Pera, R. (1986) 'Tipi dionisiaci in Sicilia e Magna Grecia', *Serta historica antiqua*: 33–67.

Riemann, H. (1983) 'Iupiter Imperator', *Mitteilungen des Deutschen Archaeologischen Instituts, Römische Abteilung* 90: 233–338.

Rutter, K. (1989) 'Athens and the Western Greeks in the fifth century B.C.: the numismatic evidence', in *Kraay-Mørkholm Essays*, Louvain, pp. 245–57.

Scurria, C.F. (1981) 'Problemi della ellenizzazione del retroterra zancleo. La questione di Agathyrno', *Rivista storica dell' antichità* 11: 53–68.

Trell, B. (1984) 'The coins of the Phoenician world, East and West', in *Ancient Coins of the Graeco-Roman World*, Waterloo, Ontario, pp. 117–39.

Tusa Cutroni, A. (1980) 'La monetazione di Siracusa sotto Dionisio I', in *Philias Charin. Miscellanea di studi classici in onore di E. Manni*, Rome, vol. 2, pp. 629–47.

— (1980–1) 'Recenti studi e ricerche sulla monetazione della Sicilia antica', *Kokalos* 26–7: 480–502.

— (1982) 'Contributi della monetazione alla identificazione dei siti menzionati nelle iscrizioni da Entella', *Annali della Scuola Normale Superiore di Pisa, classe di lettere e filosofia* 3, 12: 841–8.

— (1982) 'Il ruolo di Selinunte agli inizi della monetazione in Sicilia', *Sicilia archeologica* 15, 49–50: 27–30.

— (1982) 'Riflessioni sulla monetazione di Segesta e Erice', in *Aparchai. Nuove richerche e studi sulla Magna Grecia e la Sicilia antica in onore di Paolo Enrico Arias*, Pisa, pp. 239–42.

— (1982) 'Una officina monetale a Himera? Il problema cronologico', in *Secondo quaderno imerese*, Rome, pp. 167–74.

— (1983) 'Di una serie monetale Punica di bronzo', *Rivista Italiana di Numismatica* 84: 35–42.

— (1983) 'Rapporti tra Greci e Punici in Sicilia attraverso l'evidenza numismatica', in *Atti del I Congresso internazionale di studi fenici e punici, Roma 1979*, Rome, pp. 135–43.

— (1983) 'Studi di numismatica punica', in *Rivista di Studi Fenici*, supp. 11, pp. 37–42.

— (1984–85) 'Recenti studi e ricerche sulla monetazione della Sicilia antica', *Kokalos* 30–1: 277–97.

van der Vin, J.P.A. (1982) 'Horses from Syracuse', *Bulletin antieke beschaving* 57: 200–5.

Vassallo, S. (1983) 'La circolazione della moneta bronzea di Agrigento nel V secolo a.C.', *Rivista Italiana di Numismatica* 85: 17–34.

Visona, P. (1985) *Punic Bronze Coinage: Circulation, Mint Attribution and Chronology*, diss., Michigan.

Walker, A.S. (1984) 'Some hoards from Sicily and a Carthaginian issue of the Second Punic War', in *Festschrift für Leo Mildenberg*, pp. 269–88.

Wells, H.B. (1984) 'Observations on the Signature Kim', *Schweizer Münzblätter* 34: 57–60.

Westermark, U. (1984) 'The Bronze Hemilitra of Akragas', *Numismatica e Antichità classiche, Quaderni Ticinesi* 13: 71–84.

— (1985) 'An overstrike of Akragas on Corinth', *Schweizer Münzblätter* 35: 85–7.

Westermark, U. and Jenkins, K. (1980) *The Coinage of Kamarina*, London.

— (1982) 'Notes on some new or rare coins of Kamarina', *Numismatica e Antichità classiche, Quaderni Ticinese* 11: 47–58.

White, D. (1986) 'The Morris Coin', *Expedition* 28: pp. 13–21.

Punic

Amadasi Guzzo, M.G. (1987) 'Iscrizioni fenicie e puniche in Italia', *Bollettino d'arte* 72: 103–18.

Bondì, S.F. (1983) 'L'espansione fenicia in Italia', *Fenici e Arabi nel Mediterraneo*, Rome, pp. 63–95.

— (1985) 'La Sicilia fenicio-punica. Il quadro storico e la documentazione archeologica', *Bollettino d'arte* 70, 31–2: 13–32.

Coacci Polselli, G. (1980–1) 'L'epigrafia punica in Sicilia', *Kokalos* 26–7: 468–79.

Falsone, G. (1988) 'La Fenicia come centro di lavorazione del bronzo nell'età del ferro', *Dialoghi di archeologia* 3, 6: 79–110, on the Sciacca bronze.

Fiorentini, G. (1980) 'Santuari punici a Monte Adranone di Sambuca di Sicilia', in *Philias Charin. Miscellanea di studi classici in onore di E. Manni*, Rome, vol. 3, pp. 905–15.

Fourmont, M. (1982–3) 'Santuari punici in Sicilia',

Kokalos 28–9: 195–8.

Garbini, G. (1980) 'Riflessioni sul "segno di Tanit"', in *Philias Charin. Miscellanea di studi classici in onore di E. Manni,* Rome, vol. 3, pp. 1,033–40.

Hans, L.M. (1983) *Karthago und Sizilien. Die Enstehung und Gestaltung der Epikratie auf dem Hintergrund der Beziehungen der Karthager zu den Griechen und den nichtgriechischen Völkern Siziliens, VI.-III. Jahrhundert v. Chr.,* Hildesheim.

Joint authors (1982–3) 'I Cartaginesi in Sicilia all'epoca dei due Dionisi', *Kokalos* 28–9: 127–277.

Joint authors (1988) *I Fenici,* Milan.

Moscati, S. (1980–1) 'La Sicilia tra l'Africa fenicio-punica e il Tirreno', *Kokalos* 26–7: 80–94.

— (1987) *L'arte della Sicilia punica,* Milan.

Moscati, S. and Uberti, M.L. (1981) *Scavi a Mozia. Le Stele,* Pubblicazioni del Centro di studio per la civiltà fenicia e punica, 23, serie archeologica, 25, Rome.

Rallo, A. (1982–3) 'L'abitato di Selinunte. Il quartiere punico e la sua necropoli', *Kokalos* 28–9: 169–74.

Tamburello, I. (1980) 'Aspetti di Palermo punica. Gioielli ed amuleti', in *Philias Charin. Miscellanea di studi classici in onore di E. Manni,* Rome, vol. 6, pp. 2,067–83.

Tusa, V. (1981) 'L'aspetto punico di Selinunte con particolare riferimento all'urbanistica', in *150 Jahre Deutsches Archäologisches Institut, 1829–1979,* Berlin, pp. 99–107.

— (1982) 'La presenza fenicio-punica in Sicilia', in *Phönizier im Westen. Die Beiträge des Internationalen Symposiums über 'Die phönizische Expansion im Westlichen Mittelmeerraum' in Köln vom 24. bis 27. April 1979,* Mainz, pp. 95–108.

— (1982–3) 'I Cartaginesi nella Sicilia occidentale', *Kokalos* 28–9: 131–46.

— (1983) 'La Sicilia fenicio-punica', *Dialogues d'histoire ancienne* 9: 237–55.

— (1983) 'La Sicilia fenicio-punica. Stato attuale delle ricerche e degli studi e prospettive per il futuro', in *Atti del I Congresso internazionale di studi fenici e punici, Roma 1979,* Rome, pp. 187–97.

— (1985) 'Stato delle ricerche e degli studi fenicio-punici in Sicilia', *Bollettino d'Arte* 70, 31–2: 33–47.

INDEX